JOURNAL FOR THE STUDY OF THE NEW TESTAMENT SUPPLEMENT SERIES

59

Executive Editor
David Hill

JSOT Press
Sheffield

CLOTHED
WITH **CHRIST**

The Example and Teaching of
Jesus in Romans 12.1–15.13

Michael Thompson

Journal for the Study of the New Testament
Supplement Series 59

BS
2665.2
.T560
1991

Copyright © 1991 Sheffield Academic Press

Published by JSOT Press
JSOT Press is an imprint of
Sheffield Academic Press Ltd
The University of Sheffield
343 Fulwood Road
Sheffield S10 3BP
England

Typeset by Sheffield Academic Press
and
Printed on acid-free paper in Great Britain
by Billing & Sons Ltd
Worcester

British Library Cataloguing in Publication Data

Thompson, Michael B.
   Clothed with Christ: the example and teaching
   of Jesus in Romans 12.1–15.13.—(JSNT supplement
   series. ISSN 0143-5108; 59).
   I. Title II. Series
   227.106
   ISBN 1-85075-309-1

CONTENTS

Preface   9
Abbreviations   11
INTRODUCTION   15

Part I
ALLUSIONS AND ILLUSIONS

Chapter 1
THE MEANING AND DETECTION OF ALLUSIONS   28
   1. The Literary Phenomenon: What is an Allusion?   28
   2. Criteria for Evaluating Allusions and Echoes   30

Chapter 2
EARLY EPISTOLARY USAGE OF JESUS TRADITION OUTSIDE PAUL   37
   1. Jesus Tradition in the New Testament   37
   2. Jesus Tradition in the Apostolic Fathers   44
   3. Summary of Findings   60
   4. Conclusions   61

Chapter 3
PAUL AND JESUS TRADITION: KNOWLEDGE AND ATTITUDE   64
   1. Paul's Opportunities to Learn   64
   2. Paul's Attitude toward Jesus Tradition   66
   3. Explanations for Paul's Lack of Explicit Jesus Tradition   70

Part II
JESUS TRADITION IN ROMANS 12.1–15.13

Chapter 4
ROMANS 12.1-2: THE GREAT REVERSAL   78
   1. Exegesis   78
   2. Conclusion   85

Chapter 5
ROMANS 12.3-8: RESPONSIBILITY IN THE BODY   87

Chapter 6
ROMANS 12.9-21: LOVE IN ACTION   90
   1. Romans 12.9-13   91
   2. Romans 12.14   96
   3. Romans 12.15-21   105
   4. Summary   109

Chapter 7
ROMANS 13.1-7: RENDERING WHAT IS DUE   111
   1. Evidence for Jesus Tradition   112
   2. Possible Objections   117
   3. Conclusion   119

Chapter 8
ROMANS 13.8-10: FULFILLING THE LAW   121
   1. Evidence for Jesus Tradition   121
   2. Objections to Dominical Influence   138
   3. Conclusion   139

Chapter 9
ROMANS 13.11-14: THE DAY IS NEAR   141
   1. Romans 13.11-14 and the Teachings of Jesus   141
   2. 'Put on the Lord Jesus Christ' and the Example of Christ   149
   3. Summary   158

Chapter 10
ROMANS 14.1-13A: JUDGING   161
   1. Affinities and Differences   163
   2. Extra-Pauline Use of κρίνειν   167
   3. Summary and Conclusion   172

Chapter 11
ROMANS 14.13B: AVOIDING ΣΚΑΝΔΑΛΑ   174
   1. The Use of σκάνδαλον/σκανδαλίζειν   175
   2. Dominical Parallels   176
   3. Other Jewish Parallels   179
   4. Conclusion   183

Chapter 12
ROMANS 14.14: 'NOTHING IS UNCLEAN. . .'   185
   1. Textual Affinities   185
   2. Availability of the Gospel Tradition   188
   3. Dissimilarity   193
   4. 'Persuaded in the Lord Jesus'   194
   5. Exegetical Value   196
   6. Summary and Conclusion   198

Chapter 13
ROMANS 14.15-23: SERVING CHRIST'S KINGDOM   200
   1. Chiasm and Kingdom   201
   2. Conclusion   207

Chapter 14
ROMANS 15.1-13: THE EXAMPLE OF CHRIST   208
   1. Romans 15.1: Burden-bearing   208
   2. Romans 15.2-3: 'Christ Did Not Please Himself. . .'   212
   3. Romans 15.4: The Steadfastness   225
   4. Romans 15.5-6: In accordance with Christ Jesus   228
   5. Romans 15.7-13: Receive as Christ Received You   230
   6. Summary and Conclusion   234

SUMMARY AND CONCLUSIONS   237

Bibliography   242
Index of Biblical References   265
Index of Ancient References   281
Index of Authors   287

PREFACE

This study began life as a doctoral dissertation for the University of
Cambridge and has been slightly revised for publication. Since the
completion of the dissertation, a number of important works germane
to my subject have appeared, and I have sought to incorporate as
many of their insights as possible, given the restrictions of time and
space. It has been particularly heartening to see that Professor Dunn's
recent commentary on Romans adds further support to a number of
my conclusions.

My debt to many is enormous. Tackling a subject like Jesus and
Paul would never have been possible without the support of a host of
people. Without financial assistance from the Diocese of East
Carolina, St John's Church (Fayetteville, NC), Virginia Theological
Seminary, the Evangelical Education Society of the Episcopal Church,
Christ's College, and Tyndale House, the original project could not
have been completed. I am especially grateful to my supervisor, the
Rev. John Sweet, for his unceasing encouragement and helpful
criticisms, and also to Dr Ernst Bammel, who kindly supervised me
for a term. My examiners, Professor Morna Hooker and Professor
James Dunn, made a number of useful suggestions which have found
their way into this book. Dr Harold Hoehner, Dr Markus Bockmuehl,
Dr David Wenham, Mr Conrad Gempf, and the Rev. L.K. Lo assisted
by proofreading parts of the original dissertation. None of the above
of course are in any way responsible for errors or deficiencies which
may have remained.

I also wish to thank several other persons in particular who
provided encouragement and advice along the way: Dr Tim Savage,
Dr David Olford, Dr Murray Harris, Dr Drew Trotter, Dr Douglas
De Lacey, Dr Rainer Riesner, Dr Chuck Hill, the Rev. Dr Bruce
Winter, Mr and Mrs David Coffey, the Rev. William Loveless and Dr
Rikki Watts. The courteous staff at Tyndale House, the community of
scholars there, and the generous congregation of St Mark's Church

helped in too many ways to acknowledge here. In addition, I am grateful to the staff and students at St John's College who have encouraged me to go forward with publication of the results.

Finally I want to thank my wife Susanne, for her unfailing confidence and loving support during the last seven years. To her and to our daughters Darby and Brittany, this book is dedicated.

Michael B. Thompson
St John's College, Nottingham

ABBREVIATIONS

AB	Anchor Bible
ACNT	Augsburg Commentary on the New Testament
AF	Apostolic Fathers (the authors or their writings, depending on context)
AF	*The Apostolic Fathers* (trans. K. Lake)
AnBib	Analecta biblica
ANF	*The Ante-Nicene Fathers* (ed. A. Roberts and J. Donaldson)
ANRW	*Aufstieg und Niedergang der römischen Welt. Geschichte und Kultur Roms im Spiegel der neueren Forschung* (ed. H. Temporini and W. Haase)
ANT	*The Apocryphal New Testament* (ed. M.R. James)
ASNU	Acta seminarii neotestamentici upsaliensis
ASTI	*Annual of the Swedish Theological Institute*
ATR	*Anglican Theological Review*
BAGD	Bauer, Arndt, Gingrich and Danker (*A Greek–English Lexicon of the New Testament and Other Early Christian Literature*)
BDB	Brown, Driver and Briggs (*A Hebrew and English Lexicon of the Old Testament*)
BDF	Blass, Debrunner and Funk (*A Greek Grammar of the New Testament and Other Early Christian Literature*)
BDR	Blass, Debrunner and Rehkopf (*Grammatik des neutestamentlichen Griechisch*)
BETL	Bibliotheca ephemeridum theologicarum lovaniensium
BHT	Beiträge zur historischen Theologie
Bib	*Biblica*
BJRL	*Bulletin of the John Rylands University Library of Manchester*
BNTC	Black's New Testament Commentaries
BR	*Biblical Research*
BTB	*Biblical Theology Bulletin*
BZ	*Biblische Zeitschrift*
CBC	Cambridge Bible Commentary
CBQ	*Catholic Biblical Quarterly*
CBSC	Cambridge Bible for Schools and Colleges
CGTC	Cambridge Greek Testament Commentary
CH	Tractate in *Corpus Hermeticum* (ed. A.D. Nock and A.-J. Festugière)

ConBNT	Coniectanea biblica, New Testament
ConNT	*Coniectanea neotestamentica*
Diod. S.	Diodorus of Sicilius
EBib	Etudes bibliques
EncJud	*Encyclopedia Judaica* (ed. C. Roth)
EKKNT	Evangelisch-Katholischer Kommentar zum Neuen Testament
ETL	*Ephemerides theologicae lovanienses*
EvQ	*Evangelical Quarterly*
Exp	*Expositor*
ExpTim	*Expository Times*
FF	Foundations and Facets
FilolNT	*Filologia Neotestamentaria*
FRLANT	Forschungen zur Religion und Literatur des Alten und Neuen Testaments
GNS	Good News Studies
GNT	Grundrisse zum Neuen Testament
GTJ	*Grace Theological Journal*
HDR	Harvard Dissertations in Religion
HibJ	*Hibbert Journal*
HNT	Handbuch zum Neuen Testament
HTKNT	Herders theologischer Kommentar zum Neuen Testament
HUT	Hermeneutische Untersuchungen zur Theologie
ICC	International Critical Commentary
IDB	*The Interpreter's Dictionary of the Bible* (ed. G.A. Buttrick)
Int	*Interpretation*
JB	Jerusalem Bible
JBL	*Journal of Biblical Literature*
JBLMS	Journal of Biblical Literature Monograph Series
JETS	*Journal of the Evangelical Theological Society*
JJS	*Journal of Jewish Studies*
Jos.	Josephus
JSNT	*Journal for the Study of the New Testament*
JSNTSup	Journal for the Study of the New Testament Supplement Series
JT	Jesus tradition
JTS	*Journal of Theological Studies*
Just.	Justin Martyr
KD	*Kerygma und Dogma*
LCL	Loeb Classical Library
LD	Lectio divina
LingBib	*Linguistica Biblica*
LSJ	Liddell, Scott and Jones (*A Greek–English Lexicon*)
LTJ	*Lutheran Theological Journal*
LUÅ	Lunds universistets årsskrift

MeyerK	Kritisch-exegetischer Kommentar über das Neue Testament, founded by H.A.W. Meyer
MHT	Moulton, Howard and Turner (*A Grammar of New Testament Greek*)
MM	Moulton and Milligan (*The Vocabulary of the Greek Testament. Illustrated From the Papyri and Other Non-literary Sources*)
MNTC	Moffatt New Testament Commentary
N–A^{26}	*Novum Testamentum Graece* (ed. K. Aland *et al.*)
NICNT	New International Commentary on the New Testament
NIGTC	New International Greek Testament Commentary
NIDNTT	*The New International Dictionary of New Testament Theology* (ed. L. Goenen, E. Beyreuther and H. Bietenhard)
NKZ	*Neue kirchliche Zeitschrift*
NovT	*Novum Testamentum*
NovTSup	Novum Testamentum Supplements
NPNF	*A Select Library of Nicene and Post-Nicene Fathers of the Christian Church* (trans. H. Wace and P. Schaff)
NTAbh	Neutestamentliche Abhandlungen
NTAF	*The New Testament in the Apostolic Fathers*, by J.V. Bartlet, *et al.*
NTD	Das Neue Testament Deutsch
NTL	New Testament Library
NTS	*New Testament Studies*
NumS	Numen Supplements
OED	*The Oxford English Dictionary*
OTP	*The Old Testament Pseudepigrapha* (ed. J.H. Charlesworth)
P. Oxy.	*Oxyrhynchus Papyrus*
PerspRelStud	*Perspectives in Religious Studies*
PTMS	Pittsburgh Theological Monograph Series
RB	*Revue Biblique*
RevQ	*Revue de Qumran*
RNT	Regensburger Neues Testament
RTR	*Reformed Theological Review*
SANT	Studien zum Alten und Neuen Testament
SBLDS	Society of Biblical Literature Dissertation Series
SBLSBS	Society of Biblical Literature Sources for Biblical Study
SBT	Studies in Biblical Theology
Scr	*Scripture*
SJT	*Scottish Journal of Theology*
SM	The Sermon on the Mount/Plain (Matt 5.3–7.27; Luke 6.20-49)
SNT	Studien zum Neuen Testament
SNTSMS	Society for New Testament Studies Monograph Series

SNTW	Studies of the New Testament and its World
SQE	*Synopsis Quattuor Evangeliorum* (ed. K. Aland)
ST	*Studia Theologica*
Str–B	Strack and Billerbeck (*Kommentar zum Neuen Testament aus Talmud und Midrasch*)
SUNT	Studien zur Umwelt des Neuen Testaments
Test. XII Patr.	*Testaments of the Twelve Patriarchs*
TBü	Theologische Bücherei
TDNT	*Theological Dictionary of the New Testament* (ed. G. Kittel and G. Friedrich)
TGl	*Theologie und Glaube*
ThB	*Theologische Beiträge*
THKNT	Theologischer Handkommentar zum Neuen Testament
ThStud	*Theologische Studiën*
ThViat	Theologia viatorum. Jahrbuch der kirchlichen Hochschule Berlin
TLG	Thesaurus Linguae Graecae, a computer database of extant Greek literature from the 8th cent. BC to the 6th cent. AD
TLZ	*Theologische Literaturzeitung*
TNTC	Tyndale New Testament Commentaries
TPINTC	TPI New Testament Commentaries
TRu	*Theologische Rundschau*
TU	Texte und Untersuchungen
TWNT	*Theologisches Wörterbuch zum Neuen Testament* (ed. G. Kittel and G. Friedrich)
TynBul	*Tyndale Bulletin*
TZ	*Theologische Zeitschrift*
VC	*Vigiliae christianae*
WBC	Word Biblical Commentary
WC	Westminster Commentaries
WMANT	Wissenschaftliche Monographien zum Alten und Neuen Testament
WUNT	Wissenschaftliche Untersuchungen zum Neuen Testament
ZBNT	Zürcher Bibelkommentare NT
ZNW	*Zeitschrift für die neutestamentliche Wissenschaft*
ZTK	*Zeitschrift für Theologie und Kirche*

INTRODUCTION

Any suggestion that Paul was unfamiliar with or uninterested in the Jesus tradition must be considered improbable in view of the evidence accumulated for Paul's use of the pre-Synoptic eschatological traditions. It appears on the contrary that Paul's teaching is very heavily dependent on the teaching of Jesus, even though he does not often explicitly acknowledge this dependence.

D. Wenham (1984)[1]

It is almost impossible to forge significant links between Jesus and Paul on the basis of the sayings of Jesus which appear in the epistles: they are embarrassingly few in number, alluded to rather than quoted, perhaps known only because of their peculiar liturgical or legal status, and above all they are ignored by Paul when it suited his purpose. There is little to encourage links between Jesus and Paul here.

S.G. Wilson (1984)[2]

One of the unsolved questions in New Testament research is Paul's use of Jesus tradition (JT) in his Epistles.[3] Scholarly opinion has varied from Bultmann, who claimed 'the teaching of the historical Jesus plays no role, or practically none, in Paul', to W.D. Davies, who the same year asserted just as confidently, 'it was the words of Jesus himself that formed Paul's primary source in his work as ethical διδάσκαλος'.[4] At the end of his survey of research twenty-six years ago, Furnish allowed only a handful of probable echoes of the tradi-

---

1. D. Wenham, *Rediscovery*, p. 372.
2. Wilson, 'Contours', p. 8.
3. 'Jesus tradition' refers to traditions about the person and teaching of the historical Jesus.
4. Bultmann, *Theology*, I, p. 35; Davies, *Paul*, p. 136. Davies qualifies his view in the preface to his fourth edition, but he continues to think that JT was important for Paul (p. xxxiii; cf. p. 146 n. 1). Others adopting positions similar to Bultmann's include Schoeps (*Paul*, pp. 55-58), Klausner (*Paul*, pp. 314-15, 475-77), Schmithals ('Paulus', p.147), Bornkamm (*Paul*, p. 110), Conzelmann ('Jesus', p. 189) and Perrin (*Introduction*, p. 286).

tion, opining that the pursuit of parallels and alleged allusions to sayings of Jesus was a dead end.[1] More recently S.G. Wilson has declared, 'few would now deny that Paul's interest in the person and
teaching of Jesus is minimal'.[2] Nevertheless, a growing number of
scholars are reaffirming the earlier claim of Dodd, Davies, Hunter, *et
al.* that Paul's letters fairly bristle with echoes of dominical logia.[3]
Studies by Dungan, Fjärstedt and Wenham have argued that Paul valued and used words of Jesus.[4] Allison thinks the apostle knew blocks
of pre-Synoptic material (traditions behind Mk 6.6b-13; 9.33-50; Lk.
6.27-38, and an extended Passion narrative) as well as several isolated
sayings. He concludes, 'the persistent conviction that Paul knew next
to nothing of the teaching of Jesus must be rejected. . . the tradition
stemming from Jesus well served the apostle in his roles as pastor,
theologian, and missionary'.[5] After a century and a half of dispute,
firmly entrenched 'minimalists' and 'maximalists' continue to lob
shells into the other's camp with little apparent effect, and the battle
shows no sign of abating, although some seek shelter in an agnostic
'no-man's land' between the two extremes.[6]

   Similar skirmishes have taken place over the related question of
Paul's attitude toward Jesus as a moral exemplar. In addition to

   1. Furnish, 'Debate', p. 44.
   2. Wilson, 'Contours', pp. 6-7.
   3. Dodd, 'Catechism'; Davies, *Paul*, pp. 136-46; Hunter, *Predecessors*, pp. 45-
51. Significant earlier works include Feine, *Christus*; Knowling, *Testimony*; Moe,
Paulus; the latter two are often overlooked.
   4. Dungan, *Sayings*; Fjärstedt, *Traditions*; D. Wenham, *Rediscovery (passim)*;
idem, 'Use'; *idem*, 'Apocalypse'; *idem*, 'Echo'.
   5. Allison, 'Pattern', p. 25; criticized by Neirynck in 'Sayings', pp. 281-306. For
views similar to Allison's cf. Pfitzner, 'School'; Stanley, 'Significance'; *idem*,
'Allusions'; Bruce, 'Historical'; *idem*, *Jesus*, pp. 65-76; Fraser, *Interpreter*; Addley,
'Sayings'; Moule, 'Kerygma'; *idem*, 'Use'; Argyle, 'Parallels', p. 320; Selby, *Understanding*, pp. 298-311, 339-45.
   6. Cf., e.g., the range of views expressed in Wedderburn (*Paul*) and Richardson
and Hurd (*Studies*), the minimalist case of Neirynck ('Sayings'), and the exchange
between Tuckett ('Discourse') and Allison ('Discourse') over Paul's alleged use of
the missionary discourse. Munro (*Authority*) sees several echoes in Paul's letters,
but her thesis that this material constitutes part of an interpolated strata lacks strong
exegetical and textual evidence. For a history of the overall debate and for additional
literature see, e.g., Keegan, 'Paul'; Fraser, *Interpreter*, pp. 11-32; Dungan, *Sayings*,
p. xvii-xxix; and Furnish, 'Debate'.

challenging the significance of Jesus' *teachings* for Paul, Bultmann claimed,

> All that is important for him [Paul] in the story of Jesus is the fact that Jesus was born a Jew and lived under the Law (Gal. 4:4) and that he had been crucified (Gal. 3:1; 1 Cor. 2:2; Phil. 2:5ff., etc.). When he refers to Christ as an example, he is thinking not of the historical but of the pre-existent Jesus (Phil. 2:5ff.; 2 Cor. 8:9; Rom. 15:3).[1]

Likewise, Käsemann, Betz, Martin and others have rejected the usual understanding of Phil. 2.5-8 and related texts as appeals for Christians to imitate the character of Jesus.[2] On the other hand, Dunn writes that the ethical tradition which Paul uses '*seems to draw its force very largely (perhaps even entirely)...from the life of Jesus*, that is, from *the Jesus-tradition*, both his words... and his conduct'.[3] For Stanton, Paul's writings betray possession of 'a rich character portrait of Jesus', and others have argued that the imitation of Jesus plays some role in the apostle's ethical thought.[4] The gulf between the camps is wide, reflecting different presuppositions and methods.

The Need

Despite the ongoing discussion, crucial questions remain unanswered. Why does Paul refer to Jesus' teachings so rarely (i.e. 1 Cor. 7.10; 9.14; 11.23-25; and possibly 1 Thess. 4.15-16), if he knows more? Although diverse answers have been given, most scholars suggest only a few factors, oversimplifying the issue. Minimalists such as Wilson continue to repeat Baur's original arguments that Paul's religious experience and his strained relationship with the Jerusalem apostles explain a supposed indifference to dominical tradition;[5] granting Paul's use of tradition (cf. 1 Cor. 7.10, 12, 25, where he differentiates his own teaching from that of the Lord), some attribute his silence else-

---

1. Bultmann, *Theology*, p. 188; cf. pp. 293-94.
2. Käsemann, 'Analyse', p. 95; Betz, *Nachfolge*, pp. 137-89; Martin, *Carmen*, pp. 288-91; cf. Schrage, *Einzelgebote*, p. 240; Michaelis, *TDNT*, IV, pp. 666-74.
3. *Unity*, p. 68 (his emphasis).
4. Stanton, *Preaching*, p. 173. Cf., e.g., De Boer, *Imitation*, pp. 58-71; Tinsley, *Imitation*, pp. 134-65; Larsson, *Vorbild*; Webster, 'Imitation'; *idem*, 'Christology'.
5. Wilson, 'Contours', pp. 8-9; Baur, 'Christuspartei', esp. pp. 76-77, 83-84, 92-93; *idem, History*, I, p. 50 and n. 2.

where to ignorance.[1] Neither explanation satisfies the maximalists who reject a sharp disjunction between the Jesus of history and the risen Christ of faith, and who emphasize the opportunities Paul would have had to learn JT. Claiming that he assumed his readers' acquaintance with the tradition, they see his letters containing many 'allusions' to dominical teachings. But what constitutes an allusion, and by what criteria can we identify one? Too often writers in the past have been content simply to cite parallels as though a surface similarity in vocabulary or thought was enough to warrant confidence in a genetic relationship. What evidence there is has not usually been scrutinized with the kind of rigour necessary to convince more sceptical scholars who rightly raise questions of objectivity and method. If there *are* as many allusions as some claim, why does Paul not reveal the source of his language to make his points with greater force?[2] If he assumes a knowledge of the sayings on the part of his readers, the same could be said for the OT which he quotes often, naming his source. What is the relation of Paul to the Synoptic tradition and the direction of dependence, if any exists? M.D. Goulder for example sees a host of links between Matthew, Luke, and Paul's letters, but attributes them to the Evangelists' creative use of Paul.[3] Furthermore, did Paul think of the 'earthly' Jesus as an ethical paradigm, and if so, in what respects?

The Aims

The purpose of this book is not to try to 'solve' the Jesus–Paul problem; the complexity of the issue, the differing presuppositions of

1. From Paul's statement in 1 Cor. 7.25 that he has no command of the Lord, Bultmann drew the conclusion 'when Paul does not cite such a word where it would be expected, he knows of none' ('Significance', p. 222). Cf. Walter, who thinks Paul may not have understood Jesus' concept of the kingdom ('Jesus-Tradition', pp. 64, 79).

2. So Schweitzer: 'It is curious that...authors believe that they reduce the acuteness of the problem by pointing out in the Epistles as many reminiscences of Synoptic sayings as possible. That, of course, only makes the matter more complicated. If so many utterances of Jesus are hovering before Paul's mind, how comes it that he always merely paraphrases them, instead of quoting them as sayings of Jesus, and thus sheltering himself behind their authority?' (*Paul*, pp. 42-43).

3. Goulder, *Midrash*, pp. 153-70; *idem, Calendar*, pp. 227-40; *idem*, 'Luke'; *idem, Paradigm*. On the other hand, Orchard and Riley think Paul knew our Gospel of Matthew (*Order*, pp. 118-29).

scholars, and the limited scope of the evidence ensure that debate will continue. My goal is to seek to advance research in three respects. First, we need definitions and criteria in order to evaluate proposed 'allusions' to Jesus' teachings in Paul. The maximalist position has never fully recovered from its overstatement in Resch's *Der Paulinismus und die Logia Jesu* (1904). Resch undermined much of the credibility of the view with his epitome of parallelomania, proposing over a thousand allusions to Jesus' sayings in the Pauline corpus (including ten in Philemon!) and sixty-four in Paul's speeches in Acts. Those who discount Paul's interest in JT continue to cite his study—a lasting caricature of the potential excesses of the maximalist position. Moreover, the diverse Synoptic texts adduced by different writers as parallels for the same Pauline text do not evoke confidence in scholarly ability to detect allusions. Although criteria have been offered and discussed for judging the authenticity of JT in the Gospels and the presence of hymns/homologies in the Epistles, with few exceptions the study of Jesus–Paul parallels has enjoyed almost total freedom from controls imposed by a consistent method. The problem is well known, but little has been written to correct the deficiency.[1] Secondly, fundamental disagreement exists as to what we should expect to see in Paul's letters if he valued JT. Furnish is typical of those who make much of Paul's silence:

> One finds there [in Paul's letters] no details about Jesus' birth, no direct mention of Jesus' teaching or healing ministry, no confession at Caesarea Philippi, no transfiguration, no cleansing of the temple, no conflict with the authorities, no Gethsemane scene, no trial, no thieves crucified with Jesus, no last words from the cross, no soldiers, no weeping women, no word about the place or time of the crucifixion, no mention of Joseph or Mary, or of John the Baptist, or of Judas, or of Pilate.[2]

The author of a comparative study of Paul and Matthew observes that since Paul rarely appeals explicitly to Jesus' logia and feels free to qualify them when he does, 'It cannot be true. . . that the collected traditions of Jesus' teachings function as the primary basis of Christian morality for Paul—else we would have many more explicit references to them than we actually do'.[3] Another argues that Jesus never said

---

1. 'There is apparently no criterion by which one might determine what is or is not a substantial parallel' (Allison, 'Pattern', p. 5; cf. Bauckham, 'Study', p. 384).

2. Furnish, 'Debate', p. 43.

3. Mohrlang, *Matthew*, pp. 37-38.

'Love your enemies', partly on the basis that Paul's admonition to
bless those who persecute you in Rom. 12.14 is more primitive than
the parallels in the Synoptics, and since Paul does not cite Jesus by
name, the saying cannot have been attributed to Jesus when Paul
wrote.[1] The crucial (and common) assumption here that if a tradition
were important for Paul he would necessarily quote it and identify its
source, needs examining. The second goal of this study is to establish
some realistic expectations about Paul.

Thirdly, the bulk of the book focuses on a particular segment of
Romans as a test case in order to determine whether and how JT
served the apostle's ethics. Rom. 12.1–15.13 is often cited by those
who think Paul valued the tradition, inasmuch as it seems to echo a
number of dominical logia (especially Rom. 12.14-21; 13.7, 8-10;
14.13-14) and includes some of Paul's most direct appeals to Christ as
example (15.3, 8).[2] Surprisingly however, no one to date has studied
Rom. 12.1–15.13 *en bloc* in detail to determine whether Paul does use
JT, and if so, how it functions in his argument.[3] This book presupposes a thorough exegesis of the entire segment; only after attempting
to understand Paul on his own terms have I proceeded to examine
alleged dominical parallels. In some cases, analysis has required
consideration of critical texts outside Romans (especially Gal. 5–6;
Col. 3; Phil. 2; 1 Cor. 10–11). As a result of my research I will argue
that although Paul rarely alludes to JT, both Jesus' example and
teaching significantly influenced the shape of his admonitions.

The Limitations

My discussion of allusion could be broadened by attention to the phenomenon in Jewish texts (e.g. the use of the OT in Qumran texts,

---

1. Sauer, 'Erwägungen', p. 26.
2. So, e.g., D. Wenham, 'Use', p. 15. Cf. the surveys by J.P. Brown
('Parallels') and Talbert ('Tradition').
3. Stuhlmacher's suggestive essay touches on a number of passages in the Epistle
but is more a survey than a study, missing several important points of dispute in our
section ('Jesustradition', pp. 246, 248-50). Piper (*Enemies*), D. Wenham ('Use',
pp. 15-24) and Sauer ('Erwägungen') have explored traditions behind Rom. 12.14,
but they differ radically in their conclusions and do not investigate the segment as a
whole. The most recent (and thorough) analysis of the parallels is by Neirynck
('Sayings'); the method and conclusions here differ considerably from his. Of the
commentators, Dunn has given the question the most attention.

especially 1QH and 1QM), as well as to Paul's own use of the OT and extra-biblical sources, but to explore those areas here would take us far beyond the scope of this study. I will focus on comparing Paul's use of dominical tradition with the immediately relevant literature, that is, other NT Epistles and the earliest writings of the Apostolic Fathers (AF). Furthermore, my concern is not with the role of Jesus in Paul's theology, but in his ethical material, asking the question, how influential was the example and teaching of Jesus for Paul's understanding of how a Christian should behave? Thus there will be no attempt to recite the findings of those exploring the theological continuity and discontinuity between the two.[1] Paul's explicit references to 'words of the Lord' have already been investigated elsewhere and will not be treated here.[2]

The Assumptions

This study assumes the authenticity of the *Hauptbriefe*, Philippians, Philemon, 1 and 2 Thessalonians, and Colossians, recognizing that the two latter Epistles are widely disputed. Texts from Ephesians are not ignored because, if not by Paul, the letter attests the understanding of an early disciple or school soaked in his thought, and represents the trajectory of his theology—what the author and his audience believed Paul would have said. On occasion the testimony of Acts will be allowed as evidence (subject to refutation by the Epistles), although Luke's theological interests are not thereby denied.

In view of continuing dispute over the Synoptic problem, I am not adopting a particular stance on the order of the Gospels. There will be enough hypotheses employed here without building on a further unknown, that is, the existence of 'Q'. By avoiding as many needless assumptions as possible, it is hoped that this work may afford more lasting value.

---

1. Cf., e.g., Wedderburn, 'Problem'; *idem*, 'Similarity'; Hanson, *Paradox*; Güttgemanns, *Apostel*; Jüngel, *Paulus*.

2. On 1 Cor. 7.10-11 and 9.14 cf. Catchpole, 'Problem' (7.10-11); Dungan, *Sayings*; Fjärstedt, *Traditions*; D. Wenham, 'Use', pp. 7-15 (7.10-11); Richardson and Gooch, 'Logia'; on 1 Thess. 4.15-16 cf. Gundry, 'Hellenization'; Gewalt, 'Abgrenzung'; D. Wenham, 'Apocalypse', pp. 367-68; Waterman, 'Sources'; Hartman, *Prophecy*, pp. 181-90; Best, *Thessalonians*, pp. 189-93.

Methodological Issues

To some, study of allusions and echoes of Jesus may appear the height of folly. Not only is it impossible to *prove* that Paul is depending upon a tradition in the absence of quotation formulae or explicit statements to that effect, but questions about the availability and authenticity of the traditions seem to rule out the endeavour entirely. Classical form-criticism presupposed that the expectation of an imminent parousia and the immediacy of oracles from the risen Lord through Spirit-filled prophets so sufficiently claimed the attention of the earliest Christians that they had little need for or interest in JT, apart from missionary purposes. During an extended period of exclusively oral transmission, traditions that did go back to Jesus were passed on in isolated bits as a kind of folk literature, with little control or concern to preserve their original context. Only when the expectation of an imminent end began to fade did the tradition start to coalesce, according to this view; by that time it had come to include (as dominical) many sayings derived from prophets or freely created.

Nevertheless, this picture has been challenged from several sides.[1] Although space does not permit full discussion here, several facts deserve mention. The Qumran community's eschatological expectations did not keep them from producing and preserving a written tradition.[2] The prospect of early written collections of sayings of Jesus is not unlikely,[3] and many acknowledge that the Passion at least was transmitted as a block of material, not merely as isolated logia.[4]

---

1. For example, Ellis ('Directions'; *idem*, 'Criticism', pp. 38-43), Stuhlmacher ('Thema'), Stanton ('Criticism'), Güttgemanns (*Questions*), and Neugebauer ('Geistsprüche'), not all of whom agree in the scope of their criticisms.

2. A sense of imminency would have ensured the remembrance *at least* of those sayings of Jesus which fed that expectancy, as Christians scoured the available evidence to 'know the signs'. Moreover, this view fails to explain the writing of any Gospels datable before AD 70 (i.e. probably Mark), and it underestimates the need for traditional material in missionary work.

3. Luke 1.1-2; cf. also J.M. Robinson, 'Collections', although he does not generally accept the attribution of the sayings to Jesus. Ellis suggests that written collections were formed *before* Easter ('Directions', pp. 242-47). 'Q' (if it existed) is generally dated in the 50s. Rudimentary education (reading, writing and memorization skills) was widespread in Palestine (cf. Schürer, *History*, II, pp. 415-21; Hengel, *Judaism*, I, pp. 65-83).

4. For example, Pesch, *Markusevangelium*, II, pp. 21-22; Jeremias, *Words*, pp. 89-105; Dibelius, *Tradition*, p. 23. Robinson thinks the SM may also have had a

Eyewitnesses of Jesus were presumably still alive to tell the story and to attest the reliability of the tradition (cf. 1 Cor. 15.6), not simply to create it *ex nihilo*.[1] Riesenfeld and Gerhardsson have rightly been criticized for claiming that Jesus trained his disciples to perpetuate his teachings in rabbinic fashion, but they have shown the importance of memory and have raised the question of Jesus' work as a teacher.[2] Riesner has taken this latter point much further, stressing the nature of Jewish education, the unique authority of Jesus, and the memorable form of his teachings.[3] The need for learning and transmitting dominical teaching arose from the disciples' first mission(s) during the ministry of Jesus (the twelve, Mk 6.7-13 pars.; the seventy, Lk. 10.1-12),[4] and the concentration of apostles in Jerusalem as a centre of leadership after the resurrection ensured a measure of continuity and control over the traditioning (cf. Gal 2.2).[5] If fluid and diverse, traditions about Jesus and his teachings were surely available in Paul's day.[6]

separate existence ('Collections', pp. 391-92), a hypothesis corroborated by apparent echoes in the Epistles and early AF (see Chapter 2 below).

1. But cf. Nineham, 'Testimony I, II, III'; Teeple denies the existence of early authentic oral JT ('Tradition').

2. Riesenfeld, 'Tradition'; Gerhardsson, *Memory; idem, Transmission; idem, Origins; idem, Tradition*; cf. also Vincent, who argues that discipleship as depicted in the Gospels necessitated learning Jesus' teachings by heart ('Heart', esp. p. 116). Gerhardsson in particular has been cited *inter alia* for (1) attributing to Jesus rabbinic techniques which evolved after AD 70, (2) overlooking profound differences between the message of Jesus and that of the rabbis, (3) ignoring pervasive and significant variations in the tradition that put the lie to any *rigorous* traditioning controls, and (4) underestimating the creativity of the early Church. Cf. Smith ('Comparison'), Davies ('Reflections'), Perrin (*Rediscovering*, pp. 30-32), and Davids ('Gospels'). A targumic model for explaining the transmission of Gospel traditions (in Palestine) may prove more fruitful than Gerhardsson's mishnaic one, since the Targums are both oral and written in nature, are also specifically Jewish, are designed for popular consumption, and manifest a Synoptic relationship (Chilton, 'Transmission', pp. 28, 39-40; *idem*, 'Study').

3. Riesner, 'Elementarbildung'; *idem*, 'Ursprung'; *idem, Lehrer*.

4. Cf. Schürmann, 'Anfänge', pp. 364-65, 369-70.

5. For other factors favouring the preservation of reliable traditions cf. Stein, 'Criteria', pp. 226-27.

6. Cf. Dunn, *Unity*, pp. 70-80. One immediate source of variation is the multilingual character of early Christian tradition: 'It should not be expected that material which passed from one language and culture to another would have been so free of

The question of the authenticity of Synoptic sayings presents an obvious problem. No consensus exists as to which logia had their origin in the early Christian communities through prophetic utterance,[1] assimilation of contemporary extraneous traditions, or redaction by the writers of the Gospels. Decisions about the origin of particular logia here must thus be tentative and dependent upon the labours of others. What is clear is that by the time the Synoptics were written, the communities in which the Gospels arose had sufficient confidence to accept the teachings (in their Greek translation) as words of Jesus.[2] For our purposes we must be content to focus primarily on the relationship of parallels between Paul and sayings preserved in the Synoptics.

Since Paul rarely refers his readers to dominical teachings *per se*, all judgments about potential dependence must be couched in terms of probabilities. 'Allusions' and 'echoes' are by their nature slippery creatures; even if one can make a strong case for some relationship between two texts, to go further inevitably requires speculation. Both texts may simply draw on a popular Jewish tradition, or reflect common human reactions to similar religious conditions. Heitmüller pointed long ago to the Achilles's heel of the maximalist position: the 'Hellenistic' Christianity in which Paul's faith was formed was already (according to Heitmüller) a step removed from Palestinian JT.[3] What-

change as material which stayed in the same language and was maintained by members of a relatively small and static group [i.e. rabbinic Judaism]' (E.P. Sanders, *Tendencies*, p. 28).

1. Hill is very cautious, finding few probable instances of prophetic 'words of the Lord' placed on the lips of Jesus (*Prophecy*, pp. 160-85; *idem*, 'Evidence'). Boring identifies a considerable number of prophetic words in 'Q' and thinks Mark wrote in a 'prophetic' manner (*Sayings; idem*, 'Prophecy'). Aune concludes, 'the historical evidence in support of the theory lies largely in the creative imagination of scholars' (*Prophecy*, p. 245). It is striking that Matthew's Gospel ends with the command to observe all that ἐνετειλάμην, not ἐντέλλομαι or ἐντελοῦμαι; the focus there at least is on commands given in the past, not in the present (cf. Wilckens, 'Preaching', pp. 599-600). Clearly Paul does not feel free to produce an *ad hoc* saying of Jesus in 1 Cor. 7.25, but I find the moderate case argued by Hawthorne ('Prophets') most persuasive. For a list of Synoptic logia suspected of having been influenced/ composed and transmitted by early Christian prophets, see Aune, 'Index'.

2. Consequently, subsequent references to sayings, words, teachings, or logia as 'dominical' or 'of Jesus' are to be understood in the sense that the Gospel writers *attributed* them to Jesus, unless specified otherwise.

3. 'Problem', pp. 325-30.

ever traditions Paul knew were supposedly mediated through this grid, and furthermore, whatever parallels exist could simply reflect use of a catechetical tradition, not necessarily dominical logia known as such.[1] Despite these and other occasions for uncertainty, it is important to distinguish the sort of cumulative argument employed here from that in which each successive point is built upon an earlier hypothesis. When one constructs a case which depends upon a series of dubious conclusions, the probability that the overall hypothesis is correct diminishes as the number of necessary (and suspect) assumptions increases. In our case, however, the hypothesis that Paul was influenced by JT does not require each potential echo to be a genuine instance of influence. The higher the number of parallels with a reasonable degree of probability, the greater the likelihood that at least one or more of them preserves a genuine link.[2]

Having said that, in the course of my investigation of Romans a number of minor parallels and 'possible' links with JT will be noted, which for some may conjure up the spectre of Resch. They are included not as probative evidence (the sum of fifty zeros is still zero), but (1) for the sake of completeness, and more importantly, (2) in order to show the many lines of continuity between Jesus and Paul which one would expect if the fundamental thesis of this book is correct.

Perhaps the most compelling test for both the authenticity of a logion and, as we shall see, for Pauline dependence on that tradition— the criterion of dissimilarity—poses a crucial problem in the study of allusions and echoes, particularly in the area of ethical admonitions, where diverse religious traditions hold much in common. Recent Gospel scholarship has increasingly recognized that Jesus was much more a man of his culture than earlier writers thought.[3] The less exceptional his ethical teaching becomes, however, the more difficult

1. For theories of a primitive Christian catechism (τύπον διδαχῆς? Rom. 6.17) cf. Seeburg, *Katechismus*, pp. 1-44; Carrington, *Catechism*; Selwyn, *1 Peter*, pp. 363-466; and Dodd, 'Catechism'.

2. 'It is true that with some cumulative arguments the whole argument is no stronger than its weakest link. But in other cases. . . the argument is more like a cable with many strands, which does not depend on its weakest strands, than a chain with many links' (D. Wenham, *Rediscovery*, p. 12).

3. So, e.g., Harvey, *Constraints*; E.P. Sanders, *Jesus*; although cf. Wright ('Constraints') on Jesus' distinctive emphases.

it is to demonstrate that Paul or any other early Christian adopted a given ethical position *because it was the way of Jesus*. This is especially true in the case of OT ethical traditions, which had authority for both (cf., e.g., Rom. 13.9 and Mk 12.31). At the same time, it should not be forgotten that a saying's lack of originality by no means argues against its authenticity or its authority.

Each of the potential 'allusions' in Rom. 12–15.13 could merit a full-scale study, and the same could be said for every Synoptic parallel adduced. Any evaluation of parallels must consider extra-biblical sources that offer an alternative source of inspiration. However, whereas many Greek writings can be dated fairly accurately, rabbinic literature presents a particular problem. NT scholars have been criticized for uncritical acceptance of the dates and attribution of rabbinic parallels.[1] In this study rabbinic material will be given the benefit of the doubt, but the reservations of Vermes and others must be kept in mind.

Finally, Paul's use of Ἰησοῦς and Χριστός reveals that he did not make a neat distinction between the Jesus of history and the risen Christ of faith.[2] For the sake of clarity, however, I will maintain this distinction in terminology when evidence permits. I am on safer methodological ground if I risk error by including in my discussion some material referring only to Χρίστος by name, than if I exclude it, and the nature of the christological foundation of Paul's ethics will become more apparent in the process.

---

1. 'The use of the rabbinic data testifies. . . to a kind of historical fundamentalism; every attribution is believed, and every citation is seen to represent the truth' (Vermes, 'Reflections', p. 363); cf. Alexander, 'Judaism', and the works of Neusner.

2. In some places he clearly refers to the 'earthly' Jesus by κύριος Ἰησοῦς (1 Cor. 11.23; 1 Thess. 2.15), Χριστὸς Ἰησοῦς (Rom. 3.24-25; 6.3; 8.34), Ἰησοῦς Χριστός (Rom. 5.15), and Χριστός (Rom. 5.6, 8; 9.5; 1 Cor. 1.23; 8.11; 15.3); elsewhere he just as clearly uses Ἰησοῦς of the risen one (Rom. 4.24; cf. 1 Thess. 1.10; 4.14). Regardless of their possible pre-Pauline origins, Rom. 1.3-4 and Phil. 2.5-11 demonstrate that Paul regarded the man Jesus and the exalted Christ as one and the same person.

PART I

ALLUSIONS AND ILLUSIONS

Chapter 1

The Meaning and Detection of Allusions

1. *The Literary Phenomenon: What is an Allusion?*

Some natural tears they dropp'd, but wip'd them soon;
The World was all before them, where to choose
Thir place of rest, and Providence thir guide:
They hand in hand with wand'ring steps and slow,
Through *Eden* took thir solitary way.

(Milton, Paradise Lost XII, 645-649)[1]

The earth is all before me – with a heart
Joyous, nor scared at its own liberty,
I look about, and should the guide I chuse
Be nothing better than a wandering cloud
I cannot miss my way.

(Wordsworth, The Prelude I, 15-19)[2]

Although there is debate as to the exact nature of the comment Wordsworth is making about Milton's text, literary scholars agree that here Wordsworth is alluding to *Paradise Lost*.[3] Yet the only words shared between the texts are 'all before', 'choose', 'guide', 'wandering' and 'way'. The *OED* defines *allusion* as 'a covert, implied, or indirect reference',[4] and the word is capable of a variety of nuances, sometimes serving as a synonym for 'reference'.[5] In literary works,

1. *Complete Poems and Major Prose* (ed. M.Y. Hughes; Odyssey Press, 1957), and cited by Coombs ('Allusion', p. 476).
2. *Wordsworth: The Prelude* (ed. E. de Selincourt and rev. S. Gill; Bristol, 1970); cited by Coombs ('Allusion', p. 476).
3. Coombs, 'Allusion', p. 476.
4. *OED*, I, p. 242 col. 3. 'Allusion' has its origin in the Latin *alludere,* to joke, jest, mock, or play with (Perri, 'Alluding', p. 301).
5. Coombs, 'Allusion', pp. 475-76. H.W. Fowler however denies that 'allusion' ever involves outright or explicit mention of the referent (*Dictionary*, pp. 18-19).

allusion has a more precise meaning. One critic differentiates allusion from mere source-borrowing because the former 'requires the reader's familiarity with the original for full understanding and appreciation'; it differs from mere reference 'because it is tacit and fused with the context in which it appears'.[1] The compiler of the largest annotated bibliography to date on the phenomenon of allusion defines it as a conscious attempt on the author's part to remind readers of an earlier text, so that through their reflection on that text, the present author's meaning is enhanced in some way. In order for the allusion to be successful, the audience must *recognize* the sign, *realize* that the echo is deliberate, *remember* aspects of the original text to which the author is alluding, and *connect* one or more of these aspects with the alluding text in order to get the author's point.[2] Despite their differences, literary critics concur that allusion involves (1) the use of a sign or marker that (2) calls to the reader's mind another known text (3) for a specific purpose.[3]

Such precision in definition has somehow eluded most NT parallel hunters. Although their sources differ in kind from the Epistles and oral tradition, literary critics rightly point out that allusion is a fundamental literary technique that is not limited to poetry, and they can help us appreciate the need for caution before asserting that Paul is 'alluding' to dominical tradition in a given passage. If we insist on speaking of 'allusion', or 'allusive citation' or 'allusive quotation', we should be prepared to answer the following questions.

1. By 'allusion' do we mean that Paul is *intentionally* using language from dominical tradition, or are we thinking of 'unconscious echoes'?
2. By 'allusion' do we mean that Paul wants his readers to recognize the dominical tradition as such?
3. Is it necessary to the normal understanding of the text that the reader recognize the allusion?

1. Miner, 'Allusion', p. 18 col. 1.
2. Perri, 'Alluding', p. 301.
3. Perri bemoans the lack of agreement as to what *precisely* constitutes allusions and how they may be classified; cf. Perri, 'Alluding', pp. 289, 304-305; *idem*, 'Studies', pp. 178-225; Ben-Porat, 'Poetics', pp. 105-107; Miner, 'Allusion', p. 18 col. 1.

4. Precisely what is the sign or allusion-marker in Paul's text which echoes the tradition?
5. Is the echo sufficient to be recognized as such?
6. What is the purpose of the allusion (i.e. to give added authority, provide a springboard for contrasting thoughts, anticipate an objection, etc.)?

For the purpose of this study, I will use 'quotation' to refer to instances in which the writer uses direct quotation with an explicit citation formula (e.g. γέγραπται γάρ). 'Allusion' will refer to statements which are *intended* to remind an audience of a tradition they are presumed to know as dominical; clear examples by this definition are 1 Cor. 7.10 and 9.14. 'Echo' or 'reminiscence' will refer to cases where the influence of a dominical tradition upon Paul seems evident, but where it remains uncertain whether he was conscious of the influence at the time of dictating.

2. *Criteria for Evaluating Allusions and Echoes*

Little has been written about how to identify allusions in biblical literature. Sound method requires (1) discerning whether a significant parallel exists between the two texts, (2) determining the likelihood of their relationship, and (3) seeking to clarify the precise nature of that relationship.[1] In developing my criteria, I am dependent not only on comments by students of the Jesus–Paul issue, but also on studies of the use of the OT in the NT,[2] an essay on criteria for hymns and homologies,[3] discussions of criteria for determining authenticity of dominical logia,[4] and general essays more concerned with the parallels between Christianity and Judaism.[5] The following criteria are proposed as tests to help identify and evaluate an alleged allusion to or echo of a saying in Gospel 'G' by the author of an Epistle 'E'. No

1. Cf. Donaldson, 'Parallels'.
2. Notably Hays, *Echoes*, pp. 29-32; Reasoner, 'Relationship', pp. 34-47; Moo, *Narratives*, pp. 20-21; Gundry, *Use*, pp. 2-5; Ellis, *Use*.
3. Gloer, 'Homologies'.
4. Stein, 'Criteria'; Hooker, 'Christology'; *idem*, 'Tool'; Mealand, 'Test'; Downing, *Church*, pp. 93-131; Calvert, 'Examination'; Barbour, *Criticism*, pp. 1-27. Polkow ('Method') provides a useful overview.
5. Sandmel, 'Parallelomania'; Donaldson, 'Parallels'.

individual criterion is in itself evidence of an allusion/echo, and in most cases the judgment of the scholar is subjective.

a. *Verbal agreement.* Aside from the presence of an explicit formula, the clearest sign of possible allusion is shared vocabulary. Obviously the greater the number of significant shared words in G and E, and the greater their rarity in E and other Epistles by the same author, the higher the probability that there exists some kind of shared tradition. On the other hand, if the saying is a commonplace or the author has chosen the only appropriate way to express the idea, the significance of the parallel diminishes. Since letters were to be read aloud, words were chosen for their aural effect; we should not expect slavish repetition of a tradition unless the author's purpose is specifically to convey a tradition as such. The crucial question is whether the text contains oral signposts recalling readers to JT.

1. How many words are shared in common? Are they identical or cognates?[1]
2. How significant are the shared words? In making this judgment the following points should be considered. Do they belong to the core terminology of the logion in G or are they peripheral words (e.g. common particles)? Are they rare in E, in other Epistles by the same author, and in extra-biblical literature? What other word(s) could have been chosen? Should we have expected something different? Can a likely underlying Semitic original be identified? Are there indications elsewhere in E and other Epistles by the author that the significant word(s) come from Jesus tradition?
3. Is there a unique combination of significant words?[2]

1. Cf., e.g., 1 Pet. 5.8-9 and Lk. 22.31-32, where Gundry thinks 1 Peter's στερεοί goes back to Jesus' command, στήρισον τοὺς ἀδελφούς σου ('*Verba*', p. 344).

2. For example, the rare collocation of σημεῖον, κήρυγμα, and σοφία in 1 Cor. 1.21-22, when compared with the same combination in Mt. 12.38-42 // Lk. 11.29-32: 'Only in Q and I Corinthians does the term kerygma occur prior to the Pastorals, and only in Q and I Corinthians is Sophia clearly a Christological title, and only in Q (Luke 11.29-32, and parallel) and I Corinthians 1.17-2.7 are the two rare usages combined with each other and the rejection of signs required by "this (evil) generation" (Q), "the Jews" (I Cor.)' (J.M. Robinson, 'Shifts' pp. 85-86).

4. Are possible translation variants present? If this is claimed, an Aramaic/Hebrew original should be proposed.[1]
5. How can significant differences in vocabulary be explained, if dependence on a common source is accepted?

b. *Conceptual agreement.* Sayings in G and E can exhibit extensive verbal agreement and yet have different meanings and origins; conceptual agreement is also a prerequisite, although it would be possible for an author deliberately to use the same language in a different sense (i.e. an antithetical or contrastive allusion). The context of a saying in the Gospels may have confirming value, but as some sayings apparently circulated in isolation, Gospel context must remain a secondary consideration. On the other hand, Paul's context is primary. Allusion requires some notable allusive marker or sign, but echo does not require any shared vocabulary, as long as the shared idea(s) is sufficiently distinct. Allowance must be made for deliberate redactional adaptation, faulty memory, or use of a form of the Gospel tradition different from those available to us.[2]

1. Are the sayings in G and E similar in meaning?
2. Does a significant word(s) in E correspond in meaning to the same word(s) in G, in contrast to the usual meaning of the word(s) elsewhere in E or other Epistles by the author?[3]
3. Is there an unusual combination of ideas?[4]
4. Is there a common significance of the saying in G and E (i.e. a similar application to the community)?

c. *Formal agreement.* To what extent are G and E parallel in form (i.e. structure, number of elements)?[5]

---

1. That is, something Gundry fails to do when he compares 1 Pet. 1.4 and Lk. 12.33, calling Peter's κληρονομίαν and Luke's θησαυρόν 'translation-variants' when they show no overlap in the LXX ('*Verba*', p. 337).
2. Bauckham, 'Study', p. 384.
3. For example, εἰσέρχεσθαι used by Paul only in Rom. 11.25 of entry into God's kingdom/the community of God's people (other instances in Rom. 5.12; 1 Cor. 14.23-24); cf. the common Synoptic usage (Mk 9.43, 45, 47; 10.15, 23-25; etc.). Cf. Michel, *Römer*, p. 355.
4. For example, 'moving mountains' as an expression for doing the impossible has parallels (e.g., Isa. 54.10; Str–B, I, p. 759; cf. Lucian, *Navigium*, 45), but *faith to move mountains* does not (1 Cor. 13.2 // Mk 11.22-23 pars.).
5. For example, the contrast between being wise as. . . /innocent as. . . in

d. *Place of the Gospel saying in the tradition*. Was the logion available?

1. Is its authenticity likely? Here the usual tests for authenticity should be applied, with awareness of their assumptions and flaws. How plausible is a redactional creation? Is there evidence of dependence on the Epistle writer?

2. Is there multiple attestation? Appearance elsewhere in early Christian literature *can* indicate that a teaching was widespread in the early church (assuming the documents are independent), although the possibility always exists that the other parallels are dependent on Jewish or Greek traditions rather than on dominical logia. Similarly, if a saying is repeated within the same Gospel, the likelihood increases that it was important and well known in that community, and possibly outside. Is it alluded to elsewhere as *dominical*? Is it echoed in another source that appears to have been influenced by dominical teaching? If not, is it paralleled elsewhere as a Christian teaching outside the Gospels? Does its parallel(s) elsewhere share significant characteristics with the saying in E?

3. Is it relevant to the community? The more important the issue addressed by the logion, the more likely it is that it would have been preserved and passed on. Is it likely that the author's readers knew the tradition? Would it have any special relevance to them?[1]

e. *Common motivation, rationale*. In the case of ethical material is there a similar rationale given or implied for correct behaviour?[2]

f. *Dissimilarity to Graeco-Roman and Jewish traditions*. To what extent are sayings in G and E unparalleled outside Christian texts? Is there a more immediate and relevant parallel from another source? Is Paul more likely to know and use this source than the Jesus tradition?

Rom. 16.19 and Mt. 10.16.

1. For example, the 'Render unto Caesar' logion and its parallel in a letter addressed to *Romans* (13.7); see Chapter 7.

2. For example, the appeal to divine judgment in Rom. 14.10-11 and Mt. 7.1 par.; see Chapter 10.

The existence of an extra-Gospel parallel does not necessarily diminish the probability of a link with dominical tradition. To require sayings to be unparalleled outside early Christianity in order to be genuine or to show dependence is to isolate the idiosyncratic. This criterion thus provides a strong positive argument for dependence,[1] but it has little negative force in disproving a link unless at the same time one can show that E agrees with other traditions against G.

g. *Presence of dominical indicators.* Is there some sign in the context that the author of E is thinking about Jesus and would therefore be inclined consciously to allude to, or unconsciously to echo, his teaching? Does he use Ἰησοῦς, Χριστός, κύριος, etc. in the immediate context?[2] If so, is the formula a likely reference to the earthly Jesus?

h. *Presence of tradition indicators.*[3] There are a variety of different types of signs that an author may be using traditional material, although again no one sign in itself proves the case; it may simply reflect the author's own compositional style.

1. Grammar. Is there a disturbance in syntax or a significant change in the grammar of E to indicate the use of a new source?[4]
2. Style. Is there any abrupt change of style in E? Are there any distinctive stylistic features in E (e.g. parallelism, chiasmus, antithesis, rhythm, short pregnant polished clauses, parison [use of words which end with the same sound to produce rhythm and sometimes rhyme], isocolon [perfect equality of clauses], homoeoteleuton [repetition of the same case ending], or homoeoptoton [resemblance of cases at the beginning, middle or end of a line])?[5]

1. For example, the Lord/Day of the Lord coming as a thief in the night (1 Thess. 5.2, 4; cf. Mt. 24.43 // Lk. 12.39), unparalleled outside Christian literature; cf. D. Wenham 'Apocalypse', p. 347.
2. E.g., Rom. 14.14: ἐν κυρίῳ Ἰησοῦ; see Chapter 12.
3. Cf. Gloer, 'Homologies', pp. 124-29.
4. For example, Paul's change from participles to finite imperatives in Rom. 12.14; see Chapter 6.
5. Gloer, 'Homologies', p. 129. Cf. the alliteration, assonance, isocolon, parallelism and rhythm in Rom. 13.7:

3. Traditional formulation. Is there use of an introductory particle (e.g. ὅτι, γάρ, δέ) or introductory formulae (e.g. οὐκ οἴδατε, μὴ πλανᾶσθε)?[1] Obviously the mere use of these words does not mean that they necessarily function as introductory formulae. Is there use of indirect discourse?
4. Use of tradition words in context (ὁμολογεῖν, πιστεύειν, πίστις, μαρτυρεῖν, μάρτυς, παραλαμβάνειν, παραδιδόναι).
5. Interruption of flow of context.

i. *Presence of other dominical echoes or word/concept clusters in the immediate context.* Are significant words from other dominical logia echoed in the context? Is there evidence of conflation of material from two or more dominical sayings? Is there evidence of serial quotation of dominical sayings?[2]

j. *Likelihood the author knew the saying.* Does the author of E exhibit interest in/knowledge of Jesus tradition elsewhere?[3] Obviously in the absence of clear citations this criterion is circular, presupposing for some texts that which it seeks to prove in others. Does the author of E exhibit knowledge of a block of material (found in G) of which the logion is a part?[4]

k. *Exegetical value.* How does the saying function in the argument of E? How is the understanding of the thought of the passage and the

---

(a) τῷ τὸν φόρον τὸν φόρον, τῷ τὸ τέλος τὸ τέλος
(b) τῷ τὸν φόβον τὸν φόβον, τῷ τὴν τιμὴν τὴν τιμήν

1. οὐκ οἴδατε introduces a common proverb in 1 Cor. 5.6, and often Paul follows it with teaching he presupposes that his readers should know (cf. 1 Cor. 3.16; 6.2-3, 16, 19, etc.). This increases the likelihood that in 1 Cor. 6.9 Paul's uncharacteristic reference to inheriting the kingdom of God has traditional (dominical?) roots. μὴ πλανᾶσθε immediately precedes a quotation attributed elsewhere to Menander (*Thais*, Loeb edn, p. 356) in 1 Cor. 15.33, and a proverb in Gal. 6.7.
2. The inspiration for these criteria I owe to E.P. Sanders, although he applies them in a different context ('Dependence', p. 32).
3. 'A certain number of clear citations or allusions in a particular writer may provide not unreasonable grounds for tipping the balance in favour of more doubtful allusions, especially if these show some kind of coherence with the clearer ones' (Bauckham, 'Study', p. 384).
4. Cf. the argument of Allison, 'Pattern'.

historical situation enhanced by identifying the saying as dominical?[1]

Criteria such as these cannot be expected to *prove* dependence in a mathematical way. Although some criteria are weightier than others (e.g. verbal, conceptual or formal agreement as compared to presence of other dominical echoes), we cannot assign numerical relative values to the criteria and add them up to determine mechanically whether or not a genuine allusion or echo exists. Their value lies in assisting the judgment of relative probability. After applying these tests to a given text, the evidence should be judged and the proposed allusion/echo deemed either significant or insignificant. If significant, it may then be evaluated as to its relation to the Gospel text, and the probability of dependence on a dominical logion may be located on the following scale: virtually certain, highly probable, probable, possible, doubtful and incredible.[2] In Part II, I shall apply these tests to texts in Romans. My evaluation of the texts will be based on the criteria listed here, but the presentation of the data in each case will vary; to follow the schema outlined above in every instance would require too much repetition (citing the inapplicable criteria), and in some cases the data pertaining to several criteria are interrelated. First it is necessary to establish realistic expectations for Paul by surveying non-Pauline usage of JT.

---

1. For example, Gundry argues that dominical links in 1 Peter point to Petrine authorship ('*Verba*'; *idem*, 'Further').

2. With minor changes (dropping 'certain' and substituting 'doubtful' for 'conceivable' [virtually anything is conceivable]), the scale is adapted from E.P. Sanders, *Jesus*, p. 321.

Chapter 2

EARLY EPISTOLARY USAGE OF JESUS TRADITION
OUTSIDE PAUL

If other early Christian writers only rarely cite the teachings and example of Jesus, we should not expect to see something radically different in Paul. Most (if not all) of the other texts were written later than his letters, and some of the authors probably knew one or more of the Gospels in substantially their present form. The following section summarizes a larger investigation into other non-narrative NT writings and in the early Apostolic Fathers to serve as a backdrop for the study of Paul.[1]

1. *Jesus Tradition in the New Testament*

a. *James*
The lack of explicit quotations in James does not mean an ignorance of JT. Often observed is the frequency of its verbal and thought contacts with sayings preserved in the Synoptics; despite the uncertainties of particular cases, the author evidently knew teachings of Jesus.[2]

---

1. Not every document surveyed here is strictly an Epistle, but they are all sufficiently similar to each other and dissimilar to the Apocalypse of John, the *Shepherd of Hermas*, and the *Martyrdom of Polycarp* to warrant inclusion. The *Epistle to Diognetus* is excluded for its late date; its evidence is consistent with the conclusions reached below. For our purposes we need not argue questions of authorship, integrity and date. On JT in the Apocalypse, see Bauckham, 'Parables' and Vos, *Traditions*. Cf. Bauckham, 'Bibliography' for additional studies of JT outside the Gospels.

2. So, e.g., Mussner (*Jakobusbrief*, p. 51); Dibelius (*James*, p. 29). Davids charts and discusses the phenomena (*Epistle*, pp. 47-50); cf. also Martin, *James*, pp. lxxiv-lxxvi; Mussner, *Jakobusbrief*, pp. 48-50; Shepherd, 'James'; Kittel, 'Ort'; Moulton, 'James'; and Mayor, *James*, pp. lxxxv-lxxxviii. Hartin ('James') offers the

One parallel is particularly striking:

Jas 5.12	Mt. 5.34-37
Πρὸ πάντων δέ, ἀδελφοί μου, **μὴ ὀμνύετε μήτε τὸν οὐρανὸν μήτε τὴν γῆν μήτε ἄλλον τινὰ ὅρκον· ἤτω δὲ ὑμῶν τὸ ναὶ ναὶ καὶ τὸ οὒ οὔ**, ἵνα μὴ ὑπὸ κρίσιν πέσητε.	ἐγὼ δὲ λέγω ὑμῖν **μὴ ὀμόσαι ὅλως·** μήτε ἐν τῷ **οὐρανῷ** . . . μήτε ἐν τῇ **γῇ** . . . μήτε εἰς Ἱεροσόλυμα . . . μήτε ἐν τῇ κεφαλῇ σου ὀμόσῃς . . . **ἔστω δὲ ὁ λόγος ὑμῶν ναὶ ναί, οὒ οὔ·** τὸ δὲ περισσὸν τούτων ἐκ τοῦ πονηροῦ ἐστιν.

Justin Martyr cites this prohibition of swearing as a saying of Jesus, and the form of his positive injunction is closer to James's than to Matthew's (ἔστω δὲ ὑμῶν τὸ ναὶ ναὶ καὶ τὸ οὒ οὔ, *Apol.* I.16.5).[1] Dibelius rarely committed himself to say that the author is using JT, but he did in this case, explaining,

> the absence of a quotation formula in Jas does not qualify as evidence that the saying about swearing was not regarded as a dominical saying in the time of Jas. Other sayings of Jesus whose provenance is more assured are also used in paraenetic texts without special introductory identification [he cites Rom. 12.14]. . . . This is not surprising, for all paraenesis which is delivered by teachers who are considered bearers of the Spirit stems ultimately from the Lord, and therefore it possesses an even higher authenticity than a quotation formula can provide.[2]

It does not follow that 'bearers of the Spirit' would possess higher authenticity than an explicit quotation of Jesus, since the teachings of Christian prophets did not have unquestioned authority in the early church, but were tested (1 Thess. 5.21; 1 Cor. 14.29), among other things by their coherence with received tradition.[3] Nevertheless, Dibelius's insight into the nature of paraenesis is important. The admonitions in James are woven together to call for right behaviour, not to argue points of dogma or to establish the speaker's credentials,

most recent study of the parallels, concluding that James reflects familiarity with Q traditions as they developed within the Matthaean community.

1. Cf. Minear, 'Demand'. For other early Christian parallels see Dibelius, *James*, p. 250 n. 53. D. Wenham thinks Paul echoes the logion in 2 Cor. 1.17-18 in response to accusations that his words and actions were not consistent with those of Jesus ('Echo', pp. 275-76).

2. Dibelius, *James*, p. 251; cf. also *idem*, *Tradition*, p. 241.

3. Dunn, '"I"-Sayings', pp. 189-92, 197-98.

so quotation formulae were not required.[1] Addressing the ethical needs of his hearers, the Spirit-filled apostle spoke with authority, not needing to footnote his admonitions. Accordingly, there are few, if any, explicit clues in the text of the presence of the dozen or so dominical echoes.[2] The purpose of the document was not to give a historical account of Jesus' teaching, but to convey the will of the Lord of the Church. The letter of James *assumes* the speaker's authority, as the author probably intended to be identified by his readers as an apostle, the brother of Jesus.

Davids takes a complementary approach, interpreting the lack of quotations and abundance of echoes to indicate that the author lived in a period when the sayings were 'in the air'; the readers would have recognized the teachings as essentially those of Jesus.[3] He likens the letter to 'a halakah based on the Jesus tradition in which the oral law (the tradition) is amplified and applied to concrete situations'.[4] Almost all of the material common to James and the Synoptic tradition is ethical in nature. The Epistle does not refer to the events in Jesus' life or to his example for believers—a curiosity not only for those who posit his brother as the author but also for those assuming pseudonymous authorship, since the later the letter, the more we might expect to see evidence of increased veneration and emulation of Jesus.

b. *1 Peter*
Verba Christi in 1 Peter have been the subject of several studies.[5]

---

1. Cf. Gerhardsson, *Origins*, pp. 38-39. Regarding the quotation of OT texts, see Chapters 6 and 8.

2. Cf. the addition of βασιλικόν in 2.8 and possibly πρὸ πάντων δέ in 5.12. In addition to these, the verses most often cited as echoes are 1.2 (cf. Mt. 5.12); 1.4 (Mt. 5.48); 1.5 (Mt. 7.7); 1.6 (Mt. 21.21-22); 1.22 (Mt. 7.24); 2.5 (Mt. 5.3 // Lk 6.20); 2.13 (Mt. 5.7); 3.17-18 (Mt. 5.9); 4.4 (Mt. 6.24); 4.11-12 (Mt. 5.22; 7.1-2); 5.2-3 (Mt. 6.19-20); 5.9 (Mt. 24.33); 5.10 (Mt. 5.12).

3. Davids, *Epistle*, p. 9 n. 30.

4. 'James', p. 74; cf. Childs: 'the sayings of Jesus are not presented within the epistle by means of citation formulae, but function as the prism through which the Old Testament is now understood. In a manner paralleled to Matthew's Gospel, James understands the entire Old Testament from a Christian perspective with Christ being its true interpreter' (*Canon*, p. 437). James quotes the OT five times (2.8, 11 [twice], 23; 4.6).

5. Cf. Gundry, '*Verba*', Best's response ('Tradition'), Gundry's reply to Best ('Further'), and more recently Maier, 'Jesustradition'. If Best is too restrictive in his

There appears to be some consensus that 1 Pet. 2.12, 19-20; 3.9, 14;
4.14; and 5.3-4 derive from Jesus' teachings, or at least from a paraenetic tradition going back to him. Most of the logia are clustered in
the SM; all are ethical in nature. 'Peter' quotes the OT seven times
(1.16, 24; 2.6, 7-8; 3.10-12; 4.18; and 5.5), but never cites Jesus by
name, and none of the dominical echoes agree completely with Synoptic logia. He draws on oral tradition, displaying a freedom to adapt
traditions to the needs of his audience. Whether one sees many or few
significant parallels to JT in 1 Peter, the resulting impression is of an
author who employs traditions as a matter of course without needing
to identify their origin.

The example of Jesus features in exhortations about suffering, submission, and possibly shepherding (2.21–3.1; 3.18-22; 5.2-4). Otherwise, 'Peter' says nothing of Jesus' compassion, wisdom, or understanding, nor does he refer to events in his life, his miracles, or his
parables. If the author was an eyewitness and companion of Jesus, the
dearth of direct reference to JT has immediate implications for our
study of Paul: one could hardly expect more from a man who had
never met the earthly Jesus. If on the other hand the letter is late, it
comes from a community (Rome; 1 Pet. 5.13) which presumably
knew the Gospel of Mark and perhaps the Gospel of Luke. In either
case, the failure to quote Jesus could not possibly stem from ignorance
of the tradition.

c. *Hebrews*
Two 'quotations' from Jesus appear in Hebrews, but both consist of
texts from the OT, are unparalleled in our Gospels, and probably
reflect subsequent Christian meditation on the OT rather than logia of
Jesus (Heb. 2.12-13 citing Ps. 21[22].23 and Isa. 8.17-18; Heb. 10.5
citing Ps. 39[40].7-9). One looks in vain for allusions to dominical
parables and other teachings; verbal links are rare. By contrast,
Moffatt lists over seventy quotations or reminiscences of the OT, the
citation in 8.8-12 from Jer. 31.31-34 being the longest in the NT.[1]

---

judgments, Gundry and Maier seem too eager to find parallels (especially with
John's Gospel); the truth probably lies somewhere in between. In his commentary,
Goppelt sees echoes of over a dozen sayings (*Petrusbrief*, p. 54); Michaels is more
cautious (*1 Peter*, pp. xli-xlii).
    1. Moffatt, *Hebrews*, p. 264.

Hebrews is concerned to show how Christ is superior to the OT system which he fulfils.

The author clearly knows some details about the 'days of his flesh' (5.7) from the narrative tradition, including Jesus' descent from the tribe of Judah (7.14), the fact that he was tempted (2.18; 4.15),[1] suffered (2.10, 18) and died outside Jerusalem (13.12). The last supper tradition may be reflected in his comments about the covenant established by Jesus' blood (10.15-19; 12.24), although the source could equally be the liturgical tradition. The reference to Jesus' prayers with loud cries and tears in 5.7 suggests knowledge of the Gethsemane experience (Mk 14.32-42 pars.).[2] He mentions Jesus' faithfulness and endurance (3.2-6; 12.2), his learning of obedience (5.8), and implicitly, his humility (5.5). These brief references assume that his readers already possess knowledge of the life and character of Jesus. The Lord's obedience in temptation (4.15; cf. 5.8) and perseverance in suffering (12.1-3; 13.12-13) are foremost in his mind as qualities for Christians to emulate. Aside from his Passion, traditions of Jesus play no role in the exhortation,[3] but it would be erroneous to infer that the author did not know further details. Hebrews was not written to evangelize its readers, or to inform them of the details of one with whom they were already familiar.

d. *The Johannine Epistles*
Although 2 and 3 John are too brief to tell us anything about the author's knowledge and use of JT, the evidence of the first letter is significant.[4] There we encounter the closest thing to a direct quotation of Jesus in the NT Epistles, yet we are still far from finding the sort of citation appearing later in the AF. In 1.5 John declares what he and his companions have heard from the Lord (Jesus):[5] God is light and in

---

1. Nothing in the texts however requires knowledge of the wilderness temptation tradition.

2. So Bruce, who also cites Jn 12.27 (*Hebrews*, pp. 98-101). Nevertheless, Buchanan claims that the text in Hebrews could simply be the result of exegesis of Ps. 114 [116] (*Hebrews*, p. 253).

3. Cf. Buchanan, *Hebrews*, p. 255.

4. Whether or not the same person wrote the Epistles and Gospel, the writings appear to have come from one community.

5. The probable referent of ἀπ' αὐτοῦ; so, e.g., Smalley (*1, 2, 3 John*, p. 19) and R.E. Brown (*Epistles*, p. 194), although the latter thinks every logion in the

him there is no darkness at all. John *may* be quoting an agraphon here, but probably is summarizing teaching attributed to Jesus.[1] So also 1 Jn 2.25, where the Son is said to have promised eternal life (cf. Jn 4.14; 6.63, 68; 10.10, 28). An introductory formula similar to that in 1.5 occurs again in 3.11,[2] where the content of the message (ἵνα ἀγαπῶμεν ἀλλήλους) repeats teaching attributed to Jesus in John's Gospel (13.34; 15.12, 17). Another likely reference to Jesus' love commandment appears in 1 Jn 3.23 (cf. 4.7): Καὶ αὕτη ἐστὶν ἡ ἐντολὴ αὐτοῦ, ἵνα πιστεύσωμεν τῷ ὀνόματι τοῦ υἱοῦ αὐτοῦ Ἰησοῦ Χριστοῦ καὶ ἀγαπῶμεν ἀλλήλους, καθὼς ἔδωκεν ἐντολὴν ἡμῖν. Although God the Father could be the subject of ἔδωκεν, Jesus was the means through which the command was revealed. The aorist points back to Jesus' teaching—what Jesus said, God said (cf. Jn 8.26; 14.9-10). Finally in 1 Jn 4.21 we read: καὶ ταύτην τὴν ἐντολὴν ἔχομεν ἀπ' αὐτοῦ, ἵνα ὁ ἀγαπῶν τὸν θεὸν ἀγαπᾷ καὶ τὸν ἀδελφὸν αὐτοῦ. Here ἀπ' αὐτοῦ probably refers to God as the ultimate source, but Jesus' teaching role need not be excluded. The combination of love for God and love for the brother as *one* ἐντολή parallels Mk 12.28-31 // Mt. 22.36-39.[3] Furnish concludes, 'This is the only New Testament passage outside the Synoptic Gospels where we can be fairly sure of a direct reference to the Great Commandment with equal stress on each of its parts'.[4]

Epistle came from the Paraclete (Jn 14.26), not the historical Jesus.

1. Jesus calls himself the light of the world in Jn 8.12; 9.5; cf. 12.35-36, 46; in Matthew he speaks of his disciples in the same terms (5.14-16). His coming was interpreted as a revelation of light (Mt. 4.16; Lk. 2.32; Jn 1.4-9; etc.).

2. αὕτη ἐστὶν ἡ ἀγγελία ἣν ἠκούσατε ἀπ' ἀρχῆς. . . 'From the beginning' probably refers to his readers' first encounter with the message of Jesus (cf. 2 Jn 5-6; R.E. Brown, *Epistles*, pp. 440, 155-58).

3. Brown objects that the author does not speak of two commandments and does not give priority to love for God (*Epistles*, p. 564), but (1) Jesus insisted on giving the two together when asked for only one, and (2) John's purpose is not to introduce his readers to the teaching for the first time, but to *apply* it in a practical way to their situation. Obviously his readers already claimed to love God; the problem was that some were neglecting the practical outworking of that love in relationships with their brethren.

4. *Command*, p. 151; so also J.A.T. Robinson, *Priority*, p. 332. John's choice of ἀδελφός instead of πλησίον is understandable in the light of one of his purposes: to address heterodox members *within the community* who undervalued the importance of love (Smalley, *1, 2, 3 John*, p. 265).

In none of the above do we find a verbatim quotation from the Fourth Gospel, much less from the Synoptics, even though a concern of the author is to combat error and correct false teaching. Apparently his readers were well aware of the JT, so that only a brief reference was necessary to remind them of the teaching in order to make his points. Sayings of Jesus (particularly the love command) had obvious authority for the author, whether or not he is identified as the apostle John. Likewise, the obedience, purity, and self-sacrificing love of Jesus are characteristics he calls his readers to emulate (1 Jn 2.6; 3.2-6, 16). Yet, if we only possessed the Johannine Epistles, we could hardly demonstrate that the community had a Gospel.[1]

e. *Jude*

Jude uses OT imagery and quotes from an extra-canonical Jewish apocalypse (*1 En.* 1.9 in vv. 14-15), but affords no glimpse of JT—again, no surprise in view of the letter's brevity and the author's purpose.

f. *2 Peter*

In what is arguably the latest NT Epistle, we find for the first time clear reference to a pre-Passion event in Jesus' life—the transfiguration (2 Pet. 1.16-18; Mt. 17.1-8 pars.), and the author quotes God's declaration to Jesus on the mountain. Closest to Matthew's version, the quotation is not verbatim:

2 Pet. 1.17	ὁ υἱός μου ὁ ἀγαπητός μου οὗτός ἐστιν εἰς ὃν ἐγὼ εὐδόκησα[2]
Mt. 17.5	οὗτός ἐστιν ὁ υἱός μου ὁ ἀγαπητός, ἐν ᾧ εὐδόκησα
Mk 9.7	οὗτός ἐστιν ὁ υἱός μου ὁ ἀγαπητός
Lk. 9.35	οὗτός ἐστιν ὁ υἱός μου ὁ ἐκλελεγμένος

The evidence favours use of independent tradition (perhaps Peter's preaching) here, not a Synoptic Gospel.[3] Reference to the transfiguration functions to support the claim to certainty that Jesus will return, for 'Peter' thus had a foretaste of Christ's future honour and

1. Most date the Gospel before the Johannine Epistles (R.E. Brown, *Epistles*, p. 33); if the Gospel is later, the community would presumably have had its traditions.

2. So 𝔓[72] and B; many mss. have conformed the text to Matthew's.

3. Bauckham, *Jude, 2 Peter*, pp. 205-10.

The author does not quote teachings of Jesus, even though on the pseudonymous view Mark's Gospel (and probably Luke's, if not Matthew's also) would have been known in Rome. The clearest of the dominical echoes[1] in the letter shows his freedom to modify its application:

2 Pet. 2.20	Mt. 12.45 // Lk. 11.26
For if, after they have escaped the defilements of the world through the knowledge of our Lord and Saviour Jesus Christ, they are again entangled and overpowered, γέγονεν αὐτοῖς τὰ ἔσχατα χείρονα τῶν πρώτων.	Then he [the unclean spirit] goes and brings with him (seven) other spirits more evil than himself, and they enter and dwell there; καὶ γίνεται τὰ ἔσχατα τοῦ ἀνθρώπου ἐκείνου χείρονα τῶν πρώτων. (So shall it be also with this evil generation.)

Matthew and Luke put the saying in the context of the scribes' and Pharisees' demand for a sign and failure to believe, whereas 'Peter' applies it to false teachers who stray from the faith and become enslaved to sin (cf. also *Herm. Sim.* 9.17.5; *Mand.* 5.2.7; 12.5.4).

Concerned with the question of the delay of the *parousia*, 'Peter' knows at least one of Jesus' eschatological sayings (the coming as a thief; 2 Pet. 3.10). Yet, compared to 1 Thessalonians 4–5 there are actually fewer eschatological elements in 2 Peter paralleled by Synoptic logia, despite the fact that the letter is later than Paul's Epistle, perhaps by as much as fifty years. As with other NT letters, the contacts with *verba Christi* are fragmentary, and there are no extended parallels. The author assumes that his readers are well-instructed in the sayings of the Lord (1.12). He appears more concerned to stress the importance of maintaining the commandments of their apostles (3.2; 2.21) than to rehearse dominical logia, and he does not appeal to Jesus' example.

2. *Jesus Tradition in the Apostolic Fathers*

a. *1 Clement*
In *1 Clement* we encounter something new—two clear quotations of Synoptic logia, both introduced with a call to 'remember the words of

---

1. Bauckham sees four 'certain allusions' (1.14, 16-18; 2.20; 3.10; *Jude, 2 Peter*, p. 148; on the latter parallel cf. D. Wenham, 'Found').

the Lord Jesus' (cf. Acts 20.35).[1] A string of seven logia follow a quotation from Jer. 9.23-24 in *1 Clem.* 13.2:[2]

1 Clement	Matthew	Luke
Ἐλεᾶτε, ἵνα ἐλεηθῆτε·	μακάριοι οἱ ἐλεήμονες, ὅτι αὐτοὶ ἐλεηθήσονται (5.7)	Γίνεσθε οἰκτίρμονες, καθὼς καὶ ὁ πατὴρ ὑμῶν οἰκτίρμων ἐστίν (6.36)
ἀφίετε, ἵνα ἀφεθῇ ὑμῖν·	Ἐὰν γὰρ ἀφῆτε . . . ἀφήσει καὶ ὑμῖν ὁ πατήρ (6.14; cf. Mk 11.25)	ἀπολύετε, καὶ ἀπολυθήσεσθε (6.37)
ὡς ποιεῖτε, οὕτω ποιηθήσεται ὑμῖν·	Πάντα οὖν ὅσα ἐὰν θέλητε ἵνα ποιῶσιν ὑμῖν . . . οὕτως . . . ποιεῖτε αὐτοῖς (7.12)	Καὶ καθὼς θέλετε ἵνα ποιῶσιν ὑμῖν . . . ποιεῖτε αὐτοῖς ὁμοίως (6.31)
ὡς δίδοτε, οὕτως δοθήσεται ὑμῖν·		δίδοτε, καὶ δοθήσεται· (6.38)
ὡς κρίνετε, οὕτως κριθήσεσθε	Μὴ κρίνετε, ἵνα μὴ κριθῆτε (7.1)	Καὶ μὴ κρίνετε, καὶ οὐ μὴ κριθῆτε (6.37)
ὡς χρηστεύεσθε, οὕτως χρηστευθήσεται ὑμῖν·		ἀγαθοποιεῖτε . . . ὅτι αὐτὸς χρηστός ἐστιν (6.35)
ᾧ μέτρῳ μετρεῖτε, ἐν αὐτῷ μετρηθήσεται ὑμῖν·	ἐν ᾧ μέτρῳ μετρεῖτε, μετρηθήσεται ὑμῖν (7.2; cf. Mk 4.24)	ᾧ γὰρ μέτρῳ μετρεῖτε, ἀντιμετρηθήσεται ὑμῖν (6.38)

Except for the sixth saying, similar maxims appear in the SM.[3] None of them perfectly mirrors the Synoptics, and the order differs. Generally agreeing in thought and vocabulary, they vary in *form*. The repeated imperative + ἵνα in the first two logia followed by the

---

1. *1 Clem.* 13.1: μάλιστα μεμνημένοι τῶν λόγων τοῦ κυρίου Ἰησοῦ, οὓς ἐλάλησεν διδάσκων ἐπιείκειαν καὶ μακροθυμίαν· οὕτως γὰρ εἶπεν . . . ; *1 Clem.* 46.7: μνήσθητε τῶν λόγων τοῦ κυρίου Ἰησοῦ· εἶπεν γάρ . . .

2. See Hagner, *Use*, pp. 135-51; cf. also Pol. *Phil.* 2.3.

3. The word about 'being kind' may be Clement's paraphrase of the logion in Lk. 6.35, but the thought is different. 'Here . . . we are evidently confronted by an extra-canonical saying recorded by Clement' (Hagner, *Use*, pp. 139-40).

ὡς. . . οὕτω(ς) form in the next four favours a dependence upon oral tradition; at least it helped Clement recall and communicate the 'reciprocal' sayings. The last logion functions as a summary. Clement adduces the sayings to expound humble-mindedness (ταπεινο-φρονήσωμεν) by showing how Jesus taught ἐπιείκεια and μακροθυμία (13.1), yet none of these words appear in the logia, a fact to be remembered when considering Pauline appeals for the same qualities (i.e. Phil. 2.3; 2 Cor. 10.1; Col. 3.12; cf. Eph. 4.2).

The second citation occurs in *1 Clem.* 46.8:[1]

1 Clement	Matthew	Luke
οὐαὶ τῷ ἀνθρώπῳ ἐκείνῳ	οὐαὶ δὲ τῷ ἀνθρώπῳ ἐκείνῳ δι' οὗ ὁ υἱὸς τοῦ ἀνθρώπου παραδίδοται·	οὐαὶ τῷ ἀνθρώπῳ ἐκείνῳ δι' οὗ παραδίδοται (22.22)
καλὸν ἦν αὐτῷ εἰ οὐκ ἐγεννήθη	καλὸν ἦν αὐτῷ εἰ οὐκ ἐγεννήθη ὁ ἄνθρωπος ἐκεῖνος (26.24b; Mk 14.21b)[2]	
ἢ ἕνα τῶν ἐκλεκτῶν μου σκανδαλίσαι	ὃς δ' ἂν σκανδαλίσῃ ἕνα τῶν μικρῶν τούτων τῶν πιστευόντων εἰς ἐμέ,	
κρεῖττον ἦν αὐτῷ περιτεθῆναι μύλον	συμφέρει αὐτῷ ἵνα κρεμασθῇ μύλος ὀνικὸς περὶ τὸν τράχηλον αὐτοῦ	λυσιτελεῖ αὐτῷ εἰ λίθος μυλικὸς περίκειται περὶ τὸν τράχηλον αὐτοῦ
καὶ καταποντισθῆναι εἰς τὴν θάλασσαν ἢ ἕνα τῶν ἐκλεκτῶν μου διαστρέψαι	καὶ καταποντισθῇ ἐν τῷ πελάγει τῆς θαλάσσης (18.6; cf. Mk 9.42)[3]	καὶ ἔρριπται εἰς τὴν θάλασσαν ἢ ἵνα σκαν-δαλίσῃ τῶν μικρῶν τούτων ἕνα (17.2)

Here two sayings of Jesus are combined from different contexts in the Synoptics and applied to the problem of strife and schism, emphasizing the gravity of the offence.[4] Clement's first logion is similar to

1. See Hagner, *Use*, pp. 152-64.
2. Mark omits ἦν.
3. Mk 9.42 reads, καὶ ὃς ἂν σκανδαλίσῃ ἕνα τῶν μικρῶν τούτων τῶν πιστευόντων καλόν ἐστιν αὐτῷ μᾶλλον εἰ περίκειται μύλος ὀνικὸς περὶ τὸν τράχηλον αὐτοῦ καὶ βέβληται εἰς τὴν θάλασσαν.
4. For other Christian parallels cf. Hagner, *Use*, pp. 157-59; *Herm. Vis.* 4.2.6.

Matthew's and Mark's, lacking the former's redundant ὁ ἄνθρωπος ἐκεῖνος and the reference to Jesus' betrayal which did not suit the immediate purpose. The second saying differs from the Synoptics in vocabulary and form, but the thought is the same. Clement seems to know Matthew or his special source; καταποντίζειν is unique in the AF and occurs in the NT only at Mt. 14.30 and 18.6.

Aside from these quotations, the closest parallel with JT is *1 Clem.* 24.5, where ἐξῆλθεν ὁ σπείρων and other shared vocabulary recall the parable of the sower.[1] If, as it seems, Clement is echoing the Gospel tradition,[2] he is using familiar language to present a homily on 1 Cor. 15.36-50. He also refers to παραγγελίαι given to the apostles before Christ's resurrection (42.1-3; cf. 49.1).

Clement presumably knew narrative JT, yet rarely refers to it. In 2.1, after alluding to the agraphon recorded in Acts 20.35, he reminds the Corinthians of how they first paid attention to Jesus' words and sufferings, storing his λόγοι up carefully in their hearts, and keeping his παθήματα before their eyes. If the letter was written while he was a bishop, he would have been regarded as a tradition-bearer and expected to know and teach JT. Nevertheless, he only *shows* familiarity with details of the Passion (*1 Clem.* 16; 46.8).[3]

For Clement, Christ is the supreme example of ταπεινοφροσύνη. This appears most clearly in *1 Clement* 16, an extended discussion of Jesus' humiliation. The chapter concludes with the exhortation, 'You see, beloved, what is the example (ὑπογραμμός) which is given to us; for if the Lord was thus humble-minded (ἐταπεινοφρόνησεν), what shall we do, who through him have come under the yoke of his grace?' (cf. also 2.1; 58.2). If it is justified to deduce from this that the humility of Jesus underlies Clement's calls for ταπεινοφροσύνη

---

1. Other verbal links include ἅτινα πεσόντα (Matthew: ἃ μὲν ἔπεσεν), ξηρά (Synoptics: ἐξηράνθη); πλείονα αὔξει καὶ ἐκφέρει καρπόν (Mark: καὶ ἐδίδου καρπὸν ἀναβαίνοντα καὶ αὐξανόμενα καὶ ἔφερεν). As in Hebrews, *1 Clem.* puts OT quotations on the lips of Christ, but these probably do not go back to Jesus (16.15; 22.1-8).

2. So Lightfoot (*Fathers* 1.2, p. 83); Hagner says most commentators see Clement alluding to the Synoptics here, but he leaves open the option of dependence on oral tradition (*Use*, pp. 164-65).

3. Hagner finds several parallels to the Lukan nativity narrative, but the links are dubious (*Use*, pp. 169-70).

elsewhere in the letter, the dominical example profoundly influenced
him; the noun and related words occur thirty-one times in the
Epistle.[1]

Thus in a letter by a man who cites the OT more than any NT
author, we find two passages which quote Jesus, few certain allusions,
and no references to pre-Passion events in his life.[2] Clement's failure
to use Jesus' 'Render unto Caesar' logion in his prayer/call for submission to rulers (60.2, 4; ch. 61) cannot be due to ignorance. To
infer from this data that he was less interested in JT than the OT or
general paraenetic tradition would be erroneous. When he does
employ the sayings, he can paraphrase because he is aware that he has
written διὰ τοῦ ἁγίου πνεύματος (63.2), and because he knows his
readers have already been grounded in tradition.

b. *Barnabas*
In *Barnabas* we find a clear quotation from a written source of Jesus'
sayings. Although the formula ὡς γέγραπται does not specify a
dominical origin, the following verse introduces the suffering of Jesus
for the first time in the Epistle. The quotation is similar to a saying
twice attested in Matthew's Gospel:

Barn. 4.14	προσέχωμεν, μήποτε, ὡς γέγραπται,
	πολλοὶ κλητοί, ὀλίγοι δὲ ἐκλεκτοὶ εὑρεθῶμεν
Mt. 22.14	πολλοὶ γάρ εἰσιν κλητοί, ὀλίγοι δὲ ἐκλεκτοί
	(20.16 var.)

Given the saying's proverbial character, the author may have used an
apocryphal source unknown to us,[3] but probably he is quoting either
Matthew or a written *Vorlage*.[4] The logion is not verbatim:

---

1. ταπεινοφροσύνη in 21.8; 30.8; 31.4; 44.3; 56.1; and 58.2; ταπεινοφρονεῖν
in 2.1; 13.1, 3; 16.1-2, 17; 17.2; 19.1; 30.3; 38.2; 48.6; and 62.2; ταπεινόφρων in
19.1 and 38.2; ταπείνωσις in 16.7; 53.2; 55.6; ταπεινοῦν in 18.8, 17 and 59.3
(twice); ταπεινός in 30.2; 55.6; 59.3-4.

2. 'No writing of the NT contains as many long quotations as Clement, and in no
NT writing does the quotation material compose so large a percentage of the total
contents as it does in Clement' (Hagner, *Use*, p. 23).

3. *NTAF*, p. 18; Köster, *Überlieferung*, p. 126; cf. Kraft, *Barnabas*, p. 91. Often
cited, *4 Ezra* 8.1, 3 are not complete parallels; they contrast the fate of the many and
the few but say nothing about calling and election.

4. If he could use γέγραπται of apocryphal texts (4.3) there is no reason why he
could not do the same with words derived from a Gospel. Hagner thinks he knew

'Barnabas' drops the unnecessary γάρ, and adds εὑρεθῶμεν, emphasizing the future, making the quoted words apply directly to his generation. The citation serves to warn against over-confidence and sin (cf. 4.13). Two other quotations from the Lord introduced with φησίν (7.11) and λέγει (6.13) appear to be words from Christian prophets.

Aside from three quotations of OT texts cited by Jesus in the Synoptics (5.12; 12.10-11; 14.9), *Barnabas* clearly echoes Jesus only once:

Barn. 5.9	οὐκ ἦλθεν καλέσαι δικαίους ἀλλὰ ἁμαρτωλούς
Mk 2.17	οὐκ ἦλθον καλέσαι δικαίους ἀλλὰ ἁμαρτωλούς
Mt. 9.13	οὐ γὰρ ἦλθον καλέσαι δικαίους ἀλλὰ ἁμαρτωλούς
Lk. 5.32	οὐκ ἐλήλυθα καλέσαι δικαίους ἀλλὰ ἁμαρτωλούς

The author virtually quotes the saying, changing the verb form to fit his narrative. Since 'Barnabas' apparently possessed a written source of dominical sayings (4.14), probably a Gospel has influenced him again here.[1] He uses the saying to explain why Jesus chose as his apostles those who were 'iniquitous above all sin', a statement needing powerful justification in the early church!

In the exposition of the Way of Light (ch. 19), several short commands probably reflect Jesus' teachings and example. A Christian is to be ἁπλοῦς in heart, hating all ὑπόκρισις (followed by a reference to ἐντολαὶ κυρίου, 19.2), ταπεινόφρων instead of self-exalting (19.3), πραΰς (19.4), and loving the neighbour more than his own life (19.5). Clustered near the beginning of the Way, these exhortations are followed by many others derived from the OT.[2]

'Barnabas' mentions Jesus' τέρατα καὶ σημεῖα, his preaching, his great love for the people of Israel (5.8), and his choice of the apostles (5.9). Like Matthew, he uses Zech. 13.7 to describe Jesus' suffering (*Barn.* 5.12; cf. Mt. 26.31), and he knows that Jesus was given a scarlet robe to wear (*Barn.* 7.9 // Mt. 27.28) and vinegar and gall to drink (*Barn.* 7.3, 5; cf. Mt. 27.34, 48). He applies Ps. 21[22].19 to Jesus' Passion as the Gospels do (*Barn.* 6.6 // Mt. 27.35 pars.); the increase in narrative JT is due to his purpose in showing how Jesus

---

Matthew (*Use*, pp. 275, 281); so also Grant (*Introduction*, p. 78).

1. *Contra* Köster, *Überlieferung*, p. 145. A variant of the same logion occurs in 1 Tim. 1.15.

2. Cf. also references to τὰ δικαιώματα κυρίου (2.1; 21.1), αἱ ἐντολαὶ τῆς διδαχῆς (16.9), and τὸ ἐν παραβολαῖς κεῖσθαι (17.2), the referents of which are unclear.

fulfils the OT. On the other hand, he makes no explicit appeal to the
example of Jesus. His call for endurance (2.2; 21.5) could be compared with Christ's ὑπομονή in his suffering (5.1, 5 [twice], 6, 12;
14.4), but no direct connection is made. Perhaps the idea of Jesus'
example was so fundamental that it was assumed.

Although he apparently knew a written source of dominical tradition, 'Barnabas' quotes Jesus and echoes his teachings only once. This
cannot mean that he was ignorant or uninterested in JT. In a document
similar to Hebrews in theological tendency and use of the OT, we find
a corresponding approach to dominical tradition.

c. Didache

Didache offers two quotations of dominical logia introduced by
formulae:[1]

Did.	Mt.	Lk.	Formula
8.2	6.9-13	11.2-4	ὡς ἐκέλευσεν ὁ κύριος ἐν τῷ εὐαγγελίῳ αὐτοῦ
9.5	7.6		καὶ γὰρ περὶ τούτου εἴρηκεν ὁ κύριος

Did. 8.2 closely resembles Matthew's version of the Lord's Prayer,
differing in three particulars: ἐν τῷ οὐρανῷ for Matthew's ἐν τοῖς
οὐρανοῖς, τὴν ὀφειλήν for τὰ ὀφειλήματα, and ἀφίεμεν for ἀφή-
καμεν. This form may be more primitive than Matthew's,[2] but the τῷ
εὐαγγελίῳ in the citation formula could well refer to the First
Gospel; certainly both appear to draw on a similar source.[3] Identical
to Matthew's text, the logion 'Give not that which is holy to the dogs'
in 9.5 is used to justify barring the unbaptized from the Eucharist. It
could represent a Jewish *mashal* cited independently of Jesus (cf. *m.*

---

1. *Did.* 1.6 is an agraphon (Glover, 'Quotations', pp. 16-17) or paraphrases
Sir. 12.1-7.
2. So Draper ('Tradition', p. 279), but his arguments are inconclusive.
3. Those favouring *Didache's* knowledge of Matthew include Streeter (*Origins*,
pp. 507-11), Butler ('Relations', p. 283) and Hagner (*Use*, p. 280; but see *idem*,
'Sayings', pp. 240-42). Glover ('Quotations', pp. 27-28) and Draper ('Tradition',
pp. 283-84) think the εὐαγγέλιον was a collection of dominical sayings. Matthew
and the *Didache* probably derive from a common geographical setting (Court,
'Didache'), although one would not normally expect such textual differences in the
Lord's Prayer (repeated three times daily, *Did.* 8.3).

Tem. 6.5) with κύριος in the introductory formula referring to the Lord of the OT.[1] Against that, however, is the context of 9.5, a eucharistic prayer in which the author has referred to baptism in the Lord's name immediately before.

Unlike *1 Clement* and *Barnabas*, *Didache* also contains many probable echoes of dominical logia.[2] They tend to come in clusters, with most of the parallels occurring in 1.3–2.1; 8.1-2; 15.3-4; and ch. 16.[3] At the beginning of the Two Ways we find a catena of allusions to logia preserved in the SM which provides an introductory exposition of the 'great' commandment and the negative golden rule—the Way of Life. The context implies that the collection of sayings served in the instruction of catechumens.[4] The logia are not introduced as teachings of Jesus, yet as we have already seen, this is not surprising. The exhortations correspond closely to those of Matthew 5–7, but the order varies and sometimes Lukan particulars appear.[5]

Other logia provide guidance for prayer and fasting (8.1-2), as well as for the reproof of a brother (15.3). If the εὐαγγέλιον in 15.4 refers to collected logia, we have a strong indication of their significance: 'But your prayers and alms *and all your acts* (καὶ πάσας τὰς πράξεις) perform as ye find in the Gospel of our Lord'.[6] This is followed by a concluding chapter full of echoes of eschatological teachings attributed to Jesus in the Synoptics. Particularly striking are the links between *Did.* 16.5-8 and Matthew 24, but the verbal differences are extensive enough to encourage divergent explanations.[7]

Didache stands apart from *1 Clement* and *Barnabas* in its relatively

---

1. So Draper, 'Tradition', pp. 273, 285 n.18.

2. See Glover ('Quotations') and Draper ('Tradition') for the texts.

3. Some material in the last chapter *may* derive from an original form of the Two Ways, but if so the other clusters are later additions (still within the first century), included for the purpose of subordinating Jewish teachings of the earlier tradition to the authority of the Gospel (Draper, 'Tradition', p. 271).

4. Draper cites Justin, *Apol.* I.15-16 as another text setting out the kernel of Christian teaching for baptismal candidates ('Tradition', p. 284).

5. See Draper, 'Tradition', pp. 273-79; Köster, *Überlieferung*, pp. 217-39. Although he usually emphasizes the use of free oral tradition by the AF, Köster grants the influence of Matthew and Luke here (pp. 238-39).

6. Cf. the call to act in given ways κατὰ τὸ δόγμα τοῦ εὐαγγελίου in 11.3.

7. For detailed study see Kloppenborg, 'Tradition'; Butler, 'Relations'; Glover, 'Quotations' 25-28; and Draper, 'Tradition', pp. 282-83.

high frequency of dominical sayings. This and the absence of appeal to the example of Jesus are best explained by its purpose: the prescript states that it is Διδαχὴ κυρίου διὰ τῶν δώδεκα ἀποστόλων τοῖς ἔθνεσιν, which teaching we would expect to include words of Jesus as well as material from other sources. Although the compiler knows many Gospel traditions, he provides only one verbatim citation (9.5), and his quotation from the Lord's Prayer agrees with neither Matthew's version nor Luke's. The longest collection of dominical echoes lacks any indication of the source of the teachings, apart from the implication of the title of the whole work. *Didache*'s diversity in word choice and want of explicit reference to Jesus (only at 9.2, 3, 4; 10.2) should thus make it obvious that to expect more from Paul is unreasonable.

d. *The Epistles of Ignatius*

Only one direct citation of a dominical saying occurs in the Ignatian letters, a declaration by the risen Christ in *Smyrn.* 3.2:

> And when he came to those with Peter he said to them: 'Take, handle me and see that I am not a phantom without a body'. And they immediately touched him and believed, being mingled both with his flesh and spirit. Therefore they despised even death, and were proved to be above death. And after his Resurrection he ate and drank with them as a being of flesh, although he was united in spirit to the Father.

The saying may be compared with Lk. 24.39:

Smyrn. 3.2	Lk. 24.39
Λάβετε,	ἴδετε τὰς χεῖράς μου καὶ τοὺς πόδας μου ὅτι ἐγώ εἰμι αὐτός
ψηλαφήσατέ με καὶ ἴδετε,	ψηλαφήσατέ με καὶ ἴδετε,
ὅτι οὐκ εἰμὶ δαιμόνιον ἀσώματον	ὅτι πνεῦμα σάρκα καὶ ὀστέα οὐκ ἔχει καθὼς ἐμὲ θεωρεῖτε ἔχοντα

According to Origen, Ignatius's logion came from a *Doctrina Petri*; Jerome thought it was from the *Gospel according to the Hebrews*; and Eusebius confessed ignorance (*H.E.* 3.36.11).[1] Nevertheless, there is no reason why Ignatius could not simply be paraphrasing Lk. 24.39

---

1. Origen, *De Principiis* Preface 8 (*ANF*, IV); Jerome, *Lives of Illustrious Men* 16 (*NPNF*, III).

(or Luke's source), especially since the Lukan context has the risen Lord eating and drinking with his disciples (Lk. 24.30, 35, 41-43). Apart from the addition of λάβετε, the first half of the logion mirrors Luke's text, and ψηλαφᾶν is an Ignatian *hapax*.[1] Δαιμόνιον ἀσώματον presents no problem because it represents the position of Ignatius's docetic opponents (cf. ἀσωμάτοις καὶ δαιμονικοῖς in his description in the immediately preceding context, *Smyrn.* 2.1). By using these words in his summary of the logion he makes Jesus' rejection of their view perfectly clear.

Pol. 2.1-2 is one of several echoes of logia that appear in the Ignatian letters:[2]

Ignatius	Matthew	Luke
Καλοὺς μαθητὰς ἐὰν φιλῇς,χάρις σοι οὐκ ἔστιν...	ἐὰν γὰρ ἀγαπήσητε τοὺς ἀγαπῶντας ὑμᾶς, τίνα μισθὸν ἔχετε; (5.46)	εἰ ἀγαπᾶτε τοὺς ἀγαπῶντας ὑμᾶς, ποία ὑμῖν χάρις ἐστίν; (6.32)
φρόνιμος γίνου ὡς ὁ ὄφις ἐν ἅπασιν καὶ ἀκέραιος εἰς ἀεὶ ὡς ἡ περιστερά	γίνεσθε οὖν φρόνιμοι ὡς οἱ ὄφεις καὶ ἀκέραιοι ὡς αἱ περιστεραί (10.16)	

In this case, the first logion is closer to the Lukan form, while the second is paralleled by Matthew and does not occur in Luke at all.[3] If he is reflecting knowledge of the Synoptics here, Ignatius cannot be expected to be more exact in his quotation of dominical material than Matthew and Luke were in their use of Mark and Q (?), especially since he does not formally quote the tradition, but only alludes to it. As bishop of the third greatest city in the Empire (Jos. *War.* 3.29), he would have been aware of Matthew's Gospel, which most see written in Syria, if not Antioch; probably he was familiar with Luke as well.[4]

Besides the Lukan resurrection tradition, Ignatius mentions the virgin birth (*Eph.* 7.2; 18.2; 19.1; *Smyrn.* 1.1), Jesus' family (*Eph.* 18.2; *Trall.* 9.1), the nativity star (*Eph.* 19.2), and that the conception

---

1. Sibinga however cautions that his vocabulary is so rich that *hapax legomena* 'in no way' implies that he is borrowing ('Ignatius', p. 264).

2. See Trevett, 'Correspondence', pp. 62-63.

3. The saying also appears in *Gos. Thom.* 39 and is paralleled in a saying attributed to R. Judah (*Cant. Rab.* 2.14); it may have been a common proverb.

4. See Trevett, 'Correspondence', pp. 59-62 for the varying opinions.

and birth were *hidden* from the 'Prince of this world' (reflecting the escape from Herod?). He speaks of Jesus' baptism (*Eph.* 18.2; *Smyrn.* 1.1), anointing (*Eph.* 17.1; cf. Mt. 26.7; Jn 12.3), silence (presumably at the trial; *Eph.* 15.1-2), and suffering under Pontius Pilate and Herod the tetrarch (*Magn.* 11.1; *Trall.* 9.1; *Smyrn.* 1.1-2).[1] The relatively large number of details about Jesus should not be interpreted as evidence that Ignatius knew more than the writers of the NT Epistles or the other AF; these details generally appear as confessional items adduced to combat specific heresies (cf. esp. *Eph.* 18–21; *Trall.* 9; *Smyrn.* 1; 3.2-3).[2]

Ignatius's interest in *imitatio Christi* is well known.[3] He hopes to attain to resurrection through his own suffering as well as that of Christ (*Rom.* 4.3; 6.3; *Pol.* 7.1) and wants his end patterned after Jesus' Passion (*Smyrn.* 1.1; *Magn.* 5.2; *Phld.* 3.3; *Rom.* 6.3). He praises the Ephesian Christians for becoming μιμηταί of God (i.e. Jesus; cf. the immediately following reference to the 'blood of God' and *Eph.* 18.2), and summons them to diligence in imitating the Lord (Jesus), specifically by their ἐπιείκεια and by being πραΰς in response to others' wrath, ταπεινόφρων in answer to their proud speech, praying for their blasphemy, steadfast in faith, and not seeking to retaliate (*Eph.* 10.2-3). The language summarizes Jesus' character and teachings on non-retaliation.[4] He also cites Jesus' silence (*Eph.* 15.1-2), endurance (*Rom.* 10.3; alternatively a waiting *for* Christ), and burden-bearing (*Pol.* 1.2-3) as exemplary.[5] The readers' union with and submission to their bishop and presbyters is to be patterned after Jesus' relationship with the Father and the submission of the apostles (*Magn.* 7.1; 13.2; cf. *Phld.* 7.2; *Smyrn.* 8.1). This latter point is crucial: the community's doctrine of submission goes back to the

---

1. For a survey of the material, see Snyder, 'Jesus'.
2. Cf. Snyder, 'Jesus', p. 11.
3. See, e.g., Swartley, '*Imitatio*'; Schoedel, *Ignatius*, pp. 29-31. Grant thinks Ignatius 'almost certainly' derived his keyword 'imitation' from Paul (*Ignatius*, p. 11).
4. Schoedel thinks 10.2 is based on a 'free tradition of the words of Jesus', citing Mt. 5.39-42, 44; Lk. 6.27-28 (*Ignatius*, p. 69).
5. In *Phld.* 11.1 he states that the church in Philadelphia received (δέχεσθαι) two men even as the Lord received them [the church], but this does not *directly* refer to the earthly Jesus; cf. Paul's similar request in Rom. 15.7 (προσλαμβάνεσθαι) discussed below.

example of Jesus and to the apostles who followed his model.

Ignatius's use of Paul's writings, a collection of which he obviously knew (*Eph.* 12.2), is illuminating. He quotes or echoes 1 Corinthians alone at least forty-six times,[1] often implicitly comparing himself to the apostle (e.g. *Eph.* 17.2–18.1; 21.2; *Trall.* 12.3; 13.1; *Magn.* 14; *Rom.* 5.1; 9.2; *Smyrn.* 11.1), yet he mentions Paul by name only twice (*Eph.* 12.2; *Rom.* 4.3) and never introduces a quotation from Paul with a formula. Freely paraphrasing Paul's language, he does not confine himself to the original meanings or contexts (*Eph.* 16.1; *Phld.* 3.3). Grant writes,

> Now what does this use of 1 Corinthians show? It shows that Ignatius used the letter in several different ways and that sometimes he quoted, sometimes he alluded, sometimes he allusively quoted and sometimes he quotingly alluded. Any idea of exactness in analyzing his usage must be read in by the analyst. It does not exist in Ignatius' own writings.[2]

If Ignatius thus used the letters of a man for whom he had such high regard, it is not surprising to find a similar treatment of dominical material.

In seven letters by a bishop writing forty years after Paul's death and over a decade after the composition of the last Gospel, we encounter only one dominical citation (from the risen Christ), and a number of loose allusions or echoes which demonstrate both familiarity and freedom with the tradition. We have no conclusive *proof* that the emphasis on Jesus' example came to Ignatius through his mentor Paul, but it is interesting to note how frequently the apostle exhorts his readers to exhibit the characteristics Ignatius attributes to Jesus.

e. *Polycarp's Epistle to the Philippians*
Polycarp quotes Jesus in two passages. Chaining together several logia in 2.3, he introduces them with the formula μνημονεύοντες δὲ ὧν εἶπεν ὁ κύριος διδάσκων:

Polycarp	Matthew	Luke
Μὴ κρίνετε,	Μὴ κρίνετε,	Καὶ μὴ κρίνετε,
ἵνα μὴ κριθῆτε·	ἵνα μὴ κριθῆτε. . . (7.1)	καὶ οὐ μὴ κριθῆτε . . . (6.37a)

---

1. Grant, *Introduction*, p. 57.
2. *Introduction*, p. 59.

ἀφίετε, καὶ ἀφεθήσεται ὑμῖν·		ἀπολύετε, καὶ ἀπολυθήσεσθε (6.37c)
ἐλεᾶτε, ἵνα ἐλεηθῆτε·		δίδοτε, καὶ δοθήσεται ὑμῖν...(6.38a)
ᾧ μέτρῳ μετρεῖτε, ἀντιμετρηθήσεται ὑμῖν·	ἐν ᾧ μέτρῳ μετρεῖτε, μετρηθήσεται ὑμῖν ...(7.2)	ᾧ γὰρ μέτρῳ μετρεῖτε, ἀντιμετρηθήσεται ὑμῖν (6.38c)
καὶ ὅτι μακάριοι οἱ πτωχοὶ	Μακάριοι οἱ πτωχοὶ τῷ πνεύματι ὅτι αὐτῶν ἐστιν ἡ βασιλεία τῶν οὐρανῶν...(5.3)	Μακάριοι οἱ πτωχοί...(6.20)
καὶ οἱ διωκόμενοι ἕνεκεν δικαιοσύνης, ὅτι αὐτῶν ἐστιν ἡ βασιλεία τοῦ θεοῦ	μακάριοι οἱ δεδιωγμένοι ἕνεκεν δικαιοσύνης, ὅτι αὐτῶν ἐστιν ἡ βασιλεία τῶν οὐρανῶν (5.10)	ὅτι ὑμετέρα ἐστὶν ἡ βασιλεία τοῦ θεοῦ (6.20)

Although he had apparently seen Clement's Epistle (cf. *1 Clem.* 13.1-2),[1] Polycarp's logia are closer to the Synoptics. Given the date of his letter, he probably knew both Matthew and Luke and we see here evidence of conflation.[2] This is not to say that he had the written Gospels in front of him as he wrote; Polycarp knew oral tradition even better and relied on his memory.[3] Remarkable for its length, the quotation reveals Polycarp's liberty—he is not bound to quote with wooden precision. As in *1 Clement*, the 'remember' formula points to the fundamental role of the teachings in his readers' (baptismal?) instruction.

Warning against anyone who perverts τὰ λόγια τοῦ κυρίου and denies the resurrection and judgment, Polycarp quotes Jesus again in 7.2:[4]

> let us turn back to the word which was delivered to us in the beginning, watching unto prayer and persevering in fasting, beseeching the all-seeing

1. Not referring to Clement or to his Epistle by name, Polycarp echoes his predecessor a number of times (see Lightfoot, *Fathers*, 1.1, pp. 149-53), introducing this passage in a manner very similar to *1 Clem.* 13.1.
2. Cf. Schoedel, *Polycarp*, p. 12 n. 29.
   Cf. Grant, *Introduction*, p. 66.
   The translation is from the Loeb edition, with modified punctuation.

God in our supplications to lead us not into temptation (μὴ εἰσενεγκεῖν ἡμᾶς εἰς πειρασμόν), even as the Lord said, 'The spirit is willing, but the flesh is weak' (τὸ μὲν πνεῦμα πρόθυμον, ἡ δὲ σὰρξ ἀσθενής).

The spirit/flesh logion agrees verbatim with Jesus' saying in Mk 14.38 // Mt. 26.41, where, as here, it immediately follows an exhortation to pray not to enter εἰς πειρασμόν, although the verb in the Gospels is εἰσέρχεσθαι. Polycarp's εἰσενεγκεῖν could either be a translation variant (the two verbs translate different stems of אוב) or reflect the influence of the petition from the Lord's Prayer (Mt. 6.13; Lk. 11.4).

Polycarp rarely alludes to JT.[1] Prior to the chain of logia noted above he says Christians should 'do *his* will and walk in *his* ἐντολαί and love the things which *he* loved, refraining from all unrighteousness, covetousness, love of money, evil speaking, false witness, rendering not evil for evil, or railing for railing, or blow for blow, or curse for curse' (2.2). The aorist ἠγάπησεν favours a reference to Jesus, and the phrase μὴ ἀποδιδόντες κακὸν ἀντὶ κακοῦ ἢ λοιδορίαν ἀντὶ λοιδορίας is identical to that in 1 Pet. 3.9, corresponding closely to Rom. 12.17 (μηδενὶ κακὸν ἀντὶ κακοῦ ἀποδιδόντες). It may be that Polycarp is simply echoing the language of the Epistles as he does elsewhere, but the inclusion of these elements between a command to love the things Jesus loved and the direct citation of the Lord which follows makes it clear that Polycarp considered the words to be an accurate summary, if not an agraphon, of Jesus' words. Almost all sayings quoted or echoed come from the SM.

Aside from references to the Passion, Polycarp does not mention details of Jesus' life. He calls his readers to persevere and be imitators (μιμηταί) of Jesus' ὑπομονή, 'for this is the example [ὑπογραμμόν] which he gave us in himself' (8.1-2; cf. 1.2). He exhorts the Philippians a second time to follow the example of the Lord (*domini exemplar sequimini*), firm and unchangeable in faith and forestalling one another in the gentleness of the Lord (*mansuetudine domini alterutri praestolantes*; 10.1). διάκονοι are to walk according to the truth of the Lord, ὃς ἐγένετο διάκονος πάντων (5.2). Thus once again we find fewer references to JT than we might expect from a bishop who was thoroughly familiar with it.

---

1. εἰδότες ὅτι may introduce an allusion in 6.1 (Schoedel, *Polycarp*, p. 22 n. 58), and Polycarp apparently considers Ps. 2.11 to be a commandment of Christ (6.3).

f. 2 Clement

2 Clement is unique for the the presence of no less than eleven direct quotations of dominical logia scattered throughout the Epistle:[1]

2 *Clem.*	Synoptics	Other	Formula	Content
2.4	Mt 9.13 Mk 2.17 Lk 5.32	*Barn.* 5.9 *Just. Apol.* 15.8	καὶ ἑτέρα δὲ γραφὴ λέγει	I came not to call the right- eous but sinners
3.2	Mt 10.32 Lk 12.8		λέγει δὲ καὶ αὐτός (Χριστός)	Confession before men results in confession before the Father
4.2	Mt 7.21 Lk 6.46	*Just. Apol.* 16.9	λέγει γάρ (ὁ κύριος)	Not everyone saying 'Lord Lord' will be saved
4.5	Mt 7.23 Lk 13.27	*Gos. Eg.?* *Gos. Naz.?*	εἶπεν ὁ κύριος	Rejection for not being gathered together in his bosom and not doing his commandments
5.2	Mt 10.16 Lk 10.3		λέγει γὰρ ὁ κύριος	You will be as lambs in the midst of wolves
5.4		?	εἶπεν ὁ Ἰησοῦς τῷ Πέτρῳ	Let the lambs have no fear of the wolves after their death
	Mt 10.28 Lk 12.4f	*Just. Apol.* 19.7		Fear not those who can kill you, but him who has power to cast body and soul into hell
6.1	Mt 6.24 Lk 16.13	*Gos. Thom.* 1.47	λέγει δὲ ὁ κύριος	No servant can serve two masters
8.5	Lk 16.10- 12	?	λέγει γὰρ ὁ κύριος ἐν τῷ εὐαγγελίῳ	If you don't keep what is small, who will give you what is great? One faithful in least is faithful in much
9.11	Mt 12.50 Mk 3.35 Lk 8.21	*Gos. Eb.*[2] *Gos. Thom.* 96	καὶ γὰρ εἶπεν ὁ κύριος	My brethren are those who do the will of my Father

1. Donfried excludes 5.4 from his list, apparently because it occurs in a short nar-rative section (*Setting*, p. 49). In *2 Clem.* 6.2 a virtual citation appears with no intro-ductory formula (cf. Mk 8.36 pars.); there are no other probable echoes.
   2. Cited in Epiph. *Haer.* 30.14.5, according to Donfried (*Setting*, p. 73).

12.2		Gos. Eg.	ὁ κύριος... εἶπεν	[Kingdom] When the two will be one
		Gos. Thom.		and the outside as the
		23		inside and the male
				with the female neither
				male nor female
13.4	Lk 6.32-35	Did. 1.3	λέγει ὁ θεός	No credit to love those who love you
	Mt. 5.46, 44			A credit to you to love enemies and those who hate you

Space does not allow the parallels to be printed, and a short summary will have to suffice here.[1] *2 Clement* evidences knowledge of Luke (4.5b; 5.2; 6.1; 8.5; 13.4) and Matthew (2.4; 3.2; 4.2), their special sources, and/or a harmony of the Gospels (5.4b; 9.11).[2] It contains references to one or more sources unknown to us for some sayings, which are introduced in the same way as logia attested in the Synoptics. Extended verbatim agreement with the Synoptics is rare, and clearly the writer adjusted the language of his traditions to suit his purposes.[3]

The author quotes the OT less frequently than he does sayings of Jesus, using similar formulae (referring to γραφή three times) and showing no dependence on the Synoptics where his quotations are paralleled by dominical logia. Apart from reference to the sufferings of Christ, *2 Clement* contains no details of the life of Jesus, and there is no explicit appeal to the example of Jesus.

The sharp increase in direct quotations and the decrease in allusions in *2 Clement* is striking. What explains this profound change since the writing of *1 Clement*? Much may be attributed to the different author and purpose, but one important distinction stands out: pseudo-Clement knows a collection of dominical sayings as Scripture (2.4)—the logia are now written authorities like the OT. Even though he almost certainly possessed one or more of our Gospels, the form, vocabulary and construction of the sayings continue to vary from the Synoptics. If

1. For detailed analysis see Donfried, *Setting*, pp. 56-82.
2. Hagner usually argues for oral tradition, but here he allows for 'some knowledge' of the Synoptics ('Sayings', p. 246); cf. Grant, *Introduction*, p. 45.
3. On the function of the quotations in the argument, see Donfried, *Setting*, pp. 96-97.

this kind of freedom was characteristic of later Christians, in a time when the tendency might have been to conserve tradition in the wake of the passing of the first fathers of the Church, we could expect to see a similar freedom in Paul's letters in earlier days before the traditions had crystallized.

3. *Summary of Findings*

The only citations of dominical logia in the extra-Pauline NT Epistles appear in one of the latest letters, 1 John. Brief and summary in nature, they function to establish Jesus' teaching as a standard in the midst of controversy. Probable echoes occur in James, 1 and 2 Peter, and 1 John, but are lacking in Hebrews and the shortest letters. Like the quotations, the echoes do not verbally agree with the Gospels. In the earlier writings, they serve an ethical purpose and help to establish the eschatology. The sayings usually parallel logia in the SM or in the Olivet discourse. In later writings, they serve to establish a creed in the face of false teachings.

Direct citation occurs in every document of the early AF, but rarely (once or twice in each work) and in clusters. *2 Clement* is exceptional with eleven quotations, but this should be attributed to its late date; the written tradition was gradually becoming more important with the passing of the second and third generations of Christians. Several citations are agrapha (*Barnabas*, *Didache*, Ignatius). Two of the writings introduce quotations with a 'remember' formula (*1 Clement*, Polycarp), clearly assuming the readers' acquaintance with the tradition. The longest extended parallel is the version of the Lord's Prayer in *Did.* 8.2, and again most of the citations and echoes parallel the SM.

If some of the authors knew our Gospels, they felt no need to quote exactly. Many echoes occur in some of the AF, but they too reveal the authors' freedom in using the tradition. We hear nothing of Jesus' parables (with the exception of the eschatological parable of the Thief), although in a few cases writers seem to use parabolic imagery for another purpose.[1]

---

1. Prat suggested that Jesus' teachings were given parabolic form to avoid giving offence to Roman authorities and to correct errant notions about the kingdom of God by the Jews. Once the true notion of the kingdom began to be realized concretely in the church, the original pedagogic role of the parables came to an end, and they were

Of all the documents surveyed, only 2 Peter, Ignatius, *Barnabas*, and possibly Hebrews refer to pre-Passion events in Jesus' life; only *Barnabas* mentions Jesus' signs and wonders, none of which are specified.

Only half of the other NT Epistles and half of the early AF explicitly call Jesus an example to be followed; of the latter, two were profoundly influenced by Paul (Ignatius, Polycarp). 2 Peter, 1 and 2 John, and two letters purportedly by brothers of Jesus (James and Jude) show no interest in Jesus' example, whereas the authors of 1 Peter, Hebrews and 1 John appeal to his suffering, submission, obedience, purity, self-sacrifice and love. Of the surveyed AF, *1 Clement*, Ignatius and Polycarp cite his humility, gentleness, suffering, submission and endurance.[1]

The relative frequency of dominical logia in some works is explained by their purposes. The *Didache* purports to communicate the Lord's teachings through the twelve apostles, and *2 Clement* is so late that it reflects the growing use of written sources and reliance on authorities from the past instead of the living voice of oral tradition.

4. Conclusions

1. It is unrealistic to expect more than a few explicit references to Jesus' teachings in Paul. The important question that emerges from this survey is not why the tradition is absent,

---

preserved for historical purposes in epitomes of the life of Jesus (*Theology*, II, pp. 27-28). On later use of parabolic teaching cf. Bauckham, 'Parables'.

1. Although it belongs to a different genre, the *Shepherd of Hermas* comprises a sizeable block of text (150 pages in the Loeb edn; the *entire* Pauline corpus covers 154 pages in N-A[26]), and its evidence supports our conclusions. There are a number of echoes of JT (cf. G. Taylor, *Hermas*, pp. 25-68), the clearest of which is a reference to Jesus' teaching on divorce without the exception clause (*Man.* 4.1.6). The echoes do not figure in significant points in the argument, but indicate that the author was simply using familiar language to convey his message without intending to remind his readers of its origin. He knows that Jesus spoke in parables (*Sim.* 5.4.3) and he adopts the same method, using language similar to some dominical parables (*Sim.* 9.20.1-2; 5.5.2; cf. Snyder, *Shepherd*, p. 15). He reveals little interest in imitating Jesus' character (possibly in *Vis.* 4.1.8 and *Sim.* 6.1.2; cf. also Lake, *AF*, II, p. 275 n. 2).

but why a writer uses it when he does. What causes him to
break the 'normal' pattern of relative silence?

2.   It is unrealistic to expect exact or lengthy citations or echoes
     of Synoptic logia in Paul.

3.   We might expect echoes particularly from the SM, but noth-
     ing of Jesus' parables, except perhaps the parables of the
     Thief and the Sower.

4.   It is unrealistic to expect Paul to refer to events in Jesus' life
     prior to the Passion, especially to particular miracles.

5.   We might expect a few references to the example of Jesus in
     Paul, but primarily to characteristics seen in his Passion.
     Specifically we could expect to find something about Jesus'
     love expressed in his suffering for others, his endurance,
     humility, obedience, submission and gentleness. Some appeals
     for these qualities could well be rooted in Jesus' example,
     even though Paul does not explicitly identify him as the
     model.

The general lack of appeal to JT in early Christian writings is no
secret, but surprisingly few have seen its significance for the Jesus–
Paul debate; minimalists who emphasize the apostle's silence seem
oblivious to the data.[1] A few have taken the evidence to prove that *all*
of the early writers of Epistles were ignorant of the traditions,[2] but
this view has not commended itself to most scholars. Far more likely
is the verdict of Stuhlmacher: 'Die ausführliche oder gar vollständige
Reproduktion der Jesustradition war nicht Aufgabe oder Anliegen der
brieflichen Kommunikation'.[3] The evidence shows us that Paul is no
exception to the rule, but instead of solving a problem, it raises the
larger question of continuity between the Church's proclamation of a
risen Lord and its interest in the Jesus of history.[4]

---

1.   But see Schweitzer, *Paul*, p. 43; Schmithals, 'Paulus', pp. 156-57.
2.   For example, Strömholm ('Narrative'), Knight ('Gospels'; *idem*, 'Jesus'),
Teeple ('Tradition'), and Wells (*Jesus*, pp. 131-84).
3.   'Thema', p. 19.
4.   Cf. Schmithals, 'Paulus', p. 153; Wilckens, 'Jesusüberlieferung'; and the
comments of P.-G. Müller, *Traditionsprozeß*, pp. 205-206. Although it belongs to a
different genre altogether from the literature surveyed above, Acts makes a contribu-

The absence of direct quotation of Jesus in works attributed to people who knew him well (1 Peter, James, Jude) and the rarity of direct citations in writings composed long after our Gospels were written obviate the force of the specific argument that Paul's practice shows he did not know or was not interested in sayings of Jesus. There may be legitimate reasons for distancing Paul from Jesus, but this is not one of them.[1] Claims about specific places where an author 'should' have quoted Jesus to bolster the case do not prove ignorance or lack of interest.[2]

At least three factors help explain the phenomena summarized above: (1) it was not the authors' purpose to convey a body of traditional material but to address specific problems or to make a point not requiring the use of the tradition (e.g. Hebrews); (2) the readers' knowledge of JT was assumed as fundamental to their Christian instruction; and (3) the authority of the writer minimized the need to cite sources. In the next chapter I shall note other factors which influenced the apostle Paul.

tion to our quest. Having written a Gospel, Luke knew a great deal about the life and teachings of Jesus, yet from the evidence of Acts one could hardly suspect it (apart from 1.1-2; 2.22; 10.36-39; 20.35; for details see Barrett, 'Sayings'). Barrett observes that 'in Acts as a whole. . . important questions are not settled by appeal to the words of the Lord. . . Where they are used they are illustrative, and occasionally exemplary, rather than probative. Proof requires a step beyond the remembered saying, as when the promise of the Holy Spirit is recalled' ('Sayings', p. 706).

1. Cf. Dungan, who rightly concludes that Schweitzer's question (See p. 18 n. 2 above) was anachronistic (*Sayings*, pp. 148-50).

2. On specific passages in Paul, see p. 71 n. 2 below. Gundry writes with reference to JT in 1 Peter, 'the proper question is not, How many allusions to dominical sayings "might" the author have made but did not? It is rather, How many allusions *did* he make, and do they display such character and pattern as to constitute significant evidence concerning his identity and the quality of the dominical tradition? What the author "might have" used but did not is balanced, we should remember, by what he may have used from Jesus' *un*-recorded teaching but which has passed unnoticed through the evangelists' omissions' ('Further', p. 231). Cf., e.g., Just. *Dial*. 35.2, which attributes to Jesus a saying on the inevitability of σχίσματα and αἱρέσεις, and 1 Cor. 11.18-19.

Chapter 3

PAUL AND JESUS TRADITION:
KNOWLEDGE AND ATTITUDE

We have seen that infrequent reference to JT does not necessarily indicate lack of knowledge or interest. Before investigating the material in Rom. 12.1–15.13, it remains to establish realistic expectations of the extent of Paul's knowledge and his probable attitude toward JT. The exegesis in the following chapters will then be based on those expectations, effectively testing their reliability.

1. Paul's Opportunities to Learn

It is highly unlikely that Paul was ignorant of much JT, unless he chose to be. He probably had never seen, much less met Jesus, but as a persecutor of the Church Paul the Pharisee would certainly have heard of the Galilaean's words and deeds (Gal. 1.13-14; Phil. 3.5; Acts 7.58; 8.1-3; 23.6; 26.5), both through the Pharisaic 'grapevine' and through the direct testimony of Christians he pursued.[1] After his baptism Paul did not jump up and run out into the desert, Gal. 1.15-17

---

1. 2 Cor. 5.16 (discussed below) affords no evidence of any personal knowledge, *contra*, e.g., Weiss, who argued that Paul had seen Jesus during his last week in Jerusalem, had perhaps heard him speak and may have been a witness of his Passion, 'a supposition likely enough in the case of a passionately enthusiastic pupil of the Pharisees'. For Weiss, this explained why Paul did not consult with Peter immediately after his conversion: 'he already knew all that Peter could tell him' (*Paul*, pp. 54-55). While Acts 22.3 and 26.4-5 indicate Paul lived in Jerusalem from his early childhood (cf. van Unnik, *Tarsus*), they do not demonstrate his presence there during the Passion. We would expect some hint in 2 Cor. 11.22-23 and/or other passages had Paul been an eyewitness of Jesus (cf. C. Wolff, 'Knowledge', p. 82; Fraser, 'Knowledge', pp. 294-95); 1 Cor. 9.1 and 15.8 refer to his conversion experience.

notwithstanding.[1] In Galatians he is concerned to show his independence of the Jerusalem apostles, not his isolation from the Christian community. There is no reason to doubt that sharing his own story with fellow Christians in Damascus he listened to theirs as well, joining in their worship, and soaking up traditions conveyed through exhortation and eucharist. Paul spent considerable time there (Gal. 1.17-18; Acts 10.19-25), not far from Galilee and Judaea. He also lived and taught for at least a year in Antioch, where refugees from Jerusalem had been among the first preachers, presumably bringing JT with them (Acts 11.19-26). Moreover, the city's proximity to Palestine and importance as a major centre of trade and travel ensured a flow of Christians bearing further traditions about Jesus. The first collections of *verba Christi* translated into the Greek tongue were probably formed at this mother-city of the Christian mission,[2] if not earlier in Jerusalem as Hengel argues.[3] Sent out by the community (Acts 13.2-3), Paul carried with him Antiochene tradition. A basic stock of traditions about Jesus and his teachings would have been a prerequisite for any missionary seeking to compete with the elaborate lore of pagan cultic religions.[4] Such a need offers an explanation for the many similarities between Paul's writings and the Gospel of Matthew, links which Goulder has seen perhaps more clearly than anyone.[5] The 'M' material which parallels Paul need not be, as Goulder claims, redactional invention inspired by the apostle, but

1. When Paul says that he did not 'confer' with flesh and blood after his conversion (1.16), προσανατιθέναι connotes consultation with others with a view to discovering the meaning of the revelation (as in Diod. S. 17.116.4; cf. Dunn, 'Relationship', pp. 462-63). In other words, Paul did not need the apostles or anyone else to help him sort out his conversion and calling; the verse implies nothing about his attitude towards Christian tradition.

2. Selwyn, *1 Peter*, p. 366; cf. Dibelius, *Tradition*, pp. 30-31.

3. Hengel, 'Between', p. 27.

4. Cf. Gal. 3.1. On the importance of Gospel tradition for mission, cf., e.g., Dibelius (*Tradition*, pp. 13-15). Hengel writes, 'In antiquity it was quite impossible to proclaim as Kyrios, Son of God and Redeemer a man who had been crucified a few years—i.e. an alleged criminal—without saying something about who this man was, what he taught and did and how and why he died' ('Origins', p. 178 n. 3; cf. Moule, *Phenomenon*, p. 79; Weiss, *Paul*, pp. 17-18).

5. Goulder, *Midrash*, pp. 153-70; *idem*, *Calendar*, pp. 227-40; cf. also Argyle ('M').

probably reflects local traditions incorporated into a Syrian Gospel.[1] Finally, Paul's visits to Jerusalem,[2] his association with tradition bearers from that city (Barnabas, Silvanus, John Mark and surely many others never named in the NT), his desire to keep current with developments in the churches, and his many contacts with others through his own travels and those of his messengers ensure that he *need* not have been ignorant. But did he care to know?

2. *Paul's Attitude Towards Jesus Tradition*

A man of visions (2 Cor. 12.1-7, 9; Gal. 2.2?; cf. Acts 9.12; 16.9-10; 18.9; etc.), Paul came to faith through a direct revelation of Christ (Gal. 1.12, 16; 1 Cor. 9.1; 15.8; Acts 9.3-9 pars.). He was convinced that the risen Lord spoke through him and through Christian prophets (e.g. 1 Cor. 7.40; 14.37; 2 Cor. 13.3), so his primary interest would naturally be in the Christ whom he knew existentially. Since he had never met Jesus, he would be a further step removed from familiarity with the traditions than the first disciples. But that does not mean that Paul would be uninterested in Jesus' words and deeds (especially in view of his fascination with knowing and conforming to Christ;

1. As evidenced by studies of Sibinga ('Ignatius'), Draper ('Tradition'), Kloppenborg ('Tradition'), and Bauckham ('Study', p. 380), all of whom argue for use of 'M' (not Matthew) by other early Christian writings. A 'strong consensus' favours the composition of Matthew at or near Antioch, although Stanton demurs ('Origin', pp. 1941-42). Space precludes response to Goulder's case for Lukan dependence on Paul ('Luke'; *idem, Paradigm*), except to say that we are not confined to a choice between Paul drawing on Luke/Lukan tradition and Luke *creating* Jesus tradition from Paul's letters. If, as it seems most likely from the 'we' passages, Luke was a travelling companion of Paul, we would *expect* Paul's version of the Gospel tradition to influence the evangelist's wording. How does Goulder know that Paul was not one of Luke's many sources for pre-Easter JT (Luke 1.1-2)? Only if one presupposes the view that Paul was uninterested or ignorant in JT should there be surprise at links between the two.

2. The immediate context and Paul's three-year delay testifies against a visit to learn fundamental JT in Gal. 1.18. ἱστορῆσαι does not connote 'to get information from' Cephas (*contra*, e.g., Kilpatrick, 'Galatians 1:18'), but 'to get to know' him (Hofius, 'Gal. 1.18'; Dunn, 'Reply'), yet among the reasons for meeting Peter may well have been Paul's desire to supplement his own preaching and teaching, and to verify that his perspective on the law was not contrary to Jesus' (cf. Walter, 'Jesus-Tradition', pp. 64-66).

cf. Phil. 3.8-10), unless we assume *a priori* a radical disjunction between Christ and Jesus. The critical question is whether Paul saw pneumatic insights as supplementing existing traditions or supplanting them, a question I shall return to later in my study of Romans.

Ever since F.C. Baur, Galatians has been the quarry from which scholars have mined evidence setting Paul against his Christian predecessors. Yet alongside the references to direct revelation in Galatians and assertions of the apostle's independence, we find signs that Paul was concerned to maintain continuity with established tradition. Although he vigorously asserts that he received his gospel directly from God,[1] nowhere does he claim that it differed essentially from the faith of those who were Christians before him—after his conversion, he preached the same faith he once sought to destroy (Gal. 1.23; cf. 1 Cor. 15.11, οὕτως).[2] Paul's willingness to go to Jerusalem fourteen years later to discuss his gospel with Peter and James (Gal. 2.2) reveals that he had no desire to break away and establish separate 'Pauline' churches, but rather was concerned to preserve the unity (and thus the central tradition) of the body of Christ.[3] His quarrel was with judaizers (ψευδαδέλφοι 2.4)[4] and those inclined to elevate the

---

1. Paul's insistence that his gospel was not κατὰ ἄνθρωπον (1.11) and had no human origin (1.12, 16), that his apostleship was οὐκ ἀπ' ἀνθρώπων οὐδὲ δι' ἀνθρώπου (1.1), and that he was not seeking to please humankind (1.10) suggests that his purpose was not to vindicate the creation of something essentially new to replace the gospel already preached in general by Christians, but to answer the charge that his message and ministry lacked divine authorization. His opponents charged him with pleasing humankind, by minimizing the requirements of salvation for the Gentiles (i.e. by allowing non-Jews to continue in uncircumcision, etc.). Possibly they claimed that he got his gospel from the Hellenists who were evangelizing the Gentiles (Acts 11.20).

2. Cf. also the traces of early Aramaic traditions in Paul (μαράνα θά, 1 Cor. 16.22; ἀββά, Rom. 8.15; Gal. 4.6 // Mk 14.36).

3. Paul's choice of Silas as a travelling companion may reflect this concern (Acts 15.40). According to Luke, Silas was a prophet and capable speaker (Acts 15.32), but he had also been a trusted leader in the church at Jerusalem and knew the tradition well (Acts 15.22-27). His presence with Paul would be both helpful to their mission and reassuring to brethren in Jerusalem.

4. The 'false brethren' probably were from the ranks of the Pharisaic Christians in Jerusalem, the 'circumcision party' of Acts 11.2; 15.1, 5. Whether they are to be identified with those ἀπὸ Ἰακώβου (Gal. 2.12), is not clear. The requirements and expectations of Gentile Christians at Jerusalem were obviously different from those

'pillar apostles' over Paul (hence over his gospel), not the apostles themselves, at least not until Peter's inconsistent behaviour at Antioch (Gal. 2.11-14; cf. 2.9). What was new and threatening to conservative Jewish Christians in Jerusalem was his free association with Gentiles, his refusal to require Gentile converts to conform to distinctively Jewish customs in order to be acceptable to God, and his success in winning non-Jews to Christ. His letters show us no critical attitude towards contemporary Christian tradition, except insofar as it was interpreted by some to require more of Gentile converts than did Jesus, who had freely associated with sinners and tax collectors.[1]

In the early days of the Jesus–Paul debate, not a few thought they found an important clue in 2 Cor. 5.16, where Paul states, ὥστε ἡμεῖς ἀπὸ τοῦ νῦν οὐδένα οἴδαμεν κατὰ σάρκα· εἰ καὶ ἐγνώκαμεν κατὰ σάρκα Χριστόν, ἀλλὰ νῦν οὐκέτι γινώσκομεν.[2] Is Paul rejecting all knowledge of 'Christ [Jesus] according to the flesh'? The phrase κατὰ σάρκα should be construed not with Χριστόν but with ἐγνώκαμεν.[3] In context Paul is contrasting two attitudes towards others, the fallen 'this-worldly' way of thinking and the outlook of one who is a new creation, controlled by the love of Christ and living for others as he did (cf. the ψυχικός/πνευματικός contrast in 1 Cor. 2.14-15). The changed perspective appears most clearly in one's attitude towards Christ, the cause of that change. As a new creation, the Christian recognizes that Jesus' death was no mere crucifixion (what men would call a σκάνδαλον or μωρία; 1 Cor. 1.23), but a redemptive act ὑπὲρ πάντων (2 Cor. 5.14). A growing number of scholars on both sides of the debate would agree with Stuhlmacher's conclusion that 'Die Stelle ist bekehrungstheologisch formuliert und

---

at Antioch and in the Pauline churches, due not only to the piety of Jewish Christians in Jerusalem, but also to pressure from the Jews and the threat of suffering the same fate as those in Acts 8.1 (the 'Hellenists'?).

1. On the similarity of Paul's and Jesus' openness toward 'outsiders', see Wedderburn, 'Similarity'.

2. For a summary of views cf. Fraser, 'Knowledge'.

3. Otherwise we would expect οὐδένα κατὰ σάρκα οἴδαμεν in the first clause. When used adjectivally, κατὰ σάρκα follows the noun it modifies (Rom. 4.1; 9.3; 1 Cor. 1.26; 10.18) unless it appears in the attributive position (Rom. 8.4-5; 9.5; Gal. 4.29; Col 3.22; cf. Eph 6.5). Cf. C. Wolff, 'Knowledge', pp. 87-89, and Fraser, 'Knowledge', p. 298, for discussion.

(6.20) besagt für ein angebliches Desinteresse des Paulus am irdischen Jesus gar nichts'.[1]

We find then no compelling positive evidence that Paul stood outside mainstream Chris*anity by disregarding JT. Paul is not attacked for having a defective christology, nor for neglecting the teachings and example of Jesus. That silence is surely as significant as his non-inclusion of dominical sayings, a characteristic representing no departure from the custom of other early Christian writers who presumably knew JT. On the other hand Paul uses the vocabulary of tradition (cf. the semi-technical terms παραλαμβάνειν = קבל, παραδίδοναι = מסר), not only of his own teachings but also of that which he identifies as JT (1 Cor. 11.23-25), and he plainly alludes to JT in 1 Corinthians 7 and 9.[2] The importance of imitation in pagan and OT thought, coupled with evidence from later Jewish traditions that a rabbi's example had decisive significance for his followers, supports the *a priori* expectation that Paul too would want to know all he could about his master.[3] Paul the Pharisee had presumably imitated

---

1. Stuhlmacher, 'Thema', p. 17; C. Wolff, 'Knowledge'; so also, e.g., the minimalists Furnish (*II Corinthians*, pp. 312-14, 329-32) and Walter ('Jesus-Tradition', p. 60). Walter speaks of 'widespread agreement', but cf. Wilson, 'Contours', p. 9.

2. For the language of tradition see 1 Cor. 11.2, 23; 15.3; Rom. 6.17; Gal. 1.9; Phil. 4.9; Col. 2.6; 1 Thess. 2.13; 4.1; 2 Thess. 3.6; cf. Gerhardsson, *Memory*, p. 290; Dibelius, *Tradition*, p. 21. On 1 Cor. 11.23-25 cf. Jeremias, *Words*, pp. 103-104. Schippers writes, 'None of the other authors of the N.T. has placed such an accent on the significance of the Christian tradition as he [Paul] does' ('Tradition', p. 224). Richardson's argument that 1 Cor. 7.10 reflects a saying of the risen Christ ('Opinion') is not persuasive; there is not the slightest hint that Paul received the word through revelation, and the shared vocabulary with Mt. 19.6 // Mk 10.9 (a saying widely regarded as authentic, regardless of what one concludes about the 'exception clause') points toward knowledge of JT which surfaced later in the Synoptics. It is very unlikely that Paul was ignorant of such a tradition, since the divorce logion would obviously have constituted a fundamental part of early Christian domestic teaching.

3. On the general background of imitation, cf. Kosmala, 'Nachfolge I, II'; Tinsley, *Imitation*, pp. 27-64; for rabbinic evidence see, e.g., Aberbach, 'Relations'. Evidence suggests that *imitatio Deo* began with *imitatio rabbini*: 'Even the master's most intimate habits and activities were subjected to careful scrutiny. Disciples followed him to the privy and the bath house; they studied his bedclothes and imputed significance to when and how he sneezed' (Kirschner, 'Imitatio', p. 70; cf. *b. Ber.* 23a, 24a, 62a; *b. Shab.* 40b-41a).

Gamaliel; it is unlikely that he would totally abandon the practice of imitation when he became a follower of Jesus. No more than a half dozen years (possibly less than two) had elapsed between the death of Jesus and the conversion of Paul, leaving little time for a supposed 'Hellenistic christology' far-removed from Palestinian JT to have developed.[1] Unless we *presuppose* for him a sharp dichotomy between Jesus and Christ, we should therefore tentatively conclude that Paul would have been positively disposed toward the available JT, as well as to subsequent revelations from his risen Lord.

3. *Explanations for Paul's Lack of Explicit JT*

Paul's failure to cite JT more often has no simple answer, although Chapter 2 has made a start. The following list is not exhaustive, but surveys the most common factors given, grouping them roughly according to what I judge to be their relative significance for (1) early Christian letters in general and (2) Paul in particular. Given the limits of space, detailed evaluation of each is impossible, but their collection may prove convenient for future studies.

General factors

a. *The presupposition of earlier instruction.* This goes some way towards explaining the phenomena in all early Christian letters. Very little shared vocabulary appears in Paul's clear reference to dominical teaching in 1 Cor. 7.10-11 (none in 1 Cor. 9.14); Paul's allusiveness demonstrates that he assumes his readers are thoroughly familiar with *at least* those sayings, and his letters presuppose the recipients' knowledge of general Christian tradition (cf. Rom. 6.17; 15.14; 16.17; 1 Cor. 1.5; 11.2; 15.3; Col. 2.7; Phil. 4.9; 1 Thess 4.3; 5.1-2; 2 Thess. 2.15; 3.6). Statements such as those in Gal. 3.1; 4.4; 1 Thess. 4.2; 5.2 provide clues that he and his colleagues communicated elements of the pre-Synoptic tradition in the early instruction of congregations. Still, the depth of that instruction remains a mystery, and it remains possible to argue that Paul and other early Christian writers refrained from quoting Jesus because they were uncertain as to how much tradition their readers knew.

---

1. For criticism of Heitmüller's influential theory of a 'Hellenistic Christianity' that bypassed JT see Hengel, 'Christology'; Marshall, 'Christianity'.

b. *The nature of apostolic paraenesis.* Where argument ceased and exhortation began, apostles had little need to cite sources. Paul does not tell us that his inspiration in Phil. 4.8 is Stoic, and likewise we should not necessarily expect explicit references to JT. His primary aim in paraenesis was to remind readers of essential moral concerns, not to prove a point. Like other apostles, Paul spoke with the assurance that his message had the guidance and authority of Christ's Spirit. Given that confidence, identification of specific ethical teaching as that of Jesus would be expected only (1) when first instructing a congregation, (2) when asked particularly about the traditions, or (3) when responding to a situation where one's ways were challenged as contrary to those of Jesus.

c. *The occasional nature of the Epistles.* The purpose of the Epistles we possess is not to convey the ABCs of Christian tradition to neophytes, but to address particular problems in particular situations at particular times. It has often been observed that if it were not for misbehaviour in Corinth, we would have little evidence of the eucharist's importance for Paul. Wedderburn's comparison of Paul's lack of explicit quotation with the readiness of his contemporaries among the Jewish rabbis and Hellenistic philosophers to lard their writings with the sayings and incidents in the lives of their teachers is mistaken, not simply because of the freedom and authority given by the Spirit, but fundamentally because of the essential difference in genre between an occasional letter, Mishnah, and philosophical tracts.[1] It is worth asking exactly in what places we should expect Paul to quote JT where he does not; the number is smaller than one might think.[2] The situations Paul faced were sometimes quite

1. Wedderburn, 'Continuity', p. 100. The Cynic Epistles offer a closer parallel, yet a comparison of their contents with the New Testament letters reveals profound differences in purpose and method.
2. Wedderburn ('Similarity', pp. 117-18 n.1) cites the absence of express references to JT in (1) the controversies over the observance of certain days in Gal. 4.10 and Rom. 14.5-6; (2) the question of the 'virgins' in 1 Cor. 7.25-28 [cf. Mt. 19.10-12]; (3) the attitude towards the authorities in Rom. 13.1-7; (4) the issue of what a Christian may or may not eat in 1 Corinthians 8–10 and Romans 14 [cf. Mk 7.15, 18-19; Lk. 10.7-8]; and (5) arguments over whether a Christian is saved by grace or because it is earned [cf. the parable of the workers in the vineyard, Mt. 20.1-16]. Of these, (3) and (4) will be specifically addressed below, (5) is irrelevant in view of the

different from those addressed by Jesus.

d. *The changed historical situation after the Christ-Event.* Goppelt has observed that Jesus' ministry was knit to its particular eschatological situation which differed decisively from that of the post-Easter Church. Logia calling for repentance and behaviour in view of the approaching eschaton had to be transposed for a people who already stood in repentance on the other side of the resurrection.[1] Paraenetic sayings were therefore transmitted in a different form than their Synoptic counterparts (e.g. the similarity of Rom. 12.17a; 1 Thess. 5.15a; and 1 Pet. 3.9 as compared with Lk. 6.27a and Mt. 5.44a). Jesus' teaching became an 'orientation aid', a 'criterion of choice' helping to direct the communities to the right direction in which they were to live out their eschatological existence.[2] The problem with this view is its implication that the Synoptics' purpose was essentially historical and not paraenetic as well.

e. *The difficulty of directly applying some logia.* Some of Jesus' teachings may well have been as enigmatic and troublesome in application for the early Church as they are to us today.[3] The lack of direct reference to Jesus' parables in early epistolary literature has already been noted. It is not unlikely that Paul preferred to communicate JT in person so as to be able to answer interpretative questions and to clarify a saying's application on the spot rather than to risk misunderstanding or encourage proof-texting through liberal quotation. Letters for him were a necessary evil, a poor alternative to communication in person; hence he chose his words carefully for optimum clarity. The lack of a fixed written logia tradition and lengthy history of interpretation such as existed for the OT would also enter into consideration here.

general neglect of the parables in all early Christian epistolary literature, and (2) may well be a case in which the Corinthians already knew and misused the logion (see below). How a logion of Jesus would speak more directly than Paul's comments in (1) remains to be seen.

1. Cf. Goppelt, *Theology*, II, pp. 45-46.
2. Goppelt, *Theology*, II, pp. 45-46.
3. Cf. Dungan's study of the application of the divorce logion (*Sayings*, pp. 83-131).

Factors Affecting Paul in Particular

a. *The centrality of the cross and resurrection.* For Paul, the death and resurrection of Jesus inaugurated the eschaton, thus eclipsing in significance all of his words and deeds leading up to the Passion. Why should Paul point to an act of love, humility, or compassion during Jesus' ministry when he could cite his example of total commitment on the cross? Why should he cite a healing act of power, when he could refer to the resurrection? Everything Jesus said and did before his death and vindication paled in significance by comparison to the Christ-Event. According to Paul, the purpose of Jesus' appearance was to redeem God's people from under the law (Gal. 4.4-5) and deliver them from the present evil age (Gal. 1.4). Furthermore, other men were esteemed for their teachings or healing works,[1] but what set Jesus apart was his crucifixion, resurrection and exaltation. An overemphasis on Jesus' ministry could lead to dangerous misunderstanding and a failure to appreciate the uniqueness of his real significance.[2] That is not to say that JT was unnecessary or irrelevant, for without some tradition of what Jesus was like the gospel claim would have been incredible. Pre-Passion JT was effectively summarized and concentrated in the Christ-Event.[3]

b. *The need to assert his own apostolic authority.* Paul's particular style is not that of one given to parroting others.[4] Furthermore, the thought that he should strategically refrain from citing Jesus may never have crossed Paul's mind, but the possibility deserves mention. In a letter such as Galatians, to cite Jesus directly would open Paul up to the charge that his gospel was handed down to him from Jerusalem. He is so insistent that he did not get his gospel from humans that to begin quoting words of the historical Jesus would open him up to the obvious objection that he was taught those words at least by the apostles or churches in Judaea.[5]

---

1. E.g. Hanina ben Dosa; Vermes, *Jew*, pp. 72-80.
2. So Barrett, *Adam*, p. 91. I would disagree with his assertion that Paul 'could afford to be content with a bare assertion of the realization in historical and personal terms, that is, in Jesus, of the eschatological myth of salvation' (p. 91).
3. Cf. Weder, *Kreuz*, p. 229.
4. Cf. V. Taylor, 'Riddle', p. 288.
5. So also Wedderburn ('Continuity', p. 101).

c. *The similarity of dominical teachings to those of Judaism.* In view
of the considerable overlap between Jesus' words and the ethical ideals
of Judaism which Paul could assume for many of his readers, he had
little need to identify dominical teaching (unless he wanted to mark
out JT as such). Moreover, when Paul wrote, dominical logia may not
have occurred to him as readily as their OT roots which he had
known from childhood. Barrett conjectures that if Paul shows us only
a few of the logia he knew, 'it may be that he chose only those where
the teaching of Jesus differed sharply from that prevailing in
Judaism', that is, Paul referred to Jesus' teachings in 1 Corinthians 7
because his view on divorce differed from that of the OT.[1] This overlooks evidence that the Corinthians were particularly interested in JT
(see below) and does not explain his allusion in 1 Cor. 9.14, but it has
some force.[2]

d. *Avoidance of legalism.* Barrett thinks Paul does not quote Jesus as
his authority directly in Rom. 12.14 precisely because he did not see
Jesus as a lawgiver: 'For him the importance of Jesus was not legisla-
tive but historical and theological; accordingly he used material that
came to him from the historical tradition, but because it was intrinsically suitable, rather than to establish doctrine'.[3] Paul held Jesus'
teachings to be authoritative (1 Cor. 7.10, 25), but we do not see them
functioning quite like Paul's own pneumatic 'sentences of holy law'.[4]
Given the apostle's emphasis on grace and the gift of the Spirit
(especially when understood as the Spirit of Christ), we would not
expect to see sayings of Jesus mechanically applied to life in the
Church. On the connection between JT and the 'law of Christ', see
Chapter 8 below.

e. *Misuse of Jesus tradition.* On occasion Paul may have had difficulty
with Christians who misused JT. In some circles the words of Christ
were taken to constitute a new law (*Barn.* 2.6; Jas 2.8?; 1.25).
Wedderburn wonders if perhaps in Paul's eyes the teaching of Jesus
was 'in enemy hands', that is, being used in a legalistic way by

---

1. Barrett, *1 Corinthians*, p. 162; cf. Bultmann, *Theology*, I, pp. 34-35.
2. Cf. Best, *Paul*, p. 79.
3. Barrett, *Romans*, p. 241.
4. Cf. Käsemann, 'Sentences'.

Judaizers.[1] Others think that Paul encountered in Corinth a Jewish Christianity which emphasized pre-Synoptic traditions ('Q') presenting Jesus as a wisdom teacher and miracle-working hero or θεῖος ἀνήρ while neglecting his Passion.[2] There is evidence for special interest in JT among the Corinthians, but the specific claims of Robinson *et al.* are dubious.[3] If the root question at Corinth really were 'the adequacy of a collection of Jesus-sayings to shape the Church, a collection which provided only sayings and did not present the sacrifice of Christ and his triumph over death',[4] Paul would have addressed the issue head-on. Furthermore, this factor fails to address the general lack of JT in other early Christian writings.

f. *Sociological differences*. The specificity of some sayings would require translation and adaptation for Paul's audience, hindering the kind of immediate recognition required for allusion. Jesus lived in and spoke to a rural, Jewish culture, removed from the urban, thoroughly Hellenized life of Paul's Gentile audiences.[5] Sayings which presupposed a Palestinian milieu would sound foreign to those accustomed to

1. Wedderburn, 'Continuity', p. 100.
2. So Georgi, *Opponents*; J.M. Robinson, 'Kerygma', pp. 40-46; *idem*, 'Shifts', pp. 82-85; Köster, 'Gospels', p. 186; *idem*, 'Writings', pp. 247-49; Kuhn, 'Problem'; Balch, 'Backgrounds'; cf. Richardson, 'Thunderbolt'; *idem*, 'Traditions'; Kelber, *Gospel*, p. 176.
3. See Tuckett, '1 Corinthians'. All of Paul's explicit references to dominical sayings are clustered in 1 Corinthians, and only there does he refer to his lack of further sayings (7.25). Apparently the Corinthians had asked him what Jesus had to say about divorce and remarriage (1 Cor. 7.1). Cf. also faith to move mountains in 1 Cor. 13.2 // Mk 11.22-23 pars.; 1 Cor. 1.18–2.16 and the *Jubelruf* in Mt. 11.25-27 par.; non-resistance in 1 Cor. 6.7 // Mt. 5.39 par.; a steward being found faithful in 1 Cor. 4.2 // Lk. 12.42-43; the connection of γαμέω and the rare γαμίζω in 1 Cor. 7.36, 38 // Mk 12.25 pars.; Mt. 24.38 par.; Balch, 'Backgrounds'; etc. One need not subscribe to Robinson's hypothesis to see the potential of abuse of dominical traditions by a 'Christ party' (1.12; cf. 2 Cor. 10.7). Is this higher concentration of parallels due to a phase in Paul's life (Hurd, 'Jesus', pp. 88), or to the more practical nature of the issues Paul is addressing (Kennedy, *Theology*, p. 103)?
4. Richardson, 'Thunderbolt', p. 110.
5. Palestine was exposed to a considerable amount of Greek culture (Hengel, *Judaism*), but 'backwoods' Galilee was less Hellenized than Jerusalem (Hengel, 'Between', p. 7; *idem*, *Acts*, p. 76), and much less than Paul's communities in Greece and Asia Minor.

life in Greece. So, for example, the command to go the extra mile
when commandeered (Mt. 5.41) would hardly be understandable to
those unfamiliar with occupation by the military.

There are, of course, other factors that have been proposed, such as
the old theory that expectation of an imminent parousia tended to sus-
pend any interest in facts about Jesus of Nazareth (although *Naherwartung* would have ensured the remembrance at least of those sayings which fed that expectancy), or Riesenfeld's suggestion that Jesus'
words were considered to be particularly holy, and therefore were not
readily quoted.[1] But it should now be clear that one needs a far
stronger foundation than an argument from silence, dubious exegesis
of 2 Cor. 5.16, and a one-sided reading of Paul through the lens of
Galatians in order to build a case that JT was irrelevant to the apostle.
There are many clues, though they are not as obvious as we might
like, that the teachings and example of Jesus shaped and moulded
Paul's Christian perspective. Where and how Paul used those traditions in Rom. 12–15.13 is the subject of Part II.

---

1. Riesenfeld, 'Tradition', pp. 12, 21, 18. Paul however shows no hesitation in
citing what were some of the holiest words in the tradition in 1 Cor. 11.23-26, and a
rabbinic model for the preservation of the Synoptic tradition does not fit the facts of
the case.

PART II

JESUS TRADITION IN ROMANS 12.1–15.13

Chapter 4

ROMANS 12.1-2: THE GREAT REVERSAL

Rom. 12.1-2 serves as a heading for the exhortations in the following four chapters; if JT informs Paul's paraenesis, we might expect some indication of that here. At first glance the evidence is disappointing. No direct comparison with Jesus' behaviour is drawn and no explicit 'word of the Lord' is given, although Paul uses θεός three times in the two verses. Nevertheless, there is reason to suspect that Paul's admonitions find their basis and shape in a christology in which the obedience of Jesus was central.[1]

1. *Exegesis*

An initial question which must be answered about Rom. 12.1-2 is its relationship to Paul's argument in the first eleven chapters. Although some see the οὖν in 12.1 functioning only as a formal transitional particle, coupled with διὰ τῶν οἰκτιρμῶν τοῦ θεοῦ it points to a theological and argumentative link with the preceding material. The 'mercies of God' is more than simply a stock phrase reflecting the influence of the LXX rendering of רחמים; whether it refers to those οἰκτιρμοί enumerated in earlier sections or in the whole of the letter, it signifies the basis of appeal, as well as emphasizing urgency.[2] Paul has just finished extolling the wonder of God's plan to show mercy to all, demonstrated in the Deliverer who comes from Zion (11.26), through whom salvation has come to the Gentiles (11.11), the Lord Jesus who bestows his riches on all who call upon him (10.9-13),

---

1. Cf. Hahn, 'Foundation'.

2. Cf. Leenhardt, *Romans*, p. 301. Schlier sees the 'mercies' referring back to chs. 5–8 (*Römerbrief*, p. 351), Michel (*Römer*, p. 368) favours chs. 9–11, and Cranfield opts for the whole letter (*Romans*, II, p. 596).

through whom the grace of God abounded for many (5.15), who delivers from the body of death (7.24), and who is at the right hand of God, not condemning but interceding (8.34).[1] Now he will go on to characterize the behaviour of both Jew and Greek as the one people of God in Christ. As we shall see, there are significant vocabulary links in 12.1-2 with previous passages in the letter, which indicate that Paul is recombining ideas expressed earlier.[2]

The content of Paul's exhortation is given by the infinitive παραστῆσαι and the following words. He uses the verb five times in Romans 6 (vv. 13 [twice], 16 and 19 [twice]), and the close connection with σῶμα in 6.12-13 suggests that Paul is replaying a familiar theme:[3]

> Let not sin therefore reign in your mortal bodies (σώματι), to make you obey their passions. Do not yield (παραστάνετε) your members to sin as instruments of wickedness, but yield yourselves (παραστήσατε ἑαυτούς) to God, as men who have been brought from death to life (ὡσεὶ ἐκ νεκρῶν ζῶντας), and your members to God as instruments of righteousness.

Other similarities in vocabulary confirm the linkage of chs. 6 and 12, a connection we would expect since Paul's first imperative in the letter appears in 6.11, and the call there to sanctification is picked up and expanded in chs. 12–13. ζῶσαν in 12.1 is usually taken simply as the opposite of the dead ritual sacrifices of Judaism and Hellenistic religion, but ζῶντας in 6.13 offers an additional nuance: 'offer yourselves to God as those alive from the dead', that is, united to the life of Christ, which he (and the Christian) lives to God (6.4, 10-11; cf. 14.7-8).[4] In 6.19 Paul reminds his readers of the past when they offered their members (παραστῆσαι) as slaves to impurity/lawlessness, and he calls them to present themselves as slaves to righteousness εἰς ἁγιασμόν (cf. 6.22). This finds its counterpart in ἁγίαν in 12.1; the holiness Paul seeks is not simply cultic but ethical (cf. 1 Thess. 4.3; Rom. 15.16). Furthermore, the two chapters employ the

---

1. Cf. Corriveau, *Liturgy*, pp. 166-67; Piper, *Enemies*, pp. 103-104.

2. So also Dunn (*Romans*, II, p. 707).

3. So also Wilckens, *Römer*, III, p. 3; Furnish, *Theology*, p. 106; Leenhardt, *Romans*, p. 301.

4. Note the use of ζωή in 5.10, 17-18; 8.2, 6, 10; cf. also Corriveau, *Liturgy*, pp. 170-71; Cranfield, *Romans*, II, p. 600.

language of baptism, 6 more clearly than 12.[1]

One difference between the two passages, however, is the presence of θυσία in 12.1—it does not appear in ch. 6.[2] In contrast to the cultic sacrifices of the Jews and Greeks, the people of God in Christ are to offer themselves for obedience to God's will. Their sacrifice issues from faith (cf. Phil. 2.17), and is a sacrifice of thanksgiving in grateful response to the mercy of God seen in the sacrifice of his Son.[3] Although their sacrifice is not *explicitly* linked here with that of Jesus, there is more than a causal relation in Paul's theology.[4] The λατρεία

1. Cf. 6.3-4. ἀνακαίνωσις in 12.2 should be linked to the καινότης ζωῆς in 6.3, and occurs again only in Tit. 3.5, a probable reference to baptism. συσχη- ματίζεσθαι is found again only in 1 Pet. 1.14, another baptismal passage (cf., e.g., Evans, 'Worship', p. 14).

2. Rare in the Pauline corpus (elsewhere only in 1 Cor. 10.18; Phil. 2.17; 4.18; Eph. 5.2), θυσία here signifies the material comprising the sacrifice since Paul qualifies it with ζῶσαν (Cranfield, *Romans*, II, p. 599). The singular indicates that Paul is not viewing the presentation of his readers' bodies as a series of unrelated acts of individuals, but as a corporate offering to God (cf. 12.4-5; Barrett, 'Ethics', p. 231).

3. Cf. Seidensticker, *Opfer*, pp. 255-56; Goppelt, *Typos*, p. 150; *contra*, e.g., Olford ('Study', pp. 302-303) and Evans ('Worship', p. 14 n. 40), who deny a connection in our text. The belief that Jesus' death was in some way sacrificial goes back to the very earliest days of Christianity (Hengel, *Atonement*; Daly, *Sacrifice*, pp. 236-40; *idem*, *Origins*, pp. 59-61; Bultmann, *Theology*, I, pp. 46-47). Explicit sacrificial language with reference to Christ is rare in Paul (1 Cor. 5.7; Rom. 5.9; 8.3; 2 Cor. 5.21; cf. Eph. 5.2) but we have good evidence that he also viewed Jesus' death as an atoning sacrifice (e.g. Sykes, 'Sacrifice', pp. 73-77, esp. 76; Cranfield, *Romans*, I, pp. 216-18). Paul uses ὑπέρ and διά in the 'surrender formula' (with παραδιδόναι or δίδοναι: Rom. 4.25; 8.32; Gal. 1.4; 2.20; cf. Eph. 5.25) and in the 'dying formula' (with ἀποθνήσκειν: Rom. 5.6, 8; Gal. 2.21; 1 Cor. 8.11; 15.3; 2 Cor. 5.14-15; 1 Thess. 5.10; cf. Hengel, *Atonement*, pp. 35-37; *idem*, 'Sacrifice', pp. 458-59). 1 Cor. 15.3 reveals that this usage was a part of the Christian tradition he had inherited. In Rom. 3.25-26 he refers to Christ's death as a ἱλαστήριον, employing what is often seen as traditional language traceable at least back to Antioch and probably to Palestine, if not Jerusalem (cf. 4.25; so Bultmann, *Theology*, I, pp. 46-47; Jeremias, *Theology*, pp. 296-97 and n. 5; Stuhlmacher, 'Auferweckung', pp. 73-74; on ἱλαστήριον see Cranfield, *Romans*, I, pp. 214-18). For a possible background in Maccabaean martyr theology, cf. Williams, *Death*, pp. 203-54.

4. 'Christ is the sacrificial victim offered in favour of and in the place of the sinner, so that he may share in his death and thus no longer live for himself (2 Cor. 5:15)' (Leenhardt, *Romans*, p. 301). 'In numerous texts. . . Paul both explicitly and implicitly. . . compares the life and death of the Christian with the sacrificial

which people failed to offer by refusing to glorify him as God and give thanks (1.21) is now restored through Christ.

Although rarely observed, the connection with ch. 1 is unmistakable.[1] First, there is the theme of *worship*: in addition to the failure δοξάζειν and εὐχαριστεῖν we read of the idolatrous exchange of glory (1.23) and the choice to worship and serve (σεβάζεσθαι καὶ λατρεύειν) the creature instead of the Creator (1.25), in contrast to the proper worship offered in ch. 12 (παραστῆσαι, θυσία, λατρεία).

Secondly, we find the same emphasis on the νοῦς, once subjected to futility, darkened (καρδία) in the foolishness of idolatry (1.21-22), rejecting the truth and failing δοκιμάζειν the knowledge of God and his will (1.25, 28, 32), but now renewed, approving (δοκιμάζειν) the will of God, and seeking to please him.[2] This in turn helps to account for Paul's choice of λογικός instead of πνευματικός in 12.2: λογικὴ λατρεία stands in strongest contrast to the topsy-turvy mind that in its foolishness establishes the lie in place of the truth—the ἀδόκιμος νοῦς (1.28).[3] Paul's emphasis on the mind and thought as

---

death of Christ' (Daly, *Origins*, p. 62); cf. Rom. 8.36; 2 Cor. 4.10-11; Gal. 2.20; Col. 1.24. Note also the connection of Christ's reconciling death with his presentation of Christians as a holy offering to God in Col. 1.22; cf. Eph. 5.25-27.

1. Among the few who have noted some of the links are Furnish, *Theology*, pp. 103-104; Evans, 'Worship', pp. 30-32; Olford, 'Study', pp. 328, 346 n. 27; Hooker, 'Ethics', p. 4; Dunn, *Romans*, II, pp. 707-708.

2. Contrast the Jews who know God's will but do not fulfil it (2.18); note also 1 Thess. 4.3; 5.18; cf. Eph. 5.17. On the importance of doing God's θέλημα in the Gospels see Mk 3.35; Mt. 12.50; 6.10 // Lk. 11.2; Mt. 26.42 // Lk. 22.42. τὸ ἀγαθὸν καὶ εὐάρεστον καὶ τέλειον in 12.1 should be taken as substantival adjectives in apposition with τὸ θέλημα, i.e., 'that which is good, well-pleasing and perfect' (so Lagrange, *Romains*, p. 295). The emphasis here is on *pleasing* God (cf. εὐάρεστος in 12.1; 14.18; 2 Cor. 5.9; Col. 3.20; cf. Eph. 5.10). Matthew presents Christ as having exhorted his hearers to be τέλειος as God is τέλειος (Mt. 5.48; cf. 19.21); for Paul also this is a goal for his readers (1 Cor. 14.20; Col. 1.28; 4.12; cf. 1 Cor. 2.6). Cf. Eph. 4.13-15, where Christ is the measure of the τέλειος ἀνήρ into which believers are to grow in unity as his body.

3. This is not to say that the appearance of λογικός in 12.2 is surprising; it was a popular word in Greek philosophy (esp. Stoicism), the mystery religions and in Hellenistic Judaism (e.g. *T. Levi* 3.6; *CH* I.31; XIII.18; also 1 Pet. 2.2; cf., e.g., Kittel, *TDNT*, IV, pp. 142-43; Cranfield, *Romans*, pp. 602-605). Here the meaning is not 'rational' or 'logical' (in contrast to ecstatic worship), 'authentic' (in contrast to

directing one's behaviour comes to expression also in 8.5-10, where there are further links with chs. 1 and 12: the clustered use of φρονεῖν and cognates (8.5-7; 12.3, 16; cf. 15.5); death the result of setting the mind on the flesh (8.6; 1.32; cf. 6.21), which mind (the φρόνημα τῆς σαρκός) is hostile to God (8.7; 1.30 θεοστυγεῖς) and cannot please him (8.8),[1] in contrast to the one whose life is determined by the Spirit, who *is* capable of pleasing God (εὐάρεστον; 12.1-2), who discerns his will and fulfills the δικαίωμα of the law (8.4; 13.8ff.; cf. 1.32).[2]

Thirdly, the bodies that were dishonoured in impurity, unnatural passions, and destructive behaviour resulting from rebellion against God and deserving the sentence of death (1.24-32) are now to be presented to him as θυσίαν ζῶσαν ἁγίαν εὐάρεστον, for obedience to that divine will formerly rejected. Nowhere else does Paul link sacrifice and bodily consecration in his paraenesis. The action he calls for in 12.1-2 thus represents a reversal of the downward spiral depicted in Romans 1:

wrath	mercy
refusing to glorify or thank God	(thankful) sacrifice
dishonouring the body	offering the body
ἀσύνετος, idolatrous λατρεία	λογικὴ λατρεία
reprobate mind	renewed mind
rejecting the δικαίωμα τοῦ θεοῦ	approving the θέλημα τοῦ θεοῦ

When we recognize that this reversal represents two poles in salvation history, the pieces in a larger puzzle begin to drop into place.

The notion that Romans 1 recalls the story of Adam is not new.[3] If

---

meaningless) or 'spiritual' (in contrast to physical) but 'understanding' (Cranfield, *Romans*, II, pp. 595, 604-605) or 'reasonable', as opposed to the foolishness of wilful avoidance of the creature's responsibility to the Creator. It characterizes the behaviour of one in his 'right mind' (i.e. in right orientation to God).

1. This is the state of those who yielded themselves as slaves of ἀκαθαρσία and ἀνομία (6.19, cf. 1.24), to which we have already seen a contrast in the παραστῆσαι exhortation of 12.1.

2. Note also that to present one's body as a sacrifice is to give one's self away, i.e., to 'lose one's life'. The thought links with Rom. 6 show that the idea here is a voluntary 'enslavement' to God under a different metaphor; the slavery/service imagery is not far in thought from the teaching and example of Jesus.

3. Cf. Hyldahl, 'Reminiscence'; Hooker, 'Adam'; Wedderburn, 'Adam',

Paul is employing the language of the first chapter in 12.1-2, then the latter amounts to a call to participate in a reversal of Romans 1 in the Second Adam. Paul's Adamic theology clearly surfaces in Rom. 5.12-19 (cf. also 3.23; 7.7-11; 8.19-22; 1 Cor. 15.45-49), where the act of obedience of one man (Jesus) is said to lead to righteousness and life.[1] In the light of Jesus' obedience, life and death, Christians are to present themselves ὡσεὶ ἐκ νεκρῶν ζῶντας, δούλους εἰς ὑπακοήν (Rom. 6.13, 16; cf. 6). Now in 12.1-2 Paul calls those who have died with Jesus through baptism to join him in offering themselves completely—in effect, after his example. His sacrifice evokes the Christian sacrifice.[2] The giving up of Jesus' body as a sacrifice for the sake of others (1 Cor. 11.24) enables this reversal and provides the archetype for Christian self-offering in Rom. 12.1; both are acts in accordance with God's will (cf. Gal. 1.3-4). So Sykes sees Jesus' sacrifice as a 'climactic act of a life of self-giving, an act with a voluntary and purposive intention, whose quality is taken to be paradigmatic for all future human life. . . an offering of "himself in love for others" which Christians are also to offer in conformity with him'.[3] The obedience which Adam and his descendants failed to offer (echoed in Rom. 1), has at last been offered and enabled by the Second Adam, Jesus Christ.[4]

---

pp. 413-19; Dunn, *Christology*, pp. 101-102. On the larger issue of Adam in Paul see Schlier, *Römerbrief*, pp. 179-89; Scroggs, *Adam*, pp. 75-112; Barrett, *Adam*. '*In his most careful analysis of the plight of man he draws repeatedly on the account of Adam and his fall in Gen 2–3*' (Dunn, *Christology*, p. 105, his emphasis).

1. Hooker sees these verses as 'the key to Romans, summing up the argument of the previous chapters in terms of the contrast between Adam and Christ' ('Atonement', p. 464).

2. If it is correct to take the genitives as subjective in the phrases πίστις Ἰησοῦ (Rom. 3.26), πίστις Ἰησοῦ Χριστοῦ (Rom. 3.22; Gal. 2.16; 3.22), or πίστις Χριστοῦ (Gal. 2.16; Phil. 3.9), i.e., referring to Jesus' faith or faithfulness, the likelihood of an implied correspondence between his sacrifice and the Christian's increases. Cf., e.g., Howard, 'Notes'; *idem*, 'Faith'; *idem, Crisis*, pp. 57-58, 95-96 n. 191; D.W.B. Robinson, 'Faith'; Hays, *Faith*, pp. 157-191; Hooker, 'Suffering', pp. 75-76; *idem*, 'ΠΙΣΤΙΣ'.

3. Sykes, 'Sacrifice', p. 76.

4. 'As Adam had headed the whole line of disobedience and sin, so Christ stands at the head of a new race which lives under the sign of obedience' (Corriveau, *Liturgy*, p. 173; on obedience see Rom. 1.5; 5.8-9, 19 [cf. Phil. 2.8]; 15.18; 16.19; 2 Cor. 10.5). A similar reversal and contrast appears in Eph. 4.17-24. Although the

The link with Christ is confirmed by the reference to transformation in 12.2.[1] Although he does not specify the goal of the transformation (μεταμορφοῦσθαι), that is, the form or image (εἰκών) his readers are to assume, 2 Cor. 3.18 offers the obvious answer: Christians are being transformed into the same image (τὴν αὐτὴν εἰκόνα μεταμορφούμεθα) as that of the Lord who is beheld (cf. 2 Cor. 4.16). At the same time, Paul is not interested simply in individual transformation, but corporate renewal (θυσία, not θυσίαι). His exhortation is controlled and guided by the desire to assist those who have been incorporated into the body of Christ to grow up into the image of the one into whom they have been baptized (cf. Eph. 4.13-15). So he writes in Gal. 4.19 τέκνα μου, οὓς πάλιν ὠδίνω μέχρις οὗ μορφωθῇ Χριστὸς ἐν ὑμῖν. Corporately and individually, Christians are to move toward the goal of ultimate conformity to Christ.

Rom. 8.29 adds further support to the view that Christ is the goal in 12.2. The great reversal takes place in the present, but has its completion in the age to come. Whereas 8.29 refers to ultimate conformity to the likeness of Christ's glorious resurrection body (so Phil. 3.21, 1 Cor. 15.49), in Paul's mind there is continuity between the present

Ephesians walked ἐν ματαιότητι τοῦ νοός, ἐσκοτωμένοι τῇ διανοίᾳ, ἀπηλλοτριωμένοι τῆς ζωῆς τοῦ θεοῦ, with hardened hearts giving themselves over to licentiousness (4.17-19), having 'learned Christ' and being taught in him (4.20-21) they are to put off the old, be renewed in mind (ἀνανεοῦσθαι τῷ πνεύματι τοῦ νοός) and put on τὸν καινὸν ἄνθρωπον τὸν κατὰ θεόν . . . (4.22-24). On the 'New Man' see Chapter 9.

1. J.S. Banks's suggestion long ago that Paul's use of μεταμορφοῦσθαι echoes the transfiguration of Jesus has been ignored, but deserves consideration ('Paul', p. 413). Absent from the LXX, the word appears in the NT only in Mt. 17.2 // Mk 9.2; Rom. 12.1 and 2 Cor. 3.18. Banks cited the reference to glory in the Corinthian passage, and thought Jesus' physical transformation provided for Paul the metaphor for moral transfiguration of believers in the perfecting of character. 'As the Lord's glorified body is the type of the glorified body of believers (Phil. iii. 21), so His perfect life is the type that is to be realized in their moral life' ('Paul', p. 413). The word is common in mystery religions where it signifies deification, but NT usage is rooted in Jewish apocalyptic; transformation is 'one of the gifts of eschatological salvation' (cf., e.g., 2 Apoc. Bar. 51.3; Behm, TDNT, IV, pp. 757-58). Just as Jesus' transfiguration afforded a foretaste in the present of his coming eschatological glory, likewise the present transformation of Christians is a precursor in this age of their complete transformation at the resurrection.

life of sanctification and the ultimate state. It is to those who by perseverance ἔργου ἀγαθοῦ seek (future) glory and honour and immortality that God will give eternal life (Rom. 2.7). Conformity to Christ in the present is an *essential* part of the process leading to ultimate transformation.[1] It is expected that Christians should suffer with Christ (8.17), and Paul himself sought to be conformed to Christ's death (Phil. 3.10).[2] Unity with Christ involves participation in the likeness (τῷ ὁμοιώματι) of his death and resurrection (Rom. 6.5, cf. esp. 2 Cor. 4.10).[3]

To sum up, underpinning Rom. 12.1-2 is Jesus' foundational and exemplary sacrifice.[4] For Paul, Christ's image is the goal of the transforming process, and his Spirit enables the renewal of the mind.[5] Thus, imitating his obedience of self-offering, Christians may hope to discern and perform God's perfect will. It may be objected that this exposition overloads two verses with a christological cargo which, however consistent with Paul's theology, was not intended here. Nonetheless, the exegesis of the following chapters will corroborate this christological foundation for Paul's paraenesis.

2. Conclusion

In Rom. 12.1 Paul exhorts his readers to present their bodies to God as a sacrifice devoted to his will. But they will not be the first to do so.

---

1. Cf. Hooker, 'Suffering'; *idem*, 'Atonement', p. 474.

2. In 2 Cor. 4.16-17 the idea of an inward renewing accompanied by outward suffering which leads to future glory combines the similar thoughts in Rom. 8.17 and 12.2.

3. Paul's notion of the *necessity* of suffering with Christ and conforming to his death may well be rooted in the traditions behind Mk 8.34 // Mt. 16.24-26 // Lk. 9.23-24. Cf. the call to take up one's σταυρόν and Gal. 5.24 (Paul's cross taken up at baptism when he died with Christ? Gal 2.20; Rom. 6.3-4), and the repeated κερδαίνειν/ζημιοῦν language in Phil. 3.7-11, where Paul concludes with his desire to become like Christ in his death (lose his life) in order to attain to the resurrection from the dead (i.e. save his life).

4. Seidensticker also sees Rom. 12.1 as christological in content and inspiration (*Opfer*, pp. 256-63), although he refers λογικὴ λατρεία to spiritualized piety (in deliberate contrast to Hellenistic cultic worship, p. 262) and θυσία ζῶσα as self-offering to God with Christ (for all, p. 262).

5. For the link between ἀνακαίνωσις and Christ, cf. Col. 3.10, a verse set in the heart of christologically-controlled paraenesis (see Chapter 9).

In giving up themselves to the λατρεία befitting God they demon-strate their unity with the one whose life was fully yielded to his Father's will, with the one who knew no conformity to this age but broke its power and inaugurated a new αἰών by his death and resur-rection. Alive in the Second Adam, Christians are to succeed where the first Adam failed. This means (1) seeing their very existence as an offering in worship, not to gain God's favour, but in response to his mercy poured out in Christ; (2) glorifying God and giving thanks, following the example of the one who lived to please God and offered the ultimate sacrifice in holiness; and (3) offering the obedience of faith, joining Jesus in his nonconformity and submitting to the trans-forming power of his Spirit. The renewed νοῦς is the φρόνημα τοῦ πνεύματος (8.6), the νοῦς Χριστοῦ (1 Cor. 2.16) which they possess and yet are exhorted to possess; theirs is a foretaste of the yet future renewal, but the process of renewal must progress as long as they are in the body, if they are to discern and accomplish that will for which their Lord taught them to pray. The verses that follow give shape to that will, as they outline some characteristics of those who are being transformed into his image.

Chapter 5

ROMANS 12.3-8:
RESPONSIBILITY IN THE BODY

In Rom. 12.3-8, christology again undergirds Paul's admonitions;
here the controlling category is the body of Christ. An inflated sense
of self-importance (reflected in judgmental attitudes and boasting) is
the first area of their thinking which needs transformation (12.3).[1] 'A
particular kind of conformity to the world, of συσχηματίζεσθαι τῷ
αἰῶνι τούτῳ, is to think too highly of oneself, ὑπερφρονεῖν'.[2] The
Roman Christians must learn to view themselves as interdependent
parts of a whole, the body of Christ (12.4-5). No one can be condemned by others; all are needed. Rather, each should measure himself according to his own faithfulness in fulfilling his God-given role
by using his χάρισμα as it is intended (12.6-8). In other words, a
proper self-estimation should be derived from a right understanding
of the nature of the body of Christ, and from faithful use of one's
gift(s) in that body.[3] Whereas Gentiles φάσκουσι εἶναι σοφοί but

1. Schlier thinks ὑπερφρονεῖν is 'die Gefahr des Charismatikers' (Römerbrief,
p. 364); cf. also, e.g., Wilckens (Römer, III, p. 11); Käsemann (Romans, p. 332).
Nevertheless, miraculous gifts are not mentioned, and had there been a danger from
enthusiasts we would expect to see a much more developed discussion, as is the case
with the weak and strong in chs. 14–15. Paul is addressing Christians who are not
united in one congregation but are divided along Jew/Gentile lines by pride and a
critical spirit (cf. 3.27-28; 11.17-18, 20, 25; 12.3, 10, 16; 14.1-23; so also, e.g.,
Minear, Obedience, p. 84). The repetition of verbs of thinking (ὑπερφρονεῖν,
σωφρονεῖν, φρονεῖν) in 12.3 reveals the continuity with Paul's concern for renewal
of the νοῦς (cf. the related verbs in 12.10, 16-17; 14.6; 15.5).
2. Barrett, 'Ethics', p. 223.
3. The phrases introduced by εἴτε in 12.6-8 are most likely imperatival in force, in
view of the δέ in 12.6 and the imperatival nuance of 12.9-13, although they could be
indicative, emphasizing the particular ways in which the members differ (for the
upbuilding of the body).

have become fools (1.22) and Jews assume an air of superiority by boasting in God and confidently asserting knowledge of his will while failing to live up to it (2.17-24), Paul's readers should think soberly.

A possible reference to Christ may be found in the obscure μέτρον πίστεως (12.3).[1] Cranfield takes the phrase to mean 'a standard (by which to measure, estimate himself), namely his faith', commenting,

> to estimate oneself according to the standard which consists of one's faith
> in Christ is really to recognize that Christ Himself in whom God's judge-
> ment and mercy are revealed is the One by whom alone one must measure
> oneself and also one's fellow men, the One who is, in fact, the true
> . . . πάντων χρημάτων μέτρον.[2]

μέτρον could signify a 'standard' or 'means of measurement' (cf. 2 Cor. 10.13), but a direct connection with Christ is dubious. The absence of the article argues against it, and on Cranfield's view Paul would be using μερίζειν of Christ in a completely different sense than in 1 Cor. 1.13. Ultimately Christ is the standard for all, but that is probably not Paul's thought here. We could just as easily relate the πίστις in 12.3 to that in 14.1-2, 22-23 (cf. 14.5) and understand the standard to be one's own faith, in the sense of what one knows by faith is right before God. Nonetheless μέτρον probably means 'a measure' (i.e. a measured quantity, cf. Eph. 4.7) and πίστις refers by metonymy to that which is entrusted to each person, that is, one's χάρισμα(τα).[3] In view of the exhortation to make use of their gifts in 12.6-8, the thought is not, however, that Christians should esteem themselves by the gift(s) given them (which could still lead to pride), but that they should recognize that with the gift comes the responsibility to use it for the body of Christ.

If responsibility to put one's gift to full use clarifies the difficult phrase μέτρον πίστεως, the passage may be compared to the parable of the talents (Mt. 25.14-30).[4] The three δοῦλοι in the parable are

1. For the exegetical options, see Cranfield, *Romans*, II, pp. 613-16; *idem*, 'Μέτρον'.

2. *Romans*, II, p. 616. Earlier Cranfield was more concise: 'The μέτρον πίστεως is really Jesus Christ himself as the Standard and Norm' ('Μέτρον', p. 351); cf. K. Barth (*Romans*, p. 444).

3. Cf. Black (*Romans*, p. 152) and Pallis (*Romans*, p. 134).

4. N–A[26] margin cites Mt. 25.15 at Rom. 12.3. Far less likely is a connection with Mk 4.24 // Mt. 7.2: ἐν ᾧ μέτρῳ μετρεῖτε μετρηθήσεται ὑμῖν; cf. Lk. 6.38.

given differing sums of money, ἑκάστῳ κατὰ τὴν ἰδίαν δύναμιν (25.15), and the returning judge evaluates each person's stewardship.[1] Now 1 Pet. 4.10 asserts that Christians should employ whatever gifts they are given for one another, as good stewards of God's varied grace. The statements in the following verse are close to those in Romans, suggesting that the idea of the need to use (varied) gifts as good stewards is part of early Christian tradition.[2] If there is a relationship here, Paul (or a predecessor) has taken the parable of the talents and applied it to the new situation after the coming of the Spirit.

It is thus doubtful that any direct link may be drawn in this section to dominical teaching or example, although Paul's exhortation is not divorced from his christology.[3] He bases his admonition to humility on his understanding of the unity of believers in one body ἐν Χριστῷ, in which each person has a responsibility to fulfil a particular role.

---

1. Luke's version of the parable (19.12-27) differs: identical sums are given, and the ἑκάστῳ phrase does not appear.

2. On the independence of 1 Peter and Romans, see Goppelt, *Petrusbrief*, pp. 48-51; Selwyn, *1 Peter*, pp. 20-23, 461-62. Note that Paul apparently echoes one dominical tradition about being found to be a faithful steward in 1 Cor. 4.1-2 (οἰκονόμος πιστὸς εὑρίσκεσθαι; cf. Lk. 12.42); see Fjärstedt, *Traditions*, pp. 100-37.

3. Ellis sees Paul's concept of the body of Christ and his temple typology rooted in dominical teachings ('Traditions', pp. 487-90), but his evidence is thin and needs development. Although Resch likened Rom. 12.3 to Lk. 16.15 and Rom. 12.8 to Mt. 6.3 (*Paulinismus*, p. 86), the vocabulary and thought in both cases differ notably. The only verbal links of potential interest are πρᾶξις (12.4, cf. Mt. 16.27), διακονία (12.7, cf. Mk 9.35; 10.43, 45 par.) μεταδίδεσθαι (12.8, cf. Lk. 3.11), ἁπλότης (12.8, cf. ἁπλοῦς in Mt. 6.22 par.), and ἐλεεῖν (12.8, cf. Mt. 5.7), but these parallels are too remote to be significant.

Chapter 6

ROMANS 12.9-21: LOVE IN ACTION

After establishing the proper criterion for self-estimation and the proper context in which his readers should view their lives (service in the body of Christ), Paul now gives a series of general exhortations relating to everyday life and attitudes towards fellow believers (vv. 9-13), as well as towards those that are difficult to love (vv. 14-21).[1] The loose grammatical construction which began in 12.6 continues in a string of short, pregnant phrases, as Paul sketches an outline of the transformed life for the Roman Christians.[2] Commentators dispute whether there is continuity in thought—the passage reads like a grocery list of unrelated admonitions. One thing is certain: Paul is drawing on traditional material. Comparison with exhortations in 1 Thessalonians and 1 Peter reveals that the language and ideas of 12.9-21 are

1. The common twofold schema of relations with fellow Christians (12.9-13) and with outsiders (12.14-21) is not strictly accurate, since 12.16 speaks of attitudes εἰς ἀλλήλους. Friedrich et al. see a similar structure but put the transition at 12.16b ('Situation', pp. 150-52).

2. Daube's theory that the participles in 12.9-19 reflect dependence upon a written Hebrew–Christian code of behaviour ('Participle') may be correct, but in light of the parallel commands using *finite* verbs in 1 Thess. 5.12-22, it is doubtful that Paul has quoted from one here. More probably the syntax represents an extension of what we find in Phil. 2.2-4, where he uses four participles and an adjective in an imperatival sense, filling out the meaning of 2.2a (cf. also Col. 3.16; Eph. 5.19-20; 4.1-3). Paul's descriptive use of participles to characterize behaviour (cf. Rudberg, 'Partizipien', pp. 14-15) has been overlooked in recent discussions of the grammar of 12.9-17, and the choice of participles here may be attributable to the fact that he did not know the majority of his readers. A string of imperatives such as occurs in 1 Thess. 5 might not go down as well with strangers as the more descriptive exhortations subtly conveyed by participles. That is not to deny Semitic influence, however, in Paul's constructions.

not unique to Romans.[1] Several clues in this section suggest the influence not only of the OT and other Jewish traditions, but also of the life and teaching of Jesus.[2]

1. *Romans 12.9-13*

The first clue is the theme of ἀγάπη which introduces and summarizes the chapter.[3] The pre-eminence of ἀγάπη in Paul's ethics (e.g. Gal. 5.6; Rom. 13.10; 1 Cor. 13; the noun appears in every Epistle and the verb in all but Philippians and Philemon) certainly has its roots in the OT, but it is unlikely that the apostle fastened on love as his guiding ethical principle in ignorance of (or without interest in) the early traditions of Jesus' teachings and his example of giving himself ὑπὲρ ἡμῶν. Paul probably knew Jesus' reiteration of Lev. 19.18 (Mk 12.31 pars.; see Chapter 8). He saw his death on the cross as the supreme sign of Jesus' love (Gal. 2.20), and there is good reason to think that when he expounds love he is describing no abstract concept, but that which was exemplified in the man Jesus.[4]

A second clue in 12.9 is the adjective qualifying the love Paul

---

1. Cf. Selwyn's discussion, especially table VIIIA (*1 Peter*, pp. 365-466; table on p. 408). For studies of traditions in 12.9-21 see esp. Talbert ('Tradition'), Hanson (*Studies*, pp. 126-35), Piper (*Enemies*, pp. 4-18, 100-19).

2. With the introductory formula γέγραπται γάρ Paul cites Deut. 32.35a in 12.19 (cf. Heb. 10.30), then Prov. 25.21-22 in 12.20. Other OT echoes include 12.16c μὴ γίνεσθε φρόνιμοι παρ' ἑαυτοῖς (Prov. 3.7: μὴ ἴσθι φρόνιμος παρὰ σεαυτῷ) and 12.17b προνοούμενοι καλὰ ἐνώπιον πάντων ἀνθρώπων (Prov. 3.4: προνοοῦ καλὰ ἐνώπιον κυρίου καὶ ἀνθρώπων). Less certain are εἰρηνεύοντες in 12.18 (Ps. 33[34].15: ζήτησον εἰρήνην) and μὴ ἑαυτοὺς ἐκδικοῦντες in 12.19a (Lev. 19.18: οὐκ ἐκδικᾶται σοῦ ἡ χείρ). Cf. also Rom. 12.9b and Amos 5.15. Hanson (*Studies*, pp. 126-35) sees links between *m. Ab.* 2.9-10 and Rom. 12.9b, 13a, 17b, 18, 20c; 13.8a, 9, and posits a common tradition underlying both writings. He thinks Paul's form of the tradition was derived from Jesus, who provided the positive emphasis reflected in 12.21.

3. Cf. also 13.8-10. Love and the doing of good are central; ἀγαθός brackets the segment (12.9, 21; cf. 12.2) and is closely associated with love (1 Thess. 5.15). In a recent analysis of the rhetorical structure of 12.9-21, D.A. Black ('Command') sees 12.9a as a summary of the theme.

4. Cf. 1 Corinthians 13, which begins with a probable allusion to a saying of Jesus (13.2). It is often observed that Paul describes love in terms which find their epitome in Christ (e.g. Davies, *Paul*, p. 147).

desires for his readers: ἀνυπόκριτος. Although attested only twice in pre-Christian literature (Wis. 5.18; 18.15), it became a paraenetic theme for Paul and other early believers.[1] Since the word is so rare, why does Paul give it such a place of importance as the first exhortation in a series? In ἀνυπόκριτος ἀγάπη we see a synthesis of two important thrusts of Jesus' teaching—the need for love and the danger of hypocrisy.[2]

ὑπόκρισις here cannot be attributed to Greek influence. In classical usage the word group lacked any negative ring.[3] On the other hand, later Jewish writers employed the word almost exclusively *in sensu malo*, but rarely with the nuance of presenting a righteous appearance to disguise the face of evil.[4] In the Synoptics Jesus stresses the incongruity of his opponents' outward appearance and their actual inward condition.[5] Although Matthew's frequent application of ὑποκριτής to the Pharisees may be redactional,[6] the presence of the word and its cognates in all three Synoptics indicates that the tradition of Jesus' criticism of his contemporaries' ὑπόκρισις has early roots.[7] The

1. Cf. 2 Cor. 6.6, where again Paul applies it to ἀγάπη in the description of his behaviour as an apostle. Note also 1 Tim. 1.5 and 2 Tim. 1.5 (in both cases modifying πίστις), Jas 3.17 (describing ἡ ἄνωθεν σοφία), and 1 Pet. 1.22 (with φιλαδελφία). For non-Christian use cf. Philo, *Quaest in Gen.* 3.29; Demetrius, *Eloc.* 194; and Marcus Aurelius 8.5 (ἀνυποκρίτως).

2. Cf. Ortkemper (*Leben*, p. 86). Best cites this verse together with 2 Cor. 6.6 and 1 Pet. 1.22 as evidence that the early church knew a variant of the logion 'love your neighbour' ('Tradition', p. 97). Wilckens denies that ἀνυπόκριτος ἀγάπη is elucidated by 12.9b-21, arguing that in 2 Cor. 6.6 Paul derived ἀνυπόκριτος from Wis. 5.18, since διὰ τῶν ὅπλων κ.τ.λ. in 2 Cor. 6.7 indicates that Paul saw unhypocritical love as a part of God's spiritual weaponry (*TDNT*, VIII, p. 570). The possible influence of Wisdom in this text does not, however explain Paul's transference of ἀνυπόκριτος from κρίσις to ἀγάπη.

3. Wilckens, *TDNT*, VIII, p. 563.

4. Wilckens, *TDNT*, VIII, pp. 564-65.

5. This is especially clear in Mt. 23.3-10, 27-28. Garland argues that the hypocrisy is not simply insincerity, but includes the implication of false interpretation of the law and wrong teaching (cf. Lk. 12.1 // Mt. 16.5-12); the religious leaders have failed in their responsibility as interpreters of the truth. They do not have to be consciously insincere to be ὑποκριταί (*Intention*, pp. 96-117).

6. So, e.g., van Tilborg, *Leaders*, p. 19. Minear thinks Matthew's primary purpose in the ὑποκριτής sayings was to warn church leaders not to become false prophets ('Prophecy').

7. Cf. Wilckens, *TDNT*, VIII, p. 567 nn. 41 and 45.

presence of a theatre at the provincial capital of Sepphoris, only four miles from Nazareth, increases the likelihood that Jesus knew and used the term.[1] ὑπόκρισις and its cognates occur twenty-four times in the NT, twenty-one instances of which are in the Gospels.[2] In several cases the words appear in the same Gospel context as sayings of Jesus which are claimed to be echoed in Paul (e.g. Mk 12.15 // Mt. 22.18 and the 'Render unto Caesar' logion [see Chapter 7]; Lk. 12.56 and the importance of discerning the significance of the καιρός [see Chapter 9]).[3] Two cases are particularly relevant. Mark uses ὑποκριτής for the Pharisees who insist on outward ritual (washing of hands) but reject the commandments of God (7.6). In the same context Mark records the saying of Jesus about there being nothing outside a man that defiles him but what comes from within, a saying Mark interprets as teaching that all foods are clean (καθαρός). If Paul reflects knowledge of this logion in Rom. 14.14, 20 (see Chapter 12), he may have known the related ὑποκριταί saying as well. Furthermore, it would be natural for Paul, a former Pharisee, to be sensitive to any sayings of Jesus about Pharisees.[4]

A second tradition which has a more immediate parallel in Romans is preserved in Mt. 7.5 // Lk. 6.42, where the ὑποκριτής condemns his neighbour's shortcomings but fails to discern his own. A similar thought appears in Rom. 2.1 and the admonitions against κρίνειν in ch. 14 (see Chapter 10). If chs. 14 and 15 reflect Paul's concern over a real situation in Rome, and if we can assume that the church there knew some of Jesus' teachings about the danger of ὑπόκρισις, Paul's initial call to ἀνυπόκριτος love would be even more apt, reminding them at the outset that theirs must be a genuine love with no trace of

1. Cf. Batey, 'Theatre'; Stock, 'Hypocrites', pp. 5-7.
2. The verb is used once (Lk. 20.20), of spies pretending to be righteous. ὑπόκρισις applies to the Pharisees in the Gospels (Mt. 23.28; Mk 12.15; Lk. 12.1; cf. also Gal. 2.13; 1 Tim. 4.2; 1 Pet. 2.1). ὑποκριτής is the more common term (Mk 7.6; Lk. 6.42; 12.56; 13.15; and thirteen times in Matthew). Textual variants include Mt. 16.3; 23.14; Lk. 11.44; and Jas 5.12.
3. Cf. also Mt. 23 and the severe criticism of the Jews in 1 Thess. 2.15-16; for the similarity in thought see Schippers, 'Tradition'; Orchard, 'Thessalonians', pp. 20-23. Dominical influence explains the traditional elements in 1 Thess. 2.15-16 better than interpolation theories.
4. Three passages which may reflect the influence of Jesus' criticisms of the Pharisees are 1 Thess. 2.14-16; Rom. 2.17-24; and Gal. 6.1-5.

deceit or self-deception from a failure to examine oneself (cf. 12.3).
Such a love is not sentimental, but discerning, abhorring what is evil
and cleaving to the good (12.9b; cf. Phil. 1.9-10 and 1 Cor. 13.6).[1]

It is impossible to prove any dependence on the teaching or example
of Jesus in the exhortations of Rom. 12.10-13 (if for no other reason
than because of the phrases' brevity), although some parallels deserve
to be noted. In 12.10 Paul emphasizes the familial character of the
Christian community for the benefit of his Jewish and Gentile readers,
telling them to be devoted (ἱλόστοργοι) to one another with
φιλαδελφία. Neither word occurs in the Synoptics, and the use of
'brother' with reference to followers of the same religion was not
unique to Christianity (cf., e.g., Plutarch, *Moralia*, 478-92), but this
common Christian emphasis (1 Thess. 4.9; Heb. 13.1; 1 Pet. 1.22;
etc.) is consistent with JT. The Synoptics portray Jesus as teaching that
those who do the will/word of God are members of his family (Mk.
3.35 // Mt. 12.50 // Lk. 8.21). He taught his disciples to call God
'Father' and to consider themselves as brothers (Mt. 7.3 par.; 18.15;
18.21).[2] Paul's expression here is apparently not dominical, but the
sentiment is identical.

Behind Paul's exhortations to his readers to 'prefer one another in
honour'[3] may lie an emphasis of Jesus, although there is no verbal
link. The thought is similar to ἡγούμενοι ὑπερέχοντες ἑαυτῶν in
Phil. 2.3, the context of which features Jesus' example (see Chapter
14). Matthew and Luke record the saying, 'whoever exalts himself

---

1. Paul's prayer for growth in intelligent ἀγάπη εἰς τὸ δοκιμάζειν τὰ δια-
φέροντα in Phil. 1.9-10 shows that Rom. 12.9a and 9b are not necessarily unrelated
in theme. He may well have chosen τῷ ἀγαθῷ here in view of τὸ θέλημα τὸ
ἀγαθόν he wants his readers to prove (cf. Rom. 2.18 which combines the language
of the two passages). Especially interesting for its verbal links with our passage is a
parallel in *Did*. 4.12: μισήσεις πᾶσαν ὑπόκρισιν καὶ πᾶν ὃ μὴ ἀρεστὸν τῷ
κυρίῳ. It is followed by a command not to forsake ἐντολὰς κυρίου (other teachings of Jesus?) but to keep the traditions received.

2. Note that Paul uses the Aramaic 'Abba' in Rom. 8.15 (cf. also Gal. 4.6), in a
context not as far-removed from Gethsemane (Mk 14.36) as it might seem. In both
passages the cry comes in a context of temptation to fear, a situation of suffer-
ing/costly obedience. Are the sighs and groanings of the Spirit in Rom. 8.26-27
related to Jesus' experience of prayer in the garden?

3. The translation is Cranfield's (*Romans*, II, p. 629). τῇ τιμῇ ἀλλήλους
προηγούμενοι could be rendered in other ways (see Dunn, *Romans*, II, p. 741),
but Phil. 2.3 provides the closest parallel.

will be humbled, and whoever humbles himself will be exalted' (Mt. 23.12 // Lk. 14.11); closely connected with it in Matthew is Jesus' condemnation of those who love the place of honour (πρωτοκλισίας) at feasts and the best seats (πρωτοκαθεδρίας) in the synagogues (cf. Mk 12.39), whereas Luke puts the logion at the conclusion of a parable (told in the home of a Pharisee) about choosing the last seat at a feast instead of the πρωτοκλισία (14.7-10). Could Paul be thinking of situations in which the Romans' table-fellowship was threatened by pride and criticism?[1] Paul may be admonishing those who despised the weak in faith (cf. 14.1, 3, 10), but this cannot be demonstrated. Then again, the exhortation could reflect Jesus' teaching that the greatest must be servant of all (Mk 10.43-45 // Mt. 20.26-28 // Lk. 22.26-27; Mt. 23.11), as he himself came to serve. Our evidence here *alone*, however, cannot establish a dominical link, much less point to a specific saying.

Other remote parallels may be observed in passing. Paul's use of ὀκνηρός (12.11a) is not dissimilar to Matthew's description of the πονηρός and ὀκνηρὸς δοῦλος who failed to make use of that which was given to him, in the parable of the talents (Mt. 25.26).[2] The exhortation to rejoice in hope (12.12a), closely connected with the following call to persevere in affliction, could reflect the saying about rejoicing when reviled (Mt. 5.12 par.; cf. 1 Pet. 4.13), although the background in Romans is 5.2-5; 8.16-25. 'Persevering in affliction' (12.12b) is close to the logion ὁ δὲ ὑπομείνας εἰς τέλος οὗτος σωθήσεται (Mt. 10.22; 24.13 // Mk 13.13; cf. Lk. 21.19). Matthew's repetition of the saying and the united witness of the Synoptics testify to the importance of this tradition in early Christianity. The exhortation προσκαρτερεῖν τῇ προσευχῇ, which is repeated in Col. 4.2 (cf. Acts 1.14) we may quickly attribute to Jewish roots, but we should not forget that prayer was a vital part of Jesus' life (Mk 1.35; 6.46; 14.35; etc.) and that he not only taught his disciples to pray but commanded them to do so (e.g. Mk 14.38 pars., etc.). Wenham sees echoes of the eschatological discourse in Rom. 12.12 (Mt. 24.9, 13; Lk. 21.36; 18.1).[3] Finally, the exhortations to participate in the needs

---

1. Cf. Minear, *Obedience*, pp. 88, 90 n. 4.
2. ὀκνηρός appears elsewhere in the NT only in Phil. 3.1, but is fairly common in wisdom literature (e.g. Prov. 6.6, 9; 20.4).
3. D. Wenham, *Rediscovery*, p. 283 and n. 1.

of the saints and to pursue φιλοξενίαν could go back to the tradition giving rise to Mt. 25.35ff.: 'I was hungry and you gave me food, I was thirsty and you gave me drink, I was a ξένος and you welcomed me . . . ' Commenting on 12.13 Dunn observes, 'Hospitality was a key feature of Jesus' ministry, both in his dependence on it (Mk 1.29-31; 14.3; Lk. 10.38-42) and in his practice and commendation of it as a model of divine generosity (Mk 2.15-17; Mt. 11.19 // Lk. 7.34; Lk. 14.1-24)'.[1]

Virtually all of the above parallels suffer from a common weakness. It can be demonstrated that similar ethical admonitions appear in earlier or contemporary non-Christian writings. But when we come to 12.14 we encounter a teaching that has few parallels outside the message of Jesus, and those which do exist derive from different motivations.

2. Romans 12.14

By far the most commonly cited 'allusion' to dominical teaching (apart from the explicit texts in 1 Cor. 7, 9, 11 and 1 Thess. 4) is Rom. 12.14; one can even speak of a 'unanimity' among the commentators.[2] The text is paralleled in Matthew and Luke:

Rom. 12.14a εὐλογεῖτε τοὺς διώκοντας [ὑμᾶς],
        b εὐλογεῖτε καὶ μὴ καταρᾶσθε

Mt. 5.44a ἀγαπᾶτε τοὺς ἐχθροὺς ὑμῶν
        b καὶ προσεύχεσθε ὑπὲρ τῶν διωκόντων ὑμᾶς

Lk. 6.27a ἀγαπᾶτε τοὺς ἐχθροὺς ὑμῶν,
        b καλῶς ποιεῖτε τοῖς μισοῦσιν ὑμᾶς,
      28a **εὐλογεῖτε τοὺς καταρωμένους ὑμᾶς,**
        b προσεύχεσθε περὶ τῶν ἐπηρεαζόντων ὑμᾶς

---

1. Dunn, *Romans*, II, p. 744. On the other hand, hospitality had deep roots in Judaism; cf., e.g., Isa. 58.7; Job 31.32; Str–B, IV, pp. 565-69.

2. Neirynck, 'Sayings', p. 270; cf. Käsemann: 'Reminiszenz' (*Römer*, p. 334, cf. *idem, Romans*, p. 347); Michel: 'eine genaue Wiedergabe oder eine targumartige Paraphrase des Jesuswortes' (*Römer*, p. 386); Best, *Romans*, p. 145; Barrett, *Romans*, p. 241.

Textual Affinities

Paul's exhortation shares Luke's verb (εὐλογεῖν) and Matthew's object (οἱ διώκοντες). It is closer to Luke, since 12.14b repeats εὐλογεῖτε[1] with καταρᾶσθε which corresponds to τοὺς καταρωμέ-νους, although Luke has the enemies cursing whereas Paul prohibits Christians from cursing. The parallel ὑμᾶς in 12.14 is probably original but of minimal importance since it would be expected in context.[2] Paul's use of εὐλογεῖν in 1 Cor. 4.12-13 is significant: λοιδορούμενοι εὐλογοῦμεν, διωκόμενοι ἀνεχόμεθα, δυσφημού-μενοι παρακαλοῦμεν.[3] Although not exact synonyms, λοιδορεῖν and καταρᾶν have similar meanings, and as Paul contrasts Corinthian self-elevation with apostolic self-abasement for the sake of Christ, he describes his behaviour in terms that demonstrate his conformity with the pattern of Christ (cf. 2 Cor. 4.8-11).[4] Paul wants his readers to imitate himself (1 Cor. 4.16), but his ways are 'in Christ' (4.17) and ultimately he imitates Christ (11.1). 1 Pet. 3.9 likewise calls for responding to λοιδορία with εὐλογεῖν, and earlier in the same Epistle the author has appealed to Christ's example of not reviling in return for λοιδορία (2.23).[5]

It is not unusual to find the antonyms εὐλογεῖν and καταρᾶν in close conjunction (cf. Jas 3.9-10); in the OT, the cursings of humans are often set in contrast with the blessing of God and vice versa (e.g. Ps. 108[109].28). What does not occur however is the particular relation of the words found here. A search of the TLG database reveals that nowhere in pre-Christian Greek literature do we find humans (or God) responding to καταρᾶν or λοιδορεῖν with

---

1. Its omission in $\mathfrak{P}^{46}$ ψ[c] and bo[ms] is insufficient ground for exclusion from the text.

2. It is omitted by $\mathfrak{P}^{46}$ B vg[st] and a few other mss.; an error of homoioteleuton (διώκοντας ὑμᾶς) explains its absence just as easily as its insertion by a scribe to conform the text to the Synoptic parallel.

3. He uses the verb again in 1 Cor. 10.16; 14.16; Gal. 3.9; cf. Eph. 1.3.

4. Fee, *1 Corinthians*, p. 186. Barrett observes that Paul's language 'recalls clearly the teaching of Jesus, especially in the Sermon on the Mount (Matt. v. 5, 10 ff., 44; Luke vi. 21 ff., 35), of which there are fairly clear echoes. . . ' (*1 Corinthians*, p. 112).

5. The added ὅτι εἰς τοῦτο ἐκλήθητε ἵνα εὐλογίαν κληρονομήσητε in 1 Pet. 3.9 (cf. the macarism in Mt. 5.11-12) increases the likelihood of a dominical link.

εὐλογεῖν. The evidence from vocabulary therefore strongly supports an echo of Jesus here.

Conceptually, Paul's words parallel Luke's logion. The Christian responds to hostility with blessing. The similarity with Matthew's version is less clear, since prayer for the persecutor need not go as far as blessing him. Nevertheless, in view of the accompanying calls to love the enemy and to greet (ἀσπάζειν) him (5.46-47), we should not make much of the difference.[1] Formally the exhortation is closer to Luke's logion, but Matthew's προσεύχεσθε requires a prepositional phrase to convey a parallel idea. Grammatically the exhortations all begin with a second person plural imperative followed immediately by the object. The exact formal agreement in Luke and Paul (εὐλογεῖτε) proves nothing, since in both passages this is the form we should expect.

Availability of the Gospel Tradition

The call to love enemies is deeply imbedded in the tradition; variety begins in the exposition of that call. Lk. 6.27a is identical to Mt. 5.44a, and Lk. 6.28b corresponds to Mt. 5.44b, so we can be confident enough that these logia are early.[2] διώκοντας in Mt. 5.44b could be redactional, but the assertion that if Matthew has abridged Luke, 'Paul could not have taken διώκοντας from the Synoptic saying', is a *non-sequitur*.[3] Matthew's abridgement could well be one current in his community (Antioch?) and known to Paul.[4] More important is whether Luke 6.27b and 6.28a are pre-Lukan traditions or free compositions by the evangelist.[5] Bultmann found it hard to speak with

1. D. Wenham thinks ἀσπάσησθε 'picks up' the call to bless, noting 2 Kgs 4.29 where εὐλογεῖν is used as a salutation ('Use', pp. 16, 33 n. 20).

2. There is little dispute that the first logion goes back to Jesus (although cf. Sauer, 'Erwägungen', pp. 26-27); some (e.g. Neirynck, 'Sayings', p. 299) see Mt. 5.44b // Lk. 6.28b as an early addition.

3. Neirynck, 'Sayings', p. 296. Matthew has διώκειν in six dominical sayings and Luke in three, and Luke's ἐπηρεάζειν is very rare in the NT (elsewhere only in 1 Pet. 3.16), but this is insufficient evidence for a judgment; cf. Guelich, who thinks the variation goes back to differences in Q (*Sermon*, p. 229).

4. Cf. D. Wenham, who thinks Paul here is echoing pre-Synoptic traditions found in both Luke and Matthew ('Use', p. 17).

5. Guelich (*Sermon*, p. 228), Schürmann (*Lukasevangelium*, p. 346), D. Wenham ('Use', pp. 15-17), and Piper (with qualifications; *Enemies*, pp. 56-58)

certainty, although he viewed them as traditions since Luke tends to abridge otherwise parallel elements.[1] Nowhere is the decisive importance of presuppositions and method more clear: Seitz for example thinks the parallelism of Luke's verses demonstrates their authenticity,[2] whereas Neirynck argues just the opposite.[3] Neirynck explains 6.28a as derived from Christian paraenesis (1 Cor. 4.12; Rom. 12.14), but this begs the question at issue. Although εὐλογεῖν is common in Luke (14×; Matthew: 5×), καταρᾶν is a *hapax*, evidence (however weak) that it is not Lukan creation but tradition.[4]

Evidence from other parallels is indecisive.[5] *Did.* 1.3 offers a clear parallel to 6.28a, but Neirynck dismisses it as dependent on both Luke and Matthew:[6]

> εὐλογεῖτε τοὺς καταρωμένους ὑμῖν
> καὶ προσεύχεσθε ὑπὲρ τῶν ἐχθρῶν ὑμῶν,
> νηστεύετε δὲ ὑπὲρ τῶν διωκόντων ὑμᾶς·
> ποία γὰρ χάρις, ἐὰν ἀγαπᾶτε τοὺς ἀγαπῶντας ὑμᾶς (*Did.* 1.3)

If Neirynck is wrong, *Didache* provides strong evidence for a pre-Lukan tradition; if he is right, then in effect he attributes to the author of *Didache* the same freedom (to modify and adapt the wording of traditional language)[7] that he implicitly denies Paul.

Clearly Jesus called his followers to love their enemies. But just as

---

argue for pre-Lukan traditions; Fitzmyer (*Luke*, I, pp. 627-28, 638) and Neirynck ('Sayings', pp. 296-97) favour redactional creations.

1. Bultmann, *History*, pp. 96, 79.
2. Seitz, 'Enemies', p. 52; cf. Manson: 'The Lukan version. . . is in strict poetic form, showing parallelism and—on retranslation into Aramaic—rhythm and rhyme' (*Sayings*, p. 50).
3. Neirynck, 'Sayings', p. 297. Neirynck thinks 6.27b is a Lukan elaboration to parallel 6.27a; Fitzmyer adds that it was evoked by 6.22a (*Luke*, I, p. 638).
4. So Sauer, 'Erwägungen', p. 8.
5. Cf. Pol. *Phil.* 12.3: 'Orate etiam pro regibus et potestatibus et principibus atque pro persequentibus et odientibus vos et pro inimicis crusis. . . '; Just. *Apol.* I.15.: Εὔχεσθε ὑπὲρ τῶν ἐχθρῶν ὑμῶν καὶ ἀγαπᾶτε τοὺς μισοῦντας ὑμᾶς καὶ εὐλογεῖτε τοὺς καταρωμένους ὑμῖν καὶ εὔχεσθε ὑπὲρ τῶν ἐπηρεαζόντων ὑμᾶς; P. Oxy. 1224 (4th cent. AD): κ]αι; π[ρ]οσεύχεσθε ὑπὲρ [τῶν ἐχθ]ρῶν ὑμῶν; cf. also *SQE* 84.
6. 'Sayings', pp. 297-99.
7. προσεύχεσθε ὑπὲρ τῶν **ἐχθρῶν** ὑμῶν agrees with neither Matthew nor Luke.

the later Church would need an exposition of how that love worked
itself out, so would the first disciples, and it is hard to imagine the
simple command being all that Jesus ever taught on the subject. Which
is more likely, that he said something so unusual only once, with no
explanation, or that its gist was a regular element in his preaching? He
probably repeated this difficult to accept teaching and its applications
on different occasions. We should not be surprised to find diverse
formulations in Matthew and Luke, and unfortunately we cannot speak
with any certainty as to what has been created by the evangelists.

Dissimilarity

The criterion of dissimilarity provides further evidence that Paul's
exhortation is linked to Jesus'. Piper has thoroughly examined the
roots and use of Jesus' love command, and his study includes not only
Rom. 12.14 but also 12.17-21. His survey of extra-NT parallels
cannot be repeated here, but will be summarized. Although Seneca
calls for giving aid to one's enemies (based on imitation of the gods;
De Otio 1.4; *De Beneficiis* VII.30.2, 5; IV.26) and not returning evil
for evil (*De Ira* II.32.1-6; *De Constantia* 14.3), the motivation for
that behaviour is not selfless love, but the desire to preserve mastery
over one's passions and freedom from external threats and rewards,
so as to remain unperturbed by the actions of others.[1] Epictetus's ethic
is similar: instead of being concerned primarily for the good of the
other person, one seeks to cultivate the character and moral purpose
(προαίρεσις) of the Stoic.[2] The idea of enemy love can be traced
back to the OT (e.g. Exod. 23.4-5; 1 Kgs 3.11; Prov. 17.13; 24.17-18,
29; Lev. 19.17-18, 34; Deut. 10.18-19; and the Book of Jonah),[3] and
Paul quotes Deut. 32.35 in Rom. 12.19, and Prov. 25.21 in Rom.
12.20. What appears in the Gospels and Paul, however, is a new
eschatological context for the teachings and a selective use of the OT
in order to confirm the priority of love while avoiding the response of

1. Piper, *Enemies*, pp. 22, 24-25. Cf. *De Ira* III.5.8: 'The really great mind, the
mind that has taken the true measure of itself, fails to revenge injury only because it
fails to perceive it'. Seneca also allows for ignoring, humiliating, punishing and de-
ceiving the enemy (cf. Piper, *Enemies*, pp. 21-25).

2. Cf. *Encheiridion* 42; *Discourses* I.25.29; III.4.8-9, 20.9, 22.54; Piper,
Enemies, pp. 25-27.

3. For discussion, see Piper, *Enemies*, pp. 27-35; for further literature cf.
Schottroff, 'Non-Violence', p. 32 n. 34.

hatred, which could be derived from other OT texts.[1]

In the writings of Hellenistic Judaism we find a number of parallels to the ideas of being kind to one's enemy, but these are usually restricted in some way and/or exhibit Stoic or Christian influence.[2] The clearest parallels are in the *Testaments of the Twelve Patriarchs*, especially *T. Jos.* 18.2 ('And if anyone wishes to do you harm, you should pray for him, along with doing good, and you will be rescued by the Lord from every evil') and *T. Gad* 6.7 ('But even if he [the enemy] is devoid of shame and persists in his wickedness, forgive him from the heart and leave vengeance to God').[3] Unfortunately, no consensus exists as to the degree of interpolation and Christian redaction in these documents, and Stoic influence is not unlikely.[4] The Qumran community's practice of blessing the 'sons of light' and cursing outsiders (e.g. 1QS 2.4-10; cf. 1.9) sharply contrasts with the thought of Paul and the Gospels.[5] For Josephus, kindness to an enemy (cf. *Ap.* 2.211-12) 'means primarily offering the enemy a chance to become a proselyte'.[6] The rabbinic literature is diverse, with considerable discussion about the limits of neighbour love. The instruction to hate sectarians and others in *ARN* 16 reveals how a different ethic from that of Jesus could be developed from the 'dark' side of the OT, although *m. Ab.* 1.12 and 2.11 preserve calls to love mankind and not to hate. In short, Piper finds 'nothing so explicit and unequivocal. . . nor is it thinkable that the early church should invent

---

1. Piper, *Enemies*, pp. 34-35. Schottroff notes the Jewish and Greek parallels but writes, 'The love of the enemy is a distinctively Christian attitude, something poles apart from the non-Christian attitude of "requiting love with love" and "doing good in return"' ('Non-Violence', p. 25). On the note of retribution in Rom. 12.19-20, see below.

2. Tob. 4.14-17 preserves a negative form of the Golden Rule, but restricts generosity only to the righteous; cf. also Sir. 12.1-7; *Jub.* 36.4, 9. Stoic influence appears in *Ep. Arist.* 207, 225, 227, 232; *4 Macc* 2.14 (cf. 2.9); Philo *Virt.* 116-18 (cf. Piper, *Enemies*, pp. 35-36, 39). *2 En.* 50.3-4; 61.2; 44.4 perhaps reflect Christian influence.

3. Cf. also *T. Benj.* 4.2-3; *T. Iss.* 7.6; *T. Zeb.* 7.2-4.

4. For discussion, cf. Piper, *Enemies*, pp. 43-45.

5. Abram prays for his persecutor in 1QapGen 20.28 only after calling down God's judgment upon Pharaoh, and then only at Pharaoh's request.

6. Piper, *Enemies*, p. 47.

the saying and thus impose upon themselves such a troublesome requirement'.[1]

Dominical Indicators

After a number of participles interspersed with adjectives in verbless clauses (12.9-13), Paul shifts to an imperative with εὐλογεῖτε. Some think it no coincidence that such a clear grammatical break introduces this apparent echo of Jesus. Adopting Daube's theory of an underlying Semitic paraenetic *Vorlage*, Kanjuperambil thinks Paul's switch to a finite verb reflects concern not to portray a saying of Jesus as secondary or derivative.[2] Nevertheless, Daube's explanation of the 'imperatival participles' is open to question, and a simpler solution is at hand. Paul takes up διώκειν as a catchword, not because it was present in the tradition.[3] The kindness to strangers (ξένοι) implicit in φιλοξενία (12.13) leads naturally into the thought of relations towards outsiders, and the availability of διώκειν to connote pursuit with hostile purpose affords a smooth transition into the new subject. Together with the significance of the idea and the difficulty in carrying out the command, the change in subject warrants Paul's breaking the chain of participles in order to emphasize the admonition with a finite verb. On the other hand, in verbalizing the command Paul seems to draw εὐλογεῖν from the tradition.[4] He does not identify the source of inspiration because there is no need to; he is not concerned here with whether Jesus said it. He repeats the verb εὐλογεῖν in 12.14b for rhetorical effect, because the word has instantly recalled a more familiar logion which we know from Lk. 6.28. It is thus not the shift

---

1. Piper, *Enemies*, p. 56; cf. pp. 20-49. The idea of praying for one's enemies finds few parallels, e.g., *T. Benj.* 3.6. Ps. 108[109].4-5 is a false parallel (*contra* Piper, *Enemies*, p. 190 n. 130; cf. the textual problem and the spirit of the rest of the psalm).

2. 'Participles', p. 287; cf. Talbert, 'Tradition', pp. 87-88. Hunter cites the grammatical change as evidence that Paul has borrowed words without troubling to adapt them to their grammatical context (*Predecessors*, p. 47; followed by Allison, 'Pattern', p. 28 n. 60).

3. Cf. ὀφείλετε (13.7) after the catchword ὀφειλάς in 13.6; so also Neirynck, 'Sayings', p. 299.

4. Paul may have known (from Antiochene tradition?) the exhortation to pray for those who persecute, but he had already used προσευχή in 12.12; εὐλογεῖν provided a more vivid contrast to the enemy's behaviour.

from participles to finite verb that gives an important clue, but the repetition of εὐλογεῖτε.[1]

Possible Objections

A recent study of dominical commands to love the enemy and not to retaliate claims that the direction of dependence in Rom. 12.14 is from Paul to the Gospels, not from Jesus to Paul.[2] After reconstructing a Q text from Lk. 6.27-36 and Mt. 5.38-48, Sauer finds the oldest elements to include a four-membered series of imperatives verbally identical to Lk. 6.27b-28 (differing only in reading ὑπέρ instead of περί).[3] Comparing Lk. 6.27b-29 with Rom. 12.14-21 he sees a number of parallels in thought which suggest a relationship.[4] For Sauer, Lk. 6.28a is secondary to Paul's text, being more polished than Rom. 12.14.[5] Paul could not have known the four-membered series of Lk. 6.27-28, since he does not go on to refer to it, but grounds his exhortation in the OT.[6] Therefore, Paul's formulation of the language is the *traditionsgeschichtlichen Ausgangspunkt* for the Synoptic logia, and since Rom. 12.14 presupposes persecution of Christians, the logia cannot be authentic words of Jesus. The Synoptic traditions about enemy love and non-retaliation arose from sources reflected in the rest of ch. 12: OT wisdom literature, Hellenistic popular philosophy and Hellenistic Judaism.[7]

Though argued in great detail, Sauer's work exemplifies the dangers of false assumptions, logical fallacies, restricted focus, and (for lack of a better term) precisionism[8] in the comparison of texts. His case

---

1. Evidence for the inclusion of the second εὐλογεῖτε is overwhelming, despite its omission in a few mss. (notably $\mathfrak{P}^{46}$).

2. Sauer, 'Erwägungen'.

3. 'Erwägungen', pp. 11-16.

4. 'Erwägungen', pp. 23-25, esp. p. 24.

5. He cites Luke's addition of ὑμᾶς and thinks καταρᾶσθαι reflects the cursing of Christians by synagogue congregations ('Erwägungen', p. 26).

6. 'Erwägungen', p. 26.

7. 'Erwägungen', p. 27.

8. By 'precisionism' I mean the practice of making unwarranted deductions based on the expectation that if one author uses another tradition he must reproduce that text in *precise* detail; that is to say, the failure to allow for fluidity in word choice to convey shared material.

essentially raises two major objections against dominical influence in
12.14.[1]

a. *The silence of Paul.* Sauer assumes that had Paul known the saying
to be dominical he would have said so, and that his silence therefore
reflects ignorance. We have already seen the argument from silence to
be an extremely weak basis for evaluating knowledge of tradition.
Given the paraenetic nature of the passage and the distinctiveness of
this particular teaching Paul had no need to identify his source of
inspiration. What is more, the wording and thought in Rom. 12.14 is
actually closer to the Synoptic tradition than where Paul explicitly
identifies teachings of Jesus as such (1 Cor. 7.10; 9.14).[2]

b. *Use of the OT.* Why does Paul proceed to quote the OT in 12.19-
20,[3] if at the heart of his ethic lies the teaching of Jesus? Paul was a
man soaked in the Scriptures. OT texts were the first Hebrew he had
learned as a child, and as a Pharisee he knew chunks of it by heart;
quotations would flow naturally from him, especially when a text was
already linked in Jewish tradition with the subject he was discussing.[4]
There was no reason for the apostle to stop quoting immediately relevant ethical texts after his conversion. Although Paul does not cite the
OT at all in 1 and 2 Thessalonians, Philippians, and Colossians, this
probably says less about his interest (or lack of it) in the OT than it
does about his audience and the issues he addresses.[5] A significant
number of his readers at Rome were Jewish Christians and would
appreciate Scriptural support; use of the OT here certainly would not

---

1. Even if allowed to stand, the claim that Paul's is a more primitive form of the
tradition proves nothing; for an alternate explanation cf. D. Wenham, 'Use', p. 17.
2. Cf. Piper, *Enemies*, pp. 194-95 n. 174.
3. For discussion of the quotation from Prov. 25.21-22 in 12.20 cf., e.g., Piper
(*Enemies*, pp. 114-19), Klassen ('Coals'), Stendahl ('Hate'). The context in
Romans, Paul's exclusion of the final clause from the original proverb, and its
targumic rendering favour understanding the 'coals of fire' as a reference to burning
pangs of shame leading to contrition or a pained conscience (cf. Cranfield, *Romans*,
II, pp. 648-50).
4. Cf. the comments of Selwyn on the similar phenomenon in 1 Peter (*1 Peter*,
p. 367).
5. For discussion, cf. Ellis, *Use*, pp. 30-33. On the whole, OT quotations are
rarer in paraenetic sections of Paul's letters than in other parts.

hurt any Gentile brethren who undervalued the law. Moreover, Piper observes that love for one's enemy is the most difficult demand placed on the Christian community. It seems unjust, and many passages from the OT could be cited to contradict such a position. For Paul, following Jesus means establishing the law (Rom. 3.31) which was written διὰ τῆς παρακλήσεως (Rom. 15.4; cf. 4.23; 1 Cor. 9.10). So he cites the OT to deflect potential objections and to support the interpretative key given by Jesus' teaching, which, as we shall see, in turn controls the development of the paraenesis and determines what OT material is applicable.[1]

Conclusion
Linguistic and conceptual agreement, confirmed by the principle of dissimilarity, make it highly likely that the admonitions in 12.14 represent Paul's rephrasing of a teaching ultimately derived from Jesus, and Paul almost certainly knew it as such. For his purposes in Romans Paul did not need to emphasize its dominical origin; he was conveying what he could assume to be fundamental Christian teaching already familiar to his hearers. We should thus consider Rom. 12.14 to be a virtually certain echo, but only possibly an allusion. The influence of dominical teaching here is clear, and this teaching will go on to characterize the following exhortations in 12.15-21.

3. *Romans 12.15-21*

At first glance, Rom. 12.15-16 appear unrelated to the theme of enemy love. The verses seem to refer only to attitudes towards fellow Christians, and in a parallel passage, the author of 1 Peter links exhortation to be συμπαθής, εὔσπλαγχνος, and ταπεινόφρων with φιλαδελφία *before* addressing the issue of reponse to persecution (3.8). Piper conjectures that Rom. 12.14 and vv. 17-21 were originally joined in the paraenetic tradition, but that v. 14 was drawn away from the rest because of the common *Stichwort* διώκειν shared with

---

1. Piper, *Enemies*, pp. 113-14. Cf. Ellis: 'The OT was not one of those things which Paul counted loss for the sake of Christ; indeed, it could be understood only in the light of Christ' (*Use*, p. 32). Piper thinks the early church did not employ Jesus' sayings directly because his commands were too specific and thus unsuitable for general exhortation (*Enemies*, p. 59).

v. 13.[1] On the other hand, we would preserve the train of thought by understanding χαίρειν μετὰ χαιρόντων, κλαίειν μετὰ κλαιόντων to carry the radical spirit of 12.14 a step further. Paul's readers are not to curse their persecutors but to bless them—an action coming out of a heart of compassion that identifies with fellow men (be they friends or foes) in their joys and sorrows.[2] One who genuinely blesses his detractors cannot turn and rejoice over their distress. Although the general idea of sympathy towards one's fellows is not unusual,[3] Paul elsewhere shows some awareness of the early tradition that Jesus fully identified with humanity without compromising his holiness (Rom. 1.3-4; Phil 2.7-9).[4] Did this tradition have a corresponding influence on Paul's own life and theology (cf., e.g., 2 Cor. 2.2-4)? Possibly, but we cannot establish any definite connection in 12.15.[5]

A more likely link with JT appears in 12.16b. With μὴ τὰ ὑψηλὰ φρονοῦντες ἀλλὰ τοῖς ταπεινοῖς συναπαγόμενοι, Paul exhorts his readers to behaviour that follows the example of their Lord, who did not draw back in self-righteous pride but associated with the lowly and oppressed.[6] ταπεινοῖς could be neuter, corresponding to τὰ ὑψηλά in the preceding phrase, and συναπαγόμενοι might be taken in a different sense to mean 'to accommodate yourself (to humble ways)'.[7] Nevertheless, ταπεινός consistently applies to humble persons in the NT (Mt. 11.29; Lk. 1.52; 2 Cor. 7.6; Jas 1.9; 4.6; 1 Pet. 5.5), and τὰ ὑψηλά with φρονεῖν became virtually part of the verb (cf. ὑψηλοφρονεῖν in 1 Tim. 6.17), so no corresponding neuter

---

1. *Enemies*, p. 17.

2. Yet without compromising holiness and sharing in the presuppositions of this age (Cranfield, *Romans*, II, p. 642).

3. Cf. Sir. 7.34: 'Do not fail those who weep, but mourn with those who mourn', but that corresponds to only half of the saying in Paul. Michel (*Römer*, p. 387 n. 27) cites other Jewish and Greek parallels; cf. also Str–B, III, p. 298.

4. Cf. the Gospel accounts of Jesus' baptism, his touching the unclean and dining with sinners, etc.

5. Less than convincing is J.T. Sanders's claim that 12.15 is reminiscent of Lk. 6.21b and 25b (*Ethics*, p. 58). Coincidentally, in John's Gospel Jesus presumably joined in the rejoicing at the wedding in Cana, the setting of his first miracle; beholding those who wept (κλαίειν) at Bethany, the scene of his last sign, he wept (δακρύειν); cf. also H.C.G. Moule, *Epistle of Paul*, p. 212.

6. So Käsemann, who sees Jesus as prototype intended here (*Romans*, p. 348). See Chapter 14.

7. BAGD, p. 784.

parallel would necessarily be required; ' "associate with the lowly" thus provides a fitting contrast for "do not be haughty" '.[1] That Jesus consorted with the lowly and despised belongs to the bedrock of Synoptic tradition.[2] Paul's exhortation finds a practical application later in his discussion of the weaker brother who is to be received and not despised (Rom. 14), an application extended to the acceptance of all brethren in 15.7 καθὼς καὶ ὁ Χριστὸς προσελάβετο ὑμᾶς.[3]

Not a few claim that Paul's command not to return evil for evil in 12.17 originated from dominical teachings.[4] Although there are similarities, a definite connection is by no means clear. In *Joseph and Asenath*, the phrase μὴ ἀποδιδόντες κακὸν ἀντὶ κακοῦ occurs several times in various forms (23.9; 28.4, 14; 29.3).[5] 'In each instance it is brought forth in stereotype fashion as if it is a well-known proverb: A God-fearing man does not repay evil for evil';[6] Christian influence here is improbable.[7] This of course does not prove that Paul is not reproducing or rephrasing a logion he knows to be dominical, but it does suggest that the saying itself behind Rom. 12.17a (and its parallels, 1 Thess. 5.15a and 1 Pet. 3.9) was adapted at some point (by Jesus? cf. Pol. *Phil.* 2.2) from earlier Jewish paraenetic tradition possibly influenced by Prov. 17.13 (ὃς ἀποδίδωσιν κακὰ ἀντὶ ἀγαθῶν, οὐ κινηθήσεται κακὰ ἐκ τοῦ οἴκου αὐτοῦ).[8] If not dominical in origin, this command effectively summarizes some of Jesus' teachings and characterizes his behaviour, but Paul does not need to make that point here.

1. Cranfield, *Romans*, II, p. 644.
2. For example, E.P. Sanders, *Jesus*, p. 179. Cf. also the texts calling for humbling oneself (ταπεινοῦν Mt. 18.4; 23.12; Lk. 14.11; 18.14).
3. This would not necessarily argue against understanding τοῖς ταπεινοῖς to refer to unbelievers as well as Christians.
4. For example, Michel, *Römer*, p. 403 n. 33; Black, *Romans*, p. 161; Allison, 'Pattern', p. 12; Hunter (*Predecessors*, p. 47).
5. Cf. also the Arabic version of *Ahiqar* 2.19: 'If thine enemy wrong thee, show him kindness', but the saying is probably a later Christian addition (so Lindenberger in *OTP*, I, p. 488).
6. Piper, *Enemies*, p. 39.
7. So Piper, *Enemies*, pp. 38-39, 183-84 n.40.
8. So Piper, *Enemies*, p. 39; cf. also Prov. 24.29; 1QS 10.17-18 ('I will pay to no man the reward of evil; I will pursue him with goodness. For judgment of all the living is with God and it is He who will render to man his reward') and especially *T. Jos.* 18.2; *T. Gad* 6.7.

The exhortation εἰ δυνατὸν... μετὰ πάντων ἀνθρώπων εἰρηνεύοντες in 12.18 (cf. 1 Thess. 5.13 in a context full of dominical
echoes) has also prompted comparison with Jesus' teaching (e.g. Mk
9.50: εἰρηνεύετε ἐν ἀλλήλοις; cf. Mt. 5.9; Mk 5.34; Lk. 7.50; 8.48;
24.36 [var.]). On the other hand, Paul's call to *pursue* peace (Rom.
14.19) like Heb. 12.14 almost certainly reflects the influence of Ps.
33[34].15 (ζήτησον εἰρήνην καὶ δίωξον αὐτήν) on the paraenetic
tradition, as indicated by the quotations in 1 Pet. 3.10-12; *1 Clem.*
22.1-7.[1] Paul's addition of 'all' perhaps recalls Jesus' own emphasis on
doing good even to one's enemies (cf. Lk. 6.27, 33, 35 and Gal. 6.10;
1 Thess. 5.15),[2] but *m. Ab.* 1.12 (attributed to Hillel and Shammai)
preserves a similar call with a universal scope, so the criterion of
dissimilarity cannot be invoked to support an echo.

Paul concludes this segment with μὴ νικῶ ὑπὸ τοῦ κακοῦ ἀλλὰ
νίκα ἐν τῷ ἀγαθῷ τὸ κακόν. The idea of overcoming opposition and
the repetition of κακόν (recalling 12.17a) reveal that the command
functions as a summary of at least vv. 14-20, if not 12.9-20. Many
claim that Paul here is epitomizing Jesus' teachings on non-resistance
(Lk. 6.27-36 // Mt. 5.38-48).[3] There are no verbal parallels with the
Synoptics, however, and *T. Benj.* 4.1-3 presents strikingly similar
language:

> a good man does not have a blind eye, but he is merciful to all, even
> though they may be sinners. And even if persons plot against him for evil
> ends, *by doing good this man conquers evil* (τὸ ἀγαθὸν ποιῶν νικᾷ τὸ
> κακόν), being watched over by God. He loves those who wrong him as
> he loves his own life.[4]

The theme of ἀγάπη for one's neighbour is undeniably early in the
Testaments of the Twelve Patriarchs, but the interpretation of the
neighbour to extend beyond fellow Israelites probably reflects a later

---

1. For other Jewish parallels, see, e.g., *m. Giṭ.* 5.8-9 and Daube,
'Contributions', pp. 233-34.

2. Piper, *Enemies*, p. 63.

3. For example, Ortkemper (*Leben*, p. 124 and nn. 378-79), Schottroff ('Non-
Violence', pp. 23-24, 27), Goppelt (*Theology*, p. 114), Hunter (*Predecessors*, p.
47), Davies (*Paul*, p. 138), Allison ('Pattern', p. 12); cf. Käsemann, *Romans*, p.
347.

4. Furnish cites this parallel when rejecting the idea of dominical allusion in 12.21
(*Theology*, p. 57).

influence of Stoicism, and one cannot discount the possibility of Christian interpolation.[1] It may be significant that Paul's only other use of the νικα- root (aside from the quotation of Ps. 50[51].6 in Rom. 3.4) is in Rom. 8.37, where after speaking of the sufferings of Christians Paul writes, ἀλλ' ἐν τούτοις πᾶσιν ὑπερνικῶμεν διὰ τοῦ ἀγαπήσαντος ἡμᾶς.[2] Both passages speak of how Christians are to overcome, 8.37 giving the agent (διὰ ἀγαπήσαντος) who enables victory and 12.21 the instrument (ἐν τῷ ἀγαθῷ, with τὸ ἀγαθόν closely related to ἀγάπη).[3] For Paul, the one who overcomes evil with the good, that is, by showing ἀγάπη towards his enemy who hates, does so through the one who has supremely demonstrated love on the cross. If the teaching of Jesus is not explicitly present in the passage, the example is implied.[4]

4. *Summary*

Taken individually, the links between exhortations in 12.9-21 and JT are of varying significance. Evaluated in isolation, they provide no convincing proof of allusion to Jesus; even the strongest strand (12.14) is best classified as an echo. Nevertheless, there is more to be said for a connection. Wenham finds the sequence of ideas in 12.17-20 and Mt. 5.38-43 to be similar, concluding that Paul is dependent on pre-Synoptic dominical tradition later attested in both Matthew and Luke.[5] Allison argues that the section is closely related to the block of material in Lk. 6.27-38, a collection that was probably a self-contained unit at an early stage in the tradition.[6] Regardless of which Gospel version is more primitive, the collocation of paralleled thoughts and ideas provides corroborating evidence that JT has

---

1. Piper, *Enemies*, pp. 44-45.

2. νικᾶν occurs only in Lk. 11.22, where it applies to Jesus. The word is important, however, in the Johannine literature. The author of 1 John uses it six times, always of believers, and it occurs seventeen times in Revelation, where it refers most often to Christ and to believers (cf. also Jn 16.33; νίκη is found only in 1 Jn 5.4).

3. In 8.37 Paul focuses not on relations with outsiders but on the certainty of God's love in Christ for the believer no matter what he might experience, yet the common theme of conquering in the face of opposition justifies our comparison.

4. So also Dunn, *Romans*, II, p. 752.

5. 'Use', p. 18.

6. 'Pattern', pp. 11-12.

influenced Paul's thinking. Paul's purpose in 12.9-21 is to set forth some basic characteristics of Christian behaviour for his readers. The call to ἀνυπόκριτος ἀγάπη, manifested in brotherly love, preferment of one another in honour, response to persecution with blessing, association with the lowly, promotion of peace with others, renunciation of retribution, and positive action toward enemies, summarized by admonition to overcome evil with good, could not but remind Christians whom Paul had never met of the characteristics of the one they confessed as Lord. Whether Paul *intended* that recognition must remain an open question.

Chapter 7

ROMANS 13.1-7:
RENDERING WHAT IS DUE

Being at peace with all people (Rom. 12.17-18) includes being at peace with the ruling powers. After dealing with relations with hostile persons, Paul addresses how he thinks Christians living in the capital of the empire should relate to the state.[1] Jewish Christians may have had some negative feelings after the expulsion by Claudius in AD 49; moreover, the plight of their fellow Jews in Palestine would not have endeared the authorities to them.[2] Other Christians might have claimed that as citizens of a heavenly kingdom they were free of any earthly rule.[3] Paul's appeal in 13.6-7, however, probably reveals his primary concern: the payment of taxes was a live issue not only for others in the early Church (Mk 12.17 par.), but also for all the people of Rome.[4] The thematic link in 13.1-7 is not so much a continued exposition of how love is worked out in his readers' lives, but how they are to do what is truly God's will (12.2), what is ἀγαθόν in relation to governing authorities (cf. 13.3-4).[5] In submitting to the

1. 13.1-7 is not an interpolation (contra, e.g., Kallas, 'Interpretation'; Schmithals, Römerbrief, pp. 191-97; O'Neill, pp. 207-209); the section exhibits both verbal and thematic unity with its context, and virtually no textual evidence supports its exclusion (cf., e.g., Friedrich et al., 'Situation', pp. 146-49 and the commentaries).

2. Cf. Jos. War 2.118 on the Jews' refusal to pay tribute to Caesar. Bammel thinks that there may have been Zealot inclinations among the Roman Christians, but his evidence is not conclusive ('Romans 13', pp. 370-71).

3. So, e.g., Käsemann, Romans, p. 351.

4. In AD 58 repeated public protests over the extortionate demands of Roman knights led Nero to propose the abolition of indirect taxes collected by them (Tacitus, Annals 13.50). Cf. Friedrich et al., 'Situation', pp. 156-59; Dunn, 'Charter', pp. 60, 66; Strobel, 'Furcht', pp. 61-62.

5. The emphasis on the good here is again a continuation of that seen in 12.2, 9

authorities, the Romans are submitting to God's servants, and are thus acting in accordance with his will.[1] As an apostle charged with the spread of the gospel, Paul is concerned here not only about the well-being of the Christian communities in Rome, but also with their collective witness to the outside world (cf. 14.16).

1. *Evidence for Jesus Tradition*

Although Paul does not refer to Jesus, some possible links with the dominical teaching and example in Rom. 13.1-7 should be noted. Jesus' example of non-resistance in the payment of taxes (Mt. 17.24-27) and ultimately in his act of submission to death on the cross may have played a role in the development of Paul's thought in 13.1-7, but if so it has left no distinguishing mark as it does in 1 Pet. 2.13-25. There is, however, no evidence that Paul thought the Roman Christians were suffering or would suffer for their faith as a result of their submission to the authorities, so the example of Jesus may have been of less immediate value for Paul's situation than for Peter's. On the other hand, Dodd's suggestion that 13.2 refers to the saying preserved in Mt. 26.52 is far-fetched, with no verbal and little conceptual agreement to support it.[2]

Although many scholars claim that Paul's words in 13.7 reflect the knowledge of the 'Render unto Caesar' logion (Mk 12.17 // Mt. 22.21 // Lk. 20.25), others find the evidence inconclusive, and a few are

---

(cf. 14.16; 15.2). Another common theme is government being a means by which God avenges wrong (ἔκδικος, 13.4; cf. ἐκδικοῦν/ἐκδίκησις in 12.19) and executes his ὀργή (13.4; cf. 12.19) on the wrongdoer.

1. Cf. 1 Pet. 2.13-17. Against the view that Paul has in mind a dual reference including the heavenly powers thought to stand behind and to act through the civil authorities (so Cullmann, *State*, pp. 65-70; 95-114; Morrison, *Powers*), cf., e.g., Strobel, 'Verständnis' and Cranfield, *Romans*, II, pp. 656-59. Paul's failure to reckon with the possibility of an evil government reflects the fact that he is addressing a specific historical situation; he is not attempting to produce a full-blown philosophy of church–state relations. Cf., e.g., Dunn, 'Charter', pp. 67-69.

2. Dodd, *Romans*, p. 204.

more sceptical.[1] A comparison of the texts reveals the following similarities:

Rom.13.7	Mt. 22.21 // Lk. 20.25	Mk 12.17
ἀπόδοτε πᾶσιν τὰς	ἀπόδοτε [οὖν-Mt.]	τὰ Καίσαρος ἀπόδοτε
ὀφειλάς,	τὰ Καίσαρος Καίσαρι	Καίσαρι
τῷ τὸν φόρον τὸν φόρον,		
τῷ τὸ τέλος τὸ τέλος		
τῷ τὸν φόβον τὸν φόβον,	καὶ τὰ τοῦ θεοῦ τῷ θεῷ	καὶ τὰ τοῦ θεοῦ τῷ θεῷ
τῷ τὴν τιμὴν τὴν τιμήν		

Five points of contact should be noted. First, the occasion for both statements concerns paying taxes; the parallels advocate the payment of that which belongs to the civil authority.[2] Secondly, the same verb (ἀποδιδόναι) is used and with the identical tense, voice, mood, person and number. Thirdly, the dominical saying exhibits a two-part construction with an ellipsis of the verb: (a) the hearers are to render the things belonging to Caesar to Caesar and (b) the things belonging to God [they are to render] to God. Although the accusative/dative order is reversed in Rom. 13.7 and four members expound the

1. 'An allusion. . . cannot be ruled out' (Dunn, *Romans*, II, p. 768). Expressing confidence of an echo are Black (*Romans*, p. 161), Michel (*Römer*, p. 403 n. 33), Dodd (*Romans*, p. 205), Sanday and Headlam (*Exegetical Commentary*, pp. 371, 381), Stuhlmacher ('Jesustradition', p. 248; cf. his earlier scepticism in Friedrich *et al.*, 'Situation', p. 156), Longenecker (*Paul*, p. 189), Fannon ('Influence', p. 304), Goppelt ('Freedom', p. 192), Delling (*Römer 13, 1-7*, p. 16), Neugebauer ('Auslegung', p. 165), Stanley ('Allusions', p. 33), Davies (*Paul*, p. 138), Kittel (*Christus*, pp. 7-8), Holtzmann (*Lehrbuch*, p. 232); for others see Pohle (*Christen*, pp. 53 n. 93, 69 n. 155) and Riekkinen (*Römer*, p. 87 n. 3). Wilckens (*Römer*, III, p. 38) and Cranfield (*Romans*, II, pp. 669, 670 n. 1) favour the probability. Kuss ('Gewalt', p. 334) and Kümmel ('Urchristentum', p. 138) are less confident, and those who reject a historical link include Neirynck ('Sayings', p. 291), Riekkinen (*Römer*, pp. 89-90), Käsemann (*Romans*, p. 352), and Dibelius ('Rom', p. 179 n. 4).

2. In Romans the focus is on what is due (tax, customs duty, respect, honour), whereas in the Gospels the recipients are specified (Caesar, God). Interpreters are divided as to whether Jesus intended to support payment of taxes. The important issue for us, however, is not what Jesus intended, but how the early Church interpreted and applied his words. Justin Martyr explicity cites the saying as justification for Christians paying taxes (*Apol.* 1.17). The charge that Jesus forbade the payment of taxes in Lk. 23.2 is a false accusation from his opponents.

meaning of πᾶσιν τὰς ὀφειλάς, there is again an ellipsis of the verb
and a discernible two-part structure:

> (a) τῷ τὸν φόρον τὸν φόρον, τῷ τὸ τέλος τὸ τέλος
> (b) τῷ τὸν φόβον τὸν φόβον, τῷ τὴν τιμὴν τὴν τιμήν

Fourthly, Luke gives the saying in answer to the question of whether
the φόρος (direct tax) should be paid to Caesar (Lk. 20.22; cf. 23.2);
Matthew and Mark use the word κῆνσος ('poll-tax'), a Latin loan-
word probably used by Jesus' questioners.[1] Fifthly, the constructions
τὰ Καίσαρος and τὰ τοῦ θεοῦ in connection with Jesus' question
about whose εἰκών and ἐπιγραφή were on the coin imply the idea of
that which belongs to or is due; although neither ὀφειλή nor ὀφείλω
appear in the immediate context, the concept is present.

In addition to these similarities, three other factors favour a
dominical link. First, Rom. 13.7 shows signs of being a separate piece
of tradition with which Paul caps his exhortation. After a string of
clauses joined by particles in 13.1-6, we find asyndeton and a flat
command taking up the language of 13.6 with the *Stichwort* φόρος
without appearing to be a conclusion drawn from the preceding discussion.[2] In 13.3-4 Paul says that rulers are not a cause for φόβος to
those who do good, yet in 13.7 he insists that φόβος *is* appropriate for
the Christian.[3] Paul thus uses the word in a different way in 13.7 than
in 13.3-4 (i.e. 'respect/reverence' instead of 'fear'). Whenever he
speaks positively of φόβος, it is generally with respect to God/the
Lord and not humans.[4] ἀπόδοτε πᾶσιν τὰς ὀφειλάς reads like a
summary of the dominical saying, with the following appositional
elliptical clauses filling out its implications and providing a
commentary. The alliteration, parallelism and metre in 13.7b could be
signs of a piece of tradition shaped for easy remembrance (or simply
good rhetorical style). This may be part of what Paul might normally

---

1. Bruce, 'Caesar', pp. 257-58.
2. Paul also caps 12.9-20 with asyndeton and an imperative in 12.21.
3. Cf. Cranfield, *Romans*, II, pp. 670-73; for criticism see Murray, *Romans*, II,
p. 156.
4. E.g., Rom. 3.18; 2 Cor. 5.11; 7.1; φοβεῖσθαι, Rom. 11.20. An exception is
2 Cor. 7.15, where Paul recalls how the Corinthians received Titus 'with fear and
trembling', but fear is not *enjoined* there. Cf. also Eph. 5.33 and 6.5 (wives fearing
husbands/slaves their masters) for other exceptions, yet these are only possible ἐν
φόβῳ Χριστοῦ (Eph. 5.22).

teach after relating the logion of Jesus, that is, a practical expansion and application. Like his appeal to JT in 1 Cor. 9.14, the parallel occurs at the conclusion of his argument, climaxing Paul's case.

Secondly, the dominical saying was available and well known. Attested in the triple tradition (cf. also *Gos. Thom.* logion 100; Just. *Apol.* 1.17), the 'Render unto Caesar' saying is almost certainly authentic.[1] By virtue of its subject and relevance to every Christian, such a saying would have been a part of the earliest communication of Jesus' teachings. The logion was bound to be familiar to the Christians in Rome, where the issue of one's relation to civil authority was a primary concern. Even if Luke's account that some Romans were among Peter's audience at Pentecost (Acts 2.10) cannot be trusted, Roman believers are likely to have been among the first to learn of this particular logion in view of its direct reference to Caesar and the relative ease of travel between Jerusalem and Rome. More so than perhaps anywhere else, the assumption is safe that both Paul and his readers knew the saying, and Paul could presuppose that knowledge.[2]

Thirdly, two contextual considerations afford some evidence for a dominical link. Jesus' call to non-resistance in Mt. 5.39-42 // Lk. 6.29-30 would have functioned not only within the community to promote peace among the brethren, but also without, assuring outsiders that Christians were not revolutionaries.[3] In the latter respect its effect would thus be similar to Mk 12.17 par. and Rom. 13.1-7. Paul's transition from Rom. 12.14-21 to 13.1-7 becomes all the more understandable if his *pattern* of paraenesis was rooted in this twofold application of Jesus' teaching.[4] Secondly, the dominical sayings paral-

---

1. Bultmann saw no reason for supposing it to be a community product (*History*, p. 26), although for some its *Gattung* as a controversy-dialogue could point to that conclusion (cf. Käsemann, *Romans*, p. 352).

2. That Pharisees were allegedly behind the attempt to trap Jesus (Mk 12.13 // Mt. 22.15-16) increases the likelihood of Paul's awareness of the saying (Cf. Hunter, *Predecessors*, p. 47).

3. Schottroff, 'Non-Violence', p. 26.

4. Schottroff observes, 'The commandment to love the enemy often appears in connection with [this] type of political apology. . . In a similar vein, 1 Pet. 2:13ff. establishes a political context for the passive resistance of injustice. It hardly seems accidental that the injunctions in Rom. 12:14,17, and 19-21 inculcate in effect the love of the enemy, and that Rom. 13:1-7 regulates the Christian attitude to the state' ('Non-Violence', pp. 26-27).

leling Paul's exhortations in 13.7 and 13.8-10 are also closely linked
in the conflict stories of Matthew and Mark, appearing in the same
order (Mk 12.13-17/28-31 // Mt. 22.21/34-40).[1] The resurrection
question (Mk 12.18-27 // Mt. 22.23-33) separates them, but it is more
a matter of *haggadah* than *halakah*, and would have dropped out if the
teachings were used for paraenetic purposes. If the stories circulated
together as part of a pre-Synoptic (Passion) collection, their order and
proximity may well have influenced (subconsciously) Paul's exhortation. It is not difficult to see how easily the first could flow into the
second, for we find a similar twofold division of responsibility: that
which should be rendered to God and to humans.[2] The value of this
line of argument depends on one's evaluation of the host of hypotheses
it requires,[3] but it deserves consideration.

The principle of dissimilarity affords little evidence to confirm an
echo in 13.7, but neither does it disprove the influence of dominical
tradition. Paul's ideas in 13.1-7 as a whole are typically Jewish, and
the lack of distinctively Christian language has prompted some to
identify the passage as an interpolation.[4] Thus in Jer. 29.7 the prophet
tells the exiles in Babylon to seek the welfare of the city into which
they have been sent in exile, and to pray on its behalf, for in its welfare they would find their welfare. The idea that one should revere the
authority of a king was also not foreign to Judaism. 'My son, fear the
Lord and the king, and do not disobey either of them' (Prov. 24.21).
So also the rabbis:

> R. Jannai said: Let the awe of kingship (אימת מלכות) always be upon thee,
> for it is written, *And all these thy servants shall come down unto me*, but
> he did not say it of [Pharaoh] himself... R. Johanan said: It [that

---

1. Cf. Allison, 'Pattern', p. 17; he notes the proximity, but not the order.
2. On the omission of reference to love for God in 13.8-10, see Chapter 8.
3. That is, (1) that Paul is dependent upon Jesus in 13.8-10; (2) that the order and
proximity of the sayings is pre-Synoptic (denied by Neirynck and others he cites
['Sayings', p. 286]); (3) that Paul knew the sayings as part of a pre-Synoptic collection; (4) that no other factor primarily influenced Paul.
4. On the Jewish nature of the exhortation cf. Strobel, 'Verständnis'; Dibelius,
'Rom', pp. 183-84. Bammel sees Paul's original contribution in the uncommon
qualification διάκονος θεοῦ, in 'the blunt linking of the powers with God... the
use of the genitive, the emphasis on subordination and the stigmatisation of resistance, and insistence on paying taxes' ('Romans 13', pp. 373-74).

reverence should be shown to a king] may be inferred from the following:
And the hand of the Lord was on Elijah; and he girded up his loins, and ran before Ahab [*b. Zeb.* 102a; cf. also *b. Men.* 98a].

In *b. Abod. Zar.* 4a we read,

> Rab Judah says in the name of Samuel:. . . Just as among fish of the sea, the greater swallow up the smaller ones, so with men, were it not for fear of the government (מוראה של מלכות), men would swallow each other alive. This is just what we learnt [in *m. Ab.* 3.2]: R. Hanina, the Deputy High Priest, said, Pray for the welfare of the government, for were it not for the fear thereof, men would swallow each other alive.

2. *Possible Objections*

Omission of the Second Part of the Dominical Saying

Neirynck writes 'The main difficulty has always been that the real point of the saying is not τὰ Καίσαρος ἀπόδοτε Καίσαρι but the second half: καὶ τὰ τοῦ θεοῦ τῷ θεῷ, the debt which is owed to God, and this has no correspondence in Romans 13'.[1] Advocates of a dominical link are divided as to whether or not Paul echoes the second part of Jesus' logion. Cranfield develops the shift in meaning of φόβος to argue that perhaps Paul is thinking about his readers' obligation to God in the third member of the four elliptical clauses.[2] We have already noted that Paul rarely if ever calls for φόβος toward men.[3]

---

1. Neirynck, 'Sayings', p. 291.

2. *Romans*, II, p. 673 n. 1; cf. also Schrage, *Staat*, esp. n. 132. Origen, Gregory of Nazianus and Tertullian referred both the φόβος and τιμή clauses to God, but their interpretation was conditioned more by their historical situation than by exegesis (cf. Zsifkovits, *Staatsgedanke*, p. 101 and Schelkle, 'Staat' on other patristic views). In the parallel in 1 Pet. 2.17, however the author calls for his readers to honour (τιμᾶν) all people, particularly the king. Furthermore, Paul's usage of τιμή/τιμᾶν elsewhere and the statements in *1 Clem.* 61.1-2 and *Mart. Pol.* 10.2 make the view of Origen *et al.* unlikely.

3. *2 Clem.* 4.4 states, 'We must not fear (φοβεῖσθαι) men rather than God'. The only instances in which the AF speak positively of 'fearing' humans are *Did.* 4.11 (of slaves toward masters), *Barn.* 19.7 (fear one's master as a type of God), and Ign. *Eph.* 6.1 (fear the bishop). In the vast majority of instances of φοβεῖσθαι/φόβος the object is God. Nonetheless, Paul could easily be speaking of the appropriate respect people should pay to their governing authorities who serve as διάκονοι θεοῦ. Strobel thinks the Graeco-Roman ideal of a subject's duties

The parallel in 1 Pet. 2.17 also has four members, the third of which is a call to fear (φοβεῖσθαι) God, and the fourth an exhortation to honour (τιμᾶν) the king. This could support the application of φόβος to God in Rom. 13.7, but the author of 1 Peter exhorts servants to submit to their masters ἐν παντὶ φόβῳ in the following verse (2.18).[1] Goppelt claims that even if Paul is not referring to God in the third member of the verse, he is drawing upon the teaching of Jesus, for in obeying the civil authority one is submitting to God's servant and rendering unto God what is his.[2] Goppelt's claim on its own, however, is untestable.

No one seems to have noticed in all this that Paul is quite capable of employing only half of a tradition. Neirynck's expectation that the apostle could not use only part of a well-known two-membered saying overlooks the fact that this is precisely what Paul has done only a few verses before:

Rom. 12.17   προνοούμενοι καλὰ ἐνώπιον πάντων ἀνθρώπων
Prov. 3.4   καὶ προνοοῦ καλὰ ἐνώπιον κυρίου καὶ ἀνθρώπων

Commentators are unanimous that in 12.17 Paul picks up the language of Proverbs while dropping the reference to God since it did not suit his immediate purpose, but no one has seen the implications of this for 13.7. The explanation for his failure to reflect on the second half of the saying would be the same as for his omission of first half of the dominical summary of the law in 13.9 (see below): Paul has *already* called for total allegiance to God in 12.1-2, and in the following verses he focuses on relations with others.

Lack of Reference to Jesus

'Paul does not quote either the dominical saying or its tradition. . . it would have been easy to provide the Christological motivation which is so surprisingly absent'.[3] As we have seen, the Christians in Rome would not need reminding that Jesus had taught this duty—Paul could take that knowledge for granted. Moreover, a direct quotation would not have fitted well into the flow of his exhortation, since his concern

underlies Rom. 13.7, noting that Aristotle distinguishes two types of fear in *Oecon.* 3 ('Furcht', pp. 60-61).

1. Cf. also Neirynck, 'Sayings', pp. 287-90.
2. Goppelt, 'Freedom', pp. 192-93.
3. Käsemann, *Romans*, p. 352.

is not to compare obedience to God and to Caesar, but to seek a proper attitude before *all* authorities (πᾶσιν).

Insufficient Verbal Evidence

Those who reject a Pauline echo of Jesus observe that ἀπόδοτε would be a normal verb used for paying taxes and that φόρος is Lukan redaction (cf. 23.2).[1] Both claims are probably true, but there is more to be said here. The dominical saying is so brief that the only possible verbal/grammatical 'hooks' that would recall it are ἀπόδοτε and the following elliptical construction.[2] Paul's reference in 13.7 is wider than Καῖσαρ. φόρος would be a normal translational variant for κῆνσος, so its use in the traditioning process need not be restricted to Luke.[3] Given the subject matter, the conceptual and formal agreement between the texts, and the high probability that both Paul and the Romans knew the logion, the verbal evidence is not as insignificant as it might seem.

3. *Conclusion*

Considered in isolation, the evidence for JT in Rom. 13.7 is indecisive. A dominical echo is probable; an allusion, possible at best. Again we have a case where Paul almost certainly knew a saying of Jesus quite similar to what he declares, but the apostle seems unconcerned to acknowledge it. Rather than using a logion to establish a Christian 'law', Paul wants to reason through the logic of submission to the authorities to its practical outworking—payment of taxes.[4] This does

---

1. Neirynck, 'Sayings', p. 291; cf. Käsemann, *Romans*, p. 352. We find ἀποδιδόναι φόρον in Thucydides 5.18; also Josephus *Ant.* 14.203 and *Apion* 1.119 (φόρους).

2. Munro thinks ἐξουσία and ἀρχή provide further evidence for dominical allusion (Lk. 20.20; Rom. 13.1-3), albeit not by Paul, but the words are Lukan and too far removed from the logion to be significant (*Authority*, pp. 191-92 n. 94).

3. Fitzmyer calls this use of φόρος 'proper Greek' (*Luke*, II, p. 1290), and Derrett finds it to be 'a perfectly good word to use' (*Law*, p. 329).

4. Thus in 13.1-7 we have γάρ with the indicative in 13.1, 3, 4 [thrice], 6 [twice]; ὥστε with the indicative in 13.2; a rhetorical question in 13.3; and διό introducing a conclusion followed by two reasons in 13.5; whereas in all of 12.9-21 the only evidence of *reasoning* is the twofold use of γάρ (12.19-20). Cf. Zsifkovits, *Staatsgedanke*, p. 56; *contra* Käsemann, who evaluates 13.1-7 as traditions con-

not mean that Paul was indifferent to the saying, for of all the words of Jesus, the 'Render unto Caesar' logion would perhaps have been the most familiar to Roman Christians. Whether he intended it or not, Paul's hearers would have been reminded of Jesus' words and would recognize that this brother from Tarsus stood in continuity with their tradition. Although Jesus was understood to advocate payment of tribute in Palestine, he did not offer a rationale beyond confronting the hypocrisy of those who used Caesar's coins. In spite of their knowledge of this tradition, the Romans still needed to hear the message of 13.1-7 that God stands behind the powers that be.

nected through association and coordination, not through subordination, deduction and logic ('Principles', p. 199).

Chapter 8

ROMANS 13.8-10: FULFILLING THE LAW

In Rom. 13.8-10, Paul begins to summarize his general exhortation, returning to his original theme of love (cf. 12.9-10). Addressing Christians divided by scruples, he insists that love for one another is the only debt which should remain. Sandwiched between affirmations that to love is to fulfil the law,[1] he observes that the command to love one's neighbour (Lev. 19.18) epitomizes the intention of the ethical requirements of the Mosaic law and precludes actions which harm another. Rom. 13.8-10 in effect prepares the way for the issues of ch. 14.

1. *Evidence for Jesus Tradition*

Käsemann and many others see the influence of dominical teaching in 13.8-10.[2] Paul's thought in this section closely parallels that of Jesus,

---

1. The correspondence of πλήρωμα with ἐργάζεται in the chiastic structure of 13.10, together with the use of πληροῦν in 13.8 indicate that πλήρωμα most likely means 'fulfilling' (= πλήρωσις) instead of its more usual sense of 'fullness'. Cf., e.g., Delling (*TDNT*, VI, p. 305), Wilckens (*Römer*, III, p. 71) and M. Black (*Romans*, p. 163), who cites Theophrastus, *Char.* 27.7, where the word denotes the *full performance* of a dramatic entertainment.

2. Käsemann, *Romans*, p. 361; cf. (*inter alia*) Michel, *Römer*, p. 411; Lagrange, *Romains*, p. 316; Dodd, *Romans*, pp. 207-208, Lietzmann, *Römer*, p. 113; Bruce, *Paul*, p. 111; Davies, *Paul*, p. 138; Spicq, *Agapé*, I, p. 261; Fannon, 'Paul', pp. 54-55; Brown, 'Parallels', p. 27 n. 5; Allison, 'Pattern', p. 20; Stanley, 'Allusions', p. 32; Schrage, *Einzelgebote*, p. 243 n. 250.

Some mistakenly claim that use of the term λόγος in 13.9 (cf. also Gal. 5.14 and 1 Thess. 4.15) points specifically to a word of Jesus (Ortkemper, *Leben*, p. 131; J.T. Sanders, *Ethics*, p. 51 n. 11). The ten commandments, however, are called the ten λόγοι in Exod. 34.28 and Deut. 10.4. It was common in Paul's day to refer to them as such (Philo *Decal.* 32, 154, 176; Jos. *Ant.* 3.90-91, 138; cf. *Barn.* 15.1).

but almost every aspect of the correspondence also finds parallels in Jewish literature, leading some to doubt any dominical link.[1]

Love as a Debt

Although the admonition to owe no one anything is by no means unique,[2] Paul's linkage of love and debt may go back to Jesus. For Paul, because Christians are set free and indwelt by the Spirit they are debtors (ὀφειλέται), obliged to live by the Spirit (Rom. 8.1-13). Love is a debt owed because of the love they have received from God. Just as Christ did not please himself but lived for others, so Paul's readers are obliged to bear one another's burdens (Rom. 15.1-3). The logic is that Christians are obliged in their dealings with one another to exhibit the same love, mercy, and forgiveness which characterized God's actions in Christ. This is spelled out explicitly in Col. 3.13 (mercy); cf. also Eph. 4.32 (forgiveness) and 5.2 (love). Black thinks it 'hardly coincidental' that in Rom. 13.8 the consonants of חיב (= ὀφείλειν) also give the word in Aramaic 'to love' (חבב, piel חיבב). Observing that the resulting paronomasia is reproduced in the Peshitta Syriac, he concludes, 'this proverbial-like saying was just the kind to lend itself to a "punning" word play. Paul is probably reproducing in Greek an Aramaic *sententia*, possibly a Christian one, conceivably even a dominical pun.'[3]

We may compare the thought of Paul's statements with Lk. 6.36 ('Be merciful, even as your Father is merciful') and especially Mt. 18.32, where the debtor is required to show mercy as he received mercy, with the moral drawn that God's forgiveness requires forgiveness of one's fellows (note the use of ὀφείλω [18.28 {twice}, 30, 34], ὀφειλέτης [18.24], ὀφειλή [18.32]). Matthew also has ὀφειλέτης and ὀφείλημα in his version of the Lord's Prayer (Mt. 6.12), and his language preserves an Aramaic idiom.[4] Reception of God's love in forgiveness creates an obligation ('debt'?) for the forgiven to reflect the same love as that received. It is not improbable that Paul knew

1. So Berger, *Gesetzesauslegung*, I, p. 50 n. 1; cf. Hatch, 'Summary', p. 139; Burchard, 'Liebesgebot', p. 39 n. 1; and O'Neill, *Romans*, p. 215.

2. For parallels cf. Strobel, 'Verständnis', p. 92 and n. 129.

3. M. Black, *Romans*, pp. 161-62; cf. O'Neill, *Romans*, p. 214 for a different theory.

4. So, e.g., M. Black, *Approach*, p. 40.

Matthew's parable of the unforgiving servant (18.23-35) and/or Luke's parable of the debtor (7.36-50, linked with forgiveness and love). If not distinctively dominical, Paul's notion of love as debt coheres with a central theme of Jesus.[1]

The Command to Love One Another

In 13.8, the article τό introduces ἀλλήλους ἀγαπᾶν as 'the well-known command', something Paul expects his readers to recognize immediately.[2] The Synoptics do not preserve a call to love one another (most likely because love for the brethren was included in the love command; John's Gospel preserves no call to love the neighbour), but in the Johannine tradition ἀλλήλους ἀγαπᾶν was clearly regarded as a teaching of Jesus (Jn 13.34-35; 15.12-13, 17).[3] As we have seen, it is one of the few dominical teachings quoted as such in the NT outside Paul, a command Christians had heard ἀπ' ἀρχῆς (1 Jn 3.11; 2 Jn 5; cf. 1 Jn 3.23; 4.7, 12).[4] The author of 1 Peter knows its importance (1.22), and the phrase ἀλλήλους ἀγαπᾶν occurs also in the AF (Ign. *Magn.* 6.2; *Trall.* 13.2; *2 Clem.* 9.6).

This evidence, however, does not demonstrate Paul's dependence on dominical tradition. Although the phrase is lacking in the LXX, exhortations to love one another are not unusual in the *Testaments of the Twelve Patriarchs* (*T. Zeb.* 8.5; also *T. Gad* 6.1; 7.7; *T. Jos.* 17.2; cf. *T. Sim.* 4.7), the Qumran literature (1QS 8.2; CD 6.20-21), the

---

1. On the importance of the 'coherent language of "debt"' attributed to Jesus cf. Chilton, 'Repentance', pp. 10-12.

2. BDF, sec. 399.1: 'anaphoric'; Rekhopf thinks it less clearly anaphoric, but still *das bekannte Gebot* (BDR, sec. 399.2). Paul usually prefers the anarthrous object infinitive (235×) to the articular (12×; the figures are from A.T. Robertson, *Grammar*, p. 1424), and in the only other NT instances of εἰ μή followed by an infinitive, the article is lacking (Jn 13.10; Mt. 5.13). The phrase ἀλλήλους ἀγαπᾶν appears here for the first time in Romans.

3. Bultmann thought 13.34-35 and 15.12 to be the creations of the evangelist (*John*, pp. 525 n. 1, 542 n. 1). The resemblance to Rom. 13.8 is striking in 1 Jn 4.11: ἡμεῖς ὀφείλομεν ἀλλήλους ἀγαπᾶν, although ὀφείλειν there has a different nuance. Against the objection that John restricts the scope and perverts the character of the Synoptic concept of ἀγάπη see Furnish, *Command*, pp. 143-48.

4. *Gos. Thom.* logion 25 ('Love your brother as your soul; keep him as the apple of your eye') may represent another independent dominical tradition (cf. Quispel, 'Qumran', pp. 143-44).

Mishnah (*Ab.* 1.2) and Josephus (*War* 2.119); 'parallels abound'.[1] A call to love one another would be a natural paraphrase of the OT injunctions to love the neighbour or to love one's brother, so there is nothing unique here to mark it as a demonstrable teaching of Jesus.

Nevertheless, if (as it seems likely) the Johannine saying attributed to Jesus is authentic or was believed by the earliest disciples to be a faithful interpretation of his teaching, it would have been a fundamental teaching in any primitive Christian catechism, and a believer as well-travelled as Paul could not possibly be ignorant of it. Does Paul bypass the logion in deriving this teaching? If the apostle draws on other sources, why not from Jesus, especially when Christ is at the centre of his theology? Scholars often observe that Christ is the hermeneutical key to Paul's interpretation of the OT (as in 1 Cor. 10.4; 2 Cor. 3, etc.); we should not be surprised to find something similar in his ethics.[2]

Perhaps, however, Paul was depending simply upon the primitive 'Christian tradition' without specific reference to Jesus' teachings. That is possible and appropriate in cases in which the origin of a logion may be in doubt, for example, because the teaching lacks Gospel attestation, is anachronistic, does not cohere with established dominical sayings, or has a patent *raison d'être* in the post-Easter community. On the other hand, to deny that Paul knew as dominical that which is fundamental to our understanding of Jesus strains credulity, especially since Paul specifically links love with Jesus elsewhere. Shortly after his comments in Rom. 13.8-10, he will go on to speak about walking κατὰ ἀγάπην; in the next breath he appeals to the death of Christ (14.15; cf. Gal. 2.20; 2 Cor. 5.14-15; Rom. 8.37-38). The implicit becomes explicit in Eph. 5.2, where the author (if not Paul, an imitator much closer to the apostle than we shall ever be) exhorts περιπατεῖτε ἐν ἀγάπη, **καθὼς** καὶ ὁ Χριστὸς ἠγάπησεν ἡμᾶς καὶ παρέδωκεν ἑαυτὸν ὑπὲρ ἡμῶν.[3] Clearly Paul's understanding of Christ's love was rooted in the cross-event and not

---

1. Furnish, *Command*, p. 138.

2. Cf. Hooker: 'The significant difference between Paul and his contemporaries. . . is seen in his underlying assumption that Christ himself is the key to the meaning of scripture. . . he is himself the one about whom all scripture spoke' ('Beyond', p. 306).

3. Cf. also Eph. 5.25. Paul also sees God's love demonstrated in Christ's self-giving (Rom. 5.8; 8.39).

explicitly in any teaching of Jesus—for Paul, as for James, actions speak louder than words. But it is another thing altogether to say that Paul *ignored* the tradition of Jesus' teaching when formulating his own ethic. Thus, although the call for mutual love is not, in itself, distinctively dominical, in the light of Paul's historical/theological context, the balance of probability favours an underlying influence of JT, whether or not Paul was thinking of Jesus at the moment of dictation.

Fulfilment of the Law
In 13.8b Paul grounds his assertion that love is a lasting debt in the fact that when one loves another person, one fulfils the law.[1] Two interpretative questions raised here are the referent of νόμος, and the sense in which Paul speaks of Christians fulfilling (πληροῦν) the law. Verse 9 reveals that νόμος is not 'law as principle' (Sanday and Headlam), for Paul is thinking specifically of moral commandments. It is not simply the Decalogue, since the addition of καὶ εἴ τις ἑτέρα ἐντολή radicalizes his statement and suggests a wider scope.[2] It is not the Mosaic law in general, for he cites only commands from the second 'table' of the law, and it is unlikely that Paul considered love for the neighbour to subsume one's responsibility towards God. Instead, by νόμος he is referring to the demands of the Torah with

---

1. τὸν ἕτερον could be construed with νόμον, signifying 'the *other* law', i.e., the law of Moses, as distinct from the civil law to which Paul has already sought obedience (Marxsen, 'Rom. 13,8', followed by Leenhardt, *Romans*, pp. 337-38). Other variations of this view include the possibility that the 'other' law refers to the 'second' law in Mt. 22.39 // Mk 12.31 (so Bruce, *Romans*, p. 240; Gutbrod, *TDNT*, IV, p. 1071). Paul however consistently uses (ὁ) ἕτερος independently with reference to persons (Rom. 2.1; 2.21; 1 Cor. 4.6; 6.1; 10.24, 29; 14.17; Gal. 6.4; cf. Jas 4.12), he does not employ ἀγαπᾶν without an object elsewhere, no clear reference to 'law' appears before 13.8 in the immediate context, and νόμος occurs again by itself in 13.10 (cf. also Grosheide, 'Romans 13:8b'). His choice of τὸν ἕτερον instead of τὸν πλησίον probably points to the person who differs; 'Love for the *neighbour* can too easily be misinterpreted as "love for the like-minded man who is congenial to me"' (Barrett, *Romans*, p. 250).

The perfect πεπλήρωκεν probably has a gnomic force, referring to a customary truth well-known by the recipients (so, e.g., A.T. Robertson, *Grammar*, p. 897; cf. Rom. 14.23; 1 Cor. 7.39; 1 Jn 2.5; Jas 2.10).

2. Käsemann, *Romans*, p. 361; Michel, *Römer*, p. 410.

regard to one's relationships with others.[1] Paul's purpose here is not to provide exhaustive teaching about the law and its fulfilment, but rather to stress the imperative of love.

What Paul has said earlier about justification, grace and the law does not mean the repudiation of OT morality. The just requirement (δικαίωμα) of the law is being fulfilled (πληροῦσθαι) in the Christian who walks according to the Spirit (Rom. 8.4). As in 2.26 the δικαίωμα is what the law requires, that is, the will of God,[2] which fallen men rejected (1.21, 32) but which Jesus accomplished in his obedience unto death on the cross (5.18). πληροῦν in both 8.4 and 13.8 refers to fulfilling through doing, that is, the full accomplishment of the requirement of the law.[3] The verb offered the advantage of its connotation of perfection and fullness, ensuring Paul's readers that his approach to the law is not inferior to that of Judaism. It was also ambiguous, having all the right associations of full accomplishment without the exactitude implicit in, for example, ποιεῖν (Gal. 3.10, 12; 5.3; Rom. 2.13) and φυλάσσειν (Rom. 2.26; Gal. 6.13; cf. Acts 7.53; 21.24).[4] πληροῦν could carry an eschatological connotation as well. For Paul, the law and the prophets bear witness to Christ (Rom. 3.21; 2 Cor. 1.20; Rom. 1.2); Christ is the τέλος of the law (Rom. 10.4), that is, the embodiment of the righteousness promised by the law and the latter's fulfilment.[5] By loving the neighbour, Christians exhibit the

1. 'Man könnte geradezu sagen, daß im Glauben die Gebote der Ersten Tafel des Dekalogs erfüllt werden wie in der Liebe die der Zweiten' (Wilckens, *Römer*, III, p. 71; cf. Calvin, *Romans*, p. 285). Nowhere in very early Christianity does the Decalogue as a whole appear (first instance in *Barn.* 15.1; Wilckens, *Römer*, III, p. 69-70), only commandments from the second 'table'. The fact that νόμος lacks the article is not surprising; cf. references to the Mosaic law in Rom. 2.12-14, 17, 23, 25; 3.20-21, 31; 4.13; 6.14-15; 10.4-5; etc.

2. Cranfield, *Romans*, I, p. 384.

3. Wilckens, *Römer*, III, p. 68. πληροῦν usually renders the qal or pual of מלא in the LXX and describes an action fully accomplishing that which is spoken of earlier by God or (sometimes) a person (e.g. 1 Kgs 2.27); cf. 1 Macc. 2.55 (obeying a command) and 2 Chron. 36.22 (accomplishing [כלה] the word of the Lord). Paul uses the word in the usual sense 'to fill up' (e.g. Rom. 1.29; 15.13-14), as well as 'to fulfil' in the sense 'to bring to completion' (Rom. 15.19; 2 Cor. 10.6; Phil. 2.2; 4.19 etc.). Cf. C.F.D. Moule, 'Fulfilment-words', pp. 304-13 for related texts.

4. Barclay, *Obeying*, pp. 139-40.

5. So Badenas (*Christ*, pp. 117-18), who provides the best introduction to this difficult crux.

same love revealed in Christ; in a manner not identical to but derivative from that of Christ, Paul can speak of the law's fulfilment in them.[1] 'Strictly speaking it is the Spirit which fulfills the Law, and the Christian shares in the fulfillment by "following the Spirit" (5:25)'.[2] The δικαίωμα of the law can now be fulfilled in Christians because they are set free from the dominion of sin by the coming of Jesus (Rom. 8.3-4). What was previously impossible is now expected in the eschaton of the Spirit, for love itself is a fruit of that Spirit (Gal. 5.22). It is thus not surprising to see Paul turn immediately to an eschatological motivation for his ethics in Rom. 13.11 after speaking of the fulfilment of the law in Rom. 13.8, 10.

In Gal. 5.13-14 Paul again links love for one another with the command to love the neighbour, a command which fulfils the whole law (ὁ πᾶς νόμος).[3] Instead of quarrelling (5.15), the Galatians through love are to serve one another (δουλεύειν; 5.13).[4] As in

---

1. So Fenton: '[For Paul]. . . the law points forward to the work of Christ; it is superseded through the work of Christ; and its requirement is satisfied by the love of the Christian' ('Paul', p. 93).

2. Betz, *Galatians*, p. 300.

3. ὁ πᾶς νόμος signifies 'the law as a whole—the spirit and intention of the law' in 5.14, in contrast to the 'sum-total of the precepts of the law' (ὅλος ὁ νόμος) in 5.3 (Bruce, *Galatians*, p. 241). Hübner denies reference to the Mosaic law in 5.14 ('Gesetz', p. 246; cf. *idem*, *Law*, p. 37), but Paul cites a command from the Decalogue in 5.14 and uses νόμος in the same sense in 5.18 (cf. Barclay, *Obeying*, p. 137). He may be using the language of his opponents paradoxically to affirm that the *real* way to fulfil the Mosaic law is to love (so E.P. Sanders, *Law*, p. 97).

4. Furnish notes the distinctiveness of Paul's paradoxical formulation of freedom and slavery, observing that popular Hellenistic philosophers of his day would not agree that freedom consists or issues in a servant concern for others (*Command*, p. 97). Where did Paul get that idea? It is not unlike the example and teaching of the one who emptied himself and took the form of a δοῦλος (Phil. 2.7; cf. Rom. 15.8: Christ became a διάκονος). Albeit in different contexts, traditions as diverse as the Matthaean and Johannine preserve the dominical teaching that a δοῦλος is not greater than his κύριος (Mt. 10.24; Jn 13.16); in both instances the disciples are told to be like Jesus (Mt. 10.25; Jn 13.14-15). Matthew and Mark record the saying, 'Whoever would be first among you must be your slave' (Mt. 20.27; Mk: 'slave of all', 10.44; [cf. 1 Cor. 9.19]), and the footwashing in Jn 13 incarnates the teaching. Several of Jesus' parables employ the imagery of the householder/master/king and his δοῦλοι: the tares (Mt. 13.27-28), the unforgiving servant (Mt. 18.23-32), the wicked husbandmen (Mk 12.2, 4 // Mt. 21.34-36 // Lk. 20.10-11), the great supper

Romans 13, Paul justifies the command by asserting that the demand of the whole Mosaic law is fulfilled in love for the neighbour. He is not saying here that the law is simply 'summed up' by Lev. 19.18, for he differentiates πεπλήρωται and ἀνακεφαλαιοῦται in Rom. 13.8-9; what is more, πληροῦν never has that sense in the NT, LXX or any Greek writer.[1]

Paul's language has significance because there are few references in Jewish literature to 'fulfilling' the law.[2] Given the rarity of πληρῶ-

(Mt. 22.3-10 // Lk. 14.17-23), the faithful and the wicked servant (Mt. 24.45-50 // Lk. 12.43-47), the talents (Mk 13.34 // Mt. 25.14-30 // Lk. 19.13-27), the watchful servants (Lk. 12.37); cf. also Lk. 17.7-10. The use of the δοῦλος imagery was widespread in the Early Church (Jas 1.1; 1 Pet. 2.16; 2 Pet. 1.1; Jude 1; Rev. 1.1; 2.20; 7.3; 11.18; 19.2, 5; 22.3, 6). A Greek origin for the religious use of δοῦλος/δουλεύειν is out of the question (*TDNT*, II, pp. 261-65); on the other hand, the word group is common in the LXX, where it translates עבד. Paul sees himself and other Christian leaders as slaves of Christ/God (Gal. 1.10; Rom. 1.1; Phil. 1.1; 2 Cor. 4.5; Col. 4.12; cf. 2 Tim. 2.24; Tit. 1.1), but he does not reserve such language only for those in authority—delivered from bondage to sin, all Christians are to present themselves to God voluntarily as δοῦλοι for obedience (Rom. 6.16). Particularly striking is the similarity between Paul's language about slavery to sin and freedom (in Christ) in Rom. 6 and 7 (cf. 8.2) and the teaching in Jn 8.34-36. Writing with reference to Paul's teaching about human slavery to sin, Rengstorf notes, 'Das alles ist im Grunde nur eine Ausführung über ein Wort Jesu nach Johannes: πᾶς ὁ ποιῶν τὴν ἁμαρτίαν δοῦλός ἐστιν τῆς ἁμαρτίας. . . ' (*TDNT*, II, p. 277).

1. Cf., e.g., Burton (*Galatians*, p. 295) and Lightfoot (*Galatians*, p. 205), *contra*, e.g., the *NEB* and Mussner (*Galaterbrief*, p. 370).

2. There is no statement in the LXX linking πληροῦν with τὸν νόμον, and only a handful of texts use the verb in the sense of fulfilling a command (in addition to those cited in on p. 126 n. 3 above, see Philo, *Praem.* 83; *Sib. Or.* 3.246; ἀνα- Jos. *Ant.* 8.58), none of which use νόμος. In *m. Ab.* 4.9, R. Jonathan (c. 140, a disciple of Akiba) says 'He that fulfils the Law in poverty shall in the end fulfil it in wealth; and he that neglects the Law in wealth shall in the end neglect it in poverty'. Similarly, *Mek. Vayassa'* 1 (line 165; Lauterbach, II, p. 96; on Exod. 15.26) reads: 'if one is honest in his business dealings and the spirit of his fellow creatures takes delight in him, it is accounted to him as though he had fulfilled the whole Torah'. In both cases the verb is not מלא, but קיים (piel of קום), and means 'to establish, confirm, carry out, or keep', as in the performance of a vow (cf. *b. Yom.* 28b: 'Our father Abraham kept the whole Torah'). We would not expect to see the Greek equivalents using πληροῦν. In the LXX, קום is rendered often by ἱστάναι or βεβαιοῦν, but never by πληροῦν, whereas מלא is translated by πληροῦν but never by ἱστάναι. The situation is complicated by the fact, however, that a form of קיים renders מלא in the Targums (Ljungmann, *Gesetz*, p. 314).

σαι τὸν νόμον, Mt. 5.17 provides an important parallel: μὴ νομίσητε ὅτι ἦλθον καταλῦσαι τὸν νόμον ἢ τοὺς προφήτας· οὐκ ἦλθον καταλῦσαι ἀλλὰ πληρῶσαι.[1] Although the formula μὴ νομίσητε ὅ τι ἦλθον may be redactional (cf. Mt. 10.34 // Lk. 12.51), it seems inevitable that Jesus would have been challenged to say something about his relation to the law, and there is no compelling reason for rejecting the tradition.[2] Determining what it meant for Jesus and for the Matthaean community is more difficult, although the latter is more important for our study.[3] Moule thinks πληροῦν in Mt. 5.17 has the twofold nuance of meeting the full requirements and fulfilling prophecy. He writes, 'Insofar as the Law bears witness to the will of God as an ideal yet to be achieved, and the Prophets hold out hope of a time coming when it shall be fulfilled, one who perfectly fulfils the will of God confirms also the predictions of prophecy'.[4] If Moule is correct, and if our understanding of Paul's usage of πληροῦν in Rom. 13.8 and Gal. 5.14 is accurate, the similarity is striking.[5] The

1. The literature on Mt. 5.17-20 is vast; for extended discussions and bibliography see, e.g., Luz, 'Erfüllung'; R. Banks, *Law*, pp. 204-25; Meier, *Law*, pp. 65-89; Davies, 'Matthew 5:17-18'; Ljungmann, *Gesetz*, pp. 7-96.

2. *Contra* Bultmann, *History*, pp. 138, 163. 'The historicity of the saying is probable' (B.F. Meyer, *Aims*, p. 167); cf. R. Banks, *Law*, p. 212; Feuillet, 'Morale', p. 124; C.F.D. Moule, 'Fulfilment-words', pp. 317-18; Manson, *Sayings*, pp. 153-54; Davies, 'Matthew 5:17-18', pp. 35-37. Although πληροῦν is a favourite word of Matthew, the evangelist uses the word in a slightly different sense in 5.17 than elsewhere in his Gospel; cf. also its use in Mark (14.49) and Luke (4.21; 24.44).

3. πληρῶσαι here could mean 'to confirm or establish'; 'to bring to full expression its intention' or 'to extend its demands to a better or more transcendent righteousness'; 'to bring to completion'; 'to carry out/fully accomplish'; to 'fulfil' in the sense that the Scriptures point to Jesus; or a combination of these nuances. Of immediate relevance is the fact that it is set opposite καταλῦσαι; that it follows a saying emphasizing the importance of visible καλὰ ἔργα; that it functions as sort of heading for the material to come; and that for Matthew, *the law and prophets prophesied until John* (11.13)—they begin to find their prophetic fulfilment in Jesus' forerunner and pre-eminently in Jesus himself. Matthew almost always uses πληροῦν in a prophetic sense (Meier, *Law*, p. 80).

4. C.F.D. Moule, *IDB*, II, p. 328 col 2; *idem*, 'Fulfilment-words', p. 316. The fulfilment occurs not simply through the suffering and death of Jesus but in his teaching and practice as well, as indicated by the context (R. Banks, *Law*, p. 242).

5. Omitting the eschatological elements, Schniewind also saw a similarity: 'Jesus scheint die Ordnungen Gottes zu übertreten, in Wahrheit aber erfüllt er sie, d.h. er

language of 'fulfilment', though in itself not decisive, may favour Paul's dependence upon JT; at the very least it indicates that a presupposed christology lies behind the teaching of Gal. 5.14/Rom. 13.8-10, and that Paul's paraenesis here is not simply lifted from Jewish tradition.[1]

Galatians 6.2 and the Law of Christ

When in Gal. 6.2 Paul speaks of fulfilling (ἀναπληροῦν) the 'law of Christ', we have an explicit linkage of Christ and love (as manifested in bearing one another's burdens). It is tempting to conclude that the νόμος Χριστοῦ is none other than Lev. 19.18, cited shortly before in 5.14.[2] If that is correct, we have strong evidence that Paul knew the command not merely as an OT dictum, but as a teaching given great significance by Jesus. Unfortunately, what the apostle meant by the phrase is not so easy to unravel.

Whereas some consider the 'law of Christ' to refer to the teachings of Jesus as a new Torah,[3] others see Paul opposing just such a mentality.[4] Regardless of the source of the expression, a common interpreta-

---

hält sie und setzt sie in Geltung. . . Dasselbe zeigen Stellen wie Gal. 5,14; Röm. 13,8, wo, "das Gesetz erfüllen" so viel heisst wie: seine Forderung erfüllen, das vom Gesetz Verlangte tun' (*Matthäus*, p. 54; Ljungman, *Gesetz*, p. 33).

1. Cf. Badenas's conclusion: 'It seems that Paul's teleological understanding of the relation of Christ to the law does not differ from the view that Christ himself had of that relationship according to the gospels. . . ' (*Christ*, p. 263). Having stated that he has come to 'fulfil' the law, Jesus expounds his understanding of the righteousness that exceeds that of the Pharisees (5.20). Although Paul generally emphasizes righteousness as a gift from God, he too sees the importance of ethical righteousness beyond that of the self-confident Jew (Rom. 2; 6.16-22). Worth exploring is the possibility of a link between Jesus' declaration that he must be baptized 'to fulfil all righteousness' (πληρῶσαι πᾶσαν δικαιοσύνην; Mt. 3.15; cf. Ign. *Smyrn*. 1.1), and Paul's claim that Christ is the τέλος of the law εἰς δικαιοσύνην (Rom. 10.4); Hippolytus saw a connection (*Theoph*. 5). Hatch likens the πληροῦν/ καταλῦσαι combination in Mt. 5.17 to Paul's ἱστάνειν/καταργεῖν contrast in Rom. 3.31, but does not speak of any dependence ('Summary', p. 132).

2. Bruce sees Paul depending on Jesus' teaching in Gal. 5.14 and thinks that is perhaps why he calls this tradition 'the law of Christ' (*Galatians*, p. 242).

3. E.g., Davies, *Paul*, p. 144; cf. also Dodd, '῎Εννομος', p. 147. For criticism see, e.g., Räisänen, *Paul*, pp. 78-82.

4. So, e.g., H.D. Betz, who thinks the expression 'law of Christ' came from

tion takes it to refer to the basic principle of love. Paul nowhere defines the νόμος Χριστοῦ, but in context its application is clear: the law of Christ is fulfilled by bearing one another's burdens, a concrete act of love for the neighbour. Only a few verses before, Paul has urged that the whole law is fulfilled in one λόγος, 'You shall love your neighbour as yourself' (5.14), and there is nothing in the intervening verses to establish a higher principle that could be identified as the 'law of Christ'. Paul's passing reference to the νόμος Χριστοῦ without clarification assumes that his readers will understand. The parallel commands of mutual obligation in 5.13 (δουλεύετε ἀλλήλοις) and 6.2 (ἀλλήλων τὰ βάρη βαστάζετε) confirm the link in thought: Paul is speaking in the latter passage of a specific way in which love is worked out in the life of the church. Finally, this interpretation finds support in James' statements about the perfect law, the law of liberty (1.25; 2.12), which most likely refers to the νόμον βασιλικόν (2.8) identified closely with (if not identical to) Lev. 19.18.[1]

Despite the attractiveness of the last view, it needs to be supplemented with elements of truth from other options. Betz is probably right to say that Paul used the expression only because he did not want to be misunderstood as an antinomian; the only other time Paul refers to a 'law' of Christ is 1 Cor. 9.21, where his claim to be ἔννομος Χριστοῦ is a reaction to that which might be imputed to him. Davies is right in seeing νόμος Χριστοῦ as including teachings of Jesus which were important for Paul, but he is misleading in his implication that the law of Christ was primarily dominical logia—a code of precepts. Confident of the guidance of the Spirit of Christ, the apostles appropriated other ideas and teachings from diverse sources (e.g. the wisdom tradition, Noahic commandments, Stoic elements, prophetic revelations from the Spirit) which they added to supplement a controlling core of words of Jesus. Would they consider these 'baptized' additions something less than the will of Christ for them? The νόμος Χριστοῦ is thus probably a convenient shorthand for the way in which the early Christians perceived that the Lord Christ would have

Paul's opponents in Galatia (*Galatians*, pp. 300-301); cf. also Brinsmead, *Galatians*, pp. 175-78.

1. The phrase in 1.25 has parallels in Stoic thought, as well as in Philo and other Jewish writings (Dibelius, *James*, pp. 116-20), but the presence of so many dominical echoes in the letter supports my interpretation (cf. Davids, *Epistle*, pp. 99-100).

them walk (τὸ πῶς δεῖ ὑμᾶς περιπατεῖν καὶ ἀρέσκειν θεῷ, 1 Thess. 4.1)—a way comprising the apostolic teaching about what it meant to be a Christian.[1] As such it could also be called ἡ ὁδὸς τοῦ Κυρίου/ θεοῦ (Acts 18.25-26) or ἡ ὁδὸς τοῦ τῆς ζωῆς (*Did.* 2.2), although we do not find the expression 'the way of Christ' in the NT or the AF.[2] It is summarized and epitomized by Jesus' double commandment (cf. *Did.* 1.2), which is then interpreted by Paul in terms of faith towards God and love for the neighbour. This understanding of the νόμος Χριστοῦ is broad enough to include the ἐντολαὶ θεοῦ, the keeping of which Paul sets on a level with faith working through love and a new creation (1 Cor. 7.19; Gal. 5.6; 6.15).[3] For Paul, what the apostles say, Christ says, and what Christ says, God says (cf. 1 Thess. 4.8; 2.13).[4] Christ's word (whether from JT or Spirit-led apostolic teaching) is to be obeyed. At the same time, saying cannot be divorced from doing, and obedience to the law of Christ is effected through Spirit-enabled imitation of Christ (1 Cor. 10.33–11.1; Phil. 2.5-13), whose life, death and resurrection more than validated his teachings.[5] It is thus likely that Gal. 6.2 should be taken with 5.14 to show that the 'fulfilment' of the law by obedience to Lev. 19.18 meant for Paul obedience to the 'law of Christ', which *at least* was believed to have included Jesus' own emphasis on love.

Love for the Neighbour and the Summary of the Law
Rom. 13.8-10 most clearly parallels JT in two respects: the choice of Lev. 19.18 as the epitome of the law, and its elevation to supreme

1. It would thus include some of the παραγγελίαι given to the Thessalonians διὰ τοῦ κυρίου Ἰησοῦ (1 Thess. 4.2).
2. ἡ ὁδός stands for the Christian faith in Acts 9.2; 19.9, 23; 22.4; 24.14, 22. The metaphor appears frequently; cf. exhortations to 'walk' κατὰ ἀγάπην (Rom. 14.15; cf. Eph. 5.2), πνεύματι (Gal. 5.16), ἐν καινότητι ζωῆς (Rom. 6.4), ἀξίως τοῦ θεοῦ (1 Thess. 2.12), ὡς τέκνα φωτός (Eph. 5.8; cf. 1 Jn 1.7). Paul speaks of a better way, the way of love, in 1 Cor. 12.31. In the AF, the common expression is 'the way of righteousness' or 'the way of light' (e.g. *Barn.* 1.4; 19.1).
3. Cf. R. Banks, *Law*, p. 244. Paul can call for keeping the commands of God while rejecting circumcision because he is concerned not about previous OT commands, but with the present will of God for the Church.
4. There may be here yet another indication of dominical influence; cf. Lk. 10.16 // Mt. 10.40; Jn 5.23; 12.48; 15.23, and the parallels in *Did.* 11.2, 4; 1 Jn 2.23.
5. Barclay takes the phrase ὁ νόμος τοῦ Χριστοῦ to refer to the (Mosaic) law 'as redefined and fulfilled by Christ in love' (*Obeying*, p. 134).

importance as an ethical norm.[1] Both aspects appear in the question about the greatest commandment (Mk 12.28-34 // Mt. 22.34-40).[2] Matthew and Mark agree verbally with Paul, quoting LXX Lev 19.18 verbatim. Matthew's account is slightly closer to Paul, since he has Jesus add that all the Law and Prophets 'hang' (κρέμαται) on the two commandments (22.40), that is, are derivable from them,[3] a common rabbinic idea comparable to Paul's use of ἀνακεφαλαιοῦσθαι (Rom. 13.9). Mark's account appears to be more original insofar as Luke and Matthew turn it into a controversy dialogue by deleting the questioner's positive response and imputing to him the motive of 'tempting' Jesus. Luke has the combination of Deut. 6.5 and Lev. 19.18 in a different context (10.25-28), with a lawyer giving the answer, but it is uncertain whether he is relating the same incident. Fuller reconstructs the tradition and thinks the original contained four Semitisms, which would suggest it goes back to a Palestinian milieu, the earliest Aramaic-speaking community.[4]

Love for the neighbour was a common theme in Judaism, finding expression in Tob. 4.15 (the negative form of the 'golden rule'), *Ep. Arist.* 207, and in the *Testaments of the Twelve Patriarchs*.[5] The combination of love of God and love of the neighbour also has early Jewish roots both in the *Testaments of the Twelve Patriarchs*[6] and

---

1. So Bultmann: 'in this respect. . . Paul is in complete accord with Jesus: the real demand of the law is love, in which all the other commandments are summed up' ('Jesus', p. 189).

2. Jesus quotes Lev. 19.18 again in Mt. 5.43; 19.19b, and characterizes the 'golden rule' with the words οὗτος γάρ ἐστιν ὁ νόμος καὶ οἱ προφῆται (Mt. 7.12b) but these texts are suspected to be redactional (cf., e.g., Neirynck, 'Sayings', p. 292). Even so, they evidence the early *belief* that Jesus emphasized the centrality of Lev. 19.18.

3. So, e.g., Gerhardsson, *Memory*, p. 138; Daube, *Testament*, pp. 247-51.

4. 'Commandment', pp. 46-47. He cites as evidence the inversion of verb and subject in the introduction, the phrase 'one from', omission of copula in the question and the usage of ἐν as meaning 'with'.

5. Stauffer, *TDNT*, I, p. 40. Cf. Syriac *Menander*, 250-55; *T. Reub.* 6.9; *T. Zeb.* 5.3; 6.6; 8.3; 7.2; *T. Gad* 4.2; *T. Benj.* 4.3; and Baarda's discussion in *OTP*, II, p. 587.

6. For example, *T. Dan.* 5.3; *T. Iss.* 5.2; 7.6; *T. Benj.* 3.3-4; also possibly the two unspecified commandments of *T. Naph.* 8.9; cf. Berger, *Gesetzesauslegung*, pp. 160-62. Fitzmyer doubts the significance of the evidence from *Test. XII Patr.* in view of the problems of dating and interpolation (*Luke*, II, p. 879), but there is no

Philo,[1] although the evidence does not reflect the joining of the specific texts of Deut. 6.5 and Lev. 19.18.[2] The idea that a commandment could epitomize other laws was certainly not new. Philo states that the ten words of the Decalogue are summaries (κεφάλαια) of laws recorded in the Sacred books (*Decal.* 36, 51, 121; cf. also 156, 158, 168), and the rabbis' pursuit for the greater summarizing principle(s) of the Torah is well known.[3] R. Simlai's famous statement about the 613 precepts communicated to Moses, and the following comments about subsequent reductions of the number of virtues in *b. Mak.* 23b-24a reflect the rabbis' search for the connection between the many commands and one underlying principle (כלל). Often cited in this regard is Hillel's dictum, 'What is hateful to you, do not to your neighbour: that is the whole Torah, while the rest is the commentary thereof; go and learn it' (*b. Shab.* 31a).[4] On form-critical grounds, Neusner doubts the authenticity of this attribution, but in the light of similar teaching elsewhere in the rabbinic literature there seems no strong reason to reject the antiquity of the saying.[5] In *Gen. Rab.* 24.7 we read the words of two second-century rabbis,

reason why the combination of love for God and love for the neighbour could not have been formulated in Judaism before Jesus, as the *Test. XII Patr.* would appear to indicate. 'An interpolator is not likely to have been so subtle as to disguise in every case his reminiscence of the Gospel' (G.F. Moore, *Judaism*, II, p. 86 n. 3). The construction ἀγαπᾶν ἐν. . . καὶ ἐν with the dative in *T. Dan.* 5.3 and the discovery of fragments of some of the *Testaments* at Qumran (4QTLevi, 4QTNaph, 4QTBenj) indicate that the combination probably began on Palestinian soil (cf. Fuller, 'Commandment', p. 50).

1. For example, *Spec. Leg.* 2.63; *Virt.* 51; cf. Berger, *Gesetzesauslegung*, pp. 156-60.

2. Fuller, 'Commandment', p. 50; Fitzmyer, *Luke*, I, p. 878.

3. See Gerhardsson, *Memory*, pp. 137-40.

4. Abrahams thought the negative golden rule ultimately goes back to Ps. 14[15].3, and that it lay behind Paul's words in Rom. 13.10: ἡ ἀγάπη τῷ πλησίον κακὸν οὐκ ἐργάζεται (*Studies*, I, p. 21).

5. Cf. Hübner, 'Gesetz', p. 249 n. 40, *contra* Neusner, *Traditions*, I, pp. 338-39; III, pp. 262-63. The saying is repeated in a slightly different form in *ARN* 2.26. *Tg. Ps.-J. Lev.* 19.18, 34, and *y. Ned.* 9.41c lines 36-38 preserve the negative golden rule without the idea of summarizing, and a positive variant of Hillel's rule appears in a saying attributed to R. Eliezer in *ARN* 15.1. For other parallels see Abrahams, *Studies*, I, p. 21 and Meecham, *Version*, pp. 292-97.

Ben 'Azzai said, *This is the book of the descendants of Adam* is a great principle of the Torah (זה כלל גדול בתורה). R. Akiba said: *But thou shalt love thy neighbour as thyself* [Lev. xix, 18] is even a greater principle.[1]

The idea of Rom. 13.9 finds a further parallel in *m. Pe'ah* 4.19: 'Charity (צדקה) and deeds of loving-kindness are equal to all the mitsvot in the Torah'.[2] It would appear that in thought and expression, Paul's teaching of love for the neighbour as a summary of the whole law was probably already familiar in contemporary Jewish thought.[3]

Does this then make it any less likely that Paul was relying on dominical tradition in Romans 13? Not really. First, even if the extra-biblical parallels are allowed full weight, their existence demonstrates no more than that a good Jewish teacher could be expected to say something like that attributed to Jesus. Jesus was probably asked on many occasions what he thought was most important, and the fact that the saying could have Jewish precedents may argue against Jesus' originality, but not against the authenticity of the logion.[4] There is little reason to doubt that in his teaching, Jesus linked the *Shema* with Lev. 19.18 as a summary of the law.[5] The tradition finds support not only in the witness of the Synoptics but also in other early Christian writings (1 Jn 4.21; *Did.* 1.2; Pol. *Phil.* 3).[6] These texts support the *a priori* expectation that Paul would know Lev. 19.18

1. For other texts and exposition cf. Abrahams, *Studies*, I, pp. 18-29.
2. Cited by E.P. Sanders, *Paul*, p. 113.
3. So, e.g., Dodd, *Romans*, p. 207; E.P. Sanders, *Paul*, pp. 112-14.
4. So also E. Schweizer, *Mark*, pp. 251-52.
5. *Contra* Berger, who thinks the command for neighbour-love was subsequently added to an original *Hauptgebot* (Deut. 6.5) under the influence of paraenetic interest seen in, e.g., Rom. 13.9; Gal. 5.14; and Mt. 7.12 (*Gesetzesauslegung*, pp. 64, 189-90), and Burchard, who grants the unity of the double command but contests its authenticity in view of the extra-biblical parallels ('Liebesgebot', pp. 50-51, 61). Both stumble over Jesus' twofold answer to a question asking for one, 'but the unexpectedness of the answer does not necessarily militate against its originality' (Neirynck, 'Sayings', p. 293). Fuller considers the fact that the paraenetic tradition attests only the second half to be evidence for the authenticity for the double form ('Command', p. 47). Bornkamm (*Jesus*, pp. 99-100), Fitzmyer (*Luke*, II, p. 879), and most others favour authenticity.
6. Justin Martyr may be dependent on Matthew's Gospel, but he quotes Lev. 19.18 as one of the two commandments in which Jesus said that all righteousness and godliness was fulfilled (πληροῦσθαι; *Dial.* 93.2). Although later than Paul, this attests the belief that Jesus linked Lev. 19.18 with the fulfilment of the law.

not only from the OT but as an emphasis of Jesus.

Secondly, despite the Jewish parallels to Jesus' and Paul's summarizing of the law, alongside those summaries there always remained in Judaism the demand for obedience to the whole law.[1] The rabbis' practice of condensing and abridging the law into general principles was motivated by the desire to facilitate transmission and retention of the law's teaching, but was never an end in itself; the goal was mastery of the law in all of its particulars.[2] This is quite different from the teaching of Jesus and Paul. In neither the Synoptic Gospels nor in Paul's letters is there any expectation that the readers were expected to conform to *all* of the precise stipulations of the OT law code, Mt. 5.18-19 notwithstanding. So, for, example Morton Smith sees a difference between the thrust of the μεγάλη καὶ πρώτη ἐντολή in Mt. 22.38 and the rabbinic texts about the כלל גדול. In contrast to Matthew's text, 'great' in Akiba's saying means 'logically prior': 'that rule which includes by implication all the rest'. In Matthew, 'great' means 'morally pre-eminent'—the most important. 'In short, the two sentences have nothing in common but their structure and the word "great"'.[3] Paul adopts a rabbinic method of expression in his use of ἀνακεφαλαιοῦσθαι, but his main point is by no means the same. He speaks of neighbour-love summarizing the law in order to go on to conclude that love is what *really* matters, more so than legal scruples (cf. Mt. 9.13; 12.7; Mk 12.33). Such a perspective was without real parallel within contemporary Judaism,[4] but was at least implicit in the teaching of Jesus.[5]

1. Abrahams, *Studies*, I, pp. 24-25.
2. So Daube: 'though by the time of Jesus most Rabbis held that the entire religion was implied in a small number of first principles, or even into a single one. . . yet they never ceased to insist on the absolute and independent validity of each particular commandment' (*Testament*, p. 251; cf. Gerhardsson, *Memory*, pp. 136-48; G.F. Moore, *Judaism*, II, pp. 83-88; E.P. Sanders, *Paul*, pp. 112-14).
3. *Parallels*, p. 138; cf. R. Banks, *Law*, p. 171.
4. Berger argues for the existence of antinomian groups within Hellenistic Judaism which reduced the cultic demands of the Torah (*Gesetzesauslegung*); for refutation of his view see Hübner, 'Mark 7.1-23', pp. 326-37, and Räisänen, *Paul*, pp. 34-41. Philo (*Migr. Abr.* 89-93) speaks of some allegorizers who give up Sabbath, feast days and circumcision, but they do so for different reasons than the Christians, and Philo criticizes their failure to observe the ritual laws.
5. Davies speaks of a 'principle of reticence' in the ministry of Jesus, determined by Jesus' awareness that he could not supersede the teaching of the OT law until he

A third reason to see use of JT is the likelihood that Paul is appealing to teaching he knows is familiar to the Romans (cf. Rom. 6.17; 15.14-15). His freedom not to qualify or expand his statements about fulfilling the law makes sense if his readers already knew a similar tradition.[1] Sanders observes that Paul does not often cite commandments as the ground for his ethics; he expected correct behaviour to flow naturally from living by the Spirit. In 1 Corinthians 10, for instance, Paul does not appeal to a commandment to show idolatry to be wrong, but provides typological and christological arguments to make his point.[2] Likewise, in 1 Cor. 9.8-9 and 14.21, 34, Paul cites the law in his ethical admonition, but he uses it in an illustrative and/or confirmative fashion, rather than as the decisive argument.[3] Consequently, his choice to use a commandment in Rom. 13.9 (and Gal. 5.14) is unusual, and the commandment he chooses just happens to be that which Christ elevated to primary importance.[4] Nevertheless, against the claim that Paul is influenced by dominical tradition in Rom. 13.8-10 there lie three objections, to which I now turn.

had proved his right to do so by his death: 'This is a kind of dogmatic reason, we suggest, why there is no explicit or unequivocal public annulment of the Law on the lips of Jesus but only an implicit one: there were some things that His death alone could utter about the Law as about His own person' ('Matthew 5:17-18', p. 56).

1. Käsemann (*Romans*, p. 361) draws attention to the lack of polemic against the law here.

2. E.P. Sanders, *Law*, p. 95.

3. Gutbrod, *TDNT*, IV, p. 1077.

4. Cf. R. Banks's conclusion (*Law*, pp. 244-45 n. 4): 'The teaching of Jesus is . . . quite clearly the presupposition for Paul's teaching on the Law. In each, though its God-given nature is affirmed (Matt. 15.6; cf. Rom. 7.12, 22; Gal. 3.21), it does not form part of the primary will of God (Matt. 19.8; cf. Gal. 3.17ff.); the "love-commandment" is the "essence" of the Law (Matt. 22.40; cf. Rom. 13.9-10) and the principle of the "weaker brother" is an element in the observance or non-observance of its requirements (Matt. 17.24-7; cf. Rom. 14.1ff.); it stands as a condemnation of those who are disobedient to God (Matt. 19.8; cf. 1 Tim. 1.9ff.) yet it cannot bring eternal life (Matt. 19.21; cf. Rom. 3.20ff.; Gal. 2.16ff.) nor even sanctification (Matt. 5.21ff.; cf. Gal. 3.1ff.; Col. 2.16ff.); it is a testimony against men to his ministry (Matt. 8.4; cf. Gal. 3.24) and ultimately it finds its end in him (Matt. 5.17; cf. Rom. 10.4).'

2. *Objections to Dominical Influence*

Omission of the First Great Commandment

If Paul knew Jesus' summary of the law in the two commandments, why does he quote only the second? The simplest answer is that in context he is concerned with the ethical aspect of the Torah, for he quotes only from the second table of laws—those governing relations with one another, not with God.[1] I have already noted that when Paul alludes to Prov. 3.4 in Rom. 12.17 he preserves only half of the saying, omitting the reference to God; if Paul has echoed the Caesar logion in 13.7, he has omitted the second member of a saying yet again. This should not surprise us, because Paul's purpose here is not to educate the Romans in the Gospel tradition but to provide practical admonition about how to behave towards one another. Having begun this segment of the Epistle with a call for full commitment in order to discern and obey the will of God, Paul is focusing on the discovery of that will. There is no reference to love for God here, for the whole of Paul's ethical exhortation in chs. 12 and 13 presupposes it in faith's thankful response to God's mercies (Rom. 12.1-2).[2]

Lack of Reference to Jesus

Instead of claiming the authority of Jesus, which presumably would have immediately secured his point, Paul prefers to argue, explaining the primacy of love by appealing to the law. The fact that he grounds his case solely on reason could reflect a belief that the mere statement was not peculiar to Christianity.[3] Barrett suggests that Paul wanted to avoid a new legalism, but other factors offer a better explanation.[4] In addition to Paul's familiarity with the OT (see Chapter 6), we should observe that Jesus himself apparently appealed to the OT (including

---

1. For example, Davies, *Setting*, pp. 405-407. Philo divides the Decalogue into two sets of commands in *Decal.* 51, 121.

2. Cf. Spicq, *Agapé*, I, pp. 261-62; Furnish, *Command*, p. 110. Although he often speaks of God's (or Christ's) love for humankind (Rom. 5.5; 8.35, 39; 2 Cor. 5.14; 13.13; 2 Thess. 3.5), or human love for humankind (Rom. 13.8-9; 14.15; 1 Cor. 4.21; 2 Cor. 12.15; Gal. 5.13; Col. 1.4; 1 Thess. 4.9), Paul rarely speaks of human love for God (Rom. 8.28; 1 Cor. 2.9; 8.3; 16.22). Instead he writes primarily of *faith* towards God; for one explanation, see Davies, *Setting*, p. 407.

3. Cf. Abrahams, *Studies*, I, p. 19.

4. *Romans*, p. 241.

these very texts)—his followers could be expected to do the same. More importantly, Paul did not see Christ invalidating or nullifying the OT in general but *fulfilling* it, hence the apostle does not hesitate to use it for examples and to show how it pointed to Christ (e.g. 1 Cor. 10.4, 6, 11; Rom. 4.23-24; 15.4). This is precisely what he does in Rom. 15.3 where he quotes Psalm 68[69] with reference to the sufferings of Jesus. Paul prefers to project Jesus through the lens of the OT prophecy, to show that the coming of Christ was no rupture in God's plan of salvation, but its accomplishment.[1] Bringing in the law here in his exhortation is a master stroke, as Paul writes to Jewish Christians who scrupulously kept its precepts but condemned their Gentile brethren, and to Gentile believers who saw the law as irrelevant. Coupled with the fact that the apostle probably assumed that his readers would recognize the teaching as part of their Christian instruction, and that from the nature of paraenesis one should not expect to find sources cited by name, the objection from the absence of reference to Jesus in this passage loses its force.

The Limited Scope of Neighbour-love
H. Montefiore contrasts Jesus' call for love for *all* persons with the admonitions of Paul and other early Christians to love the brethren.[2] Nevertheless, the apostle is not excluding love for those outside the faith in Rom. 13.8-10 (cf. Rom. 12.14-21; 1 Thess. 3.12; 5.15; Phil. 4.5; Gal. 6.10), only emphasizing the importance of love among his readers. Since the NT letters were written to deal with problems within the churches, we would expect to find stress on love for the brethren. It does not follow that Paul would normally restrict the meaning of 'neighbour' to 'fellow Christian', in contrast to the teaching of Jesus.

3. Conclusion

The fact that Paul chooses to ground his call to love in the OT without appealing to Jesus, and the general absence of dominical indicators in 13.8-10 render a dominical allusion here at best only a possibility. Nevertheless, there are a number of clues which, when taken together,

---

1. Cf. Lyonnet, 'Charité', pp. 157-58.
2. 'Neighbour', pp. 161-63.

make it virtually certain that Paul is not simply reflecting traditional Jewish thought, but is applying to the Romans' situation an emphasis he knew to be that of Jesus. The call to love one another and the citation of Lev. 19.18 as the summary of the law are deeply rooted in Jewish tradition, but they have impeccable credentials as teachings of Jesus as well, and Paul was writing to a group of Christians. The centrality of Christ in his theology, Paul's understanding of the OT as bearing witness to Jesus, and the apostle's experiences as a well-travelled Christian (accompanied at times by those such as Barnabas and Silvanus, who certainly knew traditions from Jerusalem) make the supposition that he was ignorant of this central teaching as the message of Jesus incredible, and if Paul ever knew it as dominical, he would not forget that. Although the 'law of Christ' should probably not be restricted to love alone, the connection of Gal. 5.14 and 6.2, together with other early Christian texts from different traditions, indicates that the νόμος Χριστοῦ at least included love for the neighbour as the epitome of the law, a teaching most likely derived from Jesus. If Paul knew that when he wrote Galatians, he would not have overlooked it when he wrote Romans. Choosing to use πληροῦν and πλήρωμα with reference to the law puts him outside the usual Jewish conventions and squarely within the stream of Christian thought that sees full obedience to the real ethical thrust of the OT law possible only in the aeon of the messiah. Whether or not Paul knew the logion behind Mt. 5.17 (if it is not redactional), he agreed with the Synoptic writers that in Christ the purposes of God were 'fulfilled'; more than likely his notion of Christians 'fulfilling' the law derives from the belief that Jesus did so supremely, and they are to follow his example. Paul began his paraenesis with a call to progressive transformation (into the image of Christ, 12.2) and will now go on to conclude the general exhortation with the admonition ἐνδύσασθε τὸν κύριον Ἰησοῦν Χριστόν (13.14). This *inclusio* should tell us something about the shape of the admonitions that fall between. Paul is painting a portrait of Christian behaviour for the Romans, and the face on the canvas is that of Jesus.

Chapter 9

ROMANS 13.11-14: THE DAY IS NEAR

In 13.11-14 Paul turns to the Christian hope as a final motivation for the behaviour outlined in chs. 12–13. His readers are to live galvanized by the knowledge that Christ's coming is near, and with it, their full entry into resurrection life. After an eschatological *Wächterruf* in 13.11-12b, Paul draws the ethical conclusion in 13.12c-14, continuing the use of the day/night imagery. Because they belong to the day, they should put away the works of darkness and put on the armour of light, specifically avoiding drunkenness, fornication and contention. In contrast to that behaviour they should put on the Lord Jesus Christ, and stop satisfying any desires of the flesh. Recalling eschatological, baptismal, and christological themes implicit in 12.1-2, these last four verses serve as a caption for the intervening material.

1. *Romans 13.11-14 and the Teachings of Jesus*

Paul's general perspective on the parousia in Rom. 13.11 (and elsewhere) is similar to that of logia attributed to Jesus in the Gospels, inasmuch as Paul maintains a sense of urgency and expectancy while refusing to commit himself to date-setting. The return of Christ is certain, it is near, but its date cannot be calculated.[1] To ask when the coming age would arrive was natural (cf. Mt. 24.3; Acts 1.6; *4 Ezra* 4.33; 6.7; 8.63-9.2), yet in contrast to the explicitness of the author of *4 Ezra*, Paul does not even go so far as to speculate within the safety of symbolism.[2] Although this reluctance may be attributed simply to

---

1. Cf. Mk 13.32, 35; Mt. 24.44; Lk. 12.40. However, Mk 9.1; 13.30; and Mt. 10.23 can be taken as expecting the coming of the Son of Man within a generation (just as Rom. 13.11 is sometimes interpreted).

2. Contrast *4 Ezra* 14.10-13: 'the age has lost its youth, and the times begin to

the better part of wisdom, the same perspective appears elsewhere in the early Christian tradition in sources which show a knowledge of Jesus tradition (Jas 5.7-8; 1 Pet. 4.7, 13; 5.4; *Did.* 16.1); if this particular tendency goes back to Jesus,[1] the likelihood increases that Paul also knows that it does.[2] Paul most probably reflects knowledge of eschatological dominical traditions in 1 Thessalonians 4–5.[3] Strong evidence for this is the 'thief in the night' imagery of Mt. 24.43 and Lk. 12.39, which is unparalleled outside 1 Thess. 5.2, 4; 2 Pet. 3.10; Rev. 3.3; 16.15; and *Gos. Thom.* 21.[4] If Paul is aware of the thief parable, he knows its application—the necessity of staying alert—

grow old. For the age is divided into twelve parts, and nine of its parts have already passed, as well as half of the tenth part; so two of its parts remain, besides half of the tenth part.' Like the evangelists, Paul speaks of the signs which precede the coming of Messiah (cf. 2 Thess. 2), but he draws up no absolute calendar.

1. As argued by, e.g., Beasley-Murray (*Commentary*, pp. 1-18). Commenting on Mk 13.32 V. Taylor remarks, 'Of its genuineness there can be no reasonable doubt' (*Mark*, p. 522; *contra* Bultmann, *History*, pp. 125-26).

2. 'The idea that the early church, because of its eschatological and charismatic fervour, was uninterested in the historical Jesus, is hardly tenable. It is more probably the case that the early church's eschatological fervour was the *result* of its familiarity with the traditions of the eschatological discourse, since these were known and received as authoritative dominical teaching from a very early period' (D. Wenham, *Rediscovery*, p. 372)

3. Cf., e.g., D. Wenham ('Apocalypse'; *idem*, *Rediscovery* [*passim*]), Waterman ('Sources'), and Orchard ('Thessalonians'); all of the foregoing cite 2 Thess. 2 as well. On the differences in context and motivation cf. Selwyn, *1 Peter*, p. 380. Although more sceptical than any of the former, E.P. Sanders writes, 'In any case, the similarities between this passage and the Synoptic depictions of the Son of man coming with angels, accompanied by the sound of a trumpet, while some are still alive. . . are so close that it is difficult to avoid the conclusion that both reflect a tradition which, before Paul, was already attributed to Jesus. . . Paul's expectation of the coming of the Lord. . . is not his own creation, but was doubtless held in common with other Christians. The early teachers and apostles changed the expectation of the Son of man coming with his angels to the *return* of the Lord, just as in the synoptic tradition they identified the Son of Man with Jesus; but the *general* expectation probably goes back to Jesus' (*Jesus*, pp. 144-45).

4. D. Wenham, 'Apocalypse', pp. 347, 366 n. 8. The original reference to the Son of Man coming as a thief is transferred to the coming of the day of the Lord in some texts (1 Thess. 5.2; 2 Pet. 3.10), possibly because the simile was considered unseemly.

although with a slightly different nuance.[1] Rom. 13.11 parallels 1 Thessalonians 4–5 in a number of respects, and there is no reason to think that Paul has forgotten a teaching he echoed only a half dozen years before.[2] Several other clues in the passage point to the possible influence of dominical tradition.

'Knowing the Time'

Paul is concerned to remind the Romans of the significance of the time in which they live (13.11). καιρός does not refer to the 'fateful and decisive point. . . which recurs with each moment of the Christian life', 'the eternal Moment', or 'the moment of destiny'.[3] The word can mean a point in time (e.g. Rom. 5.6), but here it refers to a period— the present age (Rom. 3.26; 8.18; 11.5; 2 Cor. 8.14; cf. Mk 10.30; Lk. 18.30), the end of which will be marked by the parousia of Christ.[4] Some texts depict Jesus stressing his followers' need to be aware of the significance of the καιρός during his ministry on earth. In Mt. 16.1-4, Jesus criticizes the Pharisees and Sadduccees for seeking a sign from him; they can tell the weather from the appearance of the sky, but they are not able διακρίνειν τὰ σημεῖα τῶν καιρῶν. They should recognize that God is confronting them and calling for radical obedience, offering them a kingdom unlike that which they expect. Differing from Matthew's version in setting (the audience is now simply οἱ ὄχλοι), the Lukan version of this saying is closer to

1. That is, an appeal to those outside the group of Jesus' followers has become a warning to Church members and leaders. The change is occasioned by the new situation after the death and resurrection of Jesus.

2. Cf. περιπατῆτε εὐσχημόνως (Rom. 13.13; 1 Thess. 4.12); καιρός (Rom. 13.11; 1 Thess. 5.1 [plural]); ἡμέρα (referring to the coming day of the Lord: Rom. 13.12; 1 Thess. 5.2); σκότος (Rom. 13.12; 1 Thess. 5.4); νύξ (Rom. 13.12; 1 Thess. 5.5, 7); appeal to their belonging to the day (Rom. 13.12; 1 Thess. 5.4-5); warning against sleep (Rom. 13.11; 1 Thess. 5.6); warning against drunkenness (Rom. 13.13; 1 Thess. 5.7); call to put on armour (ἐνδύεσθαι, Rom. 13.12; 1 Thess. 5.8); appeal to future salvation (Rom. 13.11; 1 Thess. 5.9). Whereas Rom. 13.8-10 expounds the thought found in Gal. 5.13-14, Rom. 13.11-14 compresses the teaching in 1 Thess. 5.4-11.

3. The phrases are from Delling (*TDNT*, III, pp. 459-60), K. Barth (*Romans*, pp. 497-98), and Käsemann (*Romans*, p. 362), respectively. Schlier is closer: 'die eschatologische Entscheidungszeit, die jetzt angebrochen ist und in der sie jetzt leben' (*Römerbrief*, p. 396).

4. Cf. Barrett, *Romans*, p. 252.

Paul's wording. There is no request for a sign, and the 'weather fore-
casts' are different, but the criticism is the same: ὑποκριταί, τὸ
πρόσωπον τῆς γῆς καὶ τοῦ οὐρανοῦ οἴδατε δοκιμάζειν, τὸν
καιρὸν δὲ τοῦτον πῶς οὐκ οἴδατε δοκιμάζειν (Lk. 12.56). 'Here
the hearers are asked to consider the gravity of the times and the need
to "get right with God" while there is still time.'[1] A similar idea
appears when Jesus weeps over Jerusalem in Lk. 19.41-44 because the
people do not know the things that make for peace. As a result,
Jerusalem will be destroyed, ἀνθ' ὧν οὐκ ἔγνως τὸν καιρὸν τῆς
ἐπισκοπῆς σου—because they did not grasp the significance of Jesus'
presence with them. In Mk 13.33, Jesus calls his disciples to watch and
be alert, for they do not know when the time (of the coming of the
Son of Man) is (οὐκ οἴδατε γὰρ πότε ὁ καιρός ἐστιν).[2] Here we
have similar vocabulary, but a different idea—καιρός is not, as in the
examples above, the immediate object of οἴδατε, and it refers to a
future event instead of the present. Nevertheless, Paul's language
could represent an understood contrast to this:[3] although Christians do
not know the time of the parousia, they know that the present time
will eventually culminate in that future event, and that what happens
in this age has significance in the age to come. If Paul was aware of
one or more of the traditions behind these dominical sayings (the most
likely being Luke 12 and Mark 13), he uses similar language in
another sense, yet so as to reinforce the intention behind the original
logia. His could be a deliberate reorientation that calls his readers to
readiness for the future while focusing on the importance of the present. Whether or not Paul's use of this language is the conscious or
unconscious result of meditation on the words of Jesus, the Romans
are to do what the Gospel audiences failed to do—know the
significance of the time.

---

1. Manson, *Ethics*, p. 96. Although he rejects Matthew's application of the
warning to the Pharisees and Sadduccees, Bultmann does not deny the authenticity of
Luke's version, stating 'it is impossible for any Jewish tradition to provide an origin'
(*History*, pp. 53, 126, 128).

2. Cf. the response of the risen Christ when queried about the timing of the
coming kingdom: οὐχ ὑμῶν ἐστιν γνῶναι χρόνους ἢ καιρούς (Acts 1.7).

3. Paul is capable of using καιρός with reference to the parousia (e.g. 1 Cor.
4.5).

The Danger of Sleep

Paul's call to rise up from sleep (ἐξ ὕπνου ἐγερθῆναι) resembles Jesus' warning lest his sudden coming find his disciples sleeping (καθεύδοντας), that is, unprepared for his arrival (Mk 13.36). Mark's saying is sandwiched between commands to watch (γρηγορεῖν) in 13.35, 37 (cf. also 34), and Paul balances another warning not to sleep with the same positive admonition in 1 Thess. 5.6. Although γρηγορεῖν does not occur in our passage, the idea is present; to be asleep in the night of this age is to be dulled by its anaesthetizing delusions, to succumb to its temptations, and thus to be unprepared for the advent of the day of the Lord.[1] Instead of sleeping, those who belong to the day should be morally alert (cf. Rom. 13.13 ὡς ἐν ἡμέρᾳ; 1 Thess. 5.5-8).[2] Matthew's parable of the virgins provides another eschatological tradition which is paralleled in Paul; when the bridegroom is delayed, the virgins slumber, then arise (ἐγείρειν) upon hearing the cry to come out to meet him (Mt. 25.5-7).[3] In this case, however, the direction of any dependence is less certain, as Matthew alone preserves the parable.[4] Finally, similar language appears in the Markan and Matthaean accounts of the night of Jesus' betrayal. In Gethsemane, Jesus admonishes his disciples to watch and pray, but later finds them sleeping; he calls them to arise (ἐγείρεσθε), declaring that the ὥρα for betrayal is at hand (ἤγγικεν; Mk 14.37-42 // Mt. 26.40-46). Thematically linked with the eschatological discourse in Mark,[5] this Passion tradition could also have provided the inspiration for Paul's language.[6]

1. Cf. Lövestam, *Wakefulness*, pp. 34-35.

2. Cf. Mt. 24.48-50 par.; 25.1-13; Lk. 12.35-40.

3. The κραυγή which announces the appearance of the bridegroom and summons the maidens (Mt. 25.6) may be compared with the κέλευσμα of 1 Thess. 4.16, and the phrase εἰς ἀπάντησιν (1 Thess. 4.17; Mt. 25.6) is very rare in the NT (elsewhere only Mt. 27.32; Acts 28.15).

4. Sleep and rising are not mentioned in Lk. 12.35, but the idea of being alert in preparation for the eschaton is present.

5. Minear follows R.H. Lightfoot in seeing a connection between the eschatological discourse and the Passion narrative, especially contrasting the disciples, who fail to watch and pray in the garden, with Jesus, who remains alert and overcomes in his final trial through prayer. Minear finds the pattern of thought in 1 Thess. 5.2-10 to be similar to Mark's (*Commands*, pp. 152-77, esp. 165-66).

6. ἐγείρειν (41× in the Pauline corpus) refers in every other case except Rom. 13.11 and Eph. 5.14 to resurrection; ὥρα (7×) has an eschatological nuance for Paul

Extra-biblical parallels to the call to 'wake up' are not unusual, but Paul's usage differs significantly.[1] In contrast to the dualistic Gnostic conception that the soul is a divine spark from the heavenly world of light which is imprisoned in the darkness of flesh and must be awakened from its ignorance of this fact, Paul's orientation is fundamentally historical and Christocentric.[2] Furthermore, despite Jewish parallels to walking in the light (of God's Law) and the danger of slumber (with the latter's opposite being ἡ γρηγόρησις κυρίου [cf. *Pss. Sol.* 16.1, 4]), 'as far as is known, *admonitions to keep awake ...do not occur in Judaic writings with the eschatological orientation*, and referring to the absolute preparedness against the background of night and darkness, as is the case in the Synoptic Gospels and other New Testament writings'.[3] Dissimilarity here favours dominical influence on Paul.[4]

The Nearness of the Day
Twice Paul speaks of the nearness of salvation/the day (ἐγγύς/ἐγγίζειν; 13.11, 12; cf. ἐν τάχει 16.20), and in Phil. 4.5 he states ὁ κύριος ἐγγύς. This is the stuff of early Christian tradition, as is evident from the use of ἐγγίζειν in Jas 5.8 (ἡ παρουσία τοῦ Κυρίου ἤγγικεν), 1 Pet. 4.7 (πάντων δὲ τὸ τέλος ἤγγικεν) and Heb. 10.25 (βλέπετε ἐγγίζουσαν τὴν ἡμέραν; cf. Rev. 1.3; 22.10; *Barn.* 21.3, ἐγγὺς ἡ ἡμέρα... ἐγγὺς ὁ κύριος).[5] The Gospels reflect the belief that both John the Baptist and Jesus spoke of the

only here. Wakefulness is linked with prayer in Col. 4.2 (cf. Eph. 6.18), as in Mk 14.38 // Mt. 26.41 // Lk. 21.36.

1. Cf., e.g., Philo, who applies the image to those who are blind to spiritual realities; when a person comes to love and honour God it is like awakening from deep sleep (*Somn.* 1.164). *CH* I.27 likens ignorance of God with drunkenness and sleep (μέθη καὶ ὕπνος); cf. VII.1.

2. Lövestam, *Wakefulness*, pp. 39-40.

3. Lövestam, *Wakefulness*, p. 142; my italics.

4. 'It is hard to find any compelling objections against the admonition to keep awake deriving from Jesus' own teaching' (Lövestam, *Wakefulness*, p. 134; cf. p. 139).

5. Lk. 21.8 has Jesus warning *against* those who claim that the time is at hand (ὁ καιρὸς ἤγγικεν); whether or not the saying is authentic, it is intended not against expectancy (since Luke preserves other sayings; e.g., 21.28, 32), but against the claim of false prophets that the coming of the end is connected with their appearance (Marshall, *Luke*, p. 763).

nearness of the kingdom (Mt. 3.2; Mk 1.15 // Mt. 4.17; Mt. 10.7 // Lk. 10.9, 11).[1] Lk. 21.28 preserves a saying that seems close in thought to Paul's 'Salvation is nearer to us now than when we first believed'; Wenham thinks Luke preserves a pre-Synoptic transition echoed by Paul:[2]

Lk. 21.28	Rom. 13.11
ἀνακύψατε καὶ	ὥρα ἤδη
ἐπάρατε τὰς κεφαλὰς ὑμῶν	ὑμᾶς ἐξ ὕπνου ἐγερθῆναι,
διότι ἐγγίζει	νῦν γὰρ ἐγγύτερον
ἡ ἀπολύτρωσις ὑμῶν	ἡμῶν ἡ σωτηρία. . .

Supporting some connection is the fact that Lk. 21.34 goes on to warn against drunkenness and the day coming unexpectedly (cf. 1 Thess. 5.6-9).[3] On the other hand, Bultmann confidently dismisses 21.28 as a Lukan concluding formula, and 21.34 is suspect as well.[4] Ultimately the significance of this parallel will depend in large part upon one's evaluation of the Gospel tradition.

'*Naherwartung*' was the order of the day in Jewish apocalyptic literature. *4 Ezra* offers several texts which may be compared with Rom. 13.11-12. Some (e.g. *4 Ezra* 2.13, 34-36) show signs of Christian composition, and must be rejected as late; others of similar import occur in the less disputed body of *4 Ezra*, e.g., 'If you are alive, you will see, and if you live long, you will often marvel, because the age is hastening swiftly to its end' (3.26; 14.18; cf. 14.10-13 cited above).[5] *4 Ezra* 4.44-50 is similar to one interpretation of

1. In regard to Rom. 13.12, A.L. Moore comments, 'The parallel with ἤγγικεν ἡ βασιλεία τοῦ θεοῦ is obviously important. The metaphor used by Paul can only be understood Christologically' (*Parousia*, p. 122 n. 1); cf. E.P. Sanders, *Jesus*, p. 93.

2. D. Wenham, *Rediscovery*, pp. 325-26; so also Bruce, *Romans*, p. 241.

3. D. Wenham also compares Rom. 13.11-12 with Lk. 21.28, 31 (*Rediscovery*, p. 116 n. 1). He notes links between Lk. 21.36 and Eph. 6 which would strengthen the case for an echo in our passage if the evidence of Ephesians were allowed.

4. Bultmann, *History*, p. 130. Marshall thinks the use of ἀπολύτρωσις indicates use of a source (*Luke*, p. 777). Grässer writes, 'Der Schluß der Rede nach Lukas (Lc 21 34-36) verrät sich nach Form und Inhalt als späte hellenistische Bildung. . . Alle Charakteristika des lukanischen Entwurfes der Eschatologie treten hier in gehäufter Zahl in Erscheinung' (*Problem*, p. 167).

5. Although the bulk of *4 Ezra* is of Jewish origin, chs. 1–2 and 15–16 are regarded as Christian additions dating from the third century (Metzger in *OTP*, I, p. 520). Dependence on NT traditions seems clear in 2.13 and in the immediate

our passage in its insistence that a greater proportion of time has passed than that which remains before the arrival of the age to come (cf. 5.50-55). The author of *2 Apoc. Bar.* also expects the day of salvation/judgment very soon: 'truly, my salvation which comes has drawn near and is not as far away as before' (23.7; cf. 82.2; 83.1; 85.10). Thus the element of expectancy in itself cannot prove dependence upon dominical tradition.

The Day/Night, Light/Darkness Contrasts

For Paul, the night is the darkness of the *Weltzeit* before Christ returns, while ἡ ἡμέρα corresponds to the age of light which dawns with the arrival of the day of the Lord (Rom. 13.12).[1] Rejecting works characteristic of the darkness from which they have been awakened (specified in 13.13), Christians are to adopt the weapons befitting their calling to be sons of light, sons of the day (cf. 1 Thess. 5.5, 8). In the eschatological Synoptic parables, the νυμφίος/κύριος comes in the midst of the νύξ (Mt. 25.6; cf. Mk 13.35-36; Lk. 12.37-38; 17.34), and ἡμέρα can apply to the that coming (Mk 13.32 // Mt. 24.36; Lk. 12.46; 17.24, 30-31; 21.34). Furthermore, in Lk. 16.8 Jesus contrasts the sons of this age with the *sons of light*.[2]

The metaphorical use of night/day and light/darkness imagery goes back to the OT, and beyond.[3] Texts from Qumran speak of the 'sons of light' (i.e. members of the community) and 'sons of darkness' (outsiders; e.g. 1QS 1.9-10), and in a context of eschatological warfare, 1QM 15.9 provides a striking parallel to Paul's ἔργα τοῦ σκότους: ובחושך כול מעשיהם (cf. also Gal. 5.19; Eph. 5.11). In view of

---

context. From references to the desolation/humiliation of Zion in 3.2; 6.19; 10.48 (cf. the destruction of the temple in 10.19-23) Metzger dates the composition of the Hebrew original (chs. 3–14) sometime between AD 100–120 (*OTP*, I, p. 520).

1. Cf. Lovestam, *Wakefulness*, p. 33. νύξ (11× in the Pauline corpus) has an eschatological sense only here and in 1 Thess. 5, whereas almost half of the 51 instances of ἡμέρα in the Pauline corpus are eschatological in nuance.

2. The construction οἱ υἱοί with the genitive is a Semitic expression, and the parallels from Qumran support a Palestinian origin for the saying. Cf. also Jn 12.36 and Eph. 5.8 for the phrase.

3. Cf. Lövestam, *Wakefulness*, pp. 8-24; Wilckens, *Römer*, III, p. 76 n. 410. In Greek literature νύξ has mostly a negative character as something ominous and bringing fear (Hahn, *NIDNTT*, I, p. 420).

the Jewish evidence, little weight can be put on the Jesus–Paul parallels here.[1]

The Warning against Drunkenness

Rom. 13.13 finds a parallel in 1 Thess. 5.7, which appears to echo explicit warnings against drunkenness in Lk. 21.34 (μέθη) and Mt. 24.48-50 (μεθύειν; cf. Lk. 12.45), both in clear eschatological contexts.[2] If Paul is addressing a specific problem in Rome this evidence would not necessarily be weakened. Drunkenness is an obvious opposite to being alert or awake, and as in the case of other elements discussed above, extra-biblical parallels abound (e.g. *T. Jud.* 14.1-8; Philo, *Ebr.; Somn.* 2.292; *CH* I.27; VII.1-2), but drunkenness does not appear to be linked with expectation of the end outside of the NT.

2. *'Put on the Lord Jesus Christ' and the Example of Christ*

Paul introduces the climax to his exhortation in chs. 12–13 by a third set of contrasts in 13.14:[3] ἀλλὰ ἐνδύσασθε τὸν κύριον Ἰησοῦν Χριστὸν καὶ τῆς σαρκὸς πρόνοιαν μὴ ποιεῖσθε εἰς ἐπιθυμίας. Behind the two ways of life contrasted in 13.12-13 stand two dominions that war against each other—the old reign of sin through the flesh that leads to death, and the Lordship of Christ which through the Spirit breaks the power of sin and leads to life in this age and in the age to come (Rom. 6–8; Gal. 5). 'Put on the Lord Jesus Christ' not only recalls but transcends ἐνδυσώμεθα τὰ ὅπλα τοῦ φωτός (13.12d), for Paul is moving in thought from impersonal armour

---

1. For rabbinic parallels cf., e.g., *b. Hag.* 12b and Str–B, IV, pp. 853-55; III, p. 749. Stählin (*TDNT*, VI, p. 716) concludes that Paul derives his image of passing night and dawning day from exposition of Isa. 21.11-12 as in *Exod. R.* 18.12, but the language there is not parallel to that in Rom. 13.12a, and the date of the traditions cannot be determined. Lövestam rightly finds Paul using the motifs of light and darkness 'in a manner reminiscent of the Qumran writings' (*Wakefulness*, p. 136).

2. Bultmann calls this a late Hellenistic formulation and speculates that Luke was using a fragment from an unknown letter of Paul (*History*, p. 119).

3. The first two sets are the actions appropriate to darkness and light in 13.12c-12d, and day behaviour with its opposite in 13.13; so also Vögtle, 'Röm 13,11-14', p. 559.

(specific ethical qualities) to the person who embodies and enables those characteristics.[1]

The idea of clothing oneself with a person is rare, the only parallel to Paul's expression being Gal. 3.27: ὅσοι... εἰς Χριστὸν ἐβαπτίσθητε, Χριστὸν ἐνεδύσασθε.[2] After citing Paul's usage of ἐνδύεσθαι, Burton writes,

> the idiom conveyed no suggestions of putting on a mask but referred to an act in which one entered into actual relations. Used with an impersonal object, it means 'to acquire', 'to make a part of one's character or possessions'... with a personal object it signifies 'to take on the character or standing' of the person referred to, 'to become', or 'to become as'.[3]

This understanding of the idiom explains Paul's indicative in Galatians, for by virtue of their union with Christ, Christians have 'become as' Christ and are thus all children of God and of Abraham, as is Christ (3.28-29).[4] It is consistent with the figurative usage of ἐνδύεσθαι in the LXX and later Jewish texts (e.g. *Odes* 33.11-12).[5]

---

1. Cf. Schmidt, *Römer*, p. 225.

2. Cf. Oepke, *TDNT*, II, p. 320. The only pre-Pauline occurrence of ἐνδύεσθαι with a person appears in Dionysius of Halicarnassus *Ant. Rom.* 11.5 (late 1st cent. BC), where τὸν Ταρκύνιον ἐκεῖνον ἐνδυόμενοι means 'playing the role' of the person 'Tarkynios'.

3. *Galatians*, p. 204.

4. Burton, *Galatians*, p. 204. A recent Harvard dissertation argues that in Gal. 3.26-28 Paul uses a dominical saying (preserved in *2 Clem.* 12.2, *Gos. Thom.* 22 [cf. 21a, 37], and Clem. Alex. *Strom.* 3.13 [quoting Cassianus who states it is from the *Gos. Eg.*]) which had its origin in a Christian community influenced by Alexandrian Judaism (MacDonald, *Male*). MacDonald thinks the logion originally taught baptism to be the means by which one escapes the body and is restored to the primordial state of androgyny; Paul deliberately alters the saying in order to nip incipient gnosticism in the bud, changing (1) reference to putting off the fleshly body (garment of shame) to putting on Christ and (2) reference to achieving androgyny (the two sexes becoming one) to different social groups becoming a unified community in Christ (*Male*, pp. 15, 128). There *may* be a common tradition behind these texts, but MacDonald (1) reads gnosticism into early Christianity, (2) rejects the interpretations given for the logion [where they appear] in favour of a hypothetical view, and (3) fails to explain why Paul would use a dominical tradition with which he fundamentally disagreed—according to his thesis the problem was in *Corinth*, not Galatia.

5. Cf. Oepke, *TDNT*, II, pp. 319-20. ἐνδύειν usually translates לבשׁ in the LXX, referring over two dozen times to the adoption of various qualities (e.g. δικαιοσύνην [Job 29.14; etc.]).

Betz claims that only the background of ἐνδύεσθαι in the mystery religions and gnostic literature can explain Paul's use of the verb in Gal. 3.27:

> this phrase presupposes the christological-soteriological concept of Christ as the heavenly garment by which the Christian is enwrapped and transformed into a new being. . . it suggests an event of divine transformation.[1]

The evidence of 'putting on' language from the mystery religions and from gnosticism provides a less than convincing background,[2] especially since in 13.12d Paul derives the figurative use of ἐνδύεσθαι with spiritual weaponry from the LXX.[3] Nevertheless, Betz's point about transformation is on target. μεταμορφοῦν plays an important role at the outset of the ethical portion of Romans, and we have suggested that it has a goal—the image of Christ. Now at the conclusion of his general exhortation Paul summarizes his paraenesis by returning to the theme of renewal and transformation introduced in 12.1-2:

Do not be conformed to this world	Put away the works of darkness/ e.g. drunkenness, immorality, and quarrels/ Make no provision for the desires of the flesh
Be transformed by the renewal of mind	Put on the armour of light/ Walk decently/ Put on the Lord Jesus Christ

1. Betz, *Galatians*, p. 187. Often cited are parallels in the Isis community: the initiate was said to be clothed with a heavenly garment, and the priestess of Isis clothed herself like the goddess (Apuleius, *Metam.* 11.23-24); in some mystery religions initiates identified themselves with the gods by putting on ritual masks as well. Cf. Reitzenstein, *Religions*, p. 339; Schoeps, *Paul*, pp. 112-13.

2. At least three objections have been raised: (1) none of the cited parallels predates the NT; (2) most of the parallels reflect a fundamentally different theology; and (3) no literal parallel of putting on or putting off a 'man' is extant (O'Brien, *Colossians*, p. 189; cf. Schweitzer, *Mysticism*, p. 134; Oepke, *TDNT*, II, p. 320). If Paul could say that Christ is our wisdom, righteousness, sanctification and redemption (1 Cor. 1.30), as well as our life (Col. 3.4), it is no great leap to go from putting on, e.g., righteousness to putting on Christ (so Cranfield, *Romans*, II, p. 689).

3. Paul gives the armour specifically Christian content. Whereas in Isa. 59.17 the armour includes righteousness, salvation, vengeance and fury (Wis. 5.17-20: righteousness, justice, holiness and wrath), in 1 Thess. 5.8 it comprises the Christian triad of faith, love and hope (on the triad see Hunter, *Predecessors*, pp. 33-35).

To 'make provision for the flesh, to gratify its desires' is to allow sin to reign again so as to obey its ἐπιθυμίαις (6.12). The way forward is through renewal of the mind and transformation into the image of Christ through 'putting' on Christ, that is, donning his characteristics (see below). By doing so, Paul's readers will be prepared for the age to come and will demonstrate themselves fit for it (1 Thess. 2.12)—the continuity between conformity to Christ the New Man in this age and ultimate conformity through their assumption of resurrection bodies like his in the next must not be broken (Phil. 3.10-11).

As in Gal. 5.16, Paul contrasts right behaviour with doing the will of the flesh,[1] but in Rom. 13.14 the direction of Christian conduct is explicitly christological. Why? Certainly he is appealing to the one thing he knows his readers will all hold in common—their allegiance to the person of Christ; this he also does in 14.8. But Paul's silence about the role of the Spirit does not mean that he is opposing or anticipating a problem with pneumatics. A more likely explanation is that his reference to Christ is simply the tip of an iceberg—Paul's christology underlies his ethics to a far greater extent than is sometimes perceived. Many recognize that in 13.11-14 Paul echoes the eschatological and baptismal basis for his ethics which is first indicated in 12.1-2;[2] what is not often emphasized is that it is a christological basis as well. Although absent by name, Christ is there in Paul's *Wächterruf* (13.11-12), for it is precisely his coming that will put an end to the darkness of this age and bring final σωτηρία. Paul has already spoken at length to show that faith in Christ is the foundation for Christian

---

1. The links between the two passages are striking. After claiming that neighbour-love (as expressed in Lev. 19.18) is the fulfilling of the law (Rom. 13.8-10; Gal. 5.14) Paul speaks of the Christians' spiritual conflict and the need to walk (περιπατεῖν, Gal. 5.16; Rom. 13.13) properly (εὐσχημόνως, Rom. 13.13; πνεύματι in Gal. 5.16), not giving any ground to the desires of the flesh (Gal. 5.16; Rom. 13.14). The vice lists in both passages overlap (Gal. 5.19-21; Rom. 13.13b), and in both he makes an eschatological appeal (cf. Gal. 5.21).

2. E.g., Michel, *Römer*, p. 416; Cranfield, *Romans*, II, p. 679. Eschatological elements in 13.11-14 are clear; baptismal language is more or less probable in the following: (1) 'awakening from sleep' (13.11; cf. Eph. 5.14); (2) reference to when they (first) believed (13.11); (3) the 'darkness/light' contrast; (4) the 'put off/put on' contrast in 13.12; (5) the possible use of catechetical material in 13.13 (cf. Pesch, *Römerbrief*, p. 96); (6) the close parallel of 13.14a with Gal. 3.27.

hope, and we should not require him to rehearse that point again when he appeals to eschatological teaching with which he could assume his readers would be familiar in the first place.[1] As we have seen, JT has already probably influenced Paul's thinking in Romans 12–13 before he says ἐνδύσασθε τὸν κύριον, and the appeal to Christ here at the climax of his paraenesis (as again in 15.3, 5, 7-8 when Paul winds up his more specific admonitions to the weak and strong) indicates that he is no afterthought to the admonition, but its foundation, guiding influence, and goal.[2] Together with 12.1-2, 13.11-14 forms an *inclusio*, giving the whole of the exhortation in chs. 12–13 a distinct ethical direction, and comprehending ethical material with a christological focus.

A survey of Paul's use of ἐνδύεσθαι reveals that outside those passages in which the influence of the OT is clear, the verb consistently appears in christological contexts. Closely related to Gal. 3.27 is Paul's claim that Christians have put on the *new man* (Col. 3.10; cf. Eph. 4.24).[3] The νέος [ἄνθρωπος] of Col. 3.10 (Eph.: καινός) refers to the new person each believer becomes when reborn in Christ, in contrast to that former life apart from God (ὁ παλαιὸς ἄνθρωπος; Col. 3.9) which is repudiated in baptism (Col. 2.11-12). Like the inner man (ὁ ἔσω ἄνθρωπος; Rom. 7.22, cf. Eph. 3.16) being renewed daily (ἀνακαινοῦσθαι, 2 Cor. 4.16; cf. Rom. 12.2), the new man which has been put on at baptism is being renewed in knowledge after the image of its creator. Paul's concept of the 'new man' is christologically founded in two respects. First, Paul viewed Christ as the new man in contrast to the first man Adam (Rom. 5.14-19; 1 Cor. 15.20-22, 45-49), and because believers are incorporated into Christ they are a new creation (2 Cor. 5.17; Gal. 6.15). 'Just as

1. In a similar passage (1 Thess. 5.1-11), Paul explicitly refers to Christ only twice: once in the stereotypical formula 'day of the Lord' (5.2), and again with reference to obtaining future salvation (5.9); 5.10 parallels Rom. 14.8-9.

2. Although in other passages Paul focuses on the work of the Spirit, such sections reflect no lack of interest in Christ, but rather Paul's flexibility of expression in admonition. For him, the Spirit is the Spirit *of Christ* (2 Cor. 3.17-18; 1 Cor. 15.45) constituting the presence of the Lord Jesus among his people.

3. Thus taking the participles in Col. 3.9-10 as causal. Some construe them as imperatival (cf. Eph. 4.22-24, where infinitives are used), but there is no clear instance of an aorist participle having imperatival force in conjunction with a present imperative.

the "old man" is what they once were "in Adam", the embodiment of unregenerate humanity, so the "new man" is what they now are "in Christ"'.[1] Secondly, as the archetypal new man, the pattern for the ongoing renewal of the Christian is the second Adam. Although κατ' εἰκόνα τοῦ κτίσαντος αὐτόν recalls Gen. 1.27, which tells us that the first Adam was created by God 'in his own image', early in the same Epistle Paul has already called Christ the εἰκὼν τοῦ θεοῦ (1.15), and that thought cannot be far from Paul's mind in 3.10. Christians are being continually transformed into the same εἰκών, that of the risen Lord (2 Cor. 3.18), who is himself the εἰκών of God (2 Cor. 4.4; cf. also Rom. 8.29; Phil. 3.21). So Moule writes, 'when God re-creates Man, it is *in the pattern of Christ*, who is God's Likeness absolutely'.[2] Paul's thought here reflects the influence of Jewish Adamic theology which was 'baptized' into the Christian community through identification of Christ as the second Adam.

What is the concrete expression of this 'pattern'? We have already noted the ethical usage of ἐνδύεσθαι with impersonal objects in the OT,[3] and something very similar appears in Col. 3.12, although with a new content. When Paul says 'put on' σπλάγχνα οἰκτιρμοῦ, χρηστότητα, ταπεινοφροσύνην, πραΰτητα, μακροθυμίαν, most of the characteristics he chooses come from a stock of descriptions applied in various traditions to the person of Christ, and none of them appear with ἐνδύεσθαι in the OT.[4] Although some of the terms in

1. O'Brien, *Colossians*, pp. 190-91; cf. Eph. 2.15, where the καινός man is the corporate body of Christ, composed of both Jews and Gentiles.

2. *Colossians*, p. 120. Michel compares Rom. 13.12, 14 with Col. 3.9, 12: 'Der "alte Mensch" ist an seinen Werken ebenso erkennbar wie der "neue" (Röm 13,13; Kol 3,12). Indem man die Werke des "alten Menschen" ablegt, legt man ihn selbst ab, und indem man die Werke des "neuen Menschen" annimmt, zieht man den Christus als den "neuen Menschen" an (13,14)' (Michel, *Römer*, p. 415). Ignatius calls Jesus Christ τὸν καινὸν ἄνθρωπον (*Eph.* 20.1).

3. See p. 150 n. 5 above. In rabbinic literature, there are also references to clothing with spiritual and ethical qualities, e.g., the Torah clothes with humility and reverence (*m. Ab.* 6.1; cf. Str–B, II, p. 301).

4. Related to Jesus: σπλαγχνίζεσθαι (Mt. 9.36 // Mk 6.34; Mt. 14.14; 15.32 // Mk 8.2; Mt. 20.34; Mk 1.41?; Lk. 7.13); ταπεινός (Mt. 11.29); πραΰς (Mt. 11.29; 21.5; 5.5); χρηστός (Jesus' yoke, Mt. 11.30; the adjective is almost a homonym for Χριστός); οἰκτιρμός, found in his summary exhortation in Lk. 6.36 (cf. also Jas 5.11 [?]); and μακροθυμία (1 Tim. 1.16; cf. 2 Pet. 3.15). Attributed to God: χρηστότης (Rom. 2.4; 11.22; Eph. 2.7; Tit. 3.4); σπλάγχνα (Lk. 1.78);

Col. 3.12 are used more often of God than Jesus in the NT (χρηστότης, μακροθυμία), two of them are applied only to Jesus and his followers (ταπεινοφροσύνη, πραΰτης). Paul calls for ταπεινοφροσύνη in the context of the imitation of Christ (Phil. 2.3), and we have already seen the importance of Jesus' example of ταπεινοφροσύνη for Clement of Rome (see Chapter 2). Paul appeals διὰ τῆς πραΰτητος...τοῦ Χριστοῦ in 2 Cor. 10.1,[1] and speaks of the σπλάγχνα Χριστοῦ Ἰησοῦ in Phil. 1.8.[2]

> As God's chosen ones who have already put on the new man (v. 10) they must don the graces which are characteristic of him. . . The graces with which they are to be clothed are those qualities predicated of God or Christ. . . It is, thus, not unusual that Paul should exhort the Roman Christians to 'put on (ἐνδύσασθε) the Lord Jesus Christ' (Rom. 13.14).[3]

The christological context in Colossians strongly indicates a connection, as Paul has just finished reminding his readers that they have been raised with Christ and should seek the things that are above, where he is (3.1-2); their life is hidden with Christ (3.3), who is their ζωή (3.4); in view of their death (with Christ in baptism; Rom. 6.2-4)

οἰκτιρμός (Rom. 12.1; 2 Cor. 1.3; cf. οἰκτίρμων in Lk. 6.36; Jas 5.11 [?]); μακροθυμία (Rom. 2.4; 9.22; 1 Pet. 3.20; 2 Pet. 3.15). If there is a link to the Jesus tradition in Paul's choice of these words, the cluster in Mt. 11.29-30 should be noted. There is evidence elsewhere that Paul was familiar with the tradition behind Mt. 11.25-28 (1 Cor. 2.7-10; cf. Richardson, 'Thunderbolt').

1. Leivestad argues that the πραΰτης and ἐπιείκεια in 2 Cor. 10.1 refer not to the *behaviour* of the earthly Jesus but to his *state* (i.e. being a man) resulting from the kenosis of the pre-existent Christ ('Meekness', pp. 161, 164). The dichotomy however is too sharp, as Leivestad eventually acknowledges (p. 164). Whether the description of Jesus in Mt. 11.29 is redactional (Stanton, 'Words', pp. 5-6) or not, it represents an application of πραΰς and ταπεινός to *Jesus*, the ταπεινοφροσύνη in *1 Clem.* 16 plainly *cannot* refer to the incarnation, and Ignatius uses πραΰς, ταπεινόφρονες, and ἐπιείκεια together in the context of imitation of the Lord who *suffered* (*Eph.* 10.2-3).

2. In view of the Synoptic traditions which apply the word group repeatedly to Jesus, σπλάγχνα/σπλαγχνίζειν appear to be fundamental descriptions of his compassion in the early Church. Thus in Phil. 1.8 Paul would be likening his own attitude to that of Jesus described in some of the first traditions Paul passed on to his readers.

3. O'Brien, *Colossians*, p. 197; so also Grundmann, *TDNT*, VIII, p. 22; Schnackenburg, *Teaching*, p. 219.

they must put to death the old way (3.5-9); they have put on the new
man which is being renewed in accordance with the image (Christ) of
God and Christ is all and in all (3.11). In this christological light, the
οὖν of 3.12 requires not simply a string of adjectives chosen at
random, but qualities which cohere with the one in whom they have
been baptized; at the very least, Paul must have considered these
characteristics to be true of the risen Christ and of the man Jesus as
well (unless Paul sharply differentiated the two). In the following
verse he will tell his readers to forgive as the Lord has forgiven them,
possibly an appeal to dominical example or an echo of his teaching
(Mt. 18.33? the Lord's Prayer?); the thought is comparable to Rom.
15.7.[1] Above all the qualities cited in Col. 3.12-13, however, the
Colossians are to put on love (3.14), which, as in Rom. 13.8-10 and
the teachings of Jesus, is given pre-eminence (cf. 1 Cor. 13; 16.14).
That Paul is thinking of the love which has its origin in Christ
becomes evident when he immediately calls for the peace of Christ to
rule in their hearts, to which peace they were called in the one body
(of Christ) (3.15).[2] Furthermore, the word of Christ is to dwell in
them richly, and Paul sums up his general paraenesis as he does in
Romans with yet another christological admonition: καὶ πᾶν ὅ τι ἐὰν

---

1. As we have seen, Christ is the controlling theme of Paul's admonition in this
section, with Χριστός occurring eight times in seventeen verses (3.1 [twice], 3, 4,
11, 13, 15, 16). Paul rarely uses κύριος of God the Father; of the ten instances of
κύριος *solitare* in the letter, eight clearly refer to Christ, leaving only this text and
Col. 1.10. The widespread textual evidence for the variant reading Χριστός in 3.13
also favours this interpretation. Nevertheless forgiveness is the more natural
prerogative of the Father (cf. the parallel in Eph. 4.31, and esp. Col. 2.13).

Merk (*Handeln*, pp. 210-11) rejects any idea of imitation of God or Christ in Col.
3. He cites the lack of explicit appeal to God or Christ, and observes 'daß den
Lasterkatalogen in Kol 3,6. 8 als Ausdruck der Handlungsweisen der σάρξ in 3, 12
bewußt das Handeln des Christen auf Grund der Taufe gegenübergestellt wird'
(*Handeln*, p. 210 n. 72). His argument from silence expects too much from the text,
and we have already noted that the context is supremely christological. Baptismal
tradition is certainly underlying some of the language here, but it is a *non sequitur* to
deny Paul's interest in the character of Christ from that observation. There is some
similarity here to the virtues enumerated in 1QS 4.3-4, but the latter passage lacks
clothing imagery, and some of the characteristics there could not be applied to Christ.

2. On the possible influence of 'peace' sayings from JT cf. Chapter 6; but Col.
3.15 probably refers to peace with God which comes *through* Christ (Rom. 5.1; cf.
Eph. 2.14-15; 6.15), the foundation for peace with one another.

ποιῆτε ἐν λόγῳ ἢ ἐν ἔργῳ, **πάντα ἐν ὀνόματι κυρίου 'Ιησοῦ,** εὐχαριστοῦντες τῷ πατρὶ δι' αὐτοῦ. The behaviour called for derives its foundation, orientation and example from Christ; as in Rom. 13.11-14, the motivation is not simply baptism but eschatology as well.

Paul uses ἐνδύεσθαι five more times with reference to the future 'clothing' of the Christian with a resurrection/spiritual body (1 Cor. 15.53 [twice], 54 [twice]; 2 Cor. 5.3), and these have verbal/conceptual parallels in Jewish literature (1QS 4.6-8; *T. Levi* 18.14; *2 Apoc. Bar.* 49; *Apoc. Abr.* 13.14; cf. *Apoc. Zeph.* 8.3).[1] Although similar, Paul's statements about putting on a resurrection body are christologically grounded inasmuch as the new existence is described as conformity to Christ (Rom. 8.28; Phil. 3.21), so that 'as was the man of dust, so are those who are of the dust; and as is the man of heaven, so are those who are of heaven. Just as we have borne the image of the man of dust, we shall also bear the image of the man of heaven' (1 Cor. 15.49). This too Paul shares with Christian tradition.[2]

What then does it mean to 'put on Christ' in Rom. 13.14? Many refer to the moral renewal of that which began sacramentally in baptism (cf. Gal. 3.27; Rom. 6.2),[3] but can we say more? Commentators have offered a number of different ideas: 'In putting on a particular type of dress, one commits oneself and decides';[4] to put on Christ means to put on the last Adam;[5] 'Christus, durch dessen Liebe wir gerecht geworden und für das Leben gerettet worden sind, im Wandel zu entsprechen, heißt im Grunde immer konkret: einander zu lieben' (i.e. what Paul has said in 13.8-10).[6] Most include some clear element of imitation/conformity to Christ: 'It means to follow Him in the way of discipleship and to strive to let our lives be moulded according to the pattern of the humility of His earthly life';[7] 'Der Sinn des Bildes ist: lasst euch gänzlich bestimmen von Christus, dass an euch nichts zu sehen ist als seine Art';[8] 'Those who have put on Christ in baptism

---

1. Cf. also ἐπενδύεσθαι in 2 Cor. 5.2, 4.
2. Compare Col. 3.4 with 1 Jn 3.2-3.
3. So, e.g., Barrett (*Romans*, p. 254), Lövestam (*Wakefulness*, p. 42).
4. Leenhardt, *Romans*, p. 343.
5. Käsemann, *Romans*, p. 363.
6. Wilckens, *Römer*, III, p. 78.
7. Cranfield, *Romans*, II, pp. 688-89, following Chrysostom.
8. Althaus, *Römer*, p. 137.

must put on Christ by living in conformity with his mind (cf. Phil. ii.5)';[1] 'Unite yourselves in the closest fellowship of life with Christ, so that you may wholly present the mind and life of Christ in your conduct'.[2] Given Paul's tendency to exalt Christ (cf. 1 Cor. 1.30), the meaning of 'putting on Christ' should not be limited to one particular expression, but in view of the verb's background, when used figuratively it surely points to adoption of his mind, character and conduct—distinguished from mere imitation by the presence and work of his Spirit. By donning the characteristics of the second Adam, Christians reflect the true image of God and are changed into his likeness from one degree of glory to another, in anticipation of the final glory of resurrection life (2 Cor. 3.18). A more specific application can be derived from the inverse of 13.14b, since the expression is accompanied by a last appeal to make no provision for the flesh, to satisfy its desires. Putting on Christ thus corresponds to taking care to discern and fulfil the θέλημα of God, as Jesus did. Instead of self-seeking indulgence of the flesh, Christians are to imitate the self-abnegation of the one who did not please himself but bore the burdens of others (cf. 15.2-3).

3. *Summary*

Taken by itself, there is little *prima facie* indication that Rom. 13.11-14 echoes JT, save for the eschatological emphasis, which could be attributed to the shared apocalyptic milieu. The danger of sleep and drunkenness, the nearness of salvation, and the contrasts between day and night, light and darkness are all common elements in the literature of Paul's day, while parallels to 'knowing the time' are sufficiently brief and inexact to dismiss on their own merits as coincidental. The case for Pauline 'independence' seems watertight when the evidence is evaluated in an atomistic fashion; it is possible to put a finger in each of the holes in the dike. Nevertheless, if one allows the full pressure of the evidence of 1 Thessalonians 4–5 to be felt, the dike collapses, and the combination of the small bits in our passage can claim a greater significance than the sum of its parts. Wenham has argued at length for the existence of a pre-Synoptic eschatological discourse

1. Barrett, *Romans*, p. 254.
2. H.A.W. Meyer, *Romans*, II, p. 292.

known to and independently used by the Synoptic writers. He thinks Paul knew a significant chunk of Jesus' eschatological teachings:

> There is good reason to believe that Paul. . . knew the opening warning against deceivers. . ., probably the warnings about coming persecution and the saying about the preaching of the gospel. . . , certainly the description of the desolating sacrilege events and the description of the parousia itself, including perhaps the Lukan call to 'lift up your heads' because of the nearness of redemption. . . He may have known the Matthew/Mark saying about no one knowing the day or hour. . . , and he probably knew the exhortation of Lk. 21.34-36 and the following parables of the virgins, the watchmen, the thief and the steward.[1]

Here more than anywhere the probability of Paul's use of JT depends not only on criteria chosen for evaluating parallels, but also on one's assessment of the historical probability that Jesus said what is attributed to him. A tendency to assign eschatological sayings to Christian prophets or evangelists will preclude the possibility of any dependence. Nevertheless, considering the likelihood that we already have some reminiscences of JT in Rom. 12–13.10, the probability that we have the same phenomenon in Rom. 13.11-14 increases. It is not as though Paul is slavishly following dominical tradition, or repeating by rote that which his readers must recognize specifically as the teaching of Jesus; his concern is to shake the people of God in Rome and wake them up to the fact that now is the time for obedience, for the coming of their redemption in the person of Jesus Christ is nearer than ever.

Although Paul is addressing the Roman situation, the importance of his choice of a christological paraenetic emphasis in what is perhaps his least 'situational' letter should not be missed.[2] Paul's knowledge of

---

1. D. Wenham, *Rediscovery*, pp. 366-67.
2. In Colossians, Paul's general paraenesis is distinctly christological in its emphasis (see above), and it is difficult to establish whether or not he is addressing a Colossian heresy (cf. Hooker, 'Colossae'). In Philippians, Paul explicitly appeals to the example of Christ (see Chapter 14). On the other hand, his emphasis on the Holy Spirit in the Corinthian literature is easily understood from the abuses of *charismata* in that community, while the focus on the Spirit in Gal. 5 is explained by his desire to contrast life in Christ with life under the law (cf. 3.2-3). This is not to minimize the role of the Spirit in Paul's ethics (i.e. to ignore Rom. 8 and Paul's references to the Spirit in all of his letters except Philemon), but to try to maintain a balanced perspective; his is an ethic of the Spirit because it is through the Spirit that Christ is present, guiding, encouraging and empowering the Church.

his audience is second hand, and therefore without strong evidence to the contrary we should expect him to present here an ethical perspective which is less reactive than any other paraenetic section in his Epistles. He is finding common ground with his readers, re-emphasizing teachings with which he can assume familiarity (cf. 15.15; 6.17). The transformed life and the renewed mind mean conformity to Christ, taking the shape of behaviour consistent with what the Romans know to be teachings and behaviour attributed to Jesus. Paul summarizes that life as putting on Christ.

Chapter 10

ROMANS 14.1-13A: JUDGING

In Rom. 14–15.13 Paul addresses a particular problem reflecting the clash of Jewish and Gentile Christians.[1] The former maintained aspects of their Jewish heritage, while the latter stressed freedom from the law. The 'weak in faith' (14.1) were predominantly Jewish converts[2] who lacked the assurance that they no longer needed to observe rigid dietary and calendrical customs to please God, among which were OT injunctions against eating unclean meats (14.2-3) and commands to keep the Sabbath and feast days (14.5-6).[3] The majority

1. So also, e.g., Watson, *Paul*, pp. 94-97, and more recently, Wedderburn, *Reasons*. Karris presents the strongest case to the contrary, concluding that the section is a 'theoretic development' of 1 Cor. 8–10, generalized exhortation applicable to any Christian community ('Occasion'); cf. the response by Donfried ('Presuppositions'). Whatever the situation in Corinth may have been (Theissen's sociological insights are valuable ['Analysis']), there are no indications that wealth and social status determined the sides in the weak/strong controversy in Rome. The dispute over observing *days* (Rom. 14.5-6) is unparalleled at Corinth. Furthermore, the distinctively Jewish nuance of κοινός (= טמא; cf. Hauck, *TDNT*, III, p. 791; Paschen, *Rein*, pp. 167-68) and (to a lesser extent) καθαρά in Rom. 14.14, 20 reveals the *theological* concern dividing the two groups. Neither word appears in the Corinthian letters. Finally, the close connection of Rom. 15.7-13 to 14.1–15.6 (προσλαμβάνεσθε), coupled with the overall argument of Romans indicates that Paul is seeking not only to introduce himself but also to unify Christians divided along Jew/Gentile lines. On the background of the churches in Rome, cf. Wiefel 'Community'.

2. For discussion of the options cf. Cranfield, *Romans*, II, pp. 690-98. One relatively unexplored possibility is that they were Jewish Christians who had been influenced by naziritic asceticism (Num. 6.2; cf. Hegesippus's tradition that James drank no wine and ate no flesh, in Eusebius, *H.E.* II.23, and the saying of R. Nathan in *b. Pes.* 22b, cited below, Chapter 11).

3. To these customs may be added their abstinence from wine, if the reference in 14.21 is not hypothetical. On Jewish abstinence from meat in Rome cf. Jos.

Clothed with Christ

of Christians in Rome, however, were apparently Gentiles,[1] some of whom prided themselves on their strength in faith and considered the Jewish customs to be absurd. In response, the 'weak' apparently countered with the charge that their so-called 'strong' brethren were not obedient to the will of God.[2] Nevertheless, some of the weak were being tempted (by pressure from the arguments and the confidence of the strong) to compromise their integrity and to act contrary to their convictions by conforming to the majority view.

We can discern the formal structure of 14–15.13 from Paul's repetition of the command προσλαμβάνεσθε (14.1; 15.7) and his use of a prayer-wish (15.5-6; 15.13) to conclude the two major segments of the passage:[3]

> I. Receive the weak regardless of their customs, 14.1–15.6
>   A. Summary exhortation, 14.1
>   B. Body, 14.2–15.4
>   1. Instructions directed to the weak and strong together, 14.2-13a
>   2. Instructions directed primarily to the strong, 14.13b–15.4
>   C. Prayer-wish, 15.5-6
> II. Receive one another as Christ received you, 15.7-13
>   A. Summary exhortation, 15.7
>   B. Body (support for exhortation), 15.8-12
>   C. Prayer-wish, 15.13

Paul's overall concern in this section is thus about the reception of currently separated Christians into fellowship; his desire is to promote unity among divided factions. In 14.1-13a he reminds those who presume to sit in judgment on each other that ultimately they all live for and answer to the Lord, who alone will judge. In 14.13b–15.6 Paul tells the 'strong' that the spiritual welfare of their brethren is more important than their own preferences for food or drink, and that by setting the other's interests over their own they will be following the

---

Life 13-14.

1. This is inferred from 1.13, 16; 15.15-16 and the fact that the strong are to 'receive' the weak (14.1). For the opposite view, see, e.g., Brown and Meier, *Antioch*, pp. 110-12).

2. If the weak were legalists who trusted in ascetic works to earn a righteous standing before God, Paul would have adopted a much different approach.

3. Parunak gives a similar structure for the passage ('Techniques', p. 535), noting that the motive for receiving one another in both major sections is that God (14.3) or Christ (15.7) has already received them (p. 534).

example of Christ. The remaining verses generalize this admonition, continue the appeal to the example of Christ, and conclude with a cluster of OT quotations finding fulfilment in the unity Paul seeks.

κρίνειν is a crucial verb in Rom. 14.1-13. Leaving aside its neutral instances (i.e. 14.5 and 14.13b), in the first part of the section Paul uses the word consistently of the 'weak' Christians (14.3, 4, 10). Ridiculed (ἐξουθενεῖν, 14.3, 10) by the 'strong', they responded defensively by condemning their Gentile brethren, perhaps accusing them of pleasing only themselves (cf. 15.1-3; Gal. 1.10) and not being concerned to obey the Lord. Nevertheless, in 14.13a Paul addresses both 'weak' and 'strong' in the exhortation μηκέτι ἀλλήλους κρίν-ωμεν, as evidenced by the inclusion of himself. He broadens the scope of 'judging'; it applies not only to Jewish Christians who consider themselves superior because of their obedience to the law, but also to Gentile believers who view themselves as superior in their faith. Rom. 14.13a serves, therefore, as a conclusion (οὖν) and transition, as Paul moves to address the strong in particular in the following verses. If he echoes any dominical teaching here, it can most likely be seen in his prohibition of 'judging'.[1]

1. *Affinities and Differences*

Rom. 14.13a Μηκέτι οὖν ἀλλήλους κρίνωμεν
Mt. 7.1 Μὴ κρίνετε ἵνα μὴ κριθῆτε
Lk. 6.37a καὶ μὴ κρίνετε, καὶ οὐ μὴ κρίθητε

Similarities in vocabulary and grammar include the following: (1) use of the same verb; (2) agreement in tense and number; (3) absence of any qualification[2] of κρίνειν (apart from ἀλλήλους); (4) direct prohibition with μή. The Gospel sayings differ from Paul in three major respects: (1) Paul uses the hortatory subjunctive instead of the imperative; (2) he presents the ground for the prohibition before the

---

1. The Pauline *hapax* οἰκέτης (14.4), in the reminder that it is not the weak person's business to judge the *servant* of another who will stand or fall in relation to his own master, may be compared with Lk. 16.13 ('No servant can serve two masters'), and Rom. 14.8 (τῷ κυρίῳ ζῶμεν) resembles Lk. 20.38 (πάντες γὰρ αὐτῷ ζῶσιν), but these minimal similarities depend on Lukan additions.

2. That is, the verb is not accompanied by a predicate accusative (e.g. Acts 13.46 οὐκ ἀξίους κρίνετε ἑαυτούς), an infinitive (Acts 15.19), a preposition (Acts 23.3), an adverb (*Barn.* 19.11), etc.

call not to judge (14.10b-11) instead of after it; and (3) he includes a direct object (ἀλλήλους).[1] With regard to the first and third points it should be noted that if Paul had simply said, 'Stop judging', it would by no means have been clear to his readers that he was speaking to *both* the weak and the strong, since by our interpretation κρίνειν was the characteristic fault of the 'weak'. The addition of ἀλλήλους clarifies Paul's intention; he is giving a general instruction that takes in all of his readers (cf. ἀλλήλους in 12.5, 10, 16; 13.8). But why does Paul now apply κρίνειν to both groups? The second difference observed above provides the answer: when members of either group begin to find fault with their brethren they presume to do something only the Lord is qualified to do. Neither group can pass judgment on the other (and thereby effectively exclude the other from fellowship), for *all* must appear before the βῆμα of the Judge before whom every knee will bow (14.10-11). It is to God (not man) that each must give an account of himself (14.12). Since Paul has already reminded his readers of the inevitability of judgment before God (supported by his quotation of Isa. 45.23), citation of the full dominical logion (if he knows it) would be redundant.[2]

What do the parallels in the Gospels mean? Matthew puts the saying at the beginning of a new section of the SM, the negative command corresponding to the openings of the two previous segments (6.19-24, 25-34).[3] Luke sets the command in contrast to the positive exhortation that introduces his new section, 'Be merciful (οἰκτίρμονες), even as your Father is merciful' (6.36).[4] In both cases the 'judging' that is

1. A fourth difference is μηκέτι as compared with μή; if Paul is addressing a current problem for the Romans, his choice of words is easily understandable. The Gospels differ in Luke's addition of καὶ οὐ instead of ἵνα: what in Matthew is essentially a warning becomes in Luke a promise (J.P. Brown, 'Parallels', p. 36). Brown thinks Paul has turned promise into threat, with Matthew following him; it would seem more likely that the threat form is primitive, and that Luke is seeking to cast the saying in a more positive light. Bultmann thought that neither Gospel preserved the original form of the saying, but he considered Matthew's version to be earlier than Luke's (*History*, pp. 79-80, 86).
2. κριθῆτε in both Mt. 7.1 and Lk. 6.37 should be taken as a 'divine passive'; so, e.g., Dalman (*Words*, I, p. 224), Jeremias (*Theology*, p. 11 n. 3); cf. Sidebottom, 'Passive'.
3. Cf. Guelich, *Sermon*, p. 349.
4. Fitzmyer groups 6.36 with the preceding paragraph, but he sees it functioning as a transition to what follows, 'since the question of judging is a further example of

prohibited lacks qualification. It is not a call to forego discernment (cf. Lk. 7.43; 12.57), nor does the command exclude needed rebuke in discipline (Mt. 18.15-20). Luke expounds the meaning of the saying by immediately adding a parallel, καὶ μὴ καταδικάζετε, καὶ οὐ μὴ καταδικασθῆτε (6.37b).[1] Sandwiched between admonitions to be merciful and not to condemn, μὴ κρίνετε seems to signify something stronger than simply 'the human tendency to criticize and find fault with one's neighbor',[2] although it would include that. The identification of κρίνετε in Mt. 7.1 as 'censorious condemnation' is better and fits both passages.[3] After giving the basic instruction in 7.1 Matthew provides its theological justification in 7.2, 'For with the judgment you pronounce you will be judged, and the measure you give will be the measure you get'. Hill rightly comments, 'this is not simply a recommendation to be moderate in judgment on others. The meaning is that, if you condemn, you exclude yourself from God's pardon. . . "If you want to be mercifully dealt with, show mercy now".'[4] Likewise, the conclusion of the 'speck'/'log' hyperbole in 7.3-5 (cf. Lk. 6.41-42) is probably not a contradiction or qualification of the prohibition by allowing judgment of another after self-judgment has taken place, but rather an ironic restatement of the principle not to judge at all, not unlike Jn 8.7, 'Let him who is without sin among you be the first to throw a stone at her'.[5] A key word here is ὑποκριτά (Mt. 7.5 // Lk. 6.42); those who would sit in judgment of another are self-deceived, failing to see their own need for mercy from the hand of the One Judge.

Paul's usage of κρίνειν in Rom. 14.13a is therefore similar to that in the Gospel parallels. The meaning of the verb is the same, the appeal to judgment by God provides a common motivation for not judging, and Paul seems particularly concerned to correct attitudes of superiority that are hypocritical and divisive (12.3, 10, 16; cf. ἀγάπη ἀνυπόκριτος in 12.9). Furthermore, there is some shared structure and vocabulary in context; when Paul confronts the weak in 14.10, τί

the imitation of God's mercy' (*Luke*, I, p. 641).

1. Bultmann suggested that the addition was possibly an alternative translation in which the saying was also handed down (*History*, p. 80).

2. Fitzmyer, *Luke*, I, p. 641.

3. Guelich, *Sermon*, p. 350.

4. *Matthew*, p. 146.

5. Hill, *Matthew*, p. 147; Guelich, *Sermon*, pp. 352-53.

κρίνεις **τὸν ἀδελφόν σου** resembles Mt. 7.3: **τί δὲ βλέπεις τὸ κάρφος τὸ ἐν τῷ ὀφθαλμῷ τοῦ ἀδελφοῦ σου**. There are differences, to be sure. The first reason Paul gives for not condemning another focuses not on the human or divine judge, but on the one who is judged; he should not be condemned because he is received by God (14.3) and ultimately answers to him alone (14.4). In addition, Paul emphasizes the contrast between Christ, the Lord of all, and those who presume to judge or despise (14.9-10);[1] the Gospel parallels do not specify who will judge those who judge others.[2] Finally, in context both Gospels underline the importance, in one's dealings with others, of self-judgment and reflection on mercy received from God, whereas Paul seems not to include those elements.[3] However, his statement that each person shall give account of himself to God (14.12) has the effect of calling the reader to consider his own situation.[4] Moreover, in an earlier 'judgment' passage (Rom. 2.4), Paul cites the kindness (χρηστότης), forbearance (ἀνοχή) and patience (μακροθυμία) of God, the experience of which should lead one to repentance, not to a judgmental spirit.

1. σύ is emphatic in 14.10, as also in 14.4 where it is set in contrast with ὁ θεός from 14.3 (BDF, sec. 277.1). On the other hand, Paul speaks of the judgment in 14.10-12 as a judgment before God. In 14.10 the reading θεοῦ has stronger textual support than Χριστοῦ, the latter arising from the influence of 2 Cor. 5.10. Likewise τῷ θεῷ should probably be accepted as belonging to the original text in 14.12. Although M. Black (*Romans*, pp. 166-67) argues that Paul clearly intended to identify κύριος with the Lord Christ in the quotation from Isa. 45.23 (Rom. 14.11; cf. Phil. 2.10-11; also cf. ζῶ ἐγώ [Rom. 14.11] and ἔζησεν [14.9]), Cranfield correctly concludes that the quotation supports 14.10c and refers to judgment by God (*Romans*, II, p. 710).

2. But see p. 164 n. 2 above. This is not a serious difference, since Matthew and Luke present Christ functioning as a judge elsewhere (Mt. 7.21-23; 25.31-46; Acts 17.31) as does Paul (2 Cor. 5.10). All three writers closely associate God and Christ in the judgment, so little weight should be put on any supposed difference in this respect.

3. Mercy is explicit in Luke's Gospel (6.36), implied in Matthew. Guelich observes, 'This section on Judging directly corresponds with the thrust of the fifth petition regarding forgiveness in the Lord's Prayer (6:12), just as the sections 6:19-24, 25-34 have done with the preceding petitions' (*Sermon*, p. 353).

4. So also Murray, *Romans*, II, p. 185; cf. 1 Cor. 11.31: 'But if we judged ourselves truly, we should not be judged', εἰ δὲ ἑαυτοὺς διεκρίνομεν, οὐκ ἂν ἐκρινόμεθα. This would be a closer parallel (in form) to the Gospels than Rom. 14.13 were it not for the use of διακρίνειν instead of κρίνειν.

Outside Romans 2 and 14 Paul speaks three times of 'judging' one's fellows in a negative sense. κρίνειν signifies censorious judgment in 1 Cor. 10.29 (of one's liberty to act being condemned by another's scruples) and Col. 2.16: 'Therefore let no one pass judgment on you in questions of food and drink or with regard to a festival or a new moon or a sabbath'. In 1 Cor. 4.5 he tells the Corinthians not to judge anything (μὴ . . . τι κρίνετε) before the Lord comes; in context Paul is addressing his readers' attitude toward their apostolic leaders. Rather than appreciating Paul's faithfulness as servant and steward, the Corinthians are setting themselves up as judges, examining (ἀνακρίνειν) his ministry by other criteria. Their criticism is not important to Paul, since the Lord alone is the one who judges (4.3-4). Hence, his readers are not to 'reach any verdict',[1] for when the Lord comes he will bring to light every hidden thing and all will answer to him (4.5). Elsewhere he indicates that it can be appropriate to 'judge' brethren in a different sense (1 Cor. 5.3-4, 12-13). Here κρίνειν means to reach a decision in the exercise of church discipline (cf. Mt. 18.15-20), not censorious condemnation of others in day-to-day relations.

2. *Extra-Pauline Use of* κρίνειν

In secular Greek, κρίνειν was a neutral word meaning 'to part' or 'to sift out' (Homer), leading to the sense 'to divide out', 'to select', or 'to value'.[2] Acquiring a variety of nuances (discriminate, approve, estimate, prefer, etc.)[3] it most commonly signified 'to decide', and hence 'to assess', in the middle voice connoting 'to go to law' or 'to dispute with' in a legal sense.[4] Although the verb was often used as a technical legal term meaning 'to judge', 'to bring to judgment', or 'to condemn', it is difficult to find any instances in which κρίνειν applies to specifically negative personal judgments on others (i.e. outside the court context or the action of those in authority). Under the category 'pass sentence upon, condemn', LSJ cites in addition to Mt. 7.1 only Demosthenes 19.232; 4.47; and *PRyl.* 76.8, all of which are cases of

---

1. Barrett, *1 Corinthians*, p. 103.
2. Büchsel, *TDNT*, III, p. 922.
3. Schneider, *NIDNTT*, II, p. 362.
4. Büchsel, *TDNT*, III, p. 922.

judgment in court.[1] An apparent parallel appears in Epictetus 2.21.11:

> Man, at home you have fought a regular prize-fight with your slave, you
> have driven your household into the street, you have disturbed your
> neighbours' peace; and now do you come to me with a solemn air, like a
> philosopher, and sitting down pass judgment on the explanation I gave of
> the reading of the text (καθήμενος κρίνεις, πῶς ἐξηγησάμην τὴν
> λέξιν) and on the application, forsooth, of the comments I made as I
> babbled out whatever came into my head?

The meaning of κρίνειν in this case may be 'to pass a negative judgment', but in context the verb probably means 'evaluate' (a common
nuance). Epictetus is speaking about inconsistency; the imaginary
person addressed is not a man who admits that he knows nothing and
goes to his teacher like one who goes to consult an oracle, prepared to
obey (2.21.10). Instead, he fails to live like a philosopher while
insisting on acting like one, sifting his teacher's words without putting
them into practice. The object of the judgment here is not Epictetus,
but the manner (πῶς) in which he explained the text.

In Jewish literature closer analogies to Paul's concern over one man
judging (in the sense of condemning) another appear. There are no
parallels in the LXX[2], Philo,[3] or Josephus, but in 1QS 10.17-18 we
read,

> I will pay to no man the reward of evil;
> I will pursue him with goodness.
> For judgment (משפט) of all the living is with God
> and it is he who will render to man his reward.

The author of the hymn does not explicitly state that he will not judge
another, but paying the 'reward of evil' appears to be equivalent to
judging, for he recognizes that to render what is due to the evil man is

---

1. LSJ, II, p. 996.
2. Common in the LXX, κρίνειν is most often applied to God who judges (משפט);
human judges do so only by God-given authority. κρίνειν translates several other
roots, the most frequent of which is דין (e.g. Ps. 7.9). BDB cites three instances in
the MT in which משפט is used of humans condemning others: Ps. 108[109].31, where
the LXX has καταδιώκειν; Ezek. 23.45 (ἐκδικοῦν); and Ps. 140[141].6, a corrupt
text which the LXX (140.6) translates as κατεπόθησαν ἐχόμενα πέτρας οἱ κριταὶ
αὐτῶν. דין is not used in this way.
3. Philo uses κρίνειν over ninety times, but never in the sense found in our passages.

God's prerogative. The saying seems to parallel the spirit of the teachings of the Gospels, yet there is a decisive difference that surfaces in the verses that follow (1QS 10.19-20):

> I will not grapple with the men of perdition
> until the Day of Revenge,
> but my wrath shall not turn from the men of falsehood
> and I will not rejoice until judgment (משפט) is made.

With this may be compared earlier instructions in 1QS for members of the sect to 'love all that God has chosen and hate all that he has rejected', to 'love all the sons of light, each according to his lot in God's design, and hate all the sons of darkness, each according to his guilt in God's vengeance' (1QS 1.4, 9-10). Although one could not be vindictive in one's actions, hatred of outsiders was not only permitted but expected.[1] Thus any 'judging' that may be implicitly prohibited in 1QS 10.17-18 would refer only to hostile actions, not attitudes. Paul and the authors of the Gospels would hardly allow such a distinction.[2]

Rabbinic literature provides the closest parallels to NT prohibitions of judging. Rabbi Joshua ben Perachiah is quoted in *m. Ab.* 1.6 as having said,

> Provide thyself with a teacher and get thee a fellow[-disciple]; and when thou judgest (והוי דן) any man incline the balance in his favour.

Judging here however appears neutral; it is allowed, and it lacks the distinctly negative nuance it has in our texts.[3] Often cited are the words ascribed to Rabbi Hillel (*m. Ab.* 2.5):

> Keep not aloof from the congregation and trust not in thyself until the day of thy death, and judge not (ואל תדין) thy fellow until thou art come to his place. . .

Furnish thinks this saying undercuts the case for dominical influence on Paul,[4] but here דין means to judge in the sense 'to form an opinion

---

1. Cf. Piper, *Enemies*, p. 40; he comments, 'As with certain parts of the rabbinic literature. . . Qumran apparently represents a further development of that side of the Old Testament seen in Pss. 69:21-28; 109; 139:19-22' (p. 41).

2. In the Qumran writings שפט appears frequently, and is consistently used of either God or those appointed to serve in the office of judge (e.g. 1QS 6.24). דין is rare, again usually referring to God.

3. Cf. also, e.g., *Der. Er. Zut.* 3; *b. Shab.* 127b.

4. *Theology*, pp. 57-58.

of';[1] unlike Rom. 14.13 and Mt. 7.1 par., the reason for not judging is one's ignorance of the other person's situation, not the awareness that God will judge him who judges.[2] It is unclear whether Hillel is prohibiting judging another. The aphorism could mean either 'Don't judge at all' (i.e. one can never know all the facts), or 'Don't be hasty in evaluating another; know the facts first'.[3] The saying of Rabbi Ishmael ben Jose (late 2nd cent. AD) in *m. Ab.* 4.8 may seem a better parallel at first glance:

Judge not alone (אל תהי דן יחידי), for none may judge alone save One,

but in context he is giving advice to those who hold judicial office; the point is that a judge should render decisions in consultation with his peers. Probably the closest parallel is the saying of R. Isaac in *b. Ros. Has.* 16b,

Three things call a man's iniquities to mind, namely, a shaky wall, the scrutinizing of prayer, and calling for [Divine] judgment (ומוסר דין) on one's fellow man. For R. Abin said: He who calls down [Divine] judgment on his neighbour is himself punished first [for his own sins].

To call for divine judgment, however, is not quite the same thing as to judge, and dates for Rabbis Isaac and Abin are late.

In summary, outside the NT we find κρίνειν used in a variety of senses, including the more familiar meaning 'to judge' in a legal sense. It can mean 'to condemn' or 'to pass sentence upon' (where it is virtually equivalent to κατακρίνειν), but then it applies to God, kings, and those who possess the authority to judge. Sometimes men are said to have judged wrongly, but in those cases the verb is qualified with an adverb. There appears to be no instance in which κρίνειν is prohibited in secular Greek. With the possible exception of *m. Ab.* 2.5, one searches Jewish literature in vain for a case in which men are cat-

---

1. Jastrow, *Dictionary*, II, p. 301.

2. Blackman paraphrases the thought of the saying in an explanatory note: 'viz., one must not pass judgment without full knowledge of all the circumstances' (*Mishnayoth*, IV, p. 498 n. 9).

3. Büchler sees the saying as an exhortation against condemning the neighbour too hastily: 'This warning is merely a practical application of Hillel's rendering of Lev. 19.18: what is hateful to thee, do not to thy neighbour. . . which he declared to the non-Jew to be the whole Torah: not only to think oneself into the position of the fellow-man and refrain from reproaching him, but to wait till one is actually in the same trouble' (*Piety*, p. 23).

egorically prohibited from judging (דין or שׁפט) others.[1] This is not to dispute that there are many parallels to the *idea* that one should not condemn another person, but in those cases a different Greek word is employed, not κρίνειν. Paul's application of its forensic sense to everyday relations between Christians and his consequent rejection of such 'judging' appears more radical than in rabbinic thought, coming out of a strong conviction that God alone is judge. Apart from exceptions where they are given authority, people are not to usurp God's place by passing judgment upon one another.

Paul is not the only NT writer with this perspective. The author of the Epistle of James uses κρίνειν in a similar way:

> Do not speak evil against one another, brethren. He that speaks evil against a brother or judges (ὁ . . . κρίνων) his brother, speaks evil against the law and judges (κρίνει) the law. But if you judge the law, you are not a doer of the law but a judge (κριτής). There is one lawgiver and judge, he who is able to save and to destroy. But who are you that you judge (ὁ κρίνων) your neighbour? (4.11-12)

The one who 'judges' his brother sets himself above the law (i.e. the 'royal' law, 2.8; cf. the use of πλησίον in 4.12 and 2.8) by acting as though he need not love his neighbour. Here κρίνειν connotes passing negative judgment on another and is closely associated with κατα-λαλεῖν, 'to slander'. Like Paul, the author does not qualify κρίνειν with an adverb or predicate accusative; κρίνειν τὸν πλησίον is flatly prohibited. The motivation is also similar: God alone should judge.[2] Given the evidence that James knew and drew upon a number of teachings of Jesus elsewhere in his Epistle, it is not unreasonable to see in 4.12 the influence of JT attested in Mt. 7.1 // Lk. 6.37. If that is correct, we have extra-Pauline evidence corroborating the use of the

---

1. *Contra* C.G. Montefiore's assertion, 'There is nothing in these verses [Mt. 7.1-5] which is not entirely on Rabbinic lines'. Montefiore observed that instead of 'Judge not', 'the usual Rabbinic wording is rather "judge favourably"', but he did not comment on the radical force of 7.1 (*Literature*, pp. 144-45). In a polemical work intended to expose and expound the parallels in Jewish literature to the SM, G. Friedlander did not dispute the originality of the prohibition of judging; rather, he *contrasted* the wisdom of the saying with that of *m. Ab.* 1.6; 2.5, and *b. Shab.* 127b, concluding that Jesus' teaching is inferior because it is negative and impossible to carry out literally (*Sources*, pp. 212-16).

2. Davids correctly notes the uniqueness of the reasoning that judging breaks the law, but that does not affect our case (*Epistle*, p. 170).

command in question. The significance of the evidence from James depends of course on where and when the Epistle was written, but in any event we find there another case of κρίνειν with the distinctly negative nuance found in Romans 14 and the Gospel parallels.[1]

3. *Summary and Conclusion*

The vocabulary in Rom. 14.13a is similar to that of Mt. 7.1 and Lk. 6.37a. The differences are capable of explanation, and in this particular case grammatical considerations are of little assistance. Although κρίνειν is a common word, Paul's application of it to private relations between persons seems distinctly Jewish. The meaning of the parallels is essentially the same. More importantly, Paul's unqualified criticism of κρίνειν is unusual and parallels the Gospels. The rationale given and implied in the parallels reflects a common motivation, although there are some differences. In other passages where Paul speaks negatively about judging we find similar appeals to the certainty of future judgment by God (Rom. 2.1-11; 1 Cor. 4.3-5), but no hint that he is alluding to a saying of Jesus. He gives reasons for prohibiting judging, but the fact that Jesus said the same thing was apparently so basic to Christian instruction that Paul could take it for granted, leaving for him the task of driving home the inner logic of the saying. The evidence of Jas 4.11-12 supports the case that the saying attested in Mt. 7.1 // Lk. 6.37a was well known.

Paul chooses to conclude the segment of thought running from 14.1 to 14.12 with a short, pointed prohibition of κρίνειν in 14.13a. Elsewhere the apostle sometimes appeals to Christ as the climactic rationale in his arguments (cf. 1 Cor. 9.14; Rom. 13.14; and the use of Jesus' example in 15.3ff.); is it possible that he does so here? Perhaps. But what is more likely is that his language in general about judging reflects the influence of meditation on the radical teaching of Jesus.[2] In their day-to-day relations with each other, the Christians in

1. Cf. also *1 Clem*. 13.2 and Pol. *Phil*. 2.3. BAGD cites Sextus's *Sententiae* 183 (late 2nd cent. AD Christian reworking of a pagan original): ὁ κρίνων ἄνθρωπον κρίνεται ὑπὸ τοῦ θεοῦ.

2. So also Allison, 'Pattern', p. 12; Hunter, *Predecessors*, p. 48; Knowling, *Testimony*, p. 317; Feine, *Christus*, p. 254. Davies lists Rom. 14.10-11 as the passage paralleled by Mt. 7.1 // Lk. 6.37 (*Paul*, p. 138); so also Fraser (*Interpreter*, p. 97).

Rome are not to reform their standards of judgment; they are not to judge each other according to a 'scale of merit'; they are to cease 'judging' *altogether*. When Jews boast in the law, consider themselves guides to the blind, are confident that they are correctors of the foolish, and presume therefore to teach others, they set themselves up as judges, hypocritically blind to their own need for repentance (Rom. 2.1-4, 17-24; 14.10). Similarly, when Gentile Christians boast of their faith but ridicule the sincere practices of their Jewish brethren, their superior attitude leads them to 'judge' in hypocrisy (11.20, 25; 14.10). Censorious condemnation is out of the question for the Roman Christians for the same reason given in the Gospels: they will all be judged. Awareness of their own sinfulness should lead them to exhibit the same accepting spirit that they have experienced in Christ. κρίνειν ἀδελφόν is not the way of ἀνυπόκριτος ἀγάπη (12.9).

Chapter 11

ROMANS 14.13B: AVOIDING ΣΚΑΝΔΑΛΑ

With the use of paronomasia, Paul makes a smooth transition in Rom. 14.13 from admonition addressed to both weak and strong to exhortation especially directed to the latter: instead of condemning (κρίνειν) a weak brother, the strong should decide (κρίνειν) not to put a πρόσκομμα or σκάνδαλον in his way.[1] Paul does not immediately expound what he means by these words; apparently they were familiar enough for his readers to grasp their significance. Was that because they knew dominical teaching(s) that employed similar language? Over fifty years ago C.H. Dodd commented on the verse,

> It can hardly be doubted that [dominical] sayings. . . were in Paul's mind. . . The key-word is skandalon. . . It is not a good or usual Greek word, and the very fact that Paul uses it here suggests that he knew it in the tradition of the sayings of Jesus.[2]

Maximalists continue to quote Dodd,[3] although the only discussion of

---

1. So Käsemann, *Romans*, p. 374 and most commentators. Evidence for the omission of πρόσκομμα ἤ is insufficient to warrant its deletion. Jewett translates σκάνδαλον as 'hindrance' (cf. RSV), finding in the word reference to Jewish restrictions advanced by the weak (*Tolerance*, p. 135). 'Hindrance' may occasionally render πρόσκομμα but not σκάνδαλον; the latter is better translated 'trap' or 'temptation to sin' (cf. BAGD, p. 753) and signifies the threat of spiritual ruin. Paul uses the words together in Rom. 9.32-33 (cf. Isa. 8.14) where they form a virtual tautology (cf. K. Müller, *Anstoss*, pp. 32-45). In the light of subsequent comments in 14.14-21 directed particularly to the strong, Jewett's view should be rejected.

2. *Romans*, p. 218 and n. 1; cf. *idem*, '"Εννομος', p. 145; Sanday and Headlam, *Exegetical Commentary*, p. 390. Paul's use of πρόσκομμα has no significant Synoptic parallel; the context of Jn 11.9-10 links stumbling (προσκόπτειν) with Jewish unbelief and rejection of Jesus (cf. Rom. 9.32-33; 1 Pet. 2.8).

3. E.g. Allison ('Pattern', p. 15), Hunter (*Predecessors*, p. 48) and Davies (*Paul*, p. 138). For a similar view: Fraser (*Jesus*, pp. 97, 113), J.P. Brown ('Parallels', pp. 41, 46-47), Furnish (*Theology*, p. 53), and Knowling (*Testimony*, p. 317).

this claim concludes to the contrary.[1] What is the evidence?

1. *The Use of* σκάνδαλον/σκανδαλίζειν

On the basis of word frequency, Dodd's statement appears justified. σκάνδαλον does not appear outside the Jewish–Christian sphere, and aside from *Pss. Sol.* 16.7 there are no extant instances of the verb σκανδαλίζειν independent of the Bible.[2] The words do not appear in Josephus, Philo, or other Hellenistic Jewish writers, and occur in the papyri only in two 8th cent. AD mss.[3] In the LXX the noun occurs 21 times and the verb only 4, always in the passive voice.[4] σκάνδαλον most frequently renders either מוקש (8 times: 'lure', or figuratively, 'snare'; the construction usually is εἶναι or γίνεσθαι εἰς σκάνδαλον)[5] or מכשול (3 times: 'stumbling-block').[6] Proportionately, the σκάνδαλ- words are far more common in the NT (especially in the Gospels) than in the LXX. The Synoptics employ the noun 9 times and the verb 24; in contrast to the LXX, the Gospels have the active form almost as often as the passive.[7] Paul has the noun 6 times and the verb 4.[8] The verb appears twice more in John's Gospel (6.61; 16.1) and the noun once each in 1 Peter (2.8), 1 John (2.10), and Revelation (2.14).

The influence of the LXX on the NT in this respect can scarcely be overestimated. Stählin notes both formally and materially the NT use of σκάνδαλον and σκανδαλίζω is exclusively controlled by the thought and speech of the OT and Judaism. How far the words are from Greek thought may be seen not only from their absence from

1. That is, K. Müller, *Anstoss*, pp. 42-45.
2. Stählin, *TDNT*, VII, p. 340.
3. MM, p. 576.
4. I.e. Dan. 11.41 (= כשל); Sir. 9.5; 23.8; 35.15 [ET 32.15].
5. I.e. Pss. 68[69].23; 139[140].6; 140[141].9; 105[106].36; Josh. 23.13; Judg. 2.3; 8.27; 1 Sam. 18.21.
6. I.e. Lev. 19.14; 1 Sam. 25.31; Ps. 118[119].165. Cf. also Pss. 48[49].14; 49[50].20; 1 Macc. 5.4.
7. The active voice is used six times in Matthew (5.29, 30; 17.27; 18.6, 8, 9), four in Mark (9.42, 43, 45, 47) and once in Luke (17.2); Matthew has the passive eight times (11.6; 13.21; 13.57; 15.12; 24.10; 26.31, 33 [twice]), Mark four (4.17; 6.3; 14.27, 29, and Luke once (7.23).
8. In addition to texts cited below, Paul uses σκάνδαλον in an OT quotation in Rom. 11.9 (Ps. 68[69].23).

Greek literature but also from the need which the fathers repeatedly felt to explain the meaning of the NT σκάνδαλον.[1]

Although in some cases the meaning is close to that of πρόσκομμα (e.g. Rom. 9.33; 1 Pet. 2.8) σκάνδαλον continues to mean 'cause of ruin', maintaining the nuance of enticement/temptation ('snare', 'trap'; cf. מוקש) in several instances.

Two passages in the LXX are of major relevance to Rom. 14.13b. Jdt. 12.2 presents an immediate thematic parallel, inasmuch as Judith refuses to eat pagan food set before her, lest it be an offence (ἵνα μὴ γένηται σκάνδαλον), that is, lead to her ruin (cf. Rev. 2.14). The most important text however is Lev. 19.14, which features a verbal construction closer to Paul's μὴ **τιθέναι** πρόσκομμα τῷ ἀδελφῷ ἢ **σκάνδαλον** than in any of the Synoptics: 'You shall not curse the deaf or put a stumbling block (οὐ **προσθήσεις σκάνδαλον**) before the blind'.[2] As we shall see, this text probably provided the inspiration at least for the *form* of Paul's admonition in Romans.

2. Dominical Parallels

If Paul knew a logion about σκάνδαλα it would most likely be the warning that it would be better for a person to have a millstone put around his neck and to be cast into the sea than to 'scandalize' one of the little ones:

Mt. 18.6	Mk 9.42	Lk. 17.2 (inverted)
Ὃς δ' ἂν σκανδαλίσῃ	Καὶ ὃς ἂν σκανδαλίσῃ	...ἢ ἵνα σκανδαλίσῃ
ἕνα τῶν μικρῶν τούτων	ἕνα τῶν μικρῶν τούτων	τῶν μικρῶν τούτων ἕνα
τῶν πιστευόντων εἰς ἐμέ,	τῶν πιστευόντων [εἰς ἐμέ],	
συμφέρει αὐτῷ	καλόν ἐστιν αὐτῷ μᾶλλον	λυσιτελεῖ αὐτῷ
ἵνα κρεμασθῇ μύλος ὀνικὸς	εἰ περίκειται μύλος ὀνικὸς	εἰ λίθος μυλικὸς περίκειται
περὶ τὸν τράχηλον αὐτοῦ	περὶ τὸν τράχηλον αὐτοῦ	περὶ τὸν τράχηλον αὐτοῦ
καὶ καταποντισθῇ	καὶ βέβληται	καὶ ἔρριπται
ἐν τῷ πελάγει τῆς θαλάσσης	εἰς τὴν θάλασσαν	εἰς τὴν θάλασσαν...

This is the only σκανδαλ- saying recorded in all three Synoptics. Bultmann considered it to be a case in which the Church took over an

---

1. Stählin, *TDNT*, VII, p. 344.

2. Cf. also Sir. 7.6 and Hos. 4.17, both of which have τιθέναι σκάνδαλον. In the Gospels the phrase τιθέναι σκάνδαλον does not appear. Except for Mt. 13.41 where the noun is the object of συλλέγειν, σκάνδαλον appears only with ἔρχεσθαι or εἶναι.

old proverb whose origin is unrecoverable, and which appeared in Q without Christian alterations.[1] Certainly the logion is early, and a warning of this severity would not easily be forgotten.[2] Whether it originally referred to children is uncertain.[3]

Regardless of Jesus' original referents, for Matthew the μικροί are not children (cf. Mt. 10.42), and his context is more helpful in determining how the warning may have functioned in the early church. The parallels with Paul are striking. Like Paul, Matthew is concerned about the actions of people within his community which may lead to the spiritual ruin of their fellow-members.[4] Jesus has just said that he who would enter and be greatest in the kingdom must, through ταπείνωσις, become like the summoned child (18.3-4). Such a one should be received (δέχεσθαι) in Jesus' name (18.5; cf. Mk 9.37 // Lk. 9.48), and not caused to stumble (18.6). These ταπεινοί would include all those who need special help from the Church because of their defencelessness; to lead astray those who belong to God would be to incur his judgment.[5] In this light, Paul's words to the strong τί ἐξουθενεῖς τὸν ἀδελφόν σου (14.10) resemble the thought of the warning μὴ καταφρονήσητε ἑνὸς τῶν μικρῶν τούτων, among whom the weak person would be counted (Mt. 18.10).[6]

---

1. *History*, p. 144, citing in support the saying of R. Shesheth in *b. Sanh.* 55a (see below).

2. 'Die je verschiedene Überlieferungsgestalt, die das Drohwort gegen den Anstoßstifter bei den Synoptikern aufweist, gibt zu erkennen, daß es sich um ein Logion handelt, welches schon frühzeitig in unterschiedlichen Zusammenhängen heimisch geworden ist' (K. Müller, *Anstoss*, p. 44).

3. Matthew links the logion to the saying about receiving a child in Jesus' name (Mt. 18.5; cf. Mk 9.37). One would expect the application of the saying to move in time from children to the disciples, not vice-versa (V. Taylor, *Mark*, p. 411; cf. Manson, *Sayings*, p. 138). K. Müller thinks that Luke's version preserves the more primitive version of the wording; Mark has added τῶν πιστευόντων and Matthew εἰς ἐμέ (*Anstoss*, p. 43, rejecting the Markan εἰς ἐμέ variant). On the other hand, C.G. Montefiore claimed that Matthew's version was perhaps earlier than Mark's because 'the absolute use of "believe" to mean the Christian believer is secondary and late' (*Gospels*, I, p. 222).

4. Cf. also Moffatt ('Stumbling-blocks', pp. 408-409), who finds Jesus' intense care for the μικροί disciples reflected in Paul's passionate word of 2 Cor. 11.29; cf. Stählin, *TDNT*, VII, p. 356.

5. Cf. Guhrt, *NIDNTT*, II, pp. 709-10.

6. Dodd, '"Εννομος', p. 145. Dodd also notes that Mark concludes the σκαν-

Other Synoptic warnings about σκάνδαλα (Mt. 18.7 // Lk. 17.1;
Mt. 13.41-42; 16.23) are also marked by a very serious tone. Jesus is
not talking about questions of defilement or of minor transgressions,
but of spiritual life and death.[1] Paul's language is similarly strong in
his warning to take note of those who create dissensions and σκάνδαλα (Rom. 16.17). Although the noun never refers to Christ in the
Synoptics, the use of σκανδαλίζεσθαι with a causal/instrumental ἐν
phrase consistently depicts Christ as the occasion for danger, either
through rejection of him or by persecution for his sake. It is not a
long step from the declaration μακάριός ἐστιν ὃς ἐὰν μὴ
σκανδαλισθῇ ἐν ἐμοί (Mt. 11.6 // Lk. 7.23; cf. Jn 6.61b-64) for Paul
to speak of the σκάνδαλον of Christ crucified (1 Cor. 1.23; cf. Gal.
5.11).[2] σκανδαλίζεσθαι ἐν αὐτῷ (Mt. 13.57 // Mk 6.3; Mt. 15.12)
can be the opposite of πιστεῦσαι εἰς αὐτόν[3]—precisely what the Jews
and Greeks in 1 Corinthians 1 have failed to do. As in 1 Pet. 2.8, the
conflated quotation of Isa. 28.16 and Isa. 8.14 in Rom. 9.32 depicts
Christ himself as the stone over which people stumble and come to
ruin.[4]

Paul's use of the verb σκανδαλίζειν also parallels the Synoptics.
Although N–A[26] rejects the reading, ἢ σκανδαλίζεται ἢ ἀσθενεῖ
may well belong to the original text of Rom. 14.21.[5] In 2 Cor. 11.29

δαλ- sequence with the call to be at peace with one another (9.50); cf. Rom. 14.19.

1. Cf. Moffatt, 'Stumbling-blocks', p. 407.

2. Richardson and Gooch compare Paul's words in the same context about the
Jews seeking signs (1 Cor. 1.22) with Jesus' logia in Mk 8.11-12, where the
Pharisees seek a sign ('Logia', p. 47).

3. Stählin, *TDNT*, VII, p. 349. Cf. Humbert: 'Dans l'évangile, les concepts
σκάνδαλον et πίστις sont inséparablement unis. Σκάνδαλον traduit une idée
essentielle du christianisme. A la limite, la formule σκανδαλίζεσθαι ἐν ἐμοί
exprime chez le païen le refus absolu de répondre à l'appel du Christ, chez le croyant
l'apostasie. A l'actif, σκανδαλίζειν consistera à tuer la foi dans les âmes des croy-
ants' ('Essai', pp. 10-11).

4. Both authors similarly combine the texts from Isaiah without closely following
either the MT or the LXX, an indication of probable dependence upon a common tradition (cf. Lindars, *Apologetic*, pp. 175-83).

5. Metzger explains the addition as a western expansion reflecting the influence of
1 Cor. 8.11-13 (*Commentary*, p. 532), but evidence for its inclusion is widespread
and early (𝔓[46] vid ℵ[2] B D F 𝔐 lat sy[h], etc.), whereas witnesses for its omission are
confined largely to the Alexandrian text type. Furthermore, 1 Cor. 8 does not provide
a suitable parallel, as none of the three verbs are *combined* there. Paul was capable of

Paul is again thinking of the welfare of his congregation: 'Who is weak, and I am not weak? Who is *made to fall*, and I am not indignant? (τίς ἀσθενεῖ καὶ οὐκ ἀσθενῶ; τίς σκανδαλίζεται καὶ οὐκ ἐγὼ πυροῦμαι). Finally, the clearest dominical link in Paul appears in 1 Cor. 8.13, where the extremely rare transitive use of σκανδαλίζειν (elsewhere only in *Pss. Sol.* 16.7) agrees with the Synoptics (cf. Mk 9.43-47 // Mt. 18.8-9; 5.29-30; 17.27). Paul warns against setting a trap for a brother by eating food or meat:

> Therefore, if food is a cause of my brother's falling (εἰ βρῶμα σκανδαλίζει τὸν ἀδελφόν μου), I will never eat meat, lest I cause my brother to fall (ἵνα μὴ τὸν ἀδελφόν μου σκανδαλίσω).

The context (specifically 8.10) makes it clear that he has in mind any situation in which one person's confident behaviour leads another to act contrary to conscience.

3. *Other Jewish Parallels*

On the basis of the Greek evidence, a case for dependence on JT may seem fairly strong. Nevertheless, the metaphor of stumbling blocks and snares was common in other Jewish writings. In the Qumran literature, as in the OT, כשל and מכשול occur fairly frequently, the verb more so than the noun (e.g. 1QS 2.12, 17; 11.12; 1QH 17.23); מוקש is quite rare (i.e. 1QH 2.21; cf. CD 14.2). In the rabbinic writings, a new loan word from Aramaic, תקל, appears. Common in the Mishnah and Talmud, it is a synonym of כשל and probably lies behind the Synoptic σκανδαλίζειν sayings.[1] In *b. Sanh.* 55a, R. Shesheth (late 3rd–mid 4th cent. AD) states:

> We have learnt it: If in the case of trees, which neither eat nor drink nor smell, the Torah decreed that they should be burnt and destroyed, because they had proved a stumbling block (תקלה); how much more so [must thou destroy him] who seduces his neighbour from the path of life to that of death.

---

combining σκανδαλίζειν and ἀσθενεῖν (cf. 2 Cor. 11.29), and an Alexandrian copyist could have either skipped a line of text because of homoioteleuton, or shortened what he considered redundant. Stählin (*TDNT*, VII, p. 355 n. 96), Michel (*Römer*, p. 438 n. 33) and Lagrange (*Romains*, p. 333) include the text.

1. Stählin, *TDNT*, VII, p. 341; C.G. Montefiore, *Literature*, p. 259. The root does not appear in the Qumran literature.

The saying parallels Mt. 18.7 par., reflecting the seriousness with which causes of stumbling could be seen by the Rabbis. In *m. Ber.* 4.2 it is stated that R. Neḥunya b. ha-Kanah (1st cent. AD) used to pray a short prayer whenever he entered the house of study:

> When I enter I pray that no offence shall happen through me...
> (בכניסתי אני מתפלל שלא תארא תקלה על ידי)

Here תקלה refers to a wrong decision on matters of law, a failure in judgment, which leads others to commit sin.[1] In the Gemara on this passage (*b. Ber.* 28b) the saying is expanded:

> Our Rabbis taught: On entering what does a man say? 'May it be Thy will,
> O Lord my God, that no offence (תקלה) may occur through me, and that I
> may not err in a matter of *halachah* and that my colleagues may rejoice in
> me and that I may not call unclean clean or clean unclean, and that my
> colleagues may not err in a matter of *halachah* and that I may rejoice in
> them'.

In this case the תקלה does not seem quite so serious as in the saying of R. Shesheth, but what is interesting is the connection of the תקלה with the confusion of that which is considered clean and unclean. The construction does not parallel Rom. 14.13, but there is some similarity in thought: if the Rabbi were to declare that which was unclean to be clean, it would be a cause for stumbling. In Romans the πρόσκομμα/ σκάνδαλον is the temptation to compromise one's integrity wilfully, whereas in the example above the error is unintentional. Furthermore, in *b. Ber.* 28b there is some question as to what the stumbling consists of. It is possible to read the text simply as a prayer that the Rabbi might not cause his colleagues to commit sin by their rejoicing over his failure to judge rightly.[2]

There remain a number of instances in rabbinic literature in which the verb כשל appears and not a few warnings, most of which are citations of Lev. 19.14:

> You shall not curse the deaf or put a stumbling block before the blind
> (ולפני עור לא תתן מכשל), but you shall fear your God: I am the Lord.

In virtually every instance the rabbis take the injunction in a metaphorical sense (e.g. *b. Abod. Zar.* 6a; 22a; *b. B. Meṣ.* 90a). The

---

1. So Blackman, *Mishnayoth*, I, p. 49 nn. 3, 5.
2. So Blackman, *Mishnayoth*, I, p. 49 n. 5.

most frequently cited parallel is *m. B. Meṣ.* 5.11, where Lev. 19.14 is quoted in a list of injunctions as proof that those who borrow and lend are transgressors. Commenting on the passage, Abaye implies that the borrower places a stumbling block before the lender by offering interest and appealing to the creditor's greed (*b. B. Meṣ.* 75b). Of particular interest is a saying of R. Nathan (mid 2nd cent. AD) which is quoted twice in the Talmud (*b. Pes.* 22b and *b. Abod. Zar.* 6a):

> How do we know that a man must not hold out a cup of wine to a nazirite
> or the limb of a living animal to the children of Noah? Because it is stated,
> thou shalt not put a stumbling block before the blind.

The temptations of offering wine to a nazirite or meat with blood in it to a fellow Jew parallels the temptation of the weak Christians in Rome to compromise their integrity by drinking wine and eating meat of uncertain origin. Given the importance of Lev. 19.14 in rabbinic thought, the saying attributed to R. Nathan could preserve an early Jewish application of the verse, an application particularly fitting for the Roman situation. Paul certainly knows Leviticus well. He has already quoted a verse from the same chapter in Rom. 13.9 (Lev. 19.18), and if there did exist an early Christian 'holiness code' paralleling some elements of the Levitical law of ch. 19,[1] the prohibition of putting a σκάνδαλον before another would presumably be familiar to the readers. Whereas the Gospels provide no parallel to Paul's τιθέναι σκάνδαλον construction in Rom. 14.13b, Lev. 19.14 in the LXX does, although the verb there is προστιθέναι. Other similar constructions in the LXX are Ps. 139[140].6; Sir. 7.6; Hos. 4.17; Jdt. 5.1; and Isa. 29.21 (τιθέναι πρόσκομμα).

On the other hand, there are problems with this view. The Christian 'holiness code' is only a theory. Furthermore, Paul uses τιθέναι in connection with both πρόσκομμα and σκάνδαλον earlier in Rom. 9.33, where he cites Isa. 28.16.[2] The verb in the LXX is different (ἐμβάλλειν), and τίθημι does not occur as a variant in the later versions, but it is used in a citation of the same verse by the author of 1 Peter (2.6).[3] If this translation of Isa. 28.16 was not unfamiliar to

---

1. As suggested by Carrington (*Catechism*) and Selwyn (*1 Peter*).
2. Rom. 14.13 differs from 9.33 in that πρόσκομμα and σκάνδαλον are the objects of the verb in the former, but are in the genitive case modifying the objects λίθον and πέτραν, respectively, in the latter.
3. The author of 1 Peter separates his citations of Isa. 8.14 and 28.16, so that

the early Church, we have another potential source for the language of Rom 14.13b.[1] What can be said then for tracing Paul's concern about σκάνδαλον/σκανδαλίζειν back to the teaching of Jesus?

K. Müller has briefly addressed the question of the relationship of Rom. 14.13b and Mt. 18.6 par. in his dissertation on the background of Paul's use of σκάνδαλον. Citing the rabbinic parallels, he rightly concludes that the metaphorical interpretation of Lev. 19.14 was well known in the earliest rabbinic traditions. Paul's expression τιθέναι πρόσκομμα τῷ ἀδελφῷ ἢ σκάνδαλον is the equivalent of לחבירו גרם חקלה, and 'Dabei legt der Wortlaut in Röm 14,13b die Annahme nahe, daß Paulus seine Stellungnahme für den schwachen Mitbruder an den Sprachgebrauch der jüdischen Schultheologie anlehnte'.[2]

The frequency of σκάνδαλον in the LXX reduces the force of Dodd's claim by offering a probable text to inspire Paul. With the verb, however, the situation is different. Although Matthew is fond of the word, all of the σκανδαλίζειν sayings cannot be attributed to his creativity. Luke, who does not find the words helpful,[3] nevertheless joins Matthew (Q?) in preserving the logion about the blessedness of the one who is not 'scandalized' ἐν Ἰησοῦ. Mark uses the verb 8 times, and the Gospels unite in their witness to Jesus' warning against causing the 'little ones' to sin. The relative frequency of σκανδαλίζειν in the Gospels compared to the LXX and later versions of the OT is an argument, however weak in the light of the 'stumbling block' traditions in Judaism, in favour of some connection between the Synoptic tradition and Paul's statements in Rom. 14.21, 1 Cor. 8.13, and 2 Cor. 11.29. On the basis of the evidence presented thus far, it would therefore seem probable that Paul knew at least the saying preserved in Mt. 18.6 par., but also that unless further evidence from the context is adduced, he has expressed himself in Rom. 14.13 in the language of the OT.

There are, however, two factors remaining to be considered. First,

τίθημι occurs in 2.6, but πρόσκομμα and σκάνδαλον appear in 2.8.

1. Cf. Harris and Burch, *Testimonies*, I, pp. 26-32.

2. K. Muller, *Anstoss*, pp. 37, 44.

3. He uses the verb twice (7.23; 17.2) and the noun once (17.1). The rarity of σκάνδαλον and σκανδαλίζειν in his Gospel probably reflect both the difficulty his Gentile audience had understanding the words, and the importance of those σκανδαλ-sayings which he chose to include (cf. Stählin, *TDNT*, VII, pp. 344-45).

on any account one must explain how Paul expects an unknown and predominantly Gentile audience to comprehend the gravity of the Jewish words σκάνδαλον/σκανδαλίζειν.[1] When he turns to address the 'strong' in particular in 14.13b he chooses vocabulary found nowhere else outside biblical literature. πρόσκομμα (comparatively rare itself) would have been sufficient to make his point; the addition of ἢ σκάνδαλον after τὸ μὴ τιθέναι πρόσκομμα τῷ ἀδελφῷ reads almost as an afterthought, as if, having created an image, Paul is reminded of another (more striking?) word that expands and deepens his point. He obviously expects such an appeal to communicate effectively and to elicit prompt response. Paul probably derived his expressions from pre-Christian training, and the order πρόσκομμα– σκάνδαλον could derive from Isa. 8.14 (cf. Rom. 9.33), but such language would be more intelligible and compelling if the Gentile Christians in Rome (and Corinth) knew from their earlier instruction that some of Jesus' strongest warnings pertained to σκάνδαλα.

Secondly, this possible echo of Jesus appears in close conjunction with several other potential echoes. Taken individually, the exhortations not to condemn one another and not to place a σκάνδαλον before a fellow believer, and Paul's declaration that nothing is κοινός in itself (14.14, see below) may not seem impressive evidence for the influence of JT. Nevertheless, the concatenation of these parallels (as well as the appearance of more probable echoes in chs. 12–13) increases the likelihood that some link exists.

4. Conclusion

Do the rabbinic parallels reveal sufficient use of stumbling-block language to justify the important place Paul gives it in working out his ethic? Paul's imagery ultimately derives from the OT. The difficulty here (as in his use of Lev. 19.18 in 13.8-10) is in deciding whether or not the exhortation was shaped from the knowledge that Paul's Lord had stressed the importance of that OT teaching. The appearance of the unusual σκανδαλίζειν in all three Gospels indicates that Jesus used such language, and the severity of his warning makes it likely that such a saying would quickly become well known in the early

1. The same should be asked for the Corinthian congregation (cf. 1 Cor. 1.23; 8.13; 2 Cor. 11).

Church. It is doubtful that Paul would have been unaware of such a warning about community life. Whether he deliberately chose to use σκανδαλ- language because of his Lord's warning must remain uncertain and is incapable of proof. Here, as in several other so-called 'allusions' in Romans 12–15, Paul has probably been influenced by the teaching of Jesus, but he does not draw attention to the origin of the thought.

Chapter 12

ROMANS 14.14: 'NOTHING IS UNCLEAN...'

After calling for the strong to decide not to put a stumbling block or temptation to sin before a (weak) person (14.13b), Paul prefaces his explanation with a bold assertion: οἶδα καὶ πέπεισμαι ἐν κυρίῳ Ἰησοῦ ὅτι οὐδὲν κοινὸν δι' ἑαυτοῦ, confidently sweeping aside the fundamental Jewish distinction between that which is clean and unclean (Lev. 11; Deut. 14). Paul is not simply rejecting the idea of ritual defilement, a condition resulting from association with unclean things and persons; his unqualified affirmation in 14.20 πάντα μὲν καθαρά reveals his abandonment of that way of thinking which considers any type of food as intrinsically unacceptable.[1] Many see Paul alluding to JT here; others confidently deny it.[2] Who is correct?

---

1. Cf., e.g., Newton, *Concept*, p. 102. By the NT era κοινός had become a virtual synonym for ἀκάθαρτος (cf. 1 Macc. 1.47, 62; κοινοῦν in *4 Macc.* 7.6, and NT usage).

2. Those affirming an allusion echo include, *inter alia*, Deidun (*Morality*, p. 172 n. 64), Jeremias (*Sayings*, pp. 4-5), Westerholm (*Jesus*, pp. 81-82), Stuhlmacher ('Christologie', p. 215), Roetzel (*Letters*, p. 46), Lagrange (*Romains*, p. 329), Michel (*Römer*, p. 431 n. 6), Fitzmyer (*Romans*, II, p. 328 par. 128.). Denying an allusion: Zeller, *Römer*, p. 227; Neirynck, 'Sayings', pp. 307-308; E.P. Sanders, *Jesus*, p. 235; Räisänen, 'Jesus', p. 88; Ridderbos, *Romeinen*, p. 311; Lietzmann, *Römer*, p. 117.

1. *Textual Affinities*

Rom. 14.14, 20	Mk 7.15, 18b-19, 23	Mt. 15.11, 17, 20
οὐδὲν κοινὸν δι' ἑαυτοῦ,	**οὐδέν** ἐστιν ἔξωθεν τοῦ ἀνθρώπου εἰσπορευόμονον εἰς αὐτὸν ὃ **δύναται κοινῶσαι** αὐτόν,	**οὐ** τὸ εἰσερχόμενον εἰς τὸ στόμα **κοινοῖ** τὸν ἄνθρωπον,
εἰ μὴ τῷ λογιζομένῳ τι κοινὸν εἶναι, ἐκείνῳ κοινόν...	ἀλλὰ τὰ ἐκ τοῦ ἀνθρώπου ἐκπορευόμενά ἐστιν τὰ κοινοῦντα τὸν ἄνθρωπον... πᾶν τὸ ἔξωθεν εἰσπορευόμενον εἰς τὸν ἄνθρωπον **οὐ δύναται** αὐτὸν **κοινῶσαι** ὅτι οὐκ εἰσπορεύεται αὐτοῦ εἰς τὴν καρδίαν ἀλλ' εἰς τὴν κοιλίαν, καὶ εἰς τὸν ἀφεδρῶνα ἐκπορεύεται.	ἀλλὰ τὸ ἐκπορευόμενον ἐκ τοῦ στόματος, τοῦτο κοινοῖ τὸν ἄνθρωπον... πᾶν τὸ εἰσπορευ- όμενον εἰς τὸ στόμα εἰς τὴν κοιλίαν χωρεῖ καὶ εἰς ἀφεδρῶνα ἐκβάλλεται;
μὴ ἕνεκεν **βρώματος** κατάλυε τὸ ἔργον τοῦ θεοῦ. **πάντα μὲν καθαρά**...	**καθαρίζων πάντα τὰ βρώματα**	
	...πάντα ταῦτα τὰ πονηρὰ ἔσωθεν ἐκπορεύεται καὶ κοινοῖ τὸν ἄνθρωπον	...ταῦτα ἐστιν τὰ κοινοῦντα τὸν ἄνθρωπον, τὸ δὲ ἀνίπτοις χερσὶν φαγεῖν **οὐ κοινοῖ** τὸν ἄνθρωπον.

Paul's text is closer to Mark's Gospel than to Matthew's. κοινός and οὐδέν (Rom. 14.14) appear in Mark's account (7.2, 5, 15), while both

Matthew and Mark use the verb κοινοῦν.¹ μὴ ἕνεκεν βρώματος... πάντα μὲν καθαρά (Rom. 14.20) corresponds to
καθαρίζων πάντα τὰ βρώματα (Mk 7.19) and has no parallel in
Matthew. Luke records a scene in which Jesus dines with a Pharisee
and is asked why he himself did not first wash before dinner; his
response about cleansing the cup focuses on the disparity between the
Pharisees' outward purity and inward wickedness (cf. Matthew's version in 23.25-26), but there is no implicit rejection of OT purity laws
nor any solid verbal link with Romans (Lk. 11.37-41).² On the other
hand, in Mark's account Jesus is concerned not only to emphasize the
inner source of defilement but also to make a statement about what
does *not* defile. The Markan words οὐδέν ἐστιν ἔξωθεν... ὃ
δύναται κοινῶσαι (7.15), [πᾶν τὸ ἔξωθεν]... οὐ δύναται αὐτὸν
κοινῶσαι (7.18), and the editorial inference καθαρίζων πάντα τὰ
βρώματα make the denial of the Jewish clean/unclean distinction
so pointed that it could scarcely be missed, especially by Gentile
readers.³

By contrast, Matthew's version focuses on defilement arising from
the heart and plays down the implications of the antithesis for external
sources of defilement. Matthew adds the words τὸ δὲ ἀνίπτοις χερσὶν

1. The adjective in Mark's κοιναῖς χερσίν (= סהם ידים, cf. Smith, *Parallels*,
p. 32) has a slightly different nuance from that in Romans, where it applies to food.
Nevertheless, the verb's use in 7.15 is consistent with Paul's usage of κοινός.
2. Out of context, πάντα καθαρὰ ὑμῖν ἐστιν (Lk. 11.41) might seem to be a
parallel (the ὑμῖν here is similar in use to ἐκείνῳ in Rom. 14.14), but πάντα is
simply gathering up both the Pharisees' inward state and outward appearance; the
point is that if they would give attention to cleaning the inside, they would be completely clean (cf. Neusner, 'Background'). Clearly Luke has Jesus repudiating the
tradition of ritual washing, but nothing is said about food distinctions established in
the law. Luke implies the setting aside of Jewish food laws in the mission instructions (Lk. 10.8; cf. 1 Cor. 10.27).
3. So, e.g., E.P. Sanders, *Jesus*, p. 266. It is possible to construe the participle
καθαρίζων with ἀφεδρῶνα ('the latrine... purifies all foods', i.e., since all
foods eventually become excrement, there is no distinction among them; cf.
McEleney, 'Criteria', pp. 454-55, 460, following M. Black, *Approach*, pp. 217-18),
but to do so would be a breach of grammatical concord. Much more probable is the
interpretation going back to the Greek fathers that the participial phrase is grammatically dependent on καὶ λέγει αὐτοῖς in v. 18, καθαρίζων agreeing with the subject
of λέγει (Cranfield, *Mark*, p. 241). The difficulty of construing the participle occasioned the weakly attested variants for καθαρίζων (Metzger, *Commentary*, p. 95).

φαγεῖν οὐ κοινοῖ τὸν ἄνθρωπον at the conclusion of the pericope, underscoring Jesus' rejection of the traditions of men but also ensuring that his teaching would not be seen as addressing anything beyond the practice of ritual washing of hands—for Matthew, Jesus cannot set aside the law (cf. Mt. 5.18-19).[1] This does not necessarily mean that Matthew's community required keeping the kosher laws; the implication of an abrogation of purity laws is just as present in Mt. 15.11 as it is in the tradition that Jesus touched lepers (8.3) and associated with sinners.[2]

Rom. 14.14 and 20 more closely resemble Mark's account not only verbally, but also conceptually: both Paul and Jesus reject the idea that food is capable in itself of defiling a person.[3] The locus for sin is within.[4] Paul differs from the Synoptics by locating the sin in a person's decision to violate his or her faith, whereas Jesus emphasizes that the truly defiling actions originate in the heart. Paul's assertion has a more general application; 'It looks. . . like an attempt to bring out the underlying principle of Jesus' saying'.[5]

2. Availability of the Gospel Tradition

Until recently there was little question of the pre-Easter origin of Mk 7.15. The unusual assertion that uncleanness comes from within, the presence of antithetic parallelism, and the reference to the saying as a 'parable' (7.17) all support the conclusion that the saying goes back to Jesus. Some have criticized Mark's reference to the practice of hand-washing as anachronistic,[6] and it is widely accepted that in 7.1-23 he

---

1. Hill, *Matthew*, p. 252.

2. Cf. Carlston, 'Things', pp. 88-90.

3. So Neusner, *Idea*, p. 61; Hübner, *Law*, p. 84. R. Banks claims that Mark is thinking only of foods involved in idol worship (*Law*, pp. 144-45), but Räisänen rightly rejects such an interpretation as 'arbitrary' (*Paul*, p. 84 n. 211).

4. So also Leenhardt, *Romans*, p. 352. The contrast between 'inward' reality and 'outward' appearance goes back to the OT (e.g. 1 Sam. 16.7; Argyle, 'Outward').

5. Jeremias, *Sayings*, p. 5.

6. His ascription of the practice to 'all the Jews' (7.3) is surely an overstatement if pressed beyond the sense of 'pious Jews in general', and even that scope is disputed (cf., e.g., Büchler, 'Law', pp. 34-40; Margoliouth, 'Traditions', p. 263). On the early development of the practice see Lane, *Mark*, pp. 245-46.

brings together originally unconnected material,[1] but the common consensus has been that 7.15 represents historical bedrock.[2]

E.P. Sanders rejects the saying as unhistorical, doubting the common depiction of opposition between Jesus and the Pharisees. The setting of the pericope is 'extraordinarily unrealistic', and whereas the dispute in 7.1-23 arises over the issue of handwashing, the central logion around which the section is built (7.15) deals with food, so the saying fails to respond to the original question. Jesus and his disciples probably ate only kosher food, but the importance of the logion in 7.15 and Mark's comment in 7.19c for churches including Gentiles is obvious.[3] He concludes, 'as the saying [7.15] now stands it can hardly be authentic. . . it probably never had any setting outside the church's rejection of the food laws'.[4]

None of Sanders's objections are new. Neusner's studies of mishnaic traditions show that table-fellowship would have been a critical issue for the Pharisees before AD 70, so conflicts with Jesus over purity laws are not unthinkable; cf. Mt. 23.25-26 // Lk. 11.39-40; Mt. 23.27-28; Gal. 2.11-14.[5] The objection on the basis of a change in topic (from handwashing to food) overlooks Jesus' general refusal to debate issues on his opponents' terms—in the Synoptics he does not usually provide direct answers to questions, but rather gives the questioner more than he bargains for. Jesus' reply shifts the discussion to another level, in this case not so much changing the topic as broadening it, challenging his hearers to think of defilement in a much more radical

---

1. Pesch for example holds that Mark has joined the separate traditions contained in 7.1-13 and 7.14-23 because of the commmon *Stichwort* κοινοῦν/κοινός (*Markusevangelium*, I, p. 367). On the other hand, Daube argues for the unity of Mk 7.1-15, based on examples of what he considers to be the specific rabbinic form of public retort and private explanation (*Testament*, pp. 141-50). Lambrecht surveys the kaleidoscope of scholarly views on the passage's composition ('Investigation').

2. So, e.g., Bultmann, *History*, pp. 105, 147; V. Taylor, *Mark*, p. 342; McEleney, 'Criteria'; Dunn, 'Purity', p. 268; see Lambrecht, 'Investigation', p. 29 n. 10 for many others.

3. *Jesus*, pp. 265-66.

4. *Jesus*, p. 267; cf. also Schulz, 'Frage', p. 39.

5. For example, *Politics*, p. 83-86. Dunn builds on Neusner's insights, observing the sociological importance of purity rituals as 'boundary defining acts' ('Purity', pp. 269-71).

sense.[1] Mark was not so stupid as to be unaware of the shift from handwashing to food; if he were not concerned to preserve a tradition he considered authentic, one would expect him to have introduced the logion with a question that corresponded more closely to the saying he wished to highlight. Moreover, the addition of an explanatory comment in 7.19c reveals that he did not feel free to revise the tradition radically. Finally, Matthew's preservation of such a potentially controversial saying in his basically pro-law Gospel favours its probable authenticity.[2]

Räisänen highlights another objection to the reliability of Mk 7.15: the lack of a *Wirkungsgeschichte* for the saying. Comparing the tradition to Mt. 28.18-20 he suggests, 'Mk 7.15 reflects an attempt to find a theological justification for the practical step taken in the Gentile mission long before'.[3] Why else, he asks, did the saying play no role in the Jerusalem–Antioch debate; why does Peter's vision seem to be a new insight in Acts 10–11 and 15.7-9?[4] Räisänen makes hay with Paul's failure to quote the passage:

> Paul never refers to it, although it could have aided him greatly in many of his arguments. How effective it would have been to quote such a saying to Peter (a person surely sensitive to words of the historical Jesus!) and others in the heat of the Antiochian conflict (Gal. 2.11ff.), in which Paul, with all his post-Easter theological arguments, evidently was the losing party. One wonders too whether it might not have made sense to him to hint, elsewhere in Galatians. . . at the position taken by Jesus. Even more strikingly, perhaps, Paul refrains from using the saying in his discussion of meat offered to idols (1 Cor. 8); yet, immediately before and after the chapter in question, he does appeal to sayings of the historical Jesus (7.10, 9.14; cf. 7.25).[5]

Peter's vision in Acts 10 shows Luke's concern to ground this new freedom in post-Easter revelation, and Mark 7.15 is possibly the work of a Christian prophet who radicalized the Q saying about cleansing the inner part as well as the outer (Mt. 23.25-26 // Lk. 11.39-41).[6] It

---

1. R. Banks, *Law*, p. 140. This is not to deny the presence of redactional elements in 7.1-23.
2. Carlston, 'Things', p. 77.
3. 'Jesus', p. 88.
4. 'Herkunft', p. 479.
5. 'Jesus', pp. 87-88.
6. 'Herkunft', p. 483.

is doubtful that Paul knows the logion, for 'wäre es schon seltsam, daß Paulus das Herrenwort nur in einem eher peripheren Zusammenhang anführte, in dem er ein *Adiaphoron* diskutiert, nicht aber in seinen zentralen Auseinandersetzungen um das Gesetz'.[1] Thus he concludes, 'If there is a connection between Rom. 14.14 and Mk 7.15 it is just as likely that the dependence lies the other way around'.[2]

Räisänen is right to see freedom from ritual law coming largely as a result of the charismatic experience in the early Church, but that need not be set in opposition to the use of a dominical saying. He overlooks the probability that the interpretation and application of such a logion would have been disputed in the Church from the very beginning. Matthew probably preserves the logion's original intention,[3] and one can readily envisage more conservative Jewish Christians in Jerusalem claiming that instead of repudiating food laws Jesus meant to say, 'It is not so much that which enters a man's mouth that defiles him as that which proceeds from his mouth'.[4] On the other hand, Mark's interpretation probably goes back as far as the Greek-speaking Jewish Christians in Jerusalem (the Ἑλληνισταί; Acts 6.1),[5] one of whom (Stephen) was accused of speaking against Moses, the Temple and the law, as well as saying that Jesus would change τὰ ἔθη handed down by Moses (Acts 6.11, 13-14).[6] What would Paul accomplish by citing a disputed saying, especially in a letter where he cannot defend his

1. 'Herkunft', p. 481.
2. 'Jesus', p. 88.
3. So, e.g., Lohmeyer, *Markus*, p. 142, and Cranfield, *Mark*, p. 230; cf. also Farmer, *Problem*, p. 243. *Gos. Thom.* log. 14 preserves a parallel closest to Matthew but may be dependent upon the latter (Ménard, *Thomas*, p. 101). In the Synoptics Jesus usually repudiates peoples' interpretations, not the Torah itself. The idea that Jesus was perhaps unaware of his own inconsistency (e.g. Lambrecht, 'Investigation', pp. 77-78) is unconvincing.
4. So also Dunn, 'Purity', pp. 273-74. The lack of a comparative degree required Semitic speakers to set matters in antithetical contrasts (e.g. Ps. 39[40].7; Hos. 6.6; cf. Rawlinson, *Mark*, p. 96).
5. So Hengel, 'Between', pp. 23-24. On the Hellenists, I follow the perspective of Wedderburn, 'Similarity', pp. 121-24. U.B. Müller hypothesizes that the *gesetzeskritischen* sayings of Jesus were preserved by liberal Jewish circles in Galilee completely apart from the 'Hellenists' who allegedly had no interest in JT ('Rezeption', pp. 159-60, 176-82).
6. Hengel takes all of these charges to be accurate and derived from a pre-Lukan source ('Between', pp. 21-22).

interpretation at length? To include it as an argument would raise
more problems for him than it would solve, especially in Galatians,
where he wants to establish his authority as independent of the apostles
in Jerusalem. If he cited this logion, the Judaizers could immediately
retort, 'Where did he learn that? From the same apostles whose gospel
he also distorts!'[1]

Two facts defuse Räisänen's objection that Luke presents Peter's
vision as a new insight. First, Luke sometimes does not introduce a
Synoptic tradition until Acts, where a similar point can be made
through an experience in the early Church. In Matthew and Mark,
Jesus is twice charged with intending to destroy the Temple (Mk 14.58
// Mt. 26.61; Mk 15.29 // Mt. 27.40), yet Luke omits the traditions
and instead has the accusers of Stephen introduce the charge (Acts
6.14). Matthew and Mark have Jesus citing Isa. 6.9-10 to explain the
Jews' failure to understand (and accept) his message (Mk 4.12 // Mt.
13.14-15; cf. Mk 8.17-18), but Luke reserves the OT quotation for
Acts 28.26-27, where, on the lips of Paul, the verses function as a
climax to the narrative, if not to Luke–Acts as a whole. Although
Luke was familiar with these traditions, he chose to relate the thrust
of the teachings in a way that better suited his purpose.[2] Similarly,
whether one assumes Markan or Matthaean priority, Luke knew the
logion about defilement; had he wanted to, he could have employed it
in his account of Peter's vision and the Jerusalem council. Evidently
Luke sought to emphasize the initiative and guidance of the Spirit,
ignoring the implications for food laws and stressing the acceptance of
Gentiles into the believing community.[3] A second point in response to
Räisänen is simpler: the absence of the saying from Acts proves
nothing. Having written a Gospel, Luke knew a host of dominical
sayings, yet neither of the only two logia he includes in Acts (11.16;
20.35) is found in his first volume.

---

1. As for 1 Cor. 8, Paul cites the dominical saying in 1 Cor. 7 in response to a
specific request for more (dominical?) information (7.1), and he cites Jesus in 1 Cor.
9.14 only in order to set it aside (9.15). Jesus' saying addressed a Jewish issue of
κοινός food, not a Gentile problem with εἰδωλόθυτος meat.

2. These and other parallels between sayings/actions of Jesus and those of his
followers are probably part of a conscious programme in Acts (cf. Mattill,
'Parallels').

3. Cf. Blomberg: 'The Acts 10 narrative might even be Luke's "substitute" for the
Marcan passage earlier omitted' ('Law', p. 65).

There is thus no compelling reason to reject either the authenticity of the logion (as understood by Matthew) or the possibility that Paul could have been aware that such a saying existed. Mark's strong statement about the end of the OT clean/unclean food distinction shows that the issue had particular relevance for his readers, a fact with particular significance given the evidence favouring a Roman provenance for his Gospel.[1] Paul had written to the same readership (at most) only a dozen or so years before.

3. *Dissimilarity*

Arguing from texts in the *Testaments of the Twelve Patriarchs*, *Epistle of Aristeas*, Philo, Pseudo-Phocylides and *Sibylline Oracles*, Berger has claimed that there existed antinomian groups within 'Hellenistic Judaism', groups which, by their emphasis on the moral commandments, minimized the ritual law of the OT.[2] This could provide the background and inspiration for πάντα μὲν καθαρά in Rom. 14.20 and the language of Mk 7.15; the latter Berger considers to be inauthentic.[3] Nevertheless, Hübner has dismantled Berger's case from the *Testaments of the Twelve Patriarchs*, and Räisänen has weighed Berger's other evidence in the scales and found it wanting.[4] Räisänen rightly concludes: 'It is... quite unlikely that ritual laws were neglected among the Dispersion Jews'.[5] Significant parallels in rabbinic literature to the teaching that nothing is intrinsically unclean are also lacking.[6] The evidence from the dissimilarity criterion thus

---

1. Cf., e.g., Lane, *Mark*, pp. 24-25; Cranfield, *Mark*, pp. 8-9; Hengel, *Studies*, pp. 1-30.
2. *Gesetzesauslegung*, pp. 38-55 and *passim*.
3. *Gesetzesauslegung*, pp. 50-51.
4. Hübner, 'Gesetzesverständnis', pp. 326-37; *idem*, *Law*, p. 86; Räisänen, *Paul*, pp. 34-41. Hübner grants that *T. Levi* 16.2; 14.4 and *T. Asher* 7.5 reflect Isa. 29.13 in a way similar to Mark's text, but notes that the texts do not share Mark's fundamental rejection of the ceremonial law in favour of the Decalogue.
5. 'Jesus', p. 80; cf. Hengel, *Son*, p. 67 n. 123.
6. Carlston, 'Things', p. 94. The famous saying attributed to R. Johanan ben Zakkai ('No matter how it appears, the corpse does not defile, nor does the mixture of ash and water cleanse'; *Pes. R.* 14.14; *Pes. K.* 40b; *Num. R.* 19.8) is no real parallel, for he immediately proceeds to justify the observance of purity regulations (cf. Jeremias, *Theology*, p. 211).

tends towards the conclusion that there is a dominical link.

4. 'Persuaded in the Lord Jesus'

Not a few scholars think that ἐν κυρίῳ Ἰησοῦ indicates an allusion to the teaching of Jesus.[1] Whenever Paul uses Ἰησοῦς alone, he always refers to the historical person,[2] and κύριος Ἰησοῦς clearly refers to the historical Jesus in 1 Cor. 11.23 where Paul quotes JT (cf. also 1 Cor. 9.1; 1 Thess. 2.15; 2 Cor. 4.14; 11.31; and possibly 1 Thess. 4.2).[3] Furthermore, although its historical value is disputed, when Luke puts a direct quotation of a saying of Jesus on the lips of Paul, the apostle cites the words τοῦ κυρίου Ἰησοῦ (Acts 20.35). At the very least, Paul's language in Rom. 14.14 reveals his certainty that no saying of Jesus could be quoted against him.[4]

οἶδα καὶ πέπεισμαι ἐν κυρίῳ Ἰησοῦ could, however, simply express the assurance Paul has from his own experience of union with Christ.[5] Räisänen thinks the argument that the addition of Ἰησοῦ

---

1. So, e.g., Leenhardt, who also cites the 'solemn' tone of 14.14a (*Romans*, p. 352 n. †); cf. Dodd, 'Catechism', p. 25 n. 3; *idem*, '"Ἔννομος"', p. 144. Dodd had changed his mind; in his earlier commentary on Romans (1932) he took ἐν κυρίῳ Ἰησοῦ to refer to Paul's Christian experience (*Romans*, p. 215). ἐν here could have instrumental force ('by'), but this would be contrary to parallel phrases in Paul (so also Furnish, *Theology*, p. 53 n. 78). The variant reading αὐτοῦ in Rom. 14.14 replaces ἑαυτοῦ in A C* D F G C 𝔐, and could refer to Christ himself (i.e. through his teaching or through his death), but the Nestle text (attested by ℵ B C² *al*) is probably correct.

2. *Contra* Kramer, who goes too far in claiming that Jesus and Christ 'have exactly the same meaning' in Paul (*Christ*, p. 202); cf. Wright's case for Paul's use of Χριστός as a title ('Messiah', pp. 11-32). More probable is the view of Hengel, who grants that Paul used Χριστός as a proper name while remaining aware of its original significance as a title; the usage goes back at least to the pre-Pauline Hellenistic community in Jerusalem ('Christos').

3. No consensus exists among the commentators as to the specific force of διὰ τοῦ κυρίου Ἰησοῦ in 1 Thess. 4.2. It could be simply a stylistic variation equivalent to the ἐν κυρίῳ Ἰησοῦ of 4.1, a reference to Jesus as the origin (i.e. the *verba Christi*) or general inspiration for the teaching, or a way of expressing the activity of the living active Lord of the Church who instructs the hearers through Paul (e.g. Best, *Thessalonians*, p. 158).

4. Knowling, *Testimony*, p. 316.

5. So, e.g., Murray, *Romans*, II, p. 188; Räisänen, *Paul*, p. 247; Sanday and Headlam, *Exegetical Commentary*, p. 390.

points to the historical Jesus is weak because (1) Paul usually uses 'the Lord' instead of 'Jesus' when he clearly alludes to the words of the historical Jesus, and (2) (ἡμῶν) κύριος Ἰησοῦς sometimes clearly refers to the exalted Lord (1 Cor. 16.23; 2 Cor. 11.31; Phil. 2.19).[1] After citing Gal. 5.10; Phil. 1.25; 2.24; Rom. 8.38; 15.14 as parallels to Paul's confidence formula in Rom. 14.14, he concludes, 'Jedesmal bezieht sich "Vertrauen" also auf die innere Überzeugung, die aus dem Wesen der Gemeinschaft mit Christus gewonnen ist'.[2] Thus Paul would simply be making his assertion without particular reference to the specific way in which he arrived at his conclusion.[3]

The evidence is inconclusive. Räisänen's first point is irrelevant, since κύριος appears in 14.14; addition of Ἰησοῦς would not reduce the probability of reference to dominical teaching. Moreover, none of the confidence parallels he cites feature the name 'Jesus'. On the other hand, although the verb is ἐλπίζειν, not πείθειν, ἐν κυρίῳ Ἰησοῦ in Phil. 2.19 does approximate to ἐν Χριστῷ, and cannot refer to a dominical logion.[4] Unfortunately, there is nothing in Paul's use of οἶδα or πέπεισμαι that provides help in interpreting these words.[5] We must be careful not to dichotomize Paul's direct experience of the Lord and the tradition through which his Lord spoke.[6] Here he speaks confidently from his experience ἐν Χριστῷ which may well, but need not necessarily, include reflection on the teaching of Jesus. Ἰησοῦ certainly emphasizes the certainty of his statement in 14.14; whether it

1. Räisänen, *Paul*, p. 247 n. 99, continued from 246.
2. Räisänen, 'Herkunft', p. 481.
3. 1 Tim. 4.3-4 justifies the eating of any food on the basis that it is created by God.
4. Cf. also 1 Thess. 4.1, where the prepositional phrase may emphasize the urgency of the request (Best, *Thessalonians*, p. 156). The phrase occurs once more in a variant reading in 1 Cor. 4.17.
5. With the exception of 2 Tim. 1.12, the combination οἶδα καὶ πέπεισμαι is unparalled in the NT. οἶδα refers to revealed knowledge in 2 Cor. 12.2-3 and 1 Cor. 2.11-12; 13.2, but the word is the natural verb to use in such cases and cannot be pressed as any sort of technical term. The perfect tense of πέπεισμαι might point to a settled conviction as to how the teaching of Jesus should be interpreted, but the same could be said for Paul's reflection on the goodness of creation.
6. Cf. Cullmann, who rightly observes with reference to 1 Cor. 7.10 that for Paul *'It is the exalted Lord who now proclaims to the Corinthians, through the tradition, what he had taught his disciples during his incarnation on earth'* ('Tradition', p. 68; his italics).

points specifically to the historical Jesus must remain open until a final
factor is considered.[1]

5. *Exegetical Value*

How could Paul say 'Nothing is unclean in itself' and 'All things are
clean' to an unknown congregation which included a significant
number of Jewish-Christian believers? The assertion that nothing is
'naturally' κοινός, in the absence of support from Christian tradition,
would scarcely go down well with conservative Jewish Christians in
Rome, especially when Paul is concerned to show that he upholds the
law (3.31; cf. 7.12). Earlier in Romans he has sought to reassure his
readers that he values the privileges possessed by Israel; now he
confidently brushes aside a fundamental Jewish distinction. Paul wants
the united support of the Roman Christians for his future mission to
Spain (15.22-29) as well as their prayers for his journey to Jerusalem
(15.30-32). It is unlikely that he would be so foolish as to express
what was *simply* his opinion (even if it was amenable to the majority
in Rome) so flatly and without justification unless he knew that there
was some commonly accepted basis for it.[2] He does not back the
statement up with an argument such as that used in 1 Cor. 8.4-6 (cf.
1 Tim. 4.3-4); he takes for granted that both 'weak' and 'strong' will
acknowledge some justification for the assertion, even though the
'weak' obviously do not agree with it. The very brevity of the claim
in 14.14a, the confidence with which he speaks, and the parenthetical
nature of the statement[3] point to the conclusion that his readers were

1. After stating that 'In virtue of the authority of the Lord Jesus' would be a better
rendering of ἐν κυρίῳ Ἰησοῦ, Käsemann adds, 'But as in 1 Cor. 11.23 there is
reminiscence of a confessional tradition which not accidentally is linked to the name
of Jesus as guarantor. . . ' (*Romans*, p. 375). Dunn is unclear; he first says that
Paul did not know Jesus' teaching itself but 'the interpretative line of theologizing
which grew from it', yet he then seems to suggest that in fact Paul's thinking did go
back to Jesus ('Purity', p. 272)
2. Dunn similarly argues that the tradition behind Mk 2.15–3.6 must have had
some influence in developing confidence such as appears in Rom. 14.5, that Christians were no longer bound to observe holy days ('Bridge', esp. p. 413).
3. As the text stands, the γάρ of 14.15 is difficult to construe, unless one takes v.
14 as a parenthesis (see Cranfield, *Romans*, II, p. 714 n. 2). The asyndeton at 14.14
is noteworthy; Paul has used connectives continuously from 14.6b, and he goes on

already familiar with the assertion from tradition. Apparently Paul is echoing a slogan of the 'strong', anticipating an objection they will naturally raise in defence of their liberty.[1] What was their source for this teaching?

Paul's readers may have already known the tradition of Peter's vision, in which the voice declared, 'What God has cleansed (ἐκαθάρισεν), you must not call common' (σὺ μὴ κοίνου; Acts 10.15; 11.9). Even though Luke gives no clear indication that the early Church understood the vision to have abrogated the laws of Leviticus 11 and Deuteronomy 14, it would seem that Peter concluded from the revelation that if the food the Gentiles ate was no longer κοινός, the men themselves could not be regarded as unclean.[2] It is unlikely, however, that Peter had visited Rome prior to Paul's letter,[3] although it is certainly possible that the Roman Christians had learned of the vision from travellers from Jerusalem, assuming of course (a) that it had actually occurred, and (b) that it preceded Paul's letter.[4]

A more likely, if unprovable, solution is that Paul knew and agreed

to use them afterwards, with the exception of the commands in 14.15b, 20 and the statements in 21-22.

1. Cranfield thinks it 'highly likely' (*Romans*, II, p. 713 n. 2). J.P. Brown writes, 'the liberals quoted an (unoriginal) formula, "nothing is unclean". . . Paul accepts it, but counters it with two others: "don't judge". . . , "don't set stumbling-blocks"' ('Parallels', pp. 46-47). This is not, however, to say that the slogan was confined only to a group at Rome. Similar thoughts appear in 1 Tim. 4.4 and Tit. 1.15. If Paul's concern about stumbling blocks in 14.13 goes back to a dominical saying familiar to the Romans (Mk 9.42 par.), the 'strong' would presumably recognize the imagery and immediately grasp the application: the 'little ones' (οἱ μικροί) in this situation are the weak (οἱ ἀσθενοῦντες, οἱ ἀδύνατοι). To this the 'strong' might respond, 'Yes Paul, we know our Lord's concern for the "little ones", but *why* should what we do cause them to stumble at all? Didn't our Lord also say that there is nothing outside a man that can defile him? Surely no food is *really* unclean!'

2. So Blomberg, 'Law', p. 64. Blomberg cites Acts 10.28 to support his assertion that Peter interpreted the vision to mean the cancellation of dietary laws, as well as the abolition of the barriers preventing table-fellowship between Jews and Gentiles, but the verse says nothing about food.

3. So, e.g., Brown and Meier, *Antioch*, pp. 102-103. For a different view, see J. Wenham, 'Peter'.

4. Blomberg writes, 'it is not unreasonable to speculate that Mark's parenthetical comment in v. 19b came straight from Petrine tradition, which had reflected back upon the significance of Jesus' teaching in light of the later vision in Acts' ('Law', p. 65; cf. also Jackson and Lake, IV, p. 115).

with the 'strong' believers' defence of their freedom from the OT
dietary laws on the basis of an interpretation of dominical teaching
attested later by the Synoptics. This is not to say that Paul grounded
his belief in freedom only on the words of Jesus, but merely that he is
anticipating the use of that argument by the 'strong'. His language in
14.14 more closely resembles Mark's interpretation of Jesus' saying
rather than the saying itself. Paul does not quote Jesus directly, nor
does he allude to the saying to bolster his own argument. Rather, he
concedes that the 'strong' are correct in their interpretation of the
tradition, then he goes on to make his point in spite of Jesus' saying.
His use of the tradition here would thus be not unlike that in
1 Corinthians 7 and 9, where he (more directly) refers to teachings of
Jesus but proceeds to go beyond them or set them aside as not immediately applicable to the situation in question.[1] If correct, this hypothesis explains why Paul gives no justification for 14.14a and 20. His
more conservative Jewish brethren in Rome knew perfectly well that
those statements represented an interpretation of Jesus' words, but it
was an interpretation which they rejected. Hence to quote the saying
would accomplish nothing; Paul grants that the 'strong' are right in
their conclusion about food, but wrong if by the exercise of their
freedom they cause another to stumble. In this case, identifying the
teaching as dominical helps to explain the flow of Paul's thought.

6. *Summary and Conclusion*

I have argued that Paul assumes on the part of his readers at Rome a
knowledge of Christian tradition to the effect that the OT food laws
do not apply to those in Christ. An important pillar supporting that
tradition was the saying of Jesus, attested in Mk 7.15 // Mt. 15.11,
which was interpreted by more liberal Christians to mean that no food
can defile a man—thus any food is permissible to eat. Since Mark
probably wrote his Gospel in Rome, the saying and its liberal interpretation were known there not long after Paul wrote his Epistle, if

---

1. In 1 Cor. 7.10 he alludes to the Lord's teaching against divorce, yet he allows
divorce in the case of desertion by an unbelieving spouse (7.15); in 1 Cor. 9.14 he
refers to the Lord's command that those who proclaim the gospel should get their
living by the gospel, yet Paul refuses that right for the sake of the gospel. See
Dungan, *Sayings*, pp. 41-135.

not before. Objections against the authenticity of the logion are not compelling. The liberal interpretation of the saying probably did not originate from Mark, but went back perhaps as far as the early days of the church in Jerusalem, so the similarity between Rom. 14.20 and Mk 7.19 should not be attributed to Mark's dependence upon Paul. Although by itself the reference to Ἰησοῦς in Rom. 14.14 is not decisive, when coupled with the distinctive idea and similar vocabulary shared by Paul and the Gospels it supports a probable allusion; a dominical echo is virtually certain. If Paul is anticipating an appeal by the 'strong' to the dominical tradition, his response to that tradition is consistent with that shown elsewhere in 1 Corinthians. He accepts the authority and truth of the saying, but he corrects its use, in order to lead his readers into the way of Christ—walking in love.

Chapter 13

ROMANS 14.15-23: SERVING CHRIST'S KINGDOM

In the remaining verses of Romans 14, Paul appeals to the strong to consider their priorities. Their freedom to eat meat and drink wine cannot compare in importance with the spiritual welfare of their weaker fellows. Again, Paul's christology undergirds the admonition: walking in love, caring for the brother for whom Christ (Jesus) died, serving Christ requires self-denial for the sake of others, putting aside one's own rights for the benefit of the weak. In my next chapter, we shall see how Paul explicitly identifies this pattern of behaviour as following the example of Christ. No other frequently cited echoes of JT appear in Romans 14,[1] but there is good evidence for a chiasm structuring his call for self-denial. The chiasm tells us something about the importance of ἡ βασιλεία τοῦ θεοῦ for Paul and suggests again that both dominical example and teaching have influenced his thinking in the unfolding of the argument as a whole.[2]

---

1. Resch compared the famous Bezae variant after Lk. 6.4 ('On the same day he saw someone working on the Sabbath and said to him, "Man, if you know what you are doing, you are blessed; if you do not know, you are cursed and a transgressor of the law"' [my translation]) with Rom. 14.22-23 and other texts (*Agrapha*, pp. 45-48), but the only shared vocabulary is μακάριος, and the logion's origin and import are uncertain (cf. Bammel, 'Pericope'; Delobel, 'Sayings', pp. 437-39; *idem*, 'Luke 6,5'; Jeremias, *Sayings*, pp. 49-53). On the call to pursue peace (Rom. 14.19) see Chapter 6.

2. On the use and significance of chiasm cf. Welch, *Chiasmus*; Breck, 'Chiasmus'; Stock, 'Awareness'.

1. *Chiasm and Kingdom*

Parunak finds four levels of a chiasm in 14.13-21:[1]

(1) Both 14.13 and 14.21 refer to a 'brother' 'stumbling'. (2) The intrinsic harmlessness of forbidden foods is affirmed both in 14:14 and 14:20b. (3) Two thoughts are prominent in 14.15: the grief that loose conduct might cause a brother, and the damage such conduct does to one who is the object of Christ's work. The same two thoughts seem to be reflected in 14.19, 20a. Rather than grief wrought by compassionateless [*sic*] conduct we are to pursue peace and edification (14.15a, 19). Perverse are those values which would prefer food to the work of God (14.15b, 20a). (4) At the center of this symmetrical structure lies the command of 14.16, followed by two motives.

Parunak is right to see a chiasm here, but mistaken to include 14.16 at the centre, which is actually found in the two γάρ statements in 14.17-18:

(a)   τοῦτο κρίνατε μᾶλλον, τὸ μὴ τιθέναι πρόσκομμα τῷ ἀδελφῷ ἢ
       σκάνδαλον (14.13b)

(b)   οἶδα καὶ πέπεισμαι ἐν κυρίῳ Ἰησοῦ ὅτι οὐδὲν κοινὸν δι'
       ἑαυτοῦ, εἰ μὴ τῷ λογιζομένῳ τι κοινὸν εἶναι, ἐκείνῳ κοινόν
       εἰ γὰρ διὰ βρῶμα ὁ ἀδελφός σου λυπεῖται, οὐκέτι κατὰ ἀγάπην
       περιπατεῖς (14.14-15a)

(c)   μὴ τῷ βρώματί σου ἐκεῖνον ἀπόλλυε ὑπὲρ οὗ Χριστὸς
       ἀπέθανεν (14.15b)

(d)   μὴ βλασφημείσθω οὖν ὑμῶν τὸ ἀγαθόν (14.16)

(e)   οὐ γάρ ἐστιν ἡ βασιλεία τοῦ θεοῦ βρῶσις καὶ
       πόσις ἀλλὰ δικαιοσύνη καὶ εἰρήνη καὶ χαρὰ ἐν
       πνεύματι ἁγίῳ (14.17)

(e´)   ὁ γὰρ ἐν τούτῳ δουλεύων τῷ Χριστῷ εὐάρεστος
       τῷ θεῷ καὶ δόκιμος τοῖς ἀνθρώποις (14.18)

(d´)   Ἄρα οὖν τὰ τῆς εἰρήνης διώκωμεν καὶ τὰ τῆς
       οἰκοδομῆς τῆς εἰς αλλήλους (14.19)

(c´)   μὴ ἕνεκεν βρώματος κατάλυε τὸ ἔργον τοῦ θεοῦ (14.20a)

(b´)   πάντα μὲν καθαρά,
       ἀλλὰ κακὸν τῷ ἀνθρώπῳ τῷ διὰ προσκόμματος ἐσθίοντι (14.20b)

(a´)   καλὸν τὸ μὴ φαγεῖν κρέα μηδὲ πιεῖν οἶνον μηδὲ ἐν ᾧ
       ὁ ἀδελφός σου προσκόπτει [ἢ σκανδαλίζεται ἢ ἀσθενεῖ] (14.21)

---

1. 'Techniques', p. 536.

The chiasm is not exact (the lengths of the elements vary, as does the measure of correspondence), and we should be careful not to try to force Paul's thought into a rigid grid that violates the flow of his argument. Nevertheless, the parallelism is there, and no members are missing. The call not to put a πρόσκομμα or σκάνδαλον before an ἀδελφός (a) recurs in the concluding declaration of 14.21, where we find equivalent vocabulary and specification of what the stumbling blocks can be (a'). Paul gives three reasons why the strong need to reconsider their dietary habits. First, he states that although no food is unclean in itself, it nonetheless constitutes a danger to the weak brother who considers it so; if the strong brother's diet leads to a weak brother's grief (by encouraging him to eat that which he considers unclean), it is contrary to the way of love (b). This corresponds to the statement that although all things are clean, it is κακόν for the person whose eating causes another to stumble (b'),[1] and Paul has earlier said that love τῷ πλησίον **κακὸν** οὐκ ἐργάζεται (13.10a). Here we can see two sets of contrasting parallels, κοινόν (b) versus καθαρά (b') and 'walking according to love' (b) versus doing harm to the brother (b'). Secondly, Paul contrasts the strong person's desire for βρῶμα, which destroys the weak person, with God's love for the brother seen in Christ's death on his behalf (c); this agrees strikingly with the vocabulary and structure of 14.20a (c'), although the ἔργον τοῦ θεοῦ probably includes more than the death on the cross of God's Son.[2] Thirdly, and here I would differ from Parunak, Paul appeals to

---

1. κακόν could refer to πάντα καθαρά (Barrett, *Romans*, p. 265), but more likely describes τὸ ἐσθίειν, understood from τῷ ἐσθίοντι (e.g. Wilckens, *Römer*, III, p. 95 n. 470). No consensus exists as to the identity of the one whose eating is accompanied by stumbling. He could be either the 'weak' brother whose eating causes himself to stumble (e.g. Wilckens, *Römer*, III, p. 95) or the 'strong' person whose example leads a more scrupulous brother to violate what he believes is right (e.g. Käsemann, *Romans*, p. 378; Barrett allows for deliberate ambiguity [*Romans*, p. 266]). The answer depends upon how much weight one gives the immediate context (favouring address to the 'strong'), as opposed to the parallel in v. 14, where the thinking of the 'weak' is emphasized. Most prefer the former interpretation. At any rate, πρόσκομμα is used in the same way here as in 14.13, denoting that which occasions serious spiritual damage, leading to the destruction (καταλύειν) of a brother, i.e., the opposite of τὰ τῆς οἰκοδομῆς (14.19).

2. Murray (*Romans*, II, p. 195) refers it to the weak brother, who is God's workmanship (cf. Eph. 2.10). If the 'work of God' signifies not the individual Christian but the Church as a whole (so Barrett, *Romans*, p. 265), the parallel with

the disruptive effect the resulting divisions have on the witness of the Church to those outside (d). When brothers are destroyed and strife ensues, the gospel (ὑμῶν τὸ ἀγαθόν) is blasphemed by those outside the faith (especially by the non-Christian Jews of Rome).[1] Providing a contrasting parallel to this is his call to pursue peace and the upbuilding of one another (d´), which is a strong testimony to those outside (cf. Phil. 2.27-28).[2]

At the heart of the chiasm, then, is Paul's appeal to the nature of the kingdom of God and what is pleasing to him (e, e´; 14.17-18). This is attested formally by the parallel γάρ statements which contrast with the asyndetic commands which preceded and eventually follow; the ἄρα οὖν of v. 19 confirms that we have struck the centre of Paul's argument and are now on our way back out from there. Paul says that the kingdom is not food and drink, but righteousness, peace and joy in

14.15b is less clear. For Paul the ἔργον of God is the new creation, the upbuilding of the Church and those who compose it into the mature body of Christ (1 Cor. 3.9; 15.58; 16.10; Phil. 2.13, 30; cf. also Eph. 2.10); this began with the cross and resurrection.

1. So, e.g., Cranfield (*Romans*, II, p. 717), who surveys other options. The 'good thing' could refer to the strong believers' freedom in Christ to eat all things (Barrett, *Romans*, p. 264; Murray, *Romans*, II, p. 193; cf. 1 Cor. 10.30), in which case, the revilers would be the weaker brethren, but my view is more consistent with Paul's reference to behaviour that is δόκιμος τοῖς ἀνθρώποις (14.18; cf. εὐσχημόνως περιπατεῖν in 13.13; 12.17-18 and cf. 1 Thess. 4.12), reflecting his overall concern for the testimony of the gospel (note also 1 Cor. 10.32). There is, however, another viable option that I have not seen attested elsewhere. Given the introductory admonition ἡ ἀγάπη ἀνυπόκριτος (12.9a) and the nature of what follows in 12.10, τὸ ἀγαθόν in 12.9c refers primarily to that which makes for mutual love and harmony within the community of believers. Consistent with its usage in 15.2, this suggests that in 14.16 τὸ ἀγαθόν denotes the unity and peace (cf. εἰρήνη, 14.17, 19) which Christians enjoy as fellows in Christ (noting the frequency of ἀδελφός in the immediate context: 14.10 [twice], 13, 15, 21). This interpretation would make for an even stronger correspondence between (d) and (d´); cf. 1 Thess. 5.15: ὁρᾶτε μὴ κακὸν ἀντὶ κακοῦ τινι ἀποδῷ, ἀλλὰ πάντοτε **τὸ ἀγαθὸν διώκετε καὶ εἰς ἀλλήλους** καὶ εἰς πάντας. In any case, the chiastic parallel of (d) and (d´) stands, for even on Barrett's view, the call not to occasion the 'blasphemies' of the weak which would destroy what peace there existed between brethren would still find a corresponding member in the exhortation to pursue τὰ τῆς εἰρήνης. . . καὶ τὰ τῆς οἰκοδομῆς.

2. On the evangelistic importance of deference for the sake of peace in Judaism cf. Daube, 'Contributions', p. 234.

the Holy Spirit.[1] Cranfield wants to define these three elements only in relation to God,[2] but in context Paul more likely refers to an ethical righteousness (cf. 5.18; 6.19) that is an obedience of faith (14.5, 22-23), peace among the brethren who are wont to quarrel (14.19), and communal joy produced by the Spirit in their midst instead of the bickering and dissension that results from selfish indulgence.[3]

If our understanding of the chiastic structure is correct, the γάρ statement in 14.18 is thus not necessarily subordinate to v. 17, but can parallel it and refer back to the preceding verses. Obedience in the kingdom of God is to serve Christ and please God, and Paul at the outset of his paraenesis has given that which is εὐάρεστον τῷ θεῷ the highest priority (12.1-2; cf. 2 Cor. 5.9). The referent of ἐν τούτῳ has always been difficult to determine; rather than meaning 'in the Holy Spirit' (Origen), or 'in righteousness, peace and joy in the Holy Spirit' (Cranfield), it is probably best understood as 'in this way', that is, by refraining from actions which cause another brother to stumble, preserving peace and unity among the brethren, and thus seeking God's kingdom.[4] The reference to being δόκιμος τοῖς ἀνθρώποις picks up the appeal to concern for the Christians' testimony to outsiders in 14.16 (cf. 13.13 εὐσχημόνως; 12.17b, 18).[5]

1. Cf. Rom. 5.1-2 for a similar combination. ἐν πνεύματι ἁγίῳ is best taken with χαρά; alone in light of 1 Thess. 1.6 (cf. Cranfield, *Romans*, II, p. 718-19).

2. 'By δικαιοσύνη Paul probably means the status of righteousness before God which is God's gift, by εἰρήνη the state of having been reconciled with God, by χαρά the joy which is the Spirit's work in the believer' (*Romans*, II, p. 718).

3. So, e.g., Barrett, *Romans*, p. 265.

4. Cf. Barrett: 'by recognizing that food and drink are secondary matters' (*Romans*, p. 265).

5. One could see in the threefold reference δουλεύων τῷ Χριστῷ, εὐάρεστος τῷ θεῷ, δόκιμος τοῖς ἀνθρώποις an echo of the three reasons given in 14.15-16, but the correspondence of the second elements is weak; Paul is fond of threefold constructions and the resemblance may be coincidental.

The final admonition to the strong in 14.22-23 continues in a much more general way the chiasm of the previous verses, bringing together several elements found in 14.1-12. First, Paul returns to the somewhat unusual (for him) use of πίστις in the sense of 'confidence that one's faith allows one to do a particular thing' (14.22 // 14.1-2; Cranfield's rendering [*Romans*, II, p. 726]). Secondly, he affirms again that what convictions a person has in such matters is between himself and God—one's opinions are not to be pressed upon another (14.3-4; 14.22a). Thirdly, Paul uses διακρίνεσθαι in 14.23 with reference to one's personal decisions about what to eat,

It is significant for my thesis that Paul puts an appeal to the nature of the kingdom of God at the centre of his exhortation to the strong. He does not refer very often to the kingdom (1 Cor. 4.20; 6.9-10; 15.24, 50; Gal. 5.21; Col. 1.13; 4.11; 1 Thess. 2.12; 2 Thess. 1.5; cf. Eph. 5.5; 2 Tim. 4.1, 18), a fact indicating to some a lack of interest in JT, given the importance of the kingdom in the Synoptics.[1] As we have seen before, that sort of argument from silence is useless—outside the Pauline corpus and Revelation βασιλεία occurs only five times.[2] By contrast, Luke presents the apostle as vitally concerned with the kingdom (Acts 14.22; 19.8; 20.25; 28.23; and esp. 28.31). Although this could be attributed to Luke's apologetic programme to show how Paul closely corresponded to the pattern of Jesus,[3] it is hard to believe that in these passages (and especially in his summary of Paul's message in Acts 28.31) Luke has imputed to the apostle an emphasis completely foreign to his preaching and teaching. On the other hand, we should not expect to find extensive use of kingdom language in the letters of a Roman citizen who was concerned to promote obedience to civil authorities; Paul would want to avoid being misunderstood as a preacher of sedition.[4]

In several ways, Paul's understanding of the kingdom parallels

---

when he has begun the chapter by prohibiting διακρίσεις over the same issue; both words are uncommon in his Epistles. Fourthly, his statements that people who do not judge (κρίνειν) themselves with a view to condemnation in what they approve are blessed (14.22), and that one who acts in doubt κατακέκριται, recall and contrast his earlier warnings against condemning (κρίνειν) others (14.3-4, 10; cf. 13). Fifthly, the thought of 14.23b repeats in negative terms Paul's point in 14.5 that what matters most in 'grey' areas is the individual's full conviction of the rightness of his action. The theme of 14.1-12 as a whole, that differences of opinion about *adiaphora* such as those troubling the weak and strong should not divide Christians, because ultimately each person stands or falls before the Lord, the judge, thus finds a similar counterpart in 14.22-23.

1. E.g. Bultmann, 'Significance', p. 232.

2. I.e. Heb. 1.8; 11.33; 12.28; Jas 2.5; 2 Pet. 1.11. Of those, Heb. 1.8 is an OT quotation and Heb. 11.33 is a general reference to kingdoms; the frequency of incidence is certainly no higher than in Paul.

3. Cf. Mattill, 'Parallels'.

4. Cf. Dunn, *Romans*, II, p. 822, who observes how Paul's emphasis on righteousness and the Spirit effectively replaces kingdom *language* while preserving the essence.

dominical tradition.[1] Like Jesus in the Synoptics, Paul understands the kingdom as both present (1 Cor. 4.20; Col. 1.13; 4.11?; Rom. 14.17) and future (all other instances). It will be inherited (κληρο-νομεῖσθαι; 1 Cor. 6.9-10; 15.50; Gal. 5.21; cf. Eph. 5.5 // Mt. 25.24; cf. also Mt. 5.5; 19.29) only by the righteous (1 Cor. 6.9 // Mt. 5.20, 10), who lead a life fit for the kingdom (1 Thess. 2.12; 2 Thess. 1.5). Its character is not what men might normally expect. A spiritual kingdom, not spatial, its entrance is not for mere flesh and blood (1 Cor. 15.50). Paul is very clear about the sort of behaviour which disqualifies persons from entering the future kingdom—the works of the flesh instead of the fruit of the Spirit (Gal. 5.21; cf. 1 Cor. 6.9-10; and also Eph. 5.5). The kingdom does not consist in words but in power (1 Cor. 4.20); a similar linkage occurs in Lk. 11.20 // Mt. 12.28. In these uses, we can see that the kingdom had a significance for Paul far greater than the rarity of its expression might suggest.

Rom. 14.17 strikingly recalls JT. 'The Apostle's description of the kingdom of God reads like a brief summary of its description in the. . . Sermon on the Mount; the righteousness, peace, and joy which formed the contents of the Kingdom in the Apostle's conception are found side by side in the Saviour's Beatitudes.'[2] Moreover, Dunn has recently observed that in two particular respects the verse parallels Jesus' emphasis that God's eschatological rule was already being mani-fested in the present—in the powerful presence of the Spirit and in table-fellowship. Citing the linkage of Spirit and kingdom in the exorcisms of Mt. 12.28 // Lk. 11.20 and the Pauline teaching on the Spirit as the first instalment of the kingdom to be inherited (1 Cor. 6.9-11; Gal. 4.6-7; cf. Rom. 8.17), he writes, 'For both Jesus and Paul the Spirit *is* the presence of the kingdom, still future in its complete fulfilment. . . For both Jesus and Paul the character and power of the still future rule of God can provide inspiration and enabling for the present'.[3] The connection of table-fellowship and kingdom in Lk. 14.12-24 // Mt. 22.1-10 also finds an echo in Paul; the teaching

---

1. Walter ('Jesus-Tradition', p. 63 n.34) emphasizes the differences, and Haufe ('Reich') sees Paul echoing post-Easter baptismal and missionary traditions rather than JT, but cf. Johnston ('Kingdom') and Dunn ('Spirit') for analyses of the simi-larities between Paul and Jesus.

2. Knowling, *Witness*, p. 312; cf. Hunter, *Predecessors*, p. 48.

3. *Romans*, II, pp. 822-23; cf. also Dunn, 'Spirit'.

reflects an acceptance of outsiders and a protest against the sort of dining restrictions practised by the Pharisees and Essenes (cf. Lk. 14:13, 21 with 1QSa 2.3-9).[1] The likelihood of dominical influence here is increased when immediately after his appeal to the kingdom, Paul states that one who preserves the values of the kingdom by not insisting on his way in his eating and drinking thus serves Christ (14.18). This suggests that the βασιλεία is the kingdom proclaimed by the messiah, who died and was raised that he might be Lord over all (cf. 14.9).

2. Conclusion

Paul's brief reference in Rom. 14.17 reflects the assumption that his readers have been instructed in the idea of the kingdom and its nature. What he says is not new to them, but an appeal which needs no justification. It is true that the kingdom of God is an important concept in Judaism and that Paul's emphasis could be explained as deriving from his background as a Pharisee trained in the OT (the belief that in the age to come there would be neither eating nor drinking appears in *b. Ber.* 17a) but here he is presumably addressing Gentiles who thought little of OT stipulations and the scruples of their Jewish brethren. The frequency of βασιλεία τοῦ θεοῦ in the Gospels and Acts supports the hypothesis that basic Christian instruction included *at least* Jesus' teachings about the kingdom, which Paul could take for granted when writing to Christians in Rome whom he had never met before. Again we would have a case in which Paul is not alluding to the teachings of Jesus as dominical logia, but in which his ethical appeal is most likely influenced by JT.[2] Here Paul's decisive criterion corresponds to an emphasis of the historical Jesus.

1. Dunn, *Romans*, II, p. 822. For other parallels, see Johnston, 'Kingdom', pp. 152-55.
2. 'It is very likely. . . that Paul's language here is a further example of the influence of the Jesus tradition on Paul's teaching, but at the level of shaping his thought rather than as a formal yardstick' (Dunn, *Romans*, II, p. 823).

Chapter 14

ROMANS 15.1-13: THE EXAMPLE OF CHRIST

In Rom. 15.1-13 the christological direction of Paul's paraenesis comes most plainly into view. Through the imitation of Jesus' humility and love, seen in the reproach he bore in obedience to God, in his endurance, in his free acceptance of sinners, and in his adoption of the role of a servant, the divisions existing among the Jewish and Gentile Christians in Rome can be overcome, to the greater glory of God.[1]

1. Romans 15.1: Burden-bearing

With the metaphor of burden-bearing, Paul summarizes the responsibility of the strong toward the weak in 15.1-6.[2] He and the strong have a standing obligation (ὀφείλομεν; cf. 13.8) to bear the infirmities of the weak and not please themselves. In context the ἀσθενήματα refer to weaknesses, prejudices, anxieties, inhibitions and doubts, some of which have already occasioned conflict among the

---

1. On imitation of Christ in Paul see Michaelis, *TDNT*, IV, pp. 666-74; Tinsley, *Imitation*, pp. 134-65; De Boer, *Imitation*, pp. 58-71; Larsson, *Vorbild*; A. Schulz, *Nachfolgen*, pp. 270-89; Betz, *Nachfolge*, pp. 137-89; Spicq, 'L'imitation'. Following Luther, Protestant scholars usually prefer to speak of 'conformity' rather than 'imitation'. We would agree with Tinsley that *conformitas* is God's activity in the believer, through the Spirit conforming a person to Christ, whereas *imitatio* is a human activity, focusing attention on the supreme exemplar (Tinsley, 'Principles', p. 47). To speak of the example of Jesus or the imitation of Christ need not jeopardize the uniqueness of his accomplishment, threaten salvation by grace, or minimize the work of the Spirit (cf. Webster, 'Christology').

2. Romans 15.1ff. followed immediately after 14.23 in the original letter; for discussion of the complex textual problem of the letter's ending, cf. Metzger, *Commentary*, pp. 533-36 and Gamble, *History*.

Roman believers (14.1).[1] Paul's solution to the problem of division over ἀδιάφορα does not come through a change of scruples, but a change of attitude—the adoption of the mind of Christ.

The first hint of a dominical interest appears in his choice of βαστάζειν. Paul could mean that the strong should simply 'endure' or 'put up with' their fellows' scruples (cf. Mt. 20.10; Rev. 2.2-3), yet, if he intended only to say this, he could have employed one of a number of other verbs such as ἀνέχειν (2 Cor. 11.1, 19-20; 2 Thess. 1.4; cf. Acts 18.14; Heb. 13.22), ὑπομένειν (1 Cor. 13.7; cf. 2 Tim. 2.10), στέγειν (1 Cor. 9.12; 1 Thess. 3.1, 5), φέρειν (Rom. 9.22), or ὑποφέρειν (1 Cor. 10.13; cf. 2 Tim. 3.11; 1 Pet. 2.19), all of which (with the exception of στέγειν) are more common in the LXX than βαστάζειν. The description of the readers as δυνατοί and ἀδύνατοι, Paul's use of βαστάζειν elsewhere of relations between brethren (Gal. 6.2; elsewhere in Gal 5.10; 6.5, 17; Rom. 11.18), and the following appeal for the strong not to please themselves confirm that there is a more positive element here—he wants them to adopt the role of servant, by acting intentionally on behalf of their brethren, whether it be interpreted as bearing a burden alone for the weak by having patience with them, or (more likely) helping the weak carry their burden of scruples. In either case, the strong are to abandon superior, self-serving attitudes and instead act out of sympathy for the needs of others, by relinquishing the use of their Christian freedom when its exercise would lead weaker brethren to grief.

Linking this text to Jesus is the parallel in Galatians 6, where the spiritual are to restore an errant brother gently, taking care not to succumb to the temptation of considering themselves morally superior (6.1; cf. κενόδοξος in 5.26). Like the δυνατοί of Rom. 15.1, the πνευματικοί bear another's burden (βαστάζειν; and so fulfil the law of Christ) by forgoing a superior attitude, and by adopting a posture of humility in seeking to help the brother maintain his obedience to God (6.2).[2] The repentant brother burdened with guilt must be freely

1. Schmidt, *Römer*, p. 237.
2. Cf. Mussner, *Galaterbrief*, p. 399. Strelan thinks Paul is speaking about a financial burden to be shared in Gal. 6.2 (cf. 6.6), primarily the support of missionaries and teachers, and that the 'law of Christ' is the same as that in 1 Cor. 9.14 ('Burden-bearing', p. 276). Gal. 6.6 is certainly similar to 1 Cor. 9.14, but to read backwards to Gal. 6.2 violates the flow of thought and leaves 6.1 hanging without further development.

forgiven and accepted (cf. 2 Cor. 2.6-8); restoration does not include punishment or condemnation.[1] Pride and arrogance are ruled out (6.3), for the only ground for boasting is not through comparison with the failings of another man, but through one's faithfulness in bearing one's own load of responsibility before God (6.4-5; cf. Rom. 12.3-8)—which leaves little ground, if any. Jesus' attitude towards sinners finds concrete application here in burden-bearing.[2]

Paul's choice of βαστάζειν was probably impelled by Jesus' *Vorbild*.[3] βαστάζειν describes his bearing the cross (Jn 19.17) and in Lk. 14.27 Jesus warns, 'Whoever does not bear (βαστάζει) his own cross and come after me, cannot be my disciple'.[4] Moreover, Paul uses the word when he says that he bears on his body the marks of Jesus (Gal. 6.17). By itself this evidence is inconsiderable, but given the early traditions associating Jesus with Isaiah's Servant of the Lord, there is more to be said.[5] Paul's language of bearing infirmities

---

1. Betz, *Galatians*, p. 297. In Galatians the brother has actually sinned, whereas in Romans there is simply a difference of opinion, and the weak person is not expected to change his view. Nevertheless, both the errant and the weak are 'burdened', and Paul's desire is that they be received by their fellows with stronger faith. Jesus' instructions about church discipline in Mt. 18 are similarly qualified by the following teachings about forgiveness, although a pre-Easter origin for this tradition is in doubt (but cf. also Lk. 17.3-4; *Did.* 15.3).

2. So also Hays, 'Christology', pp. 286-88.

3. So, e.g., Schmidt, *Römer*, p. 237; cf. Michel, *Römer*, pp. 443 n. 6, 444 and n. 11. Betz asserts that 'no doubt' Gal. 6.2a is drawn from the Hellenistic philosophical tradition; the *idea* is paralleled, but βαστάζειν appears in none of the passages he cites (*Galatians*, p. 299 and nn. 58, 59).

4. Mt. 10.38 has λαμβάνειν. Cf. also *Gos. Thom.* log. 55.

5. Whether there existed a messianic interpretation of the Isaianic Servant passages in pre-Christian Judaism and the extent to which the early Church identified Jesus as the Servant are disputed (e.g., Zimmerli and Jeremias, *TDNT*, V, pp. 656-717; H.W. Wolff, *Jesaja*; Hanson, *Utterances*, pp. 56-59; Jeremias, Review, pp. 142-44; France, *Jesus*, pp. 110-35; in contrast to Hooker, *Servant*; Schürer, *History*, II, pp. 547-49; Koch, *Schrift*, pp. 233-39). *Targ. Isa.* applies parts of the Servant texts to the Messiah (including some of Isa. 53), but the sufferings to Israel and the Gentiles. One tradition in *b. Sanh.* 98b takes the sufferings in Isa. 53.4 to refer to the Messiah (cf. also 98a); see Chilton, *Rabbi*, p. 199-200 on *Targ. Isa.*, and Davies, *Paul*, pp. 274-83 for other Jewish evidence. All of the evangelists portray Jesus as believing that his sufferings were prophesied in the Scriptures (Mt. 26.24, 54, 56; Mk 9.12; Lk. 18.31; 24.25-27, 46), and few texts would offer a better witness than those of Isaiah. Some affirm that Jesus himself saw his ministry in

(βαστάζειν ἀσθενήματα) may recall in summary fashion the one point expressed through the Hebrew parallelism of Isa. 53.4 (as cited in Mt. 8.17):

αὐτὸς τὰς **ἀσθενείας** ἡμῶν ἔλαβεν
καὶ τὰς νόσους ἐβάστασεν[1]

An Ibycus search through the TLG database of extant Greek texts confirms that no other text links to βαστάζειν ἀσθενείαι/ ἀσθενήματα. Two verses later (15.3), Paul adduces the example of the messiah (ὁ Χριστός), whose suffering is foretold in the OT and whose service fulfils its promises (15.8).[2] What is more, when Paul speaks of Christ's death for the ungodly in Rom. 5.6, he says it was ὄντων ἡμῶν **ἀσθενῶν**. By bearing their weaker fellows' infirmities, the strong Christians would share in the servant character of Jesus, who took on himself the weaknesses of them all. So we find Ignatius writing to Polycarp and exhorting as part of his call for unity, πάντας **βάσταζε**, ὡς καὶ σὲ ὁ κύριος. . . πάντων τὰς νόσους **βάσταζε** ὡς τέλειος ἀθλητής (Ign. *Pol.* 1.2-3). Although in Rom. 15.1 Paul does not use ἀσθενήματα in the sense of physical disease or a state of sin, the bearing of those weaknesses through self-

---

terms of the Servant (cf. Mk 10.45; e.g., Kleinknecht, *Gerechtfertigte*, pp. 171-74; Cullmann, *Christology*, pp. 60-69). Philip the Evangelist found Isa. 53 fulfilled in Jesus (Acts 8.32), and later witnesses include 1 Pet. 2.22-25; *1 Clem.* 16; *Barn.* 5. Paul nowhere directly quotes the Servant songs with reference to Jesus, but he does cite some texts from the songs as fulfilled in the preaching of the gospel (Rom. 10.16 // Isa. 53.1; Rom. 15.21 // Isa. 52.15; cf. 2 Cor. 6.2 // Isa. 49.8; also Acts 13.47 // Isa. 49.6). Since Jesus is the subject of that gospel it is reasonable to expect that Paul associated him with the 'Servant' who is central to those passages. Moreover, Paul's statement that Christ died for our sins κατὰ τὰς γραφάς (1 Cor. 15.3) probably presupposes Isa. 53 as at least one of its foundational texts. Cf. also Rom. 3.25 (?); 4.25; 5.19; Phil. 2.7 (Cullmann, *Christology*, pp. 76-77; also Kleinknecht, *Gerechtfertigte*, pp. 185-88).

1. LXX: οὗτος τὰς ἁμαρτίας ἡμῶν φέρει καὶ περὶ ἡμῶν ὀδυνᾶται. See Gundry, *Use*, pp. 109-11. Michel (*Römer*, p. 443 n. 5) thinks Paul's choice of ἀσθενήματα was influenced by Isa. 53.4. Matthew's ἀσθενεία renders the Hebrew חלי, 'sickness'. βαστάζειν occurs only eight times in the LXX (rendering נשא in 2 Kgs 18.14; Job 21.3; נטה in Judg. 16.30; cf. also Ruth 2.16 [twice]; 2 Sam. 23.5; Sir. 6.25; Bel [Theodotion] 36), but Aquila's version has it in Isa. 53.11.

2. Although not conclusive in itself, the article would indicate that Χριστός has its titular sense (so, e.g., Kleinknecht, *Gerechtfertigte*, p. 358 n. 124).

renunciation and association with the weak reflects a posture identical to that of the one who did not please himself, but humbled himself in obedience to God.

2. Romans 15.2-3: 'Christ Did Not Please Himself...'

When Paul adds that the strong are not to please themselves, the roots of his admonition in the example of Christ are laid bare. He does not use μιμεῖσθαι or μιμητής, but the parallel between ὀφείλομεν... μὴ ἑαυτοῖς ἀρέσκειν and ὁ Χριστὸς οὐχ ἑαυτῷ ἤρεσεν sets up an obvious comparison, and the causal γάρ makes the logic apparent: Christians are not to please themselves but their neighbour, because Christ did not please himself.[1] The unspoken but assumed premise is that they are to adopt his attitude. Paul's thought is best expounded against the background of two other closely related passages.

1 Corinthians 10.31–11.1

Paul speaks positively of pleasing others only once more, in 1 Cor. 10.31–11.1, where it is again set in contrast to seeking one's own benefit, and is directly linked to the imitation of Christ:

> So, whether you eat or drink, or whatever you do, do all to the glory of God. Give no offence to Jews or to Greeks or to the church of God, just as I try to please (ἀρέσκω) all men in everything I do, not seeking my own advantage, but that of many (τῶν πολλῶν), that they may be saved. Be imitators of me, as I am of Christ (μιμηταί μου γίνεσθε καθὼς κἀγὼ Χριστοῦ).

This passage markedly resembles Romans 15 in other ways.[2] It occurs

---

1. πλησίον recalls the love command in 13.9-10; a desire to please the neighbour is just the opposite of the mind which ridicules or condemns. Apart from the other citation of Lev. 19.18 in Gal. 5.14 (cf. also Eph. 4.25) Paul does not use the word, which further supports the connection of neighbour-love and JT in his mind. Paul adds εἰς τὸ ἀγαθὸν πρὸς οἰκοδομήν to ensure that ἀρέσκειν τῷ πλησίον not be misunderstood. τὸ ἀγαθόν is either the neighbour's benefit (so, e.g., RSV) or (more likely) that of the community (cf. 14.16), which makes for upbuilding (πρὸς οἰκοδομήν; cf. 1 Cor. 12.7: πρὸς τὸ συμφέρον; C.F.D. Moule, *Idiom*, p. 52).

2. The earlier exhortation to seek (ζητεῖν) not one's own advantage, but the good of the neighbour (1 Cor. 10.24) immediately after his point that not all things edify (οἰκοδομεῖν) may be compared to Rom. 14.19: διώκωμεν τὰ τῆς οἰκοδομῆς τῆς εἰς ἀλλήλους; cf. also 15.2. For a full comparison, see Karris, 'Occasion', pp. 86-88.

at the conclusion of a section dealing with a related issue for 'strong' and 'weak' Christians in Corinth, and 'pleasing men' includes at least not putting a πρόσκομμα in their way (1 Cor. 10.32; Rom. 14.13, 20-21). Paul's point is that behaviour should ultimately be governed not by selfish desire, but by concern to serve the best interests of both Jew and Gentile (1 Cor. 10.32; Rom. 15.8-12), to the glory of God (1 Cor. 10.31; Rom. 15.6-7, 9).[1]

Paul's renunciation of his own rights for the sake of the salvation of others is consciously modelled after Christ (1 Cor. 11.1). This is not an isolated motif, but a statement properly summarizing what he has said about himself in 8.13–9.23 in order to set before the Corinthians his own example to follow. We cannot miss something similar when he says that although he is free from all, he has chosen to make himself a slave to all in order to win the more (1 Cor. 9.19; cf. Mk 10.44); Paul would not consider himself to be the first to do so. Even though he has dominical authority to receive support as an apostle of Christ (1 Cor. 9.14), he relinquishes that right for the sake of the gospel—a clear indication that for Paul the dominical example could take precedence over a specific teaching of Jesus in a case of possible conflict (cf. also Rom. 14.14). Rather than being an afterthought, 1 Cor. 11.1 gives us a glimpse of what ultimately shapes his attitude toward others.

What then is he referring to when he writes κἀγὼ Χριστοῦ in 1 Cor. 11.1? Perhaps the incarnation and life of Christ as a whole,[2] but most likely the emphasis is on the character exemplified in Jesus' Passion, especially since Paul's language echoes Mk 10.45 // Mt. 20.28: 'For the Son of Man also came not to be served but to serve, and to give his life as a ransom for many' (λύτρον ἀντὶ **πολλῶν** // 1 Cor. 10.33; cf. also Mk 10.44 // 1 Cor. 9.19). The early Church believed that Paul knew this logion,[3] and he refers to his master as one

---

1. Evidence from monumental inscriptions indicates that ἀρέσκειν was used to connote service for the benefit of others (MM 75; Robertson and Plummer, *1 Corinthians*, pp. 224-25).

2. E.g. Barrett, *1 Corinthians*, p. 246.

3. 1 Tim. 2.6; Tit. 2.14. Arguing for the pre-Easter origin of Mk 10.45 see Stuhlmacher, 'Existenzstellvertretung', pp. 414-15, and Jeremias, *Theology*, pp. 293-94. Meyer finds it consistent with Jesus' self-understanding (*Aims*, pp. 216-19).

who gave himself for others (Gal. 1.4; 2.20; cf. Eph. 5.2). Later on in
the same chapter he will remind the Corinthians of the words of the
Lord on the night of his betrayal (1 Cor. 11.23-26), words which
were doubtless at the core of whatever liturgical tradition they had
received from Paul.

H.D. Betz categorically denies any reference here to the earthly
Jesus:

> Der Aufruf zur Mimesis ist in keiner Weise an der ethischen und sittlichen
> Vorbildlichkeit des historischen Jesu oder einer präexistenten Christus-
> figur oder des Paulus orientiert, sondern am Christusmythos selber.
> Dieser Mythos beschreibt und bezeugt den präexistenten Christus als
> 'unteilbares Heilsgeschehen'. . . , so daß sich die Mimesis auf dieses
> Heilsgeschehen richtet.[1]

Betz's view however presupposes that Paul was not interested in the
historical Jesus, and suffers from the objection that Paul calls his
readers to imitate himself καθώς he imitates Christ. Paul is referring
to a person, not an event, and 'Christ is an object of imitation in the
same sense as Paul himself is'.[2] Self-denial for the salvation of many is
exemplified for Paul by Christ on the cross, hence Paul's emphasis is
on his own self-denial in seeking the salvation of others.

Philippians 2.1-11
Another passage which has vital links to Rom. 15.1-6 in thought and
vocabulary is Phil. 2.1-11. In context Paul is seeking unity for the
congregation, in order that they may stand firm in one spirit, striving
together for the advancement of the gospel (1.27). In the face of
opposition they should not be afraid, for their steadfast unity is a
proof (ἔνδειξις) from God of the Philippians' salvation (1.28; cf.
2 Thess 1.5). How is this so? πάσχειν ὑπὲρ Χριστοῦ is a gift from
God, a calling to share τὸν αὐτὸν ἀγῶνα which they know to be
Paul's past and present experience (1.28-30). Later in the same letter
(3.10-11) Paul will go on to stress his need to share in Christ's
παθήματα and be conformed to his death in order to attain to the
resurrection from the dead—in this Paul expected his readers to
follow his example (3.17)—and here the apostle says that the

---

1. *Nachfolge*, p. 168; cf. also Schrage, 'Ethik', pp. 198-99. Both follow
Bultmann in this respect (*Theology*, I, p. 305).
2. Dodd, *History*, p. 65 n. 6; De Boer, *Imitation*, p. 159.

Philippians have been given the same privilege. In the light of the importance of the preposition ὑπέρ for Paul's interpretation of Christ's death[1] and the word's twofold usage in 1.29, it is thus likely that Paul sees the Philippians' suffering *for* Christ as in response to the example of Christ's suffering *for* them (cf. 1 Pet. 2.21).[2] They share Christ's sufferings in this life in order to share in his glory in the age to come. The persecution they face is a gift from God, inasmuch as it is an opportunity to be further conformed to Christ. Suffering is expected; it is a sign of their salvation, it is the way of the cross.

In Phil. 2.1-4 Paul continues to pursue the theme of unity while turning to concentrate on attitudes and relations within the Church, and here the ethical admonition is increasingly dependent on the example of Christ. He appeals to the realities which the Philippians have experienced by virtue of being Christians (2.1): they have found comfort in the person of Christ[3] (who suffered for them), incentive afforded by Christ's[4] love for them, fellowship created by and enjoyed in his Spirit,[5] and they know the deep affection of Christ (Phil. 1.8)[6] together with the mercies of God received through

---

1. Rom. 5.6-8; 8.32; 14.15; 1 Cor. 1.13; 11.24; 15.3; 2 Cor. 5.14-15, 21; Gal. 1.4; 2.20; 3.13; 1 Thess. 5.10.

2. Cf. Collange, *Philippians*, pp. 75-76. The reason for suffering for Christ is not *only* the need to follow Christ's example (another would be gratitude in response to God's grace), but it at least *included* it.

3. E.g. Collange, *Philippians*, p. 78. ἐν Χριστῷ may refer to Christ's body (the community of believers), but (1) every preceding instance of Χριστός in the Epistle (with the exception of 1.1) refers to the person (1.2, 6, 8, 10, 11, 13 [ἐν Χριστῷ here signifies 'in the cause of Christ'], 15, 17, 18, 19, 20, 21, 23, 26 [ἐν Χριστῷ], 27, 29); cf. also ἐν Χριστῷ used of the person in 3.3); (2) the other three protases most likely refer to persons: the second points to Christ's love (note 4 below), the third to fellowship created by the Spirit (note 5 below), and the fourth to the compassion of Christ and mercies of God (note 6 below); (3) the immediate context argues for a continuing appeal to the characteristics of Christ (see below).

4. Cf. 2 Cor. 5.14; Gal. 2.20. So also Beare, *Philippians*, p. 71; Martin, *Philippians*, p. 86; *contra*, e.g., Stählin, who refers all of the protases to the interrelations of Christians (*TDNT*, V, pp. 822-23).

5. Cf. 1.19: τοῦ πνεύματος Ἰησοῦ Χριστοῦ. As for τοῦ πνεύματος in 2.1, the parallelism in 2 Cor. 13.13 argues for a subjective genitive, but it is difficult to rule out the objective genitive (cf. 1 Cor. 12.13).

6. So Martin: 'it is Christ's "love from the heart" reaching out to the church mem-

Christ[1]—the latter being a summary of the many blessings they enjoy (cf. Rom. 12.1). In the light of these benefits Paul desires oneness in aim, purpose and direction (τὸ αὐτὸ φρονεῖν; cf. Rom. 12.16; Phil. 4.2; 2 Cor. 13.11), which is expounded in 2.2b-4 through a series of participles and verbless clauses grammatically not unlike those which we find in Rom. 12.9-13. Paul particularly wants them to have the same ἀγάπη for one another as Christ has for them (another implicit call for imitation; cf. 2.1; 1 Jn 3.16),[2] and to be united in intent (2.2). Christlike love manifests itself in right thinking about others as well as about oneself, not in the self-seeking nor empty glory which threaten the unity of the Philippians (2.3).[3] With a humble attitude his readers should regard one another as more important than themselves (2.3). Behind ταπεινοφροσύνη is again the example of Jesus (cf. 2.8: ἐταπείνωσεν ἑαυτόν), a factor to be considered in other Pauline instances of the root (e.g. Rom. 12.16; 2 Cor. 11.7).[4] Likewise, ἡγούμενοι ὑπερέχοντας ἑαυτῶν in Phil. 2.3 parallels Rom 12.10b in its self-sacrificial character.

When Paul expounds what this means in Phil 2.4 the example of Christ is close at hand:

bers in their estrangement from one another' (*Philippians*, p. 88).

1. Cf. the combination σπλάγχνα οἰκτιρμοῦ in Col. 3.12, part of a description of Christ, the new man to be put on (see Chapter 9 above).

2. So Martin, *Philippians*, p. 88. Paul could be referring to the same love that he has for the Philippians, but the context does not favour it.

3. Note the frequency of the φρονεῖν word group in this passage (2.2 [twice], 3, 5) and in Romans (12.3 [4×], 16 [twice]; 15.5).

4. Cf. Mt. 11.29. 'The term. . . catches up what Jesus said about greatness through service' (Grundmann, *TDNT*, VIII, p. 22). Note also Lk. 14.11; 18.14; Mt. 23.12; 18.4; echoed in Jas 4.10 and 1 Pet. 5.6. The idea that God will exalt the humble goes back of course to the OT (e.g. Job 22.29; Ps. 146[147].6; Prov. 29.23; etc.), but Luke's repetition of the saying reflects his assurance of an original dominical emphasis. The word group had a generally negative connotation in the eyes of the Greeks (Grundmann, *TDNT*, VIII, pp. 1-5), so Paul is here clearly dependent upon Jewish tradition. ταπεινοῦν, ταπεινός, and ταπείνωσις are common enough in the LXX, but ταπεινοφρονεῖν occurs only once, in LXX Ps. 130[131].2 (שׁוה; cf. ταπεινόφρων in Prov. 29.23 [שׁפל־רוח]). At Qumran, ταπεινοφροσύνη finds an equivalent in ענוה (1QS 2.24; 4.3; 5.3-4, 25), but there it is not coupled with a love for outsiders. On the importance of Jesus' example of ταπεινοφροσύνη for Clement of Rome see Chapter 2.

Phil. 2.4	μὴ τὰ ἑαυτῶν ἕκαστος σκοποῦντες ἀλλὰ καὶ τὰ ἑτέρων ἕκαστοι
1 Cor. 10.24	μηδεὶς τὸ ἑαυτοῦ ζητείτω ἀλλὰ τὸ τοῦ ἑτέρου
1 Cor. 10.33–11.1	κἀγὼ πάντα πᾶσιν ἀρέσκω μὴ ζητῶν τὸ ἐμαυτοῦ σύμφορον ἀλλὰ τὸ τῶν πολλῶν ἵνα σωθῶσιν. μιμηταί μου γίνεσθε καθὼς κἀγὼ Χριστοῦ
Rom. 15.1-3	Ὀφείλομεν... μὴ ἑαυτοῖς ἀρέσκειν ἕκαστος ἡμῶν τῷ πλησίον ἀρεσκέτω εἰς τὸ ἀγαθὸν πρὸς οἰκοδομήν. καὶ γὰρ ὁ Χριστὸς οὐχ ἑαυτῷ ἤρεσεν...

The verbal and conceptual parallels are striking. Paul's prescription for unity in these central ethical texts is for Christians' actions to be determined not by their own desires, but by concern for the best interests of others. Such an attitude was incarnate in Christ, whose earthly life climaxed in an ultimate act of self-giving on the cross for others. In 1 Corinthians and Romans the parallel expressions are followed by appeal to the example of Christ himself, either directly (Romans) or indirectly through the example of Paul (1 Corinthians). This fact should help us interpret the difficult ellipsis in Phil. 2.5: τοῦτο φρονεῖτε ἐν ὑμῖν **ὃ καὶ ἐν Χριστῷ Ἰησοῦ.**

Regardless of their differences over the particulars, everyone from the Reformers through Schlatter understood Paul in 2.5-11 to be alluding to Christ as an ethical example for the Philippians to follow.[1] In this century however this has been denied by a series of scholars, including Käsemann and R.P. Martin.[2] Käsemann understands the passage as a description of the salvation-event (*Heilsgeschehen*); it is soteriological, not ethical, and Christ is *Urbild*, not *Vorbild*.[3] On this view, the point of the passage is Christ's cosmic lordship, reminding the readers not of an example to follow but rather saying to them 'Become in your conduct and church relationships the type of persons who, by that *kenosis*, death and exaltation of the Lord

---

1. Käsemann, 'Analyse', p. 53.
2. Käsemann, 'Analyse', p. 95; Martin, *Carmen*, pp. 288-91; cf. also K. Barth, *Philippians*, p. 59; Beare, *Philippians*, p. 75; J.A. Sanders, 'Deities', pp. 280, 289.
3. 'Analyse', pp. 91, 81.

of glory, have a place in His body, the Church'.[1]

Against the ethical interpretation it is claimed that (1) in order to preserve the best symmetry, the verb to be supplied after καί in 2.5 is φρονεῖτε (or φρονεῖν δεῖ), so that Paul is basing the imperative upon the indicative: 'Have this mind among yourselves [i.e. in your church-life]. . . which you have as those who are in Christ Jesus';[2] (2) ἐν Χριστῷ Ἰησοῦ thus has its more common technical sense of 'im Bereich des Christus', and does not refer to the person of Christ;[3] (3) only 2.6-8 could be applied to the readers—'if the hymn depicts an ethical example for the believer's *imitatio*, the final three verses must be treated as an appendix and so irrelevant';[4] and (4) 'Paul only rarely uses the idea of the ethical example of Jesus to enforce an exhortation'.[5] None of these arguments are compelling and all have been answered elsewhere:[6] (1) although the last word has not been spoken about the elusive verb in 2.5, there are several options that are just as plausible, if not more so, than supplying φρονεῖτε—the latter fails to account for the καί;[7] (2) Paul uses ἐν Χριστῷ elsewhere in the Epistle without its 'technical' sense (1.13, 26; 3.3; and probably 2.1), and his addition of Ἰησοῦ in 2.5 may be significant;[8] (3) although the exaltation of Christ cannot be *imitated*, Paul does speak later in the Epistle of *conformity* to Christ's glorious body (3.20-21) using language reminiscent of the 'hymn' in several respects, and a similar

1. Martin, *Carmen*, p. 291.

2. Martin, *Carmen*, p. 70.

3. Käsemann, 'Analyse', p. 57; Martin, *Carmen*, pp. 71-72.

4. Martin, *Carmen*, p. 88.

5. Martin, *Carmen*, p. 72. By the end of the book, Martin's confidence has increased: 'Then, there is the fact that Paul never uses the earthly life of Jesus as an *exemplum ad imitandum*. . . ' (p. 288).

6. Cf., e.g., Larsson, *Vorbild*, pp. 230-75; Marshall, 'Christ-Hymn', pp. 117-19; Stanton, *Preaching*, pp. 99-106; Hurtado, 'Jesus'.

7. Cf. C.F.D. Moule, who also punctures the indicative-imperative argument ('Reflexions', p. 266; cf. Stanton, *Preaching*, p. 101). Lightfoot favoured supplying ἐφρονεῖτο (*Philippians*, p. 110); Moule expands the verse to τοῦτο τὸ **φρόνημα** φρονεῖτε ἐν ὑμῖν ὃ καὶ ἐν Χριστῷ Ἰησοῦ, i.e., 'adopt towards one another, in your mutual relations, the same attitude which was found in Christ Jesus' ('Reflexions', p. 265); and Marshall suggests βλέπετε or οἴδατε after the analogy of similar relative clauses in Phil. 1.30 and 4.9 ('Christ-Hymn', p. 118).

8. Hooker, 'Philippians 2:6-11', p. 154.

idea appears in 2 Cor. 8.9 (cf. 2 Tim. 2.11).[1] 'Not only Christ's humility, but also his exaltation is relevant, for the fact that Christ was exalted is an indication that God is at work in the midst of the Philippians and that τὸ σῶμα τῆς ταπεινώσεως ἡμῶν will be exalted (3.21).'[2] As for (4), frequency of reference in Pauline Epistles is no reliable indicator as to the importance of a teaching (cf. the eucharist), and most would agree that Paul does appeal to Jesus' example more often than Käsemann, Martin *et al.* assert. 'It is only the dogma that the Jesus of History and the Christ of Faith belong in separate compartments that leads to the belief that the appeal to a Christian character appropriate to those who are in Christ is not linked to the pattern as seen in Jesus himself.'[3]

Exactly how much of Phil. 2.6-9 refers to the earthly Jesus is contested. A number of scholars have challenged the traditional view that vv. 6-7 describes the pre-existent Christ, taking the words to refer only to the human Jesus as the last Adam who humbled himself and was exalted to glory, in contrast to the first man who tried to become like God and suffered punishment (Gen. 1.26-27; 3.1-7).[4] If correct, this would make our case even stronger that Paul is appealing to Jesus here as ground and pattern for Christian experience.[5] Recently, however, Wright has argued persuasively that 2.6b means 'Christ did not consider his equality with God as something to take advantage of. . . , i.e. something to be exploited for his own gain'.[6]

---

1. Hooker points out a number of verbal links between 3.20-21 and the 'Christ-hymn': σύμμορφον reminds us of μορφή, ὑπάρχει echoes ὑπάρχων, μετασχηματίσει picks up σχῆμα, ταπεινώσεως recalls ἐταπείνωσεν, δόξα, πάντα and κύριος Ἰησοῦς Χριστός are repeated; but more important is the idea in 3.20-21 that at his appearance, the Christians' body of humiliation will be conformed to his glorious body through his power to subject all things to himself—as a result of his becoming like us we shall become like him ('Philippians 2:6-11', p. 155).

2. Stanton, *Preaching*, pp. 102-103. He observes that the humiliation-exaltation pattern is a motif commonly used in exhortation (Lk. 18.14; 14.11; Mt. 23.12; 18.4; Jas 4.10; 1 Pet. 5.6).

3. Hooker, 'Philippians 2:6-11', p. 154.

4. So, e.g., Talbert, 'Problem'; Murphy-O'Connor, 'Anthropology'; Howard, 'Human'; Dunn, *Christology*, pp. 115-21. Others rightly see a contrast with Adam in the passage but do not deny pre-existence, e.g., Hooker ('Philippians 2:6-11'). For a summary of views, see Wright, "Ἁρπαγμός'.

5. So also Hurtado, 'Jesus', p. 121 n. 32.

6. ' Ἁρπαγμός', pp. 340-41.

τὸ εἶναι ἴσα θεῷ is something Christ already possessed, yet he regarded it

> not as excusing him from the task of (redemptive) suffering and death, but actually as uniquely qualifying him for that vocation...ἐκένωσεν does not refer to the loss of divine attributes, but—in good Pauline fashion [Rom. 4.14; 1 Cor. 1.17; 9.15; 2 Cor. 9.3]—to making something powerless, emptying it of apparent significance. The real humiliation of the incarnation and the cross is that one who was himself God, and who never during the whole process stopped being God, could embrace such a vocation.[1]

The disparity between the divinity of Christ and the humanity of mankind does not mean that the example of the pre-existent Christ cannot be imitated.[2] Moreover, Paul's frequent use of δοῦλος to describe himself and other Christians (Rom. 1.1; Gal. 1.10; Phil. 1.1; 2 Cor. 4.5; Col. 4.12 etc.) and of δουλεύειν to characterize Christian behaviour (Gal. 5.13; Rom. 12.11; 14.18; etc.) ultimately goes back to the OT conception of the עבד יהוה, but most likely found its primary inspiration in the teaching and example of Jesus (cf. Mk 10.44; 13.34; Mt. 10.24-25; 18.23-32; 20.27; Jn 13.3-17; etc.); when Paul applies the language to Christ in Phil. 2.7 his language has 'rich positive overtones for him and his readers'.[3] Certainly 2.8 speaks about the experience of the man Jesus: ἐταπείνωσεν ἑαυτὸν γενόμενος ὑπήκοος μέχρι θανάτου, θανάτου δὲ σταυροῦ.[4] Although Paul focuses on the culmination of Jesus' life (as, e.g., Heb. 5.7-8), it does not follow that he is excluding the rest of that life characterized by association with the ταπεινοί and teaching about the necessity of self-humbling (Mt. 18.4; 23.12; Lk. 14.11; 18.14; cf. 2 Cor. 11.7). The obedient (ὑπήκοος) character of an entire life is presupposed, if the

---

1. ' 'Αρπαγμός', pp. 345-46. Wanamaker also argues for reference to Christ's pre-existence ('Christology').

2. Cf. Hurtado, 'Jesus', p. 121; Wright, ''Αρπαγμός', p. 351. The goddess Isis could be a pattern for piety (Plutarch, *Moralia* 361d, e; cf. Wedderburn, 'Story', pp. 169-71).

3. Hurtado, 'Jesus', pp. 122, 124. He rightly rejects Käsemann's interpretation that Christ became a slave to evil powers. For an interesting comparison of Jn 13.3-17 and Phil. 2.6-11 see Hawthorne, *Philippians*, p. 78.

4. Hurtado compares μορφὴν δούλου λαβών with ἐταπείνωσεν ἑαυτόν and γενόμενος ὑπήκοος: 'the unseen and ineffable action of heaven is described after the fashion of the observed, historical action' ('Jesus', p. 121).

exaltation and glorification of 2.9-11 would be truly appropriate, and if that obedience should become the pattern for Philippians (ὑπηκούσατε, 2.12). It is no accident that Paul uses the same terms to describe his Lord's actions in Phil. 2.6-8 as he does to characterize his own ministry and to shape his admonitions.[1]

Romans 15.3
Returning at last to Romans, we are now in a better position to evaluate the aorist ἤρεσεν in 15.3. Some connect it with Christ's self-emptying in Phil. 2.6 (cf. 2 Cor. 8.9),[2] and others deny any reference here to the earthly Jesus—Paul is thinking of the pre-existent Christ and the *Heilsgeschehen* proclaimed in the kerygma.[3] Phil. 2.6-8 is a parallel, but to assert that ὁ Χριστός excludes the earthly Jesus is to allow faulty presuppositions to precipitate an erroneous exegesis, for the 'reproaches' of 15.3b clearly fell on the Jesus of history (Mk 15.32 // Mt. 27.44), just as Phil. 2.8 can only describe the humble man who was obedient unto death on a cross in space and time. Not a few claim that the aorist is complexive/constative, encompassing the life and work of Christ.[4] Cranfield writes,

> The statement οὐχ ἑαυτῷ ἤρεσεν sums up with eloquent reticence both the meaning of the Incarnation and the character of Christ's earthly life. He most certainly did not seek to please Himself, but sought rather to please His Father and to please men εἰς τὸ ἀγαθὸν πρὸς οἰκοδομήν.[5]

Schulz compares the negative μὴ ἑαυτῷ ἀρέσκειν with the Synoptic

1. So also Hurtado, 'Jesus', p. 123.
2. E.g. Lietzmann, p. 119. Despite Buchanan's arguments that Jesus was a wealthy man ('Jesus', pp. 195-209) and Dunn's claim that 2 Cor. 8.9 is rooted in Adamic theology (*Christology*, pp. 121-23), it is difficult to deny that πλούσιος ὤν points to Christ's pre-existence. Nevertheless, Dunn has rightly questioned any limitation of ἐπτώχευσεν to the incarnation; the verb probably includes the earthly poverty of Jesus (cf. Mt. 8.20 // Lk. 9.58) as well as the spiritual destitution of Christ on the cross (Mk 15.34 // Mt. 27.46).
3. So Zeller, *Römer*, p. 228; Betz, *Nachfolge*, p. 162; Schrage, *Einzelgebote*, p. 240.
4. So BDF, sec. 332.1 'in his whole earthly life'; MHT, III, p. 73 'constantly'; Schulz, *Nachfolgen*, p. 280 n. 95; cf. Philippi, *Romans*, II, p. 358. This is an assertion, not a proof, for the grammar is not conclusive.
5. Cranfield, *Romans*, II, p. 732; also Barrett, *Romans*, p. 269; Stanton, *Preaching*; Harrisville, *Romans*, p. 230.

call ἀρνεῖσθαι ἑαυτόν (Mk 8.34 // Mt. 16.24 // Lk. 9.23).[1] The early
Church saw Jesus' life as fully pleasing to God; hence Jn 8.29: ὁ
πέμψας με μετ' ἐμοῦ ἐστιν· οὐκ ἀφῆκέν με μόνον, ὅτι **ἐγὼ τὰ
ἀρεστὰ αὐτῷ ποιῶ πάντοτε**. Used with reference to God,
ἀρέσκειν is effectively a synonym for obedience (Rom. 8.8; 1 Thess.
2.4; 4.1; Heb. 11.5; cf. εὐάρεστος in 2 Cor. 5.9; Col. 3.20), that is,
the accomplishment of his will (Heb. 13.21; Eph. 5.10), so that
progressive transformation into the image of Christ who οὐχ ἑαυτῷ
ἤρεσεν leads εἰς τὸ δοκιμάζειν τί τὸ θέλημα τοῦ θεοῦ **τὸ
εὐάρεστον** (Rom. 12.1-2). Christ's obedience found its climax and
τέλος in his self-giving on the cross, but in both Phil. 2.8 and Rom.
5.19 this obedience includes the whole of his earthly life, for
otherwise his exaltation and the justification of sinners through his
death would have been impossible—Paul could not assert that Jesus
knew no sin (2 Cor. 5.21). Paul primarily has the Passion of Jesus in
mind in 15.3, since his earlier references to Christ's death (14.9, 15),
coupled with the quotation in 15.3b from Psalm 68[69] which finds
fulfilment in the reproach Jesus endured on the cross (Mt. 27.44; Mk
15.32), favour a more limited appeal.[2] Nevertheless, there is little
justification for ruling out a summary of his character as well, despite
the quotation which follows (see below).[3]

Instead of citing deeds of Jesus or referring directly to the cross to
expound his statement, Paul quotes Ps. 68[69].10b verbatim: οἱ
ὀνειδισμοὶ τῶν ὀνειδιζόντων σε ἐπέπεσαν ἐπ' ἐμέ. Christ is the
speaker, and σε refers not to humankind, but to God (cf. Rom. 15.9;
3.4).[4] The Psalm was widely viewed in early Christianity as finding
fulfilment in the Christ-Event, not only because of its depiction of the
righteous sufferer, but also because of the description of his enemies

---

1. *Nachfolgen*, p. 279.

2. Cf. Wilckens, *Römer*, III, pp. 101-102; Leenhardt, *Romans*, p. 362. H.C.G.
Moule writes, 'Does not St. Paul here allude specially to the conflict of Gethsemane,
and to the outrages which our Lord patiently bore just afterwards? He had scarcely
said, "*Thy will be done*", when the awful "reproaches" of His night of shame and
insult began' (*Epistle to the Romans*, p. 234; cf. Heb. 5.7-8).

3. *Contra* Nababen ('Bekenntnis', p. 109) and Merk (*Handeln*, pp. 171-72), who
claim that Paul is grounding his exhortation in the *Heilstat*.

4. Hanson, 'Interpretation', pp. 69-72. 'When the pious person of the OT con-
fesses that the reproaches which are directed against God fall on him, he is thinking
of the world which rebels against its Lord' (Käsemann, *Romans*, p. 382).

(i.e. the unbelieving Jews, in the eyes of early Christians) and the curses which fall upon them.[1] The appropriateness of its use in Rom. 15.3 is less than obvious, but an examination of the context of the quotation makes the choice intelligible. Ps. 68[69].8 relates the reason that ὀνειδισμοί have fallen on the psalmist: ὅτι ἕνεκα σοῦ ὑπήνεγκα ὀνειδισμόν (MT: כי־עליך נשאתי חרפה). The psalmist is suffering and *bearing* (ὑποφέρειν = נשא; βαστάζειν can render the latter) reproach *on God's account*.[2] His suffering results from 'not pleasing himself', but seeking to serve God; zeal for another's house (not his own) has consumed him, and he thus bears the reproaches that are really directed against God. The quotation fits in Rom. 15.3 because if Christ the righteous sufferer bore a burden of reproach as a result of seeking to please God, Christians all the more should be prepared to bear a burden (including abuse from others) when they seek to please (i.e. to serve) their brethren—which ultimately is to please God (cf. 14.18; 12.1-2).[3] Specifically, in our context the strong should be ready to please the weak and accommodate themselves to their scruples when necessary, even though that would mean exposing themselves to the same reproaches and ridicule from the world which the strong had formerly heaped upon the ἀδύνατοι.[4] In bearing the abuse of people for the sake of God, Jesus serves as the supreme example for the strong, who would incur reproach for the sake of their brethren.

Why then did Paul not simply cite Isa. 53.4 or something similar to Mk 10.45? To try to answer why someone chooses one expression over another is always difficult (if not impossible), but we can make an attempt. The issue in Rom. 15.3 is not redemption and the acceptance of human guilt, but the sufferings of God's faithful

1. It is quoted in Jn 2.17; Acts 1.20; Rom. 11.9-10, and echoed in Mt. 27.34, 48; Mk 3.21; 15.23, 36; Lk. 13.35; 23.36; Jn 15.25; 19.38; Acts 3.5; 16.1; Phil. 4.3; and Heb. 11.26. Lindars considers it to be 'undoubtedly the most important' of the psalms employed in Christian apologetic, noting that 'it was found useful *as a whole* by the early Christians' (*Apologetic*, p. 99; his emphasis).

2. Cf. Ps. 68.10a: ὅτι ὁ ζῆλος τοῦ οἴκου σου κατέφαγέν με, cited in Jn 2.17.

3. Paul has laid the groundwork for this earlier when he says that no Christian lives ἑαυτῷ but κυρίῳ (14.7-8), ruling out self-pleasing as well as attitudes of condemnation or ridicule.

4. Similarly Käsemann, *Romans*, p. 382. He insists, however, that the idea is not imitation but conformity.

servant. The combination of elements associated with Ps. 68[69].10, and particularly the idea of reproach[1] as a burden which would be appropriate for the strong, apparently made it more obvious to Paul than other texts.[2] Moreover, Paul knew the verse in its context[3] as part of a larger picture of the attitude and experience of Christ: 'In diesem Gebet des Psalmisten sieht Paulus eine Weissagung auf das Wort und Werk Jesu, ja eine Beschreibung seines Weges'.[4] Failure to adduce an example from the life of Jesus is easier to explain: none of the authors of the NT Epistles and none of the early apostolic fathers refer to a specific event (aside from the cross) that would serve here—the Passion of Christ understandably eclipsed any other event in significance as a ground for ethical appeal. The decision to quote Psalm 68 instead of referring directly to the cross may be attributed to Paul's desire to emphasize that Christ fulfils the OT, to his concern to remind his Gentile readers that the latter has continuing value, and/or to the fact that the text was familiar to Paul from another context (apologetic). Dodd was probably right to say, 'it is more in Paul's manner to cite Scripture (cf. x. 11-21), because, to his mind, if you can cite Scripture for a fact, you show, not only that it *was* so, but that it *must* have been so, in the eternal purpose of God'.[5] In any

1. Note the twofold repetition of the ὀνειδιζ- root in the verse. Reproach is a topos both for the sufferings of the messiah (Ps. 88[89].51) and for the response of the world to Christians for his sake (Mt. 5.11 [cf. 1 Pet. 4.14]; Lk. 6.22; 1 Tim. 4.10; Heb. 10.33; 11.26; 13.13).

2. Cf. Chrysostom, 'And why did he not say, "He emptied Himself?". . . It is because this was not the only thing he wished to point out, that He became man, but that He was also ill-treated, and obtained a bad reputation with many, being looked upon as weak. For it says, "If Thou be the Son of God, come down from the Cross.". . . And, "He saved others, Himself He cannot save"' (*Homily*, p. 27; *NPNF*, XI, p. 536 col. 1).

3. Cf. Hanson, *Jesus*, pp. 153-55.

4. Michel, *Römer*, p. 445. He wonders whether 15.3b should be understood as a direct word from Jesus (comparing Ps. 21[22].23 in Heb. 2.12; cf. Schlier, *Römerbrief*, p. 420). Paul's language of perseverance, comfort and hope in 15.4 also appears in the psalm (ὑπομένειν in Ps. 68.7, 21; ἐλπίζειν in 68.4; παρακαλοῦν in 68.21).

5. Dodd, *Romans*, p. 221. Cf. Denney: 'Some have argued from this indirect proof of Christ's character that Paul had no acquaintance with the facts of His life; but the inference is unsound. It would condemn all the N.T. writers of the same ignorance, for they never appeal to incidents in Christ's life; and this summary of the

event, Paul's use of Scripture here shows that 'the example of Christ is more than an example; it belongs to the pattern of revelation'.[1]

3. *Romans 15.4: The Steadfastness*

In 15.4 Paul digresses to justify (γάρ) his use of Psalm 68[69], yet here too there is evidence of the importance of Jesus' example. Whatever was written beforehand, that is to say, the entirety of Jewish Scripture, including the verse he has just cited, was written for the instruction of Christians (cf. Rom. 4.24; 1 Cor. 9.10; 10.11; cf. 2 Tim. 3.16), that they might have hope. τῶν γραφῶν could be taken with διὰ τῆς ὑπομονῆς as well as with διὰ τῆς παρακλήσεως, but is best construed with the latter only.[2] Whose ὑπομονή then is in view? Cranfield dismisses too quickly Michel's suggestion that it refers to the example of steadfastness in the Passion of Jesus.[3] Paul has just spoken of the messiah's example, ὑπομένειν occurs twice in Psalm 68, and the article here may be anaphoric. The article is not unusual with abstract nouns, but in Paul's letters, ὑπομονή is regularly anarthrous after a preposition (e.g. Rom. 8.25: δι' ὑπομονῆς ἀπεκδεχόμεθα);[4] in the one clear exception the reference is probably to Christ's own steadfastness (2 Thess. 3.5), which engenders endurance in the members of his body.[5] Christ stands as the

whole character of Christ, possessing as it did for Paul and his readers the authority of inspiration, was more impressive than any isolated example of non-self-pleasing could have been' (*Romans*, p. 708).

1. Barrett, *Romans*, p. 269.
2. So, e.g., Käsemann (*Romans*, p. 383), who adduces 1 Macc. 12.9 as a parallel. Favouring the independence of διὰ τῆς ὑπομονῆς is the repetition of διά (evidence for the omission of the second διά is limited primarily to western witnesses) and the fact that the parallelism is not exact: the Scriptures offer comfort but not endurance, and the latter is always a characteristic of *persons* in Paul.
3. Cranfield, *Romans*, II, p. 735; Michel, *Römer*, p. 445.
4. Other instances with a preposition in Paul are Rom. 2.7; 2 Cor. 1.6; 6.4; 12.12; Col. 1.11. In 2 Thess. 1.4 the article appears with a preposition, but it is required to link ὑπομονή with πίστις.
5. So, e.g., Marshall, *Thessalonians*, p. 218. τοῦ Χριστοῦ could be an objective genitive, i.e., the steadfastness directed towards Christ, patient waiting for his coming (cf. Ign. *Rom.* 10.3; Rev. 1.9), but the parallel τοῦ θεοῦ favours a subjective genitive. Best refers it to the steadfastness which Christ imparts (*Thessalonians*, pp. 330-31), and the thought may well include the notion of Christ

supreme example of ὑπομονή in a stream of various traditions from 1 Pet. 2.20-21 through Heb. 12.1-3 to Pol. *Phil.* 8.2, where we find the clearest exposition of the theme. It is not difficult to see how '*the* steadfastness' could have recalled Jesus' definitive endurance in his sufferings (foretold in the Scriptures), as well as the ὑπομονή which he was believed to have expected from his followers for salvation (Lk. 21.19; Mk 13.13; Mt. 24.13; 10.22; cf. Rev. 3.10; *Did.* 16.5; Heb. 10.36).[1] A logion such as 'He who endures to the end will be saved' would have relevance for all in early Christian διδασκαλία, regardless of the original reference of the σωτηρία.[2] Matthew's repetition of the saying evinces its importance, as does the emphasis on ὑπομονή in 1 Tim. 6.11;[3] 2 Tim. 2.12;[4] 2 Pet. 1.6; Rev. 1.9; 2.2-3, 19; 13.10; 14.12. All of these texts are distinguished from the ὑπομονή of Stoicism by an eschatological perspective, a note of expectancy characteristic of 'hopeful perseverance that endures with faithfulness to God with an eye on the future'.[5] On the other hand, even if διὰ τῆς ὑπομονῆς is independent of τῶν γραφῶν, the article can point just as easily to the Romans (12.12; Paul has just said that Scripture was written for ἡμετέραν instruction; cf. ἔχωμεν), or it could be added simply to balance τῆς παρακλήσεως which follows.[6] Moreover, when Paul speaks of steadfastness he is usually thinking

as the source of endurance. If comparison with τὰ παθήματα τοῦ Χριστοῦ is appropriate (2 Cor. 1.5; cf. Phil. 3.10), Paul calls them to participate as members of the body of Christ in that which Christ himself experienced in his earthly life (cf. Rigaux, *Epîtres*, p. 700).

1. The *idea* of steadfastness appears in many other dominical sayings besides those employing ὑπομονή. Thus the logia about the cross to be borne by disciples presupposes faithful endurance through suffering (Mk 8.34; Lk. 9.23; 14.27; Mt. 10.38; 16.24), as do the beatitudes for the persecuted and hated (Mt. 5.10-12 // Lk. 6.22-23) and the warnings against denying him (e.g. Mt. 10.33; Lk. 12.9).

2. On the other hand, *4 Ezra* 6.25 reveals that this teaching was not peculiar to Christ.

3. Cf. Col. 3.12, where a similar list of qualities were likely applied first to Christ.

4. 2 Tim. 2.12 almost certainly echoes dominical tradition (Mt. 10.22, 33 pars.), and the introductory formula πιστὸς ὁ λόγος preceding it points to the Christian tradition. Cf. Knight, *Sayings*, p. 132.

5. Knight, *Sayings*, p. 121.

6. Cf. Käsemann, *Romans*, p. 383.

specifically of the experience of believers—not explicitly of their Lord (e.g. Rom. 2.7; 5.3-4; 8.25; 2 Cor. 1.6; Col. 1.11; 1 Thess. 1.3).

Before dismissing any dominical link in 15.4, it should be remembered that for Paul, the general idea of steadfastness is part and parcel of his theology of dying and rising with Christ (Rom. 6.3-4). Through baptism Christians have become a part of his body (1 Cor. 12.13; Gal. 3.27-28), and just as the head endured suffering and tribulation on the way to glory, so inevitably must the members of that body. If the παθήματα which the Corinthians endure are the same sufferings as those of Paul and his companions, both share in the παθήματα τοῦ Χριστοῦ which abound to them (2 Cor. 1.5-6), sufferings which are not simply for the sake of Christ but are Christ's own sufferings, both in the sense of living after his example and continuing and completing his παθήματα, insofar as those who suffer are members of his body. Hence Paul can say that he carries in his body the death of Jesus (2 Cor. 4.10; cf. the call to take up the cross in Mk 8.34 par.) and that he fills up τὰ ὑστερήματα τῶν θλίψεων τοῦ Χριστοῦ ἐν τῇ σαρκί μου (Col. 1.24).[1] So his call to 'persevere in affliction' (τῇ θλίψει ὑπομένοντες, Rom. 12.12) is more than a commonplace of paraenesis—it is fundamental to being a Christian. Defending his ministry he describes the behaviour of himself and his colleagues as συνιστάντες ἑαυτοὺς ὡς θεοῦ διάκονοι ἐν ὑπομονῇ πολλῇ, ἐν θλίψεσιν, ἐν ἀνάγκαις (2 Cor. 6.4), language which could hardly fail to remind his readers of the image of the righteous Servant of God from the OT, who found concrete form in the person of Christ (cf. 1 Thess. 1.6). ὑπομονή is the distinguishing characteristic of a true apostle (2 Cor. 12.12) who carries in himself as well as in his teaching the tradition of Christ; the 'superlative apostles' might have miracles, but Paul bears the true dominical likeness in his perseverance. Paul's attitude towards steadfastness in suffering thus involves more than *imitatio*, although it certainly includes it (1 Thess. 1.6).[2] It is an *extension* of Jesus' experience, and

---

1. According to Luke, the germ of the insight that Christ continues to suffer through the sufferings of his people goes back to Paul's conversion: 'Saul, Saul, why do you persecute *me*?' (Acts 9.4; 22.7; 26.14)

2. Tinsley emphasizes this: 'The frequent exhortations to patience and endurance, in fact, indicate that for Paul ὑπομονή is laid upon all Christians, not only because it is a good thing in itself, but because it is a necessary part of the Christian life if the latter is to be an evident *imitatio Christi*. The Lord Jesus himself was the perfect

a necessary part of conformity to Christ in the present in order to be fit for ultimate conformity to the glory of the Son at the resurrection (Phil. 3.10-11; Rom. 8.18, 29).

4. *Romans 15.5-6: In accordance with Christ Jesus*

From the digression in v. 4 Paul returns to his concern for unity with a prayer in 15.5-6, and now clearly he is addressing both the strong and the weak. His desire is that they be of the same attitude in accordance with Christ Jesus. κατὰ Χριστὸν Ἰησοῦν could signify simply 'according to the *will* of Christ', that is, 'the most important criterion of the way taught in Scripture is that it runs under Christ's lordship'.[1] Support for this is claimed from κατὰ Χριστόν in Col. 2.8 (cf. also κατὰ κύριον in 2 Cor. 11.17, and κατὰ θεόν in 2 Cor. 7.9-10; Eph. 4.24), as well as Paul's emphasis in context on the lordship of Christ (14.4, 6, 7-9; cf. τοῦ *κυρίου* ἡμῶν Ἰησοῦ Χριστοῦ, 15.6). On the other hand, others have interpreted most of these examples of κατά + accusative to mean 'in accordance with the character or manner',[2] and Col. 3.10 definitely has this force (cf. Mt. 23.3; Gal. 4.28; Eph. 4.24; Heb. 8.5; Jas 3.1; 1 Pet. 1.15). A parallel closer in thought to Rom. 15.5 than Col. 2.8 is Phil. 2.5, where τοῦτο φρονεῖτε ἐν ὑμῖν ὃ καὶ ἐν Χριστῷ Ἰησοῦ gives concrete direction to the desire for τὸ αὐτὸ φρονεῖν and τὸ ἓν φρονεῖν (Phil. 2.4; cf. 4.2; 2 Cor. 13.11). Thus in 15.5 Paul wants the Romans to find unity of intent in conformity with that attitude found in Christ *Jesus*, their *Vorbild*.[3] Schulz comments,

exemplar of it; their ὑπομονή is a *semeion* of his. . . ' (*Imitation*, p. 144).

1. Käsemann, *Romans*, p. 382; Cranfield, *Romans*, II, p. 737 n. 4; Michaelis, *TDNT*, IV, p. 669 n. 18; Betz, *Nachfolge*, p. 162 n. 2.

2. E.g. Sanday and Headlam (*Exegetical Commentary*, p. 396). Dunn sees both ideas of 'modeled on and obedient to' implicit in the κατά phrases, observing that Col. 2.8 follows the exhortation in 2.6: 'as you received the traditions concerning Christ Jesus the Lord, so walk in him' (Dunn, *Romans*, II, p. 840).

3. Michel, *Römer*, p. 446; A. Schulz: 'ein sicheres Vorbildzeugnis' (*Nachfolgen*, p. 280). The addition of Ἰησοῦς here is suggestive. Philippi (*Romans*, II, p. 362) objects that an individual cannot be adduced as an example of concord, but Paul's point in context is that by imitating Christ they will achieve unity (cf. Phil. 2.1-5). On Philippi's view κατὰ Χριστὸν Ἰησοῦν becomes redundant, for τὸ αὐτὸ φρονεῖν is Paul's request from God and plainly would be the will of Christ anyway.

Der vorausgehende Bezug auf Christi vorbildliches Verhalten in Rö 15,3 und der nachstehende Vergleich der Christenpflicht mit dem Beispiel Jesu in Rö 15,7 legen es an sich schon nahe, daß Paulus auch bei dem Zusatz κατὰ Χριστὸν Ἰησοῦν in Rö 15,5 an das Vorbild seines Herrn denkt, wenn er Gott um die einmütige Geschlossenheit der römischen Kirche bittet.[1]

Cranfield wants to see Paul praying here for a 'common sincere determination to seek to obey the Lord Jesus Christ', but Paul has already presupposed that in his argument in 14.6.[2] The problem is not an unwillingness on the part of the strong and weak to obey Christ—both were sincerely convinced of the rightness of their intention—but of their failure to exhibit his self-sacrificing love for the other. τὸ αὐτὸ φρονεῖν ἐν ἀλλήλοις κατὰ Χριστὸν Ἰησοῦν leads to **κατὰ ἀγάπην** περιπατεῖν (14.15), for Christ is the supreme manifestation of God's love in Paul's mind. At the same time, the pattern for the Romans is also their Lord (Phil. 2.12; Rom. 13.14). Following Christ's example and obeying him because he is Lord are not mutually exclusive but intimately related. The same humility, love, steadfastness and obedience that led to Jesus' exaltation to lordship make Christ Paul's example. Such an attitude is not proud or self-exalting; it does not preclude association with the lowly-esteemed, but rather seeks them out and welcomes them into full fellowship (14.1; 15.7).

The ultimate aim (ἵνα) of this unity is that the Roman Christians may glorify the God and Father of the one whose attitude they are to adopt (15.6). Mouths once full of ridicule and condemnation toward others (cf. 3.14) are to be full of praise. There is no room for antagonistic 'fellowships' or a divided 'chorus' in Rome; Paul wants them to glorify God just as Christ himself did by becoming a servant (15.7-9). Paul's concern for the δόξα of God here is echoed again in 15.7, 9 and in the following OT quotations, where it represents a complete reversal of humanity's failure to glorify God (cf 1.21), made possible through the last Adam into whose image the readers are to be transformed (12.2; 8.29). Whereas humans suppressed

---

1. A. Schulz, *Nachfolgen*, p. 283. Although he differs from my interpretation of 15.5, Betz rightly sees Paul calling for imitation in the phrase κατὰ Χριστὸν Ἰησοῦν; he thinks the reference here as elsewhere is to 'der Heilstat Gottes in Christus' (*Nachfolge*, p. 178; cf. also p. 162).

2. Cranfield, *Romans*, II, pp. 737-38.

τὴν ἀλήθειαν in unrighteousness (1.18), the last Adam became a servant to establish God's truth (15.8).

5. *Romans 15.7-13: Receive as Christ Received You*

With διό Paul introduces a summary exhortation (15.7-13) which concludes his formal *paraclesis* to the Romans. The fact that Paul repeats the call to receive (προσλαμβάνεσθαι, cf. 14.1), this time broadened (ἀλλήλους), reveals that he is thinking not only of the parties addressed in 14.1–15.6, but of all his readers scattered in communities across the capital of the empire.[1] He wants them to accept each other freely in Christian fellowship, and the apostle probably has an eye on Phoebe's and his own eventual reception by the Romans as well (προσδέξησθε αὐτήν, 16.2; cf. Phil. 2.29; Phlm 17; Acts 28.2). The predominantly Jewish–Gentile Christian conflict addressed in ch. 14 reflects in a microcosm some of the difficulties Paul has had in his overall ministry to the Gentiles, a ministry which he has sought to introduce in his letter. Thus in this concluding section,

> St Paul has a double object. He writes to remind the Gentiles that it is through the Jews that they are called, the Jews that the aim and purpose of their existence is the calling of the Gentiles. The Gentiles must remember that Christ became a Jew to save them; the Jews that Christ came among them in order that all the families of the earth might be blessed: both must realize that the aim of the whole is to proclaim God's glory.[2]

Paul justifies his final imperative with καθὼς καὶ ὁ Χριστὸς προσελάβετο ὑμᾶς εἰς δόξαν τοῦ θεοῦ. Regardless of whether καθώς is primarily causal or comparative,[3] given the context and the repetition of the verb προσλαμβάνειν in the first two clauses the thought of Christ at least as example is assured here. 'The example of Christ, once again invoked, is not, strictly speaking, to be imitated. But here again they are to consider the situation created by the

---

1. Käsemann, *Romans*, p. 384; for other views on the relation of 15.1-6 and 15.7-13 see Karris, 'Occasion', p. 93 and n. 73.

2. Sanday and Headlam, *Exegetical Commentary*, p. 397.

3. Käsemann claims it must be causal, for otherwise εἰς δόξαν τοῦ θεοῦ would be redundant (*Romans*, p. 385). A comparative καθώς, however, better explains the addition of the preposition, since Paul has just prayed that his readers will *glorify* God by finding unity in their emulation of Christ.

ministry of Christ, and on that basis to behave in the same spirit, in harmony with their pattern.'[1] As in 15.3 the aorist προσελάβετο looks back, but is Paul thinking of an action of the earthly Jesus, or of the acceptance of his readers[2] by the risen Christ at their conversion/ justification? Verbal parallels decisively favour the latter: in 14.3 the strong are warned not to despise (the opposite of 'receiving', 14.1) those who eat vegetables ὁ θεὸς γὰρ αὐτὸν προσελάβετο, and in 11.15 the anticipated conversion of the Jews is called their πρόσλημψις.[3] And yet, although the Romans would see their experience of acceptance by Christ into his fellowship as a subsequent event, for Paul their justification is founded upon the fact that 'while we were yet helpless, at the right time Christ died for the ungodly. . . while we were yet sinners Christ died for us. . . while we were enemies we were reconciled to God by the death of his Son' (5.6, 8, 10). In other words, Christ's (and God's, 14.3) reception of the readers is rooted in and inseparable from the salvific death of the historical Jesus. When he took to himself the sins of others on the cross, it was an act of 'receiving sinners', as his acceptance of the repentant thief illustrates (Lk. 23.42-43). According to the Synoptic tradition, reception of sinners was a characteristic of Jesus' life and teaching; Stuhlmacher compares this with Paul's doctrine of justification by grace:

> Von der Rechtfertigung der gottlosen Sünder allein aus Gnaden spricht Paulus *ganz im Sinne Jesu*. Dies zeigen über die sühnetheologischen Traditionen hinaus Jesu Gleichnisse vom Verlorenen in Lk 15, sein Gleichnis von Pharisäer und Zöllner (Lk 18,9-14) und der Umgang Jesu mit den Sündern allgemein (vgl. Lk 19,10). *Es ist kaum ein Zufall, daß Paulus in Röm 15,7ff. Jesu Verhalten gegenüber den Sündern aus Heiden und Juden mit demselben Stichwort der 'Annahme' beschreibt, das schon in Lk 15,2 für Jesu Verhalten gebraucht wird!* Was die Rechtfertigungsbotschaft anbetrifft, ist Paulus im Römerbrief mit Jesus

---

1. Leenhardt, *Romans*, p. 364.
2. The reading ἡμᾶς has strong support in B D* P etc., but ὑμᾶς is better attested (ℵ A C F G Ψ 𝔐 etc.), has a wider geographical distribution of mss., and should probably be preferred here.
3. Paul does not use the verb outside Rom. 14.1, 3; 15.7 and Phlm 17, and the noun is *hapax legomenon* in the NT.

(und der christologischen Tradition der Gemeinden von Jerusalem und
Antiochien) durchaus im Einklang![1]

The verb is different (προσδέχεσθαι)[2] and the verse is unparalleled
in Mark and Matthew, but Lk. 15.2 summarizes reliable Synoptic
tradition.[3] Despite its possible influence on Paul's doctrine of justification, however, we cannot be so sure that Paul is alluding to this
tradition in Rom. 15.7. He is thinking about the work of Jesus (cf.
15.8), but the focus is again primarily on the Passion (see below).
Thus we read in what may be an early commentary on our text,

> In love did the Master receive us (προσελάβετο ἡμᾶς ὁ δεσπότης); for
> the sake of the love which he had towards us did Jesus Christ our Lord
> give his blood by the will of God for us, and his flesh for our flesh, and
> his soul for our souls (*1 Clem.* 49.6).

The reception of sinners which began during Jesus' ministry was most
clearly manifested on the cross, and continues in the present as Christ
forgives and receives those who come to him in faith.[4]

In vv. 8-9 Paul reminds his readers of what Christ has done for
both the Jews and the Gentiles. The λέγω γάρ thus expresses not an
additional reason for the imperative in 15.7, but expands and explains
Paul's previous assertion. His central point is that Christ became a
servant to the Jews[5] for the sake of God's faithfulness to fulfil two

1. 'Jesustradition', p. 246; emphasis mine.
2. Like their roots, προσδέχεσθαι and προσλαμβάνειν can be virtual synonyms (cf. B. Siede, *NIDNTT*, III, pp. 744-45, 750).
3. Criticizing various interpretations of this phenomenon, E.P. Sanders nevertheless recognizes that 'Jesus offered the truly wicked. . . admission to *his*
group. . . *if* they accepted him' (*Jesus*, p. 210; his emphasis).
4. Notice that Paul does not appeal to the *teaching* of Jesus here, i.e., that he
reportedly spoke more than once of receiving and being received (δέχεσθαι, Mk
6.11 // Mt. 10.14 // Lk. 9.5; Mt. 10.40-41 // Jn 13.20 [λαμβάνειν]; Mk 9.37 // Mt.
18.5 // Lk. 9.48; Lk. 10.8, 10) although elsewhere he shows an awareness of the
missionary discourse (cf. 1 Thess. 4.8 // Lk. 10.16; 1 Cor. 9.14; Allison, 'Pattern',
pp. 12-13). Again it is the *example* of Christ that is ultimately more compelling for
Paul than his words.
5. This is to take περιτομῆς as an objective genitive referring to the Jews by way
of the sign of the old covenant (so, e.g., Barrett, *Romans*, p. 271; cf. Rom. 3.30;
Gal. 2.7-9; Eph. 2.11). Sanday and Headlam paraphrase διάκονον γεγενῆσθαι
περιτομῆς as meaning 'to carry out the promises implied in that covenant the seal of

ends: (1) to confirm the promises made to the (Jewish) fathers, and (2) so that the Gentiles should glorify God for his mercy (cf. 11.30).[1] The statement Χριστὸν διάκονον γεγενῆσθαι περιτομῆς is significant for four reasons. First, Paul is clearly referring to the earthly Jesus who fulfilled the promises made in the Jewish Scriptures (βεβαιῶσαι τὰς ἐπαγγελίας τῶν πατέρων; cf. 9.4).[2] Secondly, διάκονον γεγενῆσθαι[3] recalls the dominical saying that the Son of Man 'did not come to be served but to serve' (οὐκ ἦλθεν διακονηθῆναι ἀλλὰ διακονῆσαι; Mk 10.45 // Mt. 20.28); the word Paul chooses to characterize the Lord's work is precisely that which Jesus reputedly applied to himself. Thirdly, Paul's claim that Christ became a servant to the Jews coheres with Jesus' claim to have been sent to the lost sheep of the house of Israel (Mt. 15.24).[4] Fourthly, inasmuch as the description of his work is an expansion of καθὼς καὶ ὁ Χριστὸς προσελάβετο ὑμᾶς (15.7) and διάκονον γεγενῆσθαι corresponds to ὁ δουλεύων in 14.18 we have another appeal to the example of Jesus. If Christ became a servant to the Jews, how can the 'strong' refrain from doing the same for their Jewish brethren? And if he became a servant in order that ultimately the Gentiles might be included in God's family, how can Jewish Christians complain about their eating habits?

> Consider, then, Christ your pattern, says Paul to both groups. What else did He do but 'please' by bringing to each what he most needed, by adapting Himself to the situation of each in order to give a like welcome to all? For the people of Israel, He confirmed in His ministry and accomplished (βεβαιοῦν) the promises made to their forefathers. . . Christ

which was circumcision' (*Exegetical Commentary*, pp. 397-98; cf. Murray, *Romans*, II, p. 205).

1. Winer construes τὰ δὲ ἔθνη. . . δοξάσαι κ.τ.λ. as directly subordinate to λέγω, with ὑπὲρ ἐλέους answering ὑπὲρ ἀληθείας (*Grammar*, p. 417), but most take τὰ δὲ ἔθνη. . . δοξάσαι κ.τ.λ. to be subordinate to εἰς τό and coordinate with βεβαιῶσαι.

2. Cf. Cranfield, *Romans*, II, p. 464. The likelihood of a pre-Easter origin for Mt. 15.24 is high, given its discontinuity with the universal mission of the later Church (B.F. Meyer, *Aims*, p. 167 and n. 129).

3. The perfect tense points to the lasting result of his having become a servant—Christ remains a servant of the Jews (Barrett, *Romans*, p. 271).

4. Cf. also Rom. 1.3 (τοῦ υἱοῦ αὐτοῦ γενομένου ἐκ σπέρματος Δαυὶδ κατὰ σάρκα) and the primitive emphasis on the gospel 'to the Jew first' (Acts 3.26; 13.46; Rom. 1.16; cf. 2.9-10).

opened up to the pagan world the way of divine mercy. . . to bring them
too in their turn to glorify God. . . Thus Christ. . . has welcomed both
groups and especially those who were the weakest, the most
underprivileged, the most remote. The inspiring example is divine. In the
church, the strongest are not those who show their superiority, but those
who hide it out of love for the weak, and in order to give them a more
assured welcome.[1]

Again, although his servant character is seen most clearly in his death
on the cross, the thought of Jesus' ministry as a whole cannot be
excluded from 15.8.[2]

In 15.9b-12 Paul proceeds to support his claim in v. 9a with a
demonstration from Scripture that the divine plan envisages the union
of Gentiles and the Jews in praise to God. The chaining of citations in
a *haraz* (הרז) was a rabbinic method which Paul seldom employs in his
letters (cf. Rom. 9–11).[3] His last quotation from Isa. 11.10 in 15.12
recalls a theme sounded at the outset (Rom. 1.3)—that the messiah is
descended from David, Jesse's son.[4] Together with the concluding
prayer-wish in 15.13, Paul's *haraz* reveals that he has moved beyond
the thought of chs. 12–15 and is summarizing the concern of his
Epistle, as well as his ministry to the Gentiles. With its themes of
hope, joy, peace, faith and the power of the Spirit, it gathers together
Paul's desire for his readers, and provides a fitting climax for the
letter.

6. *Summary and Conclusion*

In summary, Paul directly and indirectly asserts in 15.1-13 that Christ
is the example for the Christians in Rome to follow. Jesus did not

1. Leenhardt, *Romans*, pp. 364-65. Karris compares the whole of 15.7-13 with
1 Cor. 10.32-33, which gives content to the injunction to imitate Christ in 1 Cor.
11.1: 'The stress of Rom. 15:7-13, therefore, is on the servant nature of
Christ. . . who makes the two one. Christ is all things to all men, to Jews and
Gentile,. . . so that he might save them all, so that they might give glory to God'
('Occasion', p. 94).
2. So Michel (*Römer*, p. 448 n. 23), citing Gal. 4.4.
3. Ellis, *Use*, pp. 49-51.
4. Barrett (*Romans*, p. 272) minimizes the significance of the Davidic descent of
Jesus for Paul, but its twofold appearance in Romans is no accident (cf. Sweet,
'Seed'); Paul is working to help a Gentile majority better appreciate their Jewish
brethren.

please himself, but bore the reproach of men for the sake of God. Christians are to follow his example by seeking the benefit of their brethren, even if it means incurring derision from others for their compromises (15.3). They can find encouragement in the Scriptures, which depict the sufferings of the righteous one, knowing that through perseverance (after his example) their sacrifice is not without hope (15.4). Paul's prayer for them is that they may be of one mind in accordance with that of Christ, their example and Lord, so that in unison they may glorify his God and Father. This too is Christ's goal. Just as Christ received them, which required becoming a servant, so they are to receive one another, for the ultimate aim is that both Jews and Gentiles may praise God together. In short, Christ provides the paradigm on which the weak and strong may focus in order to find the unity which is ultimately their destiny, to the glory of God.

Paul's clear use of the example of Jesus here reveals something significant about the apostle's paraenetic method. Appeal to Christ is not unparalleled in his other Epistles (cf. 1 Cor. 11.1; Phil. 2.7-8; 2 Cor. 8.9), yet it stands in contrast with his more common practice of referring to his own example. No doubt that is due to the fact that he did not found the church(es) of Rome and was unknown to the great majority of Christians there. But it tells us that when he *does* refer to his own example in other letters, it is not because he has an aversion to the *Vorbild* of Jesus. Rather, he presupposes basic instruction in the character and career of the earthly Jesus (at the very least, details of his Passion) for his own converts, just as he assumes a knowledge of the tradition (cf. 6.17; 16.17) for his Roman readers.

It is striking that Paul adduces the appeal to the example of Christ at both the conclusion of his discussion of the specific problem of the weak and the strong (15.1-6), and also at the climax of his paraenesis in general (15.7-8). Christ's example is no afterthought here, tacked on to give essentially Hellenistic-Jewish ethical maxims a Christian veneer. With the example of Christ in 15.7-8, Paul is not adducing a new argument, but summarizing the force of his previous admonitions. His specific appeals not to despise or condemn each other (14.3, 10, 13), not to destroy but to build up (14.15-16, 19-20), to place first not food or drink but that which is truly characteristic of the kingdom of God (14.17), to deny self for the sake of a weaker brother (14.21), to bear the burdens of another (15.1) and thus to serve Christ (δουλεύειν τῷ Χριστῷ, 14.18) are all effectively exhortations to be imitators of Christ who also became a servant (διάκονος); inasmuch as 15.7-13 summarize the general paraenesis of chs. 12–13, the same may be said for those admonitions as well (cf. 13.14a). As in 1 Cor. 9.14 and Rom. 13.14, Paul has saved his most powerful ground of appeal for last; after this there is nothing more to say, no further exhortation, only the promises of Scripture and prayer for God's provision (15.9-13), before some closing remarks.

SUMMARY AND CONCLUSIONS

I began this study by seeking to clarify the meaning of allusion and by offering some criteria to help evaluate alleged parallels. Next I investigated other early Christian epistolary literature to see how JT was used, in order to establish realistic expectations for Paul. After postulating the probability that Paul knew and was positively inclined towards JT, I examined Romans 12.1-15.13 as a test case. I will now state my conclusions in the form of theses.

1. There is at most only one probable allusion to a dominical logion in Rom. 12.1–15.13. Coupled with the verbal parallels, Paul's language of certainty and his addition of 'Ιησοῦς in 14.14 slightly favours an allusion, although the alternate explanation is attractive. The repetition of εὐλογεῖτε in Rom. 12.14b and the unusual character of the admonition make it probable that at the time of dictating, Paul was conscious that his teaching went back to Jesus, but he shows little sign of any concern for his readers to recognize the exhortation as a dominical saying. The other so-called 'allusions' are even less certain.

2. Three virtually certain echoes and several probable echoes of Jesus' teaching do appear. The influence of dominical teaching on Paul in 12.14, 13.8-10, and 14.14 is virtually certain. A highly probable echo occurs in the prohibition of judging (14.13a). Less certain but still probable echoes include the use of βασιλεία θεοῦ as a criterion for behaviour (14.17), the warning against putting a σκάνδαλον before a brother (14.13b), Paul's calls for rendering to everyone what is due (13.7), for non-retaliation (12.17-19) and for ἀνυπόκριτος love (12.9), and the eschatological emphases in 13.11-12. The influence of Jesus' sayings may appear in Paul's themes of responsibility for the use of varied gifts (12.3-8), brotherly love (12.10), putting the honour of another first (12.10), peace (12.18; 14.19), and service (14.18; cf. 12.11).

3. The cumulative effect of the more probable echoes decisively favours the conclusion that dominical teachings significantly influenced Paul. Leaving aside completely the many 'possible' links and minor points of coherence with JT, the combination of teachings found in 12.9, 14, 17-19; 13.7, 8-10, 11-12; 14.13a, 14, 17 has probative value for my working hypothesis, providing christological contours to his admonition that would be familiar to unknown Romans readers from their earliest instruction as Christians (Rom. 6.17; 15.15; 16.17). Identifying specific sources of those sayings (an oral/written 'Q', 'M', 'L', etc.) is problematical in view of the limited agreement in vocabulary, but it deserves attention in future studies of Paul.

4. The explicit example of Christ in 15.3, 7 is only the tip of a thematic iceberg for Paul. The garment metaphor in 13.14 points to Christ's moral characteristics, which by *inclusio* are implied as the goal of the transformation in 12.2. The obedience of the second Adam (5.19) who accomplished the will of God is presupposed in the appeal for the renewed obedience and reasonable worship where the first Adam failed (12.1). Christ's example is probably implied in the call for associating with the lowly (12.16), in the way of love (14.15), in burden-bearing (15.1), in bearing reproach (15.3), in the common attitude readers are to seek (15.5), in receiving sinners/outsiders (15.7), and in serving others (15.8). Christ's character is probably assumed in calls for ὑπομονή (15.4; 12.12). Paul's goal for his hearers is that individually and collectively they should be transformed progressively into the image of the person of Jesus Christ, the last Adam, and so reflect the character of God, as he did.

5. The example of Christ is not limited to the pre-existent or the risen Christ, but has at its focus the character of Jesus, seen most clearly in his death on the cross. Paul's use of Χριστός instead of Ἰησοῦς reflects his conviction that the man Jesus was the messiah, and does not imply any disregard for his earthly life. Most of the time, Paul naturally speaks of Christ *as he is*, in view of the apostle's belief in Jesus as raised from the dead and living Lord of the present. We should not expect Paul to look back to the earthly career of Jesus unless he had specific reason to do so. Paul's is first and foremost a *theologia crucis*, and the same emphasis in his ethics is not surprising. Why should Paul

adduce as an example Jesus' compassion and humility in touching a leper or eating with sinners, when he was convinced that he *died* for us while we were yet sinners (Rom. 5.8)? The particular characteristics of Jesus that we see influencing Paul in general (there probably were others but we lack evidence) are shown at the cross: his humble-mindedness (ταπεινοφροσύνη), his meekness (πραΰτης), his gentleness (ἐπιεικείας), his love (ἀγάπη), his compassion (σπλάγχνα), his endurance (ὑπομονή) through suffering, his forgiving Spirit seen in receiving sinners (προσλαμβάνειν), and above all in his attitude as a servant (διάκονος, δοῦλος).

6. In rarely citing JT explicitly Paul does not represent a special case, but is typical of what we find in early Christianity. The view that he was uninterested in JT rests primarily on the flimsy foundation of a faulty exegesis of 2 Cor. 5.16, an argument from silence based on unjustified expectations, and a reading of Paul through the distorted lens of Gal. 1.11-12, an affirmation made in the heat of his most polemical letter and balanced by 1 Cor. 15.3-7. The proper question is not why does Paul not quote or directly refer to JT more often, but why he does so at all. Significant work remains to be done especially in the Corinthian literature to explain the increased frequency of allusions and echoes there.

7. There are many reasons why we see little explicit JT in Paul's exhortations. The most important include: (1) the presupposition of earlier instruction; (2) the nature of apostolic paraenesis; (3) the purpose of the Epistles (i.e. to build upon fundamental Christian tradition, developing the inner logic of the gospel imperatives); (4) the centrality of the cross and resurrection as the supreme statement of the character of Jesus; (5) Paul's own religious experience; (6) the lack of a fixed written tradition and the consequent need for interpretation. Other factors are summarized in Chapter 3.

8. The example of Christ does not signify for Paul any kind of mechanical reproduction of Jesus' life and deeds, any more than the teachings of Jesus constituted a new Torah. Imitation means Spirit-enabled following of Jesus' spirit and attitude as exemplified and characterized on the cross. In some respects Christ could not be imitated, for example, in his lordship and consequent right to judge

(Rom. 14.9). Paul's ethic is free from bondage under the law, but is (1) impelled by the Spirit (of Christ) towards the effective fulfilment of the law's moral demands, and (2) informed by the teachings of Jesus which, together with prophetic words of the Lord, helped to delineate the boundaries within which OT hortatory texts could continue to function. Where it provides a fitting example or buttresses an argument, Paul freely uses the OT, but we do not find him insisting on an OT principle when it contradicts the Synoptic picture of Jesus.

Paul is free in his use of JT, but it is a freedom within limits. On a formal level, he shows great liberty in (unconsciously?) adapting the language to fit into the flow of his exhortation and shows no constraint to quote the tradition in a wooden fashion. This, and his freedom to qualify the *application* of dominical teachings reflects his profound awareness of having the indwelling Spirit of Jesus. On the other hand, the *essence* of Jesus' teachings had evident authority for Paul, and he plainly does not feel free to 'create' JT (cf. 1 Cor. 7.25).

9. Although both have authority for Paul, ultimately the example of Jesus carries more significance for the apostle than dominical logia. His references to dominical examples are more explicit than to sayings of Jesus as such, and at times he feels free to qualify or set aside the teachings (1 Cor. 7.10; 9.14; 13.2; Rom. 14.14) for the sake of behaviour that will advance the gospel. Paul probably would not want to distinguish sharply between the teachings and example of Jesus, but he sees the Christian's goal as conformity to the *person* of Christ.

10. If progress in the Jesus–Paul debate is to be made, maximalists must recognize that many of their points have been over-argued, and minimalists that in establishing the non-necessity of dominical reference the enquiry has only just begun. If some maximalists have been guilty of lack of precision in defining their terms, ignoring the Pauline context, and overemphasizing the significance of particular pieces of evidence to prove a dominical allusion (e.g. the change from participle to verb in 12.14 and the rarity of σκάνδαλον in 14.13b), minimalists have likewise failed in method, coming to the text with unrealistic expectations, missing subtle clues in context, and evaluating the parallels in isolation from related passages in the Pauline corpus. Study of parallels requires not only analytical skill to identify particulars, but synthetic ability as well, taking into consideration

chronological factors, avoiding precisionism, and seeking to understand Paul in relation to other writers. Given the lack of clear, decisive evidence, a break in the present impasse will not come through brief and 'conclusive' arguments, but only by close examination of the whole texture of Paul's letters against the background of the rest of early Christian (as well as non-Christian) writings.

BIBLIOGRAPHY

1. *Primary Sources*

Aland, K. (ed.), *Synopsis Quattuor Evangeliorum* (13th rev. edn; Stuttgart, 1985).

Aland, K. *et al.* (eds.), *Novum Testamentum Graece* (26th edn; Stuttgart, 1979).

Allinson F.G. (ed. and trans.), *Menander with an English Translation* (LCL; London, 1921).

Basore, J.W. (trans.), *Seneca. Moral Essays with an English Translation* (3 vols.; LCL; London, 1928–35).

Blackman, P., *Mishnayoth with an English Translation* (7 vols.; 2nd edn; New York, 1963–64).

Braude, W.G. (ed.), *Pesikta Rabbati* (2 vols.; Yale Judaica Series, 18; New Haven, 1968).

Butcher, S.H., and W. Rennie (eds.), *Demosthenes. Orationes* (4 vols.; Scriptorum classicorum bibliotheca oxoniensis; Oxford, 1903–31).

Charlesworth, J.H. (ed.), *The Old Testament Pseudepigrapha* (2 vols.; Garden City, NY, 1983–85).

Cohen, A. (ed.), *Minor Tractates*, in *Hebrew–English Edition of the Babylonian Talmud* (London, 1984).

Colson, F.H. *et al.* (trans.), *Philo with an English Translation* (12 vols.; LCL; London, 1929–53).

Danby, H. (trans.), *The Mishnah* (London, 1933).

Elliger, K., and W. Rudolph (eds.), *Biblia Hebraica Stuttgartensia* (12th edn; Stuttgart, 1961). Βιβλιοθήκη Ἑλλήνων Πατέρων καὶ Ἐκκλησιαστικῶν Συγγραφεῶν (62 vols.; Athens, 1955–82).

Epstein, I. (ed.), *Hebrew–English Edition of the Babylonian Talmud* (20 vols.; ed.; London, 1969–84).

Farquharson, A.S.L. (ed. and trans.), *The Meditations of the Emperor Marcus Antoninus*. I. *Text and Translation* (Oxford, 1944).

Freedman, H., and M. Simon, (eds.), *Midrash Rabbah* (10 vols.; London, 1939).

Ginsburger, M. (ed.), *Pseudo-Jonathan. Thargum Jonathan ben Usiël zum Pentateuch* (Berlin, 1903).

Goldschmidt, L. (ed.), *Der babylonische Talmud* (2nd edn; 8 vols.; Leipzig, 1906).

Grenfell, B.P., A.S. Hunt, *et al.* (eds.), *The Oxyrhynchus Papyri* (51 vols.; London, 1898–1984).

Harmon, A.M., M.D. Macleod and K. Kilburn (ed. and trans.), *Lucian with an English Translation* (8 vols.; LCL; London, 1913–67).

James, M.R. (ed.), *The Apocryphal New Testament* (Oxford, 1924). *Jerusalem Talmud with Commentary from the Cracow Edition of 1609* (Krotoschin, 1866).

Jones, H.S. (ed.), *Thucydides* (2 vols.; 2nd edn; Scriptorum classicorum bibliotheca oxoniensis; Oxford, 1942–63).

Jonge, M. de (ed.), *The Testaments of the Twelve Patriarchs. A Critical Edition of the Greek Text* (PVTG; Leiden, 1978).

Lake, K. (ed.), *The Apostolic Fathers, with an English Translation* (2 vols.; LCL; London, 1912–13).

Lauterbach, J.Z. (ed. and trans.), *Mekilta de-Rabbi Ishmael with an English Translation* (3 vols.; Philadelphia, 1933–61).

Lohse, E. (ed.), *Die Texte aus Qumran. Hebräisch und Deutsch* (2nd edn; Darmstadt, 1981).

Moore, C.H., and J. Jackson (trans.), *Tacitus with an English Translation* (4 vols.; LCL; London, 1925–37).

Neusner, J. (trans.), *Genesis Rabbah. The Judaic Commentary to the Book of Genesis. A New American Translation* (3 vols.; Brown Judaic Studies; Atlanta, 1985).

Nock, A.D., and A.-J. Festugière (ed. and trans.), *Corpus Hermeticum* (4 vols.; Paris, 1945–54).

Oldfather, C.H. *et al.* (eds.), *Diodorus of Sicily, with an English Translation* (12 vols.; LCL; London, 1933–67).

Oldfather, W.A. (ed. and trans.), *Epictetus, with an English Translation* (2 vols; LCL.; London, 1925–28).

Rahlfs, A. (ed.), *Septuaginta* (9th edn; Stuttgart, 1935).

Roberts, W.R. (ed.), *Demetrius on Style. The Greek Text of Demetrius De Elocutione. Edited after the Paris Manuscript* (Cambridge, 1902).

Roberts, A., and J. Donaldson (eds.), *The Ante-Nicene Fathers* (rev. edn A.C. Coxe; 10 vols.; Grand Rapids, n.d.).

Thackeray, H.StJ. *et al.* (ed. and trans.), *Josephus with an English Translation* (9 vols.; LCL; London, 1926–65).

Vermes, G. (ed.), *The Dead Sea Scrolls in English* (3rd edn; New York, 1975).

Wace, H, and P. Schaff (trans.), *A Select Library of Nicene and Post-Nicene Fathers of the Christian Church* (14 vols.; Second Series; Oxford, 1890–1900).

2. *Commentaries on the Epistle to the Romans*

Althaus, P., *Der Brief an die Römer* (10th edn; NTD; Göttingen, 1966).

Barrett, C.K., *A Commentary on the Epistle to the Romans* (BNTC; London, 1957).

Barth, K., *The Epistle to the Romans* (trans. E.C. Hoskyns; London, 1933).

Best, E., *The Letter of Paul to the Romans* (CBC; Cambridge, 1967).

Black, M., *Romans* (NCB; London, 1973).

Bruce, F.F., *The Epistle of Paul to the Romans. An Introduction and Commentary* (TNTC; London, 1963).

Calvin, J., *The Epistles of Paul the Apostle to the Romans and to the Thessalonians* (trans. R. Mackenzie; ed. D.W. and T.F. Torrance; Edinburgh, 1960).

Cranfield, C.E.B., *A Critical and Exegetical Commentary on the Epistle to the Romans* (2 vols.; ICC; Edinburgh, 1975–79).

Denney, J., 'St Paul's Epistle to the Romans', in *The Expositor's Greek Testament*, II (ed. W.R. Nicoll; London, 1900).

Dodd, C.H., *The Epistle of Paul to the Romans* (MNTC; London, 1932).

Dunn, J.D.G., *Romans* (2 vols.; WBC; Dallas, 1988).

Fitzmyer, J.A., 'The Letter to the Romans', in *The Jerome Biblical Commentary* (2 vols.; ed. R.E. Brown, J.A. Fitzmyer and R.E. Murphy; Englewood Cliffs, 1968).

Harrisville, R.A., *Romans* (ACNT; Minneapolis, 1980).

Käsemann, E., *An die Römer* (HNT; 3rd edn; Tübingen, 1973; ET: *Commentary on Romans* [trans. and ed. G.W. Bromiley; Grand Rapids, 1980]).

Lagrange, M.-J., *Saint Paul. Epître aux Romains* (EBib; Paris, 1950).

Leenhardt, F.J., *The Epistle to the Romans* (trans. H. Knight; London, 1961).

Lietzmann, H., *An die Römer* (HNT; 3rd edn; Tübingen, 1928).

Meyer, H.A.W., *Critical and Exegetical Handbook to the Epistle to the Romans* (2 vols.; trans. J.C. Moore and E. Johnson; Edinburgh, 1879).

Michel, O., *Der Brief an die Römer* (5th edn; MeyerK; Göttingen, 1978).

Moule, H.C.G., *The Epistle to the Romans* (3rd edn; The Expositor's Bible; London, 1896).

—*The Epistle of Paul the Apostle to the Romans* (CBSC; Cambridge, 1903).

Murray, J., *The Epistle to the Romans* (2 vols.; NICNT; Grand Rapids, 1960–65).

O'Neill, J.C., *Paul's Letter to the Romans* (London, 1975).

Pallis, A., *To the Romans. A Commentary* (Liverpool, 1920).

Pesch, R., *Römerbrief* (Die Neue Echter Bibel; Würzburg, 1983).

Philippi, F.A., *Commentary on St Paul's Epistle to the Romans* (2 vols.; trans. J.S. Banks; Clark's Foreign Theological Library; Edinburgh, 1878–79).

Ridderbos, H., *Aan de Romeinen* (Commentaar op het Nieuwe Testament; Kampen, 1977).

Sanday, W., and A.C. Headlam, *A Critical and Exegetical Commentary on the Epistle to the Romans* (5th edn; ICC; Edinburgh, 1902).

Schlier, H., *Der Römerbrief* (HTKNT; Freiburg, 1977).

Schmidt, H.W., *Der Brief des Paulus an die Römer* (THKNT; Berlin, 1963).

Wilckens, U., *Der Brief an die Römer* (3 vols.; EKKNT; Zürich, 1978–82).

Zeller, D., *Der Brief an die Römer* (RNT; Regensburg, 1984).

Ziesler, J., *Paul's Letter to the Romans* (TPINTC; London, 1989).

3. *Articles, Books, Dissertations, et cetera*

Aberbach, M., 'The Relations between Master and Disciple in the Talmudic Age', in *Essays Presented to Chief Rabbi Israel Brodie on the Occasion of his Seventieth Birthday* (ed. H.J. Zimmels, J. Rabbinowitz and I. Finestein; Jews' College Publications; London, 1967), pp. 1-24.

Abrahams, I., *Studies in Pharisaism and the Gospels* (2 vols.; Cambridge, 1917–1924).

Addley, W.P., 'The Sayings of Jesus in the Epistles of St Paul' (ThM thesis, University of Edinburgh, 1971).

Alexander, P.S., 'Rabbinic Judaism and the New Testament', *ZNW* 74 (1983), pp. 237-46.

Allison, D.C., Jr, 'Paul and the Missionary Discourse', *ETL* 61 (1985), pp. 369-75.

—'The Pauline Epistles and the Synoptic Gospels: The Pattern of the Parallels', *NTS* 28 (1982), pp. 1-32.

Argyle, A.W., 'M and the Pauline Epistles', *ExpTim* 81 (1969–70), pp. 340-42.

—' "Outward" and "Inward" in Biblical Thought', *ExpTim* 68 (1956–57), pp. 196-99.

—'Parallels between the Pauline Epistles and Q', *ExpTim* 60 (1948–49), pp. 318-20.

Aune, D.E., 'Christian Prophecy and the Sayings of Jesus: An Index to Synoptic Pericopae Ostensibly Influenced by Early Christian Prophets', in *SBL 1975 Seminar Papers* (ed. G. MacRae; Missoula, MT, 1975), pp. 131-42.

—*Prophecy in Early Christianity and the Ancient Mediterranean World* (Grand Rapids, 1983).

Badenas, R., *Christ the End of the Law. Romans 10.4 in Pauline Perspective* (JSNTSup, 10; Sheffield: JSOT Press, 1985).

Balch, D.A., 'Backgrounds of I Cor. VII: Sayings of the Lord in Q; Moses as an Ascetic θεῖος ἀνήρ in II Cor. III', *NTS* 18 (1971–72), pp. 351-64.

Bammel, E., 'The Cambridge Pericope. The Addition to Luke 6.4 in Codex Bezae', *NTS* 32 (1986), pp. 404-26.

—'Romans 13', in *Jesus and the Politics of his Day* (ed. E. Bammel and C.F.D. Moule; Cambridge, 1984), pp. 365-83.

Banks, J.S., 'St Paul and the Gospels', *ExpTim* 5 (1893–94), pp. 413-15.

Banks, R., *Jesus and the Law in the Synoptic Tradition* (SNTSMS; Cambridge, 1975).

Barbour, R.S., *Traditio-Historical Criticism of the Gospels: Some Comments on Current Methods* (Studies in Creative Criticism, 4; London, 1972).

Barclay, J.M.G., *Obeying the Truth. A Study of Paul's Ethics in Galatians* (SNTW; Edinburgh, 1988).

Barrett, C.K., *A Commentary on the First Epistle to the Corinthians* (BNTC; London, 1968).

—'Ethics and Eschatology: a résumé', in *Dimensions de la vie chrétienne (Rom 12–13)* (ed. L. De Lorenzi; Série Monographique de 'Benedictina'; Section Biblico-Oecuménique, 4; Rome, 1979), pp. 221-35.

—*From First Adam to Last: A Study in Pauline Theology* (London, 1962).

—'Sayings of Jesus in the Acts of the Apostles', in *A cause de l'évangile. Etudes sur les synoptiques et les Actes offertes au P. Jacques Dupont, O.S.B. à l'occasion de son 70e anniversaire* (LD, 123; Paris, 1985), pp. 681-708.

Barth, K., *The Epistle to the Philippians* (trans. J.W. Leitch; London, 1962).

Bartlet, J.V. *et al.*, *The New Testament in the Apostolic Fathers* (Oxford, 1905).

Batey, R.A., 'Jesus and the Theatre', *NTS* 30 (1984), pp. 563-74.

Bauckham, R.J., 'A Bibliography of Recent Work on Gospel Traditions outside the Canonical Gospels', in *The Jesus Tradition outside the Gospels* (Gospel Perspectives, 5; ed. D. Wenham; Sheffield: JSOT Press, 1984), pp. 405-19.

—*Jude, 2 Peter* (WBC; Waco, TX, 1983).

—'The Study of Gospel Traditions outside the Canonical Gospels: Problems and Prospects', in *The Jesus Tradition outside the Gospels* (Gospel Perspectives, 5; ed, D. Wenham; Sheffield: JSOT Press, 1984), pp. 369-403.

—'Synoptic Parousia Parables and the Apocalypse', *NTS* 23 (1976–77), pp. 162-76.

Bauer, W., *A Greek–English Lexicon of the New Testament and Other Early Christian Literature* (trans. W.F. Arndt, F.W. Gingrich and F.W. Danker; Chicago, 1979).

Baur, F.C., 'Die Christuspartei in der korinthischen Gemeinde, der Gegensatz des petrinischen und paulinischen Christentums in der ältesten Kirche, der Apostel Petrus in Rom', *Tübinger Zeitschrift für Theologie* 3/4 (1831), pp. 61-206.

—*The Church History of the First Three Centuries* (2 vols.; trans. A. Menzies; 3rd edn; London, 1878).

Beare, F.W., *The Epistle to the Philippians* (BNTC; London, 1959).

Beasley-Murray, G.R., *A Commentary on Mark Thirteen* (London, 1957).

Ben-Porat, Z., 'The Poetics of Literary Allusion', *PTL: A Journal for Descriptive Poetics and Theory of Literature* 1 (1976), pp. 105-28.

Berger, K., *Die Gesetzesauslegung Jesu. Ihr historischer Hintergrund im Judentum und im Alten Testament*. I. *Markus und Parallelen* (WMANT; Neukirchen–Vluyn, 1972).

Best, E., *A Commentary on the First and Second Epistles to the Thessalonians* (BNTC; London, 1977).

—*Paul and his Converts* (Edinburgh, 1988).

—'1 Peter and the Gospel Tradition', *NTS* 16 (1969–70), pp. 95-113.

Betz, H.D., *Galatians. A Commentary on Paul's Letter to the Churches in Galatia* (Hermeneia; Philadelphia, 1979).

—*Nachfolge und Nachahmung Jesu Christi im Neuen Testament* (BHT; Tübingen, 1967).

Black, D.A., 'The Pauline Love Command: Structure, Style, and Ethics in Romans 12:9-21', *FilolNT* 1/II (1989), pp. 3-22.

Black, M., *An Aramaic Approach to the Gospels and Acts* (3rd edn; Oxford, 1967).

Blass, F. and A. Debrunner, *Grammatik des neutestamentlichen Griechisch* (ed. F. Rehkopf; 15th edn; Göttingen, 1979).

—*A Greek Grammar of the New Testament and Other Early Christian Literature* (trans. and ed. R.W. Funk; Chicago, 1961).

Blomberg, C.L., 'The Law in Luke–Acts', *JSNT* 22 (1984), pp. 53-80.

Boring, M.E., 'Christian Prophecy and the Sayings of Jesus: The State of the Question', *NTS* 29 (1983), pp. 104-12.

—*Sayings of the Risen Jesus. Christian Prophecy in the Synoptic Tradition* (SNTSMS; Cambridge, 1982).

Bornkamm, G., *Jesus of Nazareth* (trans. Irene and Fraser McLuskey with J. Robinson; London, 1960).

—*Paul* (trans. D.M.G. Stalker; London, 1971).

Breck, J., 'Biblical Chiasmus: Exploring Structure for Meaning', *BTB* 17 (1987), pp. 70-73.

Brinsmead, B.H., *Galatians—Dialogical Response to Opponents* (SBLDS; Chico, CA, 1982).

Brown, F., S.R. Driver and C.A. Briggs, *A Hebrew and English Lexicon of the Old Testament* (Oxford, 1953).

Brown, J.P., 'Synoptic Parallels in the Epistles and Form-History', *NTS* 10 (1963–64), pp. 27-48.

Brown, R.E., *The Epistles of John* (AB; Garden City, NY, 1982).

Brown, R.E., and J.P. Meier, *Antioch and Rome: New Testament Cradles of Catholic Christianity* (London, 1983).

Bruce, F.F., *Commentary on the Epistle to the Hebrews* (NICNT; London, 1964).

—*The Epistle of Paul to the Galatians. A Commentary on the Greek Text* (NIGTC; Exeter, 1982).

—'Paul and the Historical Jesus', *BJRL* 56 (1974), pp. 317-35.

—*Paul and Jesus* (London, 1974).

—'Render unto Caesar', in *Jesus and the Politics of his Day* (ed. E. Bammel and C.F.D. Moule; Cambridge, 1984), pp. 249-63.

Buchanan, G.W., 'Jesus and the Upper Class', *NovT* 7 (1964–65), pp. 195-209.

—*To the Hebrews* (AB; Garden City, NY, 1972).

Büchler, A., 'The Law of Purification in Mark vii. 1-23', *ExpTim* 21 (1909–10), pp. 34-40.

—*Types of Jewish-Palestinian Piety from 70 B.C.E. to 70 C.E. The Ancient Pious Men* (New York, 1968; repr. of 1922 edn).

Bultmann, R., *The Gospel of John. A Commentary* (trans. G.R. Beasley-Murray; ed. R.W.N. Hoare and J.K. Riches; Oxford, 1971).

—*The History of the Synoptic Tradition* (trans. J. Marsh; rev. edn; Oxford, 1968).

—'Jesus and Paul', in *Existence and Faith. Shorter Writings of Rudolf Bultmann* (trans. S.M. Ogden; London, 1960), pp. 183-201.

—'The Significance of the Historical Jesus for the Theology of Paul', in *Faith and Understanding*, I (ed. R.W. Funk; trans. L.P. Smith; London, 1966), pp. 220-46.

—*Theology of the New Testament* (2 vols.; trans. K. Grobel; London, 1952, 1955).

Burchard, C., 'Das doppelte Liebesgebot in der frühen christlichen Überlieferung', in *Der Ruf Jesu und die Antwort der Gemeinde: Exegetische Untersuchungen Joachim Jeremias zum 70. Geburtstag gewidmet von seinen Schülern* (ed. E. Lohse with C. Burchard and B. Schaller; Göttingen, 1970), pp. 39-62.

Burton, E.D., *A Critical and Exegetical Commentary on the Epistle to the Galatians* (ICC; Edinburgh, 1921).

Butler, B.C., 'The Literary Relations of Didache, Ch. XVI', *JTS* ns 11 (1960), pp. 265-83.

Buttrick, G.A. (ed.), *The Interpreter's Dictionary of the Bible* (4 vols. with supplement; Nashville, 1962–1976).

Calvert, D.G.A., 'An Examinaton of the Criteria for Distinguishing the Authentic Words of Jesus', *NTS* 18 (1971–72), pp. 209-19.

Carlston, C.E., 'The Things that Defile (Mark vii. 14) and the Law in Matthew and Mark', *NTS* 15 (1968–69), pp. 75-96.

Carrington, P., *The Primitive Christian Catechism. A Study in the Epistles* (Cambridge, 1940).

Catchpole, D.R., 'The Synoptic Divorce Material as a Traditio-Historical Problem', *BJRL* 57 (1974–75), pp. 92-127.

Childs, B.S., *The New Testament as Canon: An Introduction* (London, 1984).

Chilton, B.D., 'A Comparative Study of Synoptic Development: The Dispute between Cain and Abel in the Palestinian Targums and the Beelzebul Controversy in the Gospels', *JBL* 101 (1982), pp. 553-62.

—*A Galilean Rabbi and his Bible. Jesus' Use of the Interpreted Scripture of his Time* (GNS; Wilmington, DE, 1984).

—'Jesus and the Repentance of E.P. Sanders', *TynBul* 39 (1988), pp. 1-18.

—'Targumic Transmission and Dominical Tradition', in *Studies of History and Tradition in the Four Gospels* (Gospel Perspectives, 1; ed. R.T. France and D. Wenham; Sheffield: JSOT Press, 1980), pp. 21-45.

Collange, J.-F., *The Epistle of Saint Paul to the Philippians* (trans. A.W. Heathcote; London, 1979).

Conzelmann, H., 'Jesus von Nazareth und der Glaube an den Auferstandenen', in *Der historische Jesus und der kerygmatische Christus. Beiträge zum Christusverständnis in Forschung und Verkündigung* (ed. H. Ristow and K. Matthiae; Berlin, 1962), pp. 188-99.

Coombs, J.H., 'Allusion Defined and Explained', *Poetics* 13 (1984), pp. 475-88.

Corriveau, R., *The Liturgy of Life: A Study of the Ethical Thought of St Paul in his Letters to the Early Christian Communities* (Studia Travaux de recherche, 25; Brussels, 1970).

Court, J.M., 'The Didache and St Matthew's Gospel', *SJT* 34 (1981), pp. 109-20.

Cranfield, C.E.B., *The Gospel according to Saint Mark: An Introduction and Commentary* (CGTC; Cambridge, 1959).

—'Μέτρον πίστεως in Romans xii. 3', *NTS* 8 (1961–62), pp. 345-51.

Cullmann, O., *The Christology of the New Testament* (trans. S. Guthrie and C.A.M. Hall; London, 1959).

—*The State in the New Testament* (London, 1957).

—'The Tradition', in *The Early Church* (ed. A.J.B. Higgins; London, 1956), pp. 59-99.

Dalman, G., *The Words of Jesus*. I. *Introduction and Fundamental Ideas* (trans. D.M. Kay; Edinburgh, 1902).

Daly, R.J., *Christian Sacrifice. The Judaeo-Christian Background before Origen* (The Catholic University of American Studies in Christian Antiquity; Washington, DC, 1978).

—*The Origins of the Christian Doctrine of Sacrifice* (London, 1978).

Danell, G.A., 'Did St Paul know the Tradition about the Virgin Birth?', *ST* 4 (1950), pp. 94-101.

Daube, D., *The New Testament and Rabbinic Judaism* (London, 1956).

—'Participle and Imperative in I Peter', in *The First Epistle of St Peter* (ed. E.G. Selwyn; London, 1946), pp. 467-88.

—'Pauline Contributions to a Pluralistic Culture: Re-creation and Beyond', in *Jesus and Man's Hope*, II (ed. D.G. Miller and D.Y. Hadidian; Pittsburgh, 1971), pp. 223-45.

Davids, P.H., *The Epistle of James. A Commentary on the Greek Text* (NIGTC; Exeter, 1982).

—'The Gospels and Jewish Tradition: Twenty Years after Gerhardsson', in *Studies of History and Tradition in the Four Gospels* (Gospel Perspectives, 1; ed. R.T. France and D. Wenham; Sheffield: JSOT Press, 1980), pp. 75-99.

—'James and Jesus', in *The Jesus Tradition outside the Gospels* (Gospel Perspectives, 5; ed. D. Wenham; Sheffield: JSOT Press, 1984), pp. 63-84.

Davies, W.D., 'Matthew 5:17-18', in *Christian Origins and Judaism* (London, 1962), pp. 31-66.

—*Paul and Rabbinic Judaism. Some Rabbinic Elements in Pauline Theology* (4th edn; Philadelphia, 1980).

—'Reflections on a Scandinavian Approach to "The Gospel Tradition" ', in *The Setting of the Sermon on the Mount* (Cambridge, 1964), pp. 464-80.

—*The Setting of the Sermon on the Mount* (Cambridge, 1964).

De Boer, W.P., *The Imitation of Paul. An Exegetical Study* (Kampen, 1962).

Deidun, T.J., *New Covenant Morality in Paul* (AnBib; Rome, 1981).

Delling, G., *Römer 13,1-7 innerhalb der Briefe des Neuen Testaments* (Berlin, 1962).

Delobel, J., 'Luke 6, 5 in Codex Bezae: The Man who Worked on Sabbath', in *A cause de l'évangile. Etudes sur les synoptiques et les Actes offertes au P. Jacques Dupont, O.S.B. à l'occasion de son 70e anniversaire* (LD; Paris, 1985), pp. 453-77.

—'The Sayings of Jesus in the Textual Tradition. Variant Readings in the Greek Manuscripts of the Gospels', in *Logia. Les paroles de Jésus—The Sayings of Jesus. Mémorial Joseph Coppens* (ed. J. Delobel; BETL; Leuven, 1982), pp. 431-57.

Derrett, J.D.M., *Law in the New Testament* (London, 1970).

Dibelius, M., *A Commentary on the Epistle of James* (11th edn, rev. H. Greeven; trans. M.A. Williams; ed. H. Koester; Hermeneia; Philadelphia, 1976).

—*From Tradition to Gospel* (trans. B.L. Woolf; London, 1934).

—'Rom und die Christen im ersten Jahrhundert', in *Botschaft und Geschichte. Gesammelte Aufsätze von Martin Dibelius. Zweiter Band: Zum Urchristentum und zur hellenistischen Religionsgeschichte* (ed. G. Bornkamm; Tübingen, 1956), pp. 177-228.

Dodd, C.H. ' "Εννομος Χριστοῦ', in *More New Testament Studies* (Manchester, 1968), pp. 134-48.

—*History and the Gospel* (London, 1938).

—'The Primitive Catechism and the Sayings of Jesus', in *More New Testament Studies* (Manchester, 1968), pp. 11-29.

Donaldson, T.L., 'Parallels: Use, Misuse and Limitations', *EvQ* 55 (1983), pp. 193-210.

Donfried, K.P., 'False Presuppositions in the Study of Romans', in *The Romans Debate* (ed. K.P. Donfried; Minneapolis, 1977), pp. 120-48.

—*The Setting of Second Clement in Early Christianity* (NovTSup; Leiden, 1974).

Downing, F.G., *The Church and Jesus. A Study in History, Philosophy and Theology* (SBT; London, 1968).

Draper, J., 'The Jesus Tradition in the Didache', in *The Jesus Tradition outside the Gospels* (Gospel Perspectives, 5; ed. D. Wenham; Sheffield: JSOT Press, 1984), pp. 269-87.

Dungan, D.L., *The Sayings of Jesus in the Churches of Paul: The Use of the Synoptic Tradition in the Regulation of Early Church Life* (Oxford, 1971).

Dunn, J.D.G., *Christology in the Making. A New Testament Inquiry into the Origins of the Doctrine of the Incarnation* (London, 1980).

—'Jesus and Ritual Purity. A Study of the Tradition History of Mk 7, 15', in *A cause de l'évangile. Etudes sur les synoptiques et les Actes offertes au P. Jacques Dupont, O.S.B. à l'occasion de son 70ᵉ anniversaire* (LD; Paris, 1985), pp. 251-76.

—'Mark 2.1–3.6: A Bridge Between Jesus and Paul on the Question of the Law', *NTS* 30 (1983–84), pp. 395-415.

—'Once More—Gal 1.18: ἱστορῆσαι Κηφᾶν. In Reply to Otfried Hofius', *ZNW* 76 (1985), pp. 138-39.

—'Prophetic "I"-Sayings and the Jesus Tradition: The Importance of Testing Prophetic Utterances within Early Christianity' *NTS* 24 (1978–79), pp. 175-98.

—'The Relationship between Paul and Jerusalem according to Galatians 1 and 2', *NTS* 28 (1982), pp. 461-78.

—'Romans 13.1-7—A Charter for Political Quietism?', *Ex Auditu* 2 (1986), pp. 55-68.

—'Spirit and Kingdom', *ExpTim* 82 (1970–71), pp. 36-40.

—*Unity and Diversity in the New Testament. An Inquiry into the Character of Earliest Christianity* (London, 1977).

Ellis, E.E., 'Gospels Criticism: A Perspective on the State of the Art', in *Das Evangelium und die Evangelien. Vorträge vom Tübinger Symposium 1982* (ed. P. Stuhlmacher; WUNT, 28; Tübingen, 1983), pp. 27-54.

—'New Directions in Form Criticism', in *Prophecy and Hermeneutic in Early Christianity. New Testament Essays* (WUNT, 18; Tübingen, 1978), pp. 237-53.

—*Paul's Use of the Old Testament* (Edinburgh, 1957).

—'Traditions in 1 Corinthians', *NTS* 32 (1986), pp. 481-502.

Evans, C., 'Romans 12.1-2. The True Worship', in *Dimensions de la vie chrétienne (Rom 12–13)* (ed. L. De Lorenzi; Série Monographique de 'Benedictina'; Section Biblico-Oecuménique, 4; Rome, 1979), pp. 7-33.

Fannon, P., 'The Influence of Tradition in St Paul', in *Studia Evangelica. IV. Part I: The New Testament Scriptures* (ed. F.L. Cross; TU; Berlin, 1968), pp. 292-307.

—'Paul and Tradition in the Primitive Church', *Scr* 16 (1964), pp. 47-56.

Farmer, W., *The Synoptic Problem. A Critical Analysis* (New York, 1964).

Fee, G., *The First Epistle to the Corinthians* (NICNT; Grand Rapids, 1987).

Feine, D.P., *Jesus Christus und Paulus* (Leipzig, 1902).

Fenton, J.C., 'Paul and Mark', in *Studies in the Gospels. Essays in Memory of R.H. Lightfoot* (ed. D.E. Nineham; Oxford, 1955), pp. 89-112.

Feuillet, A., 'Morale ancienne et morale chrétienne d'après Mt V. 17-20; comparaison avec la doctrine de l'épître aux Romains', *NTS* 17 (1970–71), pp. 123-37.

Fitzmyer, J.A., *The Gospel according to Luke* (2 vols.; AB; Garden City, NY, 1981, 1985).

Fjärstedt, B., *Synoptic Traditions in 1 Corinthians. Themes and Clusters of Theme Words in 1 Corinthians 1–4 and 9* (Uppsala, 1974).

Fowler, H.W., *A Dictionary of Modern English Usage* (2nd edn; rev. E. Gowers; Oxford, 1983).

France, R.T., *Jesus and the Old Testament. His Application of Old Testament Passages to himself and his Mission* (London, 1971).

Fraser, J.W., *Jesus and Paul. Paul as Interpreter of Jesus from Harnack to Kümmel* (Abingdon, 1974).

—'Paul's Knowledge of Jesus: II Cor V.16 Once More', *NTS* 17 (1970–71), pp. 293-313.

Friedlander, G., *The Jewish Sources of the Sermon on the Mount* (New York, 1969).

Friedrich, J., W. Pöhlmann and P. Stuhlmacher, 'Zur historischen Situation und Intention von Röm 13, 1–7', *ZTK* 73 (1976), pp. 131-66.

Fuller, R.H., 'The Double Commandment of Love: A Test Case for the Criteria of Authenticity', in *Essays on the Love Commandment* (trans. R.H. Fuller and I. Fuller; Philadelphia, 1978), pp. 41-56.

Furnish, V.P., *II Corinthians* (AB; Garden City, NY, 1984).

—'The Jesus–Paul Debate: From Baur to Bultmann', in *Paul and Jesus. Collected Essays* (ed. A.J.M. Wedderburn; JSNTSup, 37; Sheffield: JSOT Press, 1989), pp. 17-50.

—*The Love Command in the New Testament* (NTL; London, 1972).

—*Theology and Ethics in Paul* (Nashville, 1968).

Gamble, H., Jr, *The Textual History of the Letter to the Romans. A Study in Textual and Literary Criticism* (Studies and Documents; Grand Rapids, 1977).

Garland, D.E., *The Intention of Matthew 23* (NovTSup; Leiden, 1979).

Georgi, D., *The Opponents of Paul in Second Corinthians* (Philadelphia, 1986).

Gerhardsson, B., *The Gospel Tradition* (ConBNT; Malmö, 1986).

—*Memory and Manuscript. Oral Tradition and Written Transmission in Rabbinic Judaism and Early Christianity* (ASNU; Lund, 1961).

—*The Origins of the Gospel Traditions* (London, 1979).

—*Tradition and Transmission in Early Christianity* (ConBNT, 20; Lund, 1964).

Gewalt, D., '1 Thes 4,15-17; 1 Kor 15,51 und Mk 9,1—Zur Abgrenzung eines "Herrenwortes"', *LingBib* 51 (1982), pp. 105-13.

Gloer, W.H., 'Homologies and Hymns in the New Testament: Form, Content and Criteria for Identification', *PerspRelStud* 11 (1984), pp. 115-32.

Glover, R., 'The Didache's Quotations and the Synoptic Gospels', *NTS* 5 (1958–59), pp. 12-29.

Goenen, L., E. Beyreuther, and H. Bietenhard (eds.), *The New International Dictionary of New Testament Theology* (trans. and ed. C. Brown; Grand Rapids, 1975–79).

Goppelt, L., *Der Erste Petrusbrief* (MeyerK; Göttingen, 1978).

—'The Freedom to Pay the Imperial Tax (Mark 12, 17)', in *Studia Evangelica*. II. *Part I: The New Testament Scriptures* (ed. F.L. Cross; TU; Berlin, 1964).

—*Theology of the New Testament* (2 vols.; trans. J.E. Alsup; Grand Rapids, 1982).

—*Typos. The Typological Interpretation of the Old Testament in the New* (trans. D.H. Madvig; Grand Rapids, 1982).

Goulder, M.D., 'Did Luke Know Any of the Pauline Letters?', *PerspRelStud* 13 (1986), pp. 97-112.

—*The Evangelist's Calendar. A Lectionary Explanation of the Development of Scripture* (London, 1978).

—*Luke: A New Paradigm* (2 vols.; JSNTSup, 20; Sheffield: JSOT Press, 1989).

—*Midrash and Lection in Matthew* (London, 1974).

Grant, R.M., *The Apostolic Fathers. A New Translation and Commentary*. I. *An Introduction* (New York, 1964).

—*The Apostolic Fathers. A New Translation and Commentary*. IV. *Ignatius of Antioch* (Camden, NJ, 1966).

—'Scripture and Tradition in St Ignatius of Antioch', *CBQ* 25 (1963), pp. 322-35.

Grässer, E., *Das Problem der Parusieverzögerung in den synoptischen Evangelien und in der Apostelgeschichte* (3rd edn; Berlin, 1977).

Grosheide, F.W., 'Romans 13:8b', *Theologische Studiën* [Utrecht] 31 (1913), pp. 345-48.

Guelich, R.A., *The Sermon on the Mount. A Foundation for Understanding* (Waco, TX, 1982).

Gundry, R.H., 'Further *Verba* on *Verba Christi* in First Peter', *Bib* 55 (1974), pp. 211-32.

—'The Hellenization of Dominical Tradition and Christianization of Jewish Tradition in the Eschatology of 1–2 Thessalonians', *NTS* 33 (1987), pp. 161-78.

—*The Use of the Old Testament in St Matthew's Gospel: With Special Reference to the Messianic Hope* (NovTSup; Leiden, 1967).

—' "*Verba Christi*" in 1 Peter: Their Implications concerning the Authorship of 1 Peter and the Authenticity of the Gospel Tradition', *NTS* 13 (1966–67), pp. 336-50.

Güttgemanns, E., *Candid Questions concerning Gospel Form Criticism. A Methodological Sketch of the Fundamental Problematics of Form and Redaction Criticism* (trans. W.G. Doty; PTMS; Pittsburgh, 1979).

—*Der leidende Apostel und sein Herr: Studien zur paulinischen Christologie* (FRLANT; Göttingen, 1966).

Hagner, D.A., 'The Sayings of Jesus in the Apostolic Fathers and Justin Martyr', in *The Jesus Tradition outside the Gospels* (Gospel Perspectives, 5; ed. D. Wenham; Sheffield: JSOT Press, 1984), pp. 233-68.

—*The Use of the Old and New Testaments in Clement of Rome* (NovTSup; Leiden, 1973).

Hahn, F., 'The Christological Foundation of Early Christian Parenesis', in *Christological Perspectives. Essays in Honor of Harvey K. McArthur* (trans. H.K. McArthur; ed. R.F. Berkey and S.A. Edwards; New York, 1982), pp. 71-78, 267-71.

Hanson, A.T., 'The Interpretation of the Second Person Singular in Quotations from the Psalms in the New Testament: A Note on Romans XV, 3', *Hermathena* 73 (1949), pp. 69-72.

—*Jesus Christ in the Old Testament* (London, 1965).

—*The Living Utterances of God. The New Testament Exegesis of the Old* (London, 1983).

—*The Paradox of the Cross in the Thought of St Paul* (JSNTSup, 17; Sheffield: JSOT Press, 1987).

—*Studies in Paul's Technique and Theology* (London, 1974).

Harris, R., and V. Burch, *Testimonies*, Parts I and II (Cambridge, 1916/1920).

Hartin, P.J., 'James and the Q Sermon on the Mount/Plain', in *Society of Biblical Literature 1989 Seminar Papers* (ed. D.J. Lull; Atlanta, 1989), pp. 440-57.

Hartman, L., *Prophecy Interpreted. The Formation of Some Jewish Apocalyptic Texts and of the Eschatological Discourse Mark 13 Par.* (ConBNT, 1; Uppsala, 1966).

Harvey, A.E., *Jesus and the Constraints of History. The Bampton Lectures, 1980* (London, 1982).

Hatch, W.H.P., 'Jesus' Summary of the Law and the Achievement of the Moral Ideal according to St Paul', *ATR* 18 (1936), pp. 129-40.

Haufe, G., 'Reich Gottes bei Paulus und in der Jesustradition', *NTS* 31 (1985), pp. 467-72.

Hawthorne, G.F., *Philippians* (WBC; Waco, TX, 1983).

—'The Role of Christian Prophets in the Gospel Tradition', in *Tradition and Interpretation in the New Testament. Essays in Honor of E. Earle Ellis* (ed. G.F. Hawthorne and O. Betz; Grand Rapids and Tübingen, 1987), pp. 119-33.

Hays, R.B., 'Christology and Ethics in Galatians: The Law of Christ', *CBQ* 49 (1987), pp. 268-90.

—*Echoes of Scripture in the Letters of Paul* (New Haven and London, 1989).

—*The Faith of Jesus Christ: An Investigation of the Narrative Structure of Galatians 3:1– 4:11* (Chico, CA, 1983).

Heitmüller, W., 'Zum Problem Paulus und Jesus', *ZNW* 13 (1912), pp. 320-37.

Hengel, M., *Acts and the History of Earliest Christianity* (trans. J. Bowden; London, 1979).

—*The Atonement. The Origins of the Doctrine in the New Testament* (trans. J. Bowden; Philadelphia, 1981).

—'Between Jesus and Paul. The "Hellenists", the "Seven" and Stephen (Acts 6.1-15; 7.54– 8.3', in *Between Jesus and Paul. Studies in the Earliest History of Christianity* (trans. J. Bowden; London, 1983), pp. 1-29, 133-56.

—'Christology and New Testament Chronology. A Problem in the History of Earliest Christianity', in *Between Jesus and Paul. Studies in the Earliest History of Christianity* (trans. J. Bowden; London, 1983), pp. 30-47, 156-66.

—' "Christos" in Paul', in *Between Jesus and Paul. Studies in the Earliest History of Christianity* (trans. J. Bowden; London, 1983), pp. 65-77, 179-88.

—'The Expiatory Sacrifice of Christ', *BJRL* 62 (1979–80), pp. 454-75.

—*Judaism and Hellenism. Studies in their Encounter in Palestine during the Early Hellenistic Period* (2 vols.; trans. J. Bowden; London, 1974).

—'The Origins of the Christian Mission', in *Between Jesus and Paul. Studies in the Earliest History of Christianity* (trans. J. Bowden; London, 1983), pp. 48-64, 166-79.

—*The Son of God. The Origin of Christology and the History of Jewish-Hellenistic Religion* (trans. J. Bowden; London, 1976).

—*Studies in the Gospel of Mark* (trans. J. Bowden; London, 1985).

Hill, D., *The Gospel of Matthew* (NCB; London, 1972).

—*New Testament Prophecy* (London, 1979).

—'On the Evidence for the Creative Role of Christian Prophets', *NTS* 20 (1974), pp. 262-74.

Hofius, O., 'Gal 1.18: ἱστορῆσαι Κηφᾶν', *ZNW* 75 (1984), pp. 73-85.

—' "Unbekannte Jesusworte" ', in *Das Evangelium und die Evangelien. Vorträge vom*

Tübinger Symposium 1982 (ed. P. Stuhlmacher; WUNT; Tübingen, 1983), pp. 355-82.

Holtzmann, H.J., *Lehrbuch der neutestamentlichen Theologie* (2 vols.; ed. D.A. Jülicher and W. Bauer; 2nd edn; Tübingen, 1911).

Hooker, M.D., 'Adam in Romans 1', *NTS* 6 (1959–60), pp. 297-307.

—'Beyond the Things That Are Written? St Paul's Use of Scripture', *NTS* 27 (1980–81), pp. 295-309.

—'Christology and Methodology', *NTS* 17 (1970–71), pp. 480-87.

—'Interchange and Atonement', *BJRL* 60 (1977–78), pp. 462-81.

—'Interchange and Suffering', in *Suffering and Martyrdom in the New Testament. Studies Presented to G.M. Styler by the Cambridge New Testament Seminar* (ed. W. Horbury and B. McNeil; Cambridge, 1981), pp. 70-83.

—'Interchange in Christ and Ethics', *JSNT* 25 (1985), pp. 3-17.

—*Jesus and the Servant: The Influence of the Servant Concept of Deutero-Isaiah in the New Testament* (London, 1959).

—'On Using the Wrong Tool', *Theology* 75 (1972), pp. 570-81.

—'Philippians 2:6-11', in *Jesus und Paulus: Festschrift für Werner Georg Kümmel zum 70. Geburtstag* (ed. E.E. Ellis and E. Grässer; Göttingen, 1975), pp. 151-64.

—'ΠΙΣΤΙΣ ΧΡΙΣΤΟΥ', *NTS* 35 (1989), pp. 321-42.

—'Were there False Teachers in Colossae?', in *Christ and Spirit in the New Testament. Studies in Honour of Charles Francis Digby Moule* (ed. B. Lindars and S.S. Smalley; Cambridge, 1973), pp. 315-31.

Howard, G., 'The "Faith of Christ" ', *ExpTim* 85 (1973–74) , pp. 212-15.

—'Notes and Observations on the "Faith of Christ" ', *HTR* 60 (1967), pp. 459-65.

—*Paul: Crisis in Galatia. A Study in Early Christian Theology* (SNTSMS; Cambridge, 1979).

—'Phil 2:6-11 and the Human Christ', *CBQ* 40 (1978), pp. 368-87.

Hübner, H., 'Das ganze und das eine Gesetz. Zum Problemkreis Paulus und die Stoa', *KD* 21 (1975), pp. 239-56.

—*Law in Paul's Thought* (trans. J.C.G. Greig; ed. J. Riches; Edinburgh, 1984).

—'Mark. VII. 1-23 und das "jüdisch-hellenistische" Gesetzesverständnis', *NTS* 22 (1976), pp. 319-45.

Humbert, A., 'Essai d'une théologie du scandale dans les synoptiques', *Bib* 35 (1954), pp. 1-28.

Hunter, A.M., *Paul and his Predecessors* (rev. edn; London, 1961).

Hurd, J.C., ' "The Jesus Whom Paul Preaches" (Acts 19:13)', in *From Jesus to Paul. Studies in Honour of Francis Wright Beare* (ed. P. Richardson and J.C. Hurd; Waterloo, 1984), pp. 73-89.

Hurtado, L.W., 'Jesus as Lordly Example in Philippians 2.5-11', in *From Jesus to Paul: Studies in Honour of Francis Wright Beare* (ed. P. Richardson and J.C. Hurd; Waterloo, 1984), pp. 113-26.

Hyldahl, N., 'A Reminiscence of the Old Testament at Romans i. 23', *NTS* 2 (1956), pp. 285-88.

Jackson, F.J.F. and K. Lake (eds.), *The Beginnings of Christianity* (5 vols.; London, 1920–33).

Jastrow, M. (ed.), *A Dictionary of the Targumim, the Talmud Babli and Yerushalmi, and the Midrashic Literature* (2 vols.; New York, 1950).

Jeremias, J., *The Eucharistic Words of Jesus* (trans. N. Perrin; NTL; London, 1960).

—*New Testament Theology* (trans. J. Bowden; NTL; London, 1971).

—Review of *Jesus and the Servant: The Influence of the Servant Concept of Deutero-Isaiah in the New Testament,* by M.D. Hooker, *JTS* ns 11 (1960), pp. 140-44.

—*Unknown Sayings of Jesus* (trans. R.H. Fuller; London, 1958).

Jewett, R., *Christian Tolerance. Paul's Message to the Modern Church* (Philadelphia, 1982).

Johnston, G., ' "Kingdom of God" Sayings in Paul's Letters', in *From Jesus to Paul: Studies in Honour of Francis Wright Beare* (edited by P. Richardson and J.C. Hurd; Waterloo, 1984), pp. 143-56.

Jüngel, E., *Paulus und Jesus: Eine Untersuchung zur Präzisierung der Frage nach dem Ursprung der Christologie* (4th edn; HUT; Tübingen, 1972).

Kallas, J., 'Romans XIII. 1-7: an Interpolation', *NTS* 11 (1964–65), pp. 365-74.

Kanjuperambil, P., 'Imperatival Participles in Rom 12:9-21', *JBL* 102 (1983), pp. 285-88.

Karris, R.J., 'The Occasion of Romans: A Response to Professor Donfried', in *The Romans Debate* (ed. K.P. Donfried; Minneapolis, 1977), pp. 149-51.

Käsemann, E., 'Kritische Analyse von Phil. 2, 5-11', in *Exegetische Versuche und Besinnungen* , I (Göttingen, 1967), pp. 51-95.

—'Principles of the Interpretation of Rom 13', In *New Testament Questions of Today* (trans. W.J. Montague; Philadelphia, 1969), pp. 196-216.

—'Sentences of Holy Law in the New Testament', in *New Testament Questions of Today* (trans. W.J. Montague; Philadelphia, 1969), pp. 66-81.

Keegan, T.J., 'Paul and the Historical Jesus', *Angelicum* 52 (1975), pp. 302-39, 450-84.

Kelber, W.H., *The Oral and the Written Gospel. The Hermeneutics of Speaking and Writing in the Synoptic Tradition, Mark, Paul, and Q* (Philadelphia, 1983).

Kennedy, H.A.A., *The Theology of the Epistles* (London, 1919).

Kilpatrick, G.D., 'Galatians 1:18 ΙΣΤΟΡΗΣΑΙ ΚΗΦΑΝ', in *New Testament Essays. Studies in Memory of Thomas Walter Manson, 1893–1958* (ed. A.J.B. Higgens; Manchester, 1959), pp. 144-49.

Kirschner, R., 'Imitatio Rabbini', *JSJ* 17 (1986), pp. 70-79.

Kittel, G., *Christus und Imperator* (Stuttgart, 1939).

—'Der geschichtliche Ort des Jakobusbriefes' *ZNW* 41 (1942), pp. 71-105.

Kittel, G. and G. Friedrich (eds.), *Theological Dictionary of the New Testament* (10 vols.; trans. and ed. G. W. Bromiley; Grand Rapids, 1964–76).

Klassen, W., 'Coals of Fire: Sign of Repentance or Revenge?', *NTS* 9 (1962–63), pp. 337-50.

Klausner, J., *From Jesus to Paul* (trans. W.F. Stinespring; London, 1944).

Kleinknecht, K.T., *Der leidende Gerechtfertigte. Die alttestamentlich-jüdische Tradition vom "leidenden Gerechten" und ihre Rezeption bei Paulus* (WUNT; Tübingen, 1984).

Kloppenborg, J.S., 'Didache 16.6-8 and Special Matthean Tradition', *ZNW* 70 (1979), pp. 54-67.

Knight, G.W., *The Faithful Sayings in the Pastoral Letters* (Kampen, 1968).

Knight, R., 'Gospels and Epistles', *HibJ* 45 (1947), pp. 304-308.

—'Jesus or Paul? In Continuation of Gospels and Epistles', *HibJ* 47 (1948), pp. 41-49.

Knowling, R.J., *The Testimony of St Paul to Christ* (2nd edn; London, 1906).

—*The Witness of the Epistles* (London, 1892).

Koch, D.-A., *Die Schrift als Zeuge des Evangeliums. Untersuchungen zur Verwendung und zum Verständnis der Schrift bei Paulus* (BHT, 69; Tübingen, 1986).

Kosmala, H., 'Nachfolge und Nachahmung Gottes. I. Im griechischen Denken', *ASTI* 2 (Leiden, 1963), pp. 38-85.

—'Nachfolge und Nachahmung Gottes. II. Im jüdischen Denken', *ASTI* 3 (Leiden, 1964), pp. 65-110.

Köster, H., 'Gnostic Writings as Witnesses for the Development of the Sayings Tradition', in *The Rediscovery of Gnosticism. I. The School of Valentinus* (ed. B. Layton; NumS; Leiden, 1980), pp. 238-61.

—'One Jesus and Four Primitive Gospels', in *Trajectories through Early Christianity* (ed. J. Robinson and H. Köster; Philadelphia, 1971), pp. 158-204.

—*Synoptische Überlieferung bei den Apostolischen Vätern* (TU; Berlin, 1957).

Kraft, R.A., *The Apostolic Fathers. A New Translation and Commentary.* III. *Barnabas and the Didache* (New York, 1965).

Kramer, W., *Christ, Lord, Son of God* (trans. B. Hardy; SBT; London, 1966).

Kuhn, H.-W., 'Der irdische Jesus bei Paulus als traditionsgeschichtliches und theologisches Problem', *ZTK* 67 (1970), pp. 295-320.

Kümmel, W.G., 'Das Urchristentum IV', *ThR* 17 (1948–49), pp. 133-42.

Kuss, O., 'Paulus über die staatliche Gewalt', *TGl* 45 (1955), pp. 321-34.

Lambrecht, J., 'Jesus and the Law. An Investigation of Mk 7.1-23', *ETL* (1977), pp. 24-82.

Lane, W.L., *The Gospel according to Mark* (NICNT; Grand Rapids, 1974).

Larsson, E., *Christus als Vorbild* (ASNU; Uppsala, 1962).

Lattey, C., 'How Do you Account for the Lack of Direct Quotations in the Epistles from our Lord's Actual Sayings?', *Scr* 4 (1949), pp. 22-24.

Lee, J.-Y., 'The Problem of Paul's Understanding of the Historical Jesus in Critical Study. A Historico-Critical Study of the Jesus–Paul Problem in the Nineteenth Century and First Half of Twentieth Century' (PhD dissertation, University of St Andrews, 1975).

Leivestad, R., ' "The Meekness and Gentleness of Christ" II Cor. X.1', *NTS* 12 (1965–66), pp. 156-64.

Liddell, H.G. and R. Scott (eds.), *A Greek–English Lexicon* (9th edn, rev. H.S. Jones, with a Supplement; Oxford, 1968).

Lightfoot, J.B., *The Apostolic Fathers* (2 parts in 5 vols.; London, 1889–90).

—*Saint Paul's Epistle to the Galatians* (10th edn; London, 1896).

—*Saint Paul's Epistle to the Philippians* (4th edn; London, 1898).

Lindars, B., *New Testament Apologetic. The Doctrinal Significance of the Old Testament Quotations* (London, 1961).

Ljungmann, H., *Das Gesetz erfüllen: Matth. 5,17ff. und 3,15 untersucht* (Lund, 1954).

Lohmeyer, E., *Das Evangelium des Markus* (12th edn; MeyerK; Göttingen, 1953).

Longenecker, R.N., *Paul: Apostle of Liberty* (New York, 1967).

Lövestam, E., *Spiritual Wakefulness in the New Testament* (trans. W.F. Salisbury; LUÅ; Lund, 1963).

Luz, U., 'Die Erfüllung des Gesetzes bei Matthäus (Mt 5, 17-20)', *ZTK* 75 (1978), pp. 398-435.

Lyonnet, S., 'La charité plénitude de la loi (Rm 13, 8-10)', in *Dimensions de la vie chrétienne (Rm 12–13)* (ed. L. De Lorenzi; Série Monographique de 'Benedictina'; Section Biblico-Oecuménique, 4; Rome, 1979), pp. 151-72.

MacDonald, D.R., *There is No Male and Female. The Fate of a Dominical Saying in Paul and Gnosticism* (HDR; Philadelphia, 1987).

Maier, G., 'Jesustradition im 1. Petrusbrief?', in *The Jesus Tradition outside the Gospels* (Gospel Perspectives, 5; ed. D. Wenham; Sheffield: JSOT Press, 1984), pp. 85-128.

Manson, T.W., *Ethics and the Gospel* (London, 1966).

—*The Sayings of Jesus* (London, 1949).

Margoliouth, G., ' "The Traditions of the Elders" (St Mark vii. 1-23)', *ExpTim* 22 (1910–11), pp. 261-64.

Marshall, I.H., 'The Christ-Hymn in Philippians 2:5-11. A Review Article', *TynBul* 19 (1968), pp. 104-27.

—*The Gospel of Luke. A Commentary on the Greek Text* (NIGTC; Exeter, 1978).

—'Palestinian and Hellenistic Christianity: Some Critical Comments', *NTS* 19 (1972–73), pp. 271-87.

—*1 and 2 Thessalonians* (NCB; London, 1983).

Martin, R.P., *Carmen Christi. Philippians ii. 5-11 in Recent Interpretation and in the Setting of Early Christian Worship* (rev. edn; Grand Rapids, 1983).

—*James* (WBC; Waco, TX, 1988).

—*Philippians* (NCB; Grand Rapids, 1976).

Marxsen, W., 'Der ἕτερος νόμος Röm 13,8', *TZ* 11 (1955), pp. 230-37.

Mattill, A.J., Jr, 'The Jesus–Paul Parallels and the Purpose of Luke–Acts: H.H. Evans Reconsidered', *NovT* 17 (1975), pp. 15-46.

Mayor, J.B., *The Epistle of St James. The Greek Text with Introduction, Notes and Comments* (3rd edn; London, 1910).

McEleney, N.J., 'Authenticating Criteria and Mark 7:1-23', *CBQ* 34 (1972), pp. 431-60.

Mealand, D.L., 'The Dissimilarity Test', *SJT* 31 (1978), pp. 41-50.

Meecham, H.G., *The Oldest Version of the Bible: 'Aristeas' on its Traditional Origin. A Study in Early Apologetic* (The Thirty-Second Hartley Lecture; London, 1932).

Meier, J.P., *Law and History in Matthew's Gospel: A Redactional Study of Mt. 5:17-48* (Rome, 1976).

Ménard, J.E., *L'évangile selon Thomas* (Nag Hammadi Studies; Leiden, 1975).

Merk, O., *Handeln aus Glauben: die Motivierungen der paulinischen Ethik* (Marburger Theologische Studien; Marburg, 1968).

Metzger, B.M., *A Textual Commentary on the Greek New Testament. A Companion Volume to the United Bible Societies' Greek New Testament* (3rd edn; Stuttgart, 1971).

Meyer, B.F., *The Aims of Jesus* (London, 1979).

Michaels, J.R., *1 Peter* (WBC; Waco, TX, 1988).

Minear, P.S., *Commands of Christ* (Edinburgh, 1972).

—'False Prophecy and Hypocrisy in the Gospel of Matthew', in *Neues Testament und Kirche* (ed. J. Gnilka; Freiburg, 1974), pp. 76-93.

—*The Obedience of Faith. The Purposes of Paul in the Epistle to the Romans* (SBT; London, 1971).

—'Yes or No: The Demand for Honesty in the Early Church', *NovT* 13 (1971), pp. 1-13.

Miner, E., 'Allusion', in *Princeton Encyclopedia of Poetry and Poetics* (enlarged edn; London, 1974), p. 18 col. 1.

Moe, O., *Paulus und die evangelische Geschichte* (Leipzig, 1912).

Moffatt, J., *A Critical and Exegetical Commentary on the Epistle to the Hebrews* (ICC; Edinburgh, 1924).

—'Jesus upon "Stumbling-Blocks" ', *ExpTim* 26 (1914–15), pp. 407-409.

Mohrlang, R., *Matthew and Paul. A Comparison of Ethical Perspectives* (SNTSMS; Cambridge, 1984).

Montefiore, C.G., *Rabbinic Literature and Gospel Teachings* (London, 1930).

—*The Synoptic Gospels. Edited with an Introduction and a Commentary* (2 vols.; 2nd edn; London, 1927).

Montefiore, H., 'Thou Shalt Love the Neighbour as Thyself ', *NovT* 5 (1962), pp. 157-70.

Moo, D.J., *The Old Testament in the Gospel Passion Narratives* (Sheffield: Almond Press, 1983).

Moore, A.L., *The Parousia in the New Testament*.(NovTSup, 18; Leiden, 1966).

Moore, G.F., *Judaism in the First Centuries of the Christian Era* (3 vols.; Cambridge, MA, 1927–30).

Morrison, C.D., *The Powers That Be. Earthly Rulers and Demonic Powers in Romans 13.1-7* (SBT; London, 1960).

Moule, C.F.D., *The Epistles of Paul the Apostle to the Colossians and to Philemon* (CGTC; Cambridge, 1957).

—'Fulfilment-Words in the New Testament: Use and Abuse', *NTS* 14 (1967–68) 293-320.

—'Further Reflexions on Philippians 2,5-11 ', in *Apostolic History and the Gospel. Biblical and Historical Essays Presented to F.F. Bruce on his 60th Birthday* (ed. W.W. Gasque and R.P. Martin; Grand Rapids: Eredamns, 1970), pp. 264-76.

—*An Idiom Book of New Testament Greek* (2nd edn; Cambridge, 1959).

—'Jesus in New Testament Kerygma', in *Verborum Veritas. Festschrift für Gustav Stählin zum 70. Geburtstag* (ed. O. Böcher and K. Haacker; Wuppertal, 1970), pp. 15-26.

—*The Phenomenon of the New Testament* (SBT; London, 1967).

—'The Use of Parables and Sayings as Illustrative Material in Early Christian Catechesis', *JTS* ns 3 (1952), pp. 75-79.

Moulton, J.H., 'The Epistle of James and the Sayings of Jesus', *Exp* 7/4 (1907), pp. 45-55.

Moulton, J.H. and G. Milligan (eds.), *The Vocabulary of the Greek Testament. Illustrated from the Papyri and Other Non-literary Sources* (London, 1930).

Müller, K., *Anstoss und Gericht: Eine Studie zum jüdischen Hintergrund des paulinischen Skandalon-Begriffs* (SANT; München, 1969).

Müller, P.-G., *Der Traditionsprozeß im Neuen Testament. Kommunikationsanalytische Studien zur Versprachlichung des Jesusphänomens* (Freiburg, 1982).

Müller, U.B., 'Zur Rezeption gesetzeskritischer Jesusüberlieferung im frühen Christentum', *NTS* 27 (1980–81), pp. 158-85.

Munro, W., *Authority in Paul and Peter. The Identification of a Pastoral Stratum in the Pauline Corpus and 1 Peter* (SNTSMS; Cambridge, 1983).

Murphy-O'Connor, J., 'Christological Anthropology in Phil. 2:6-11 ', *RB* 83 (1976), pp. 25-50.

Mussner, F., *Der Galaterbrief* (2nd edn; HTKNT; Freiburg, 1974).

—*Der Jakobusbrief* (2nd edn; HTKNT; Freiburg, 1975).

Nababen, A.E.S., 'Bekenntnis und Mission in Römer 14 und 15' (doctoral dissertation, Heidelberg, 1963).

Neirynck, F., 'Paul and the Sayings of Jesus', in *L'apôtre Paul. Personnalité, style et conception du ministère* (ed. A. Vanhoye; BETL; Leuven, 1986), pp. 265-321.

Nepper-Christensen, P., 'Das verborgene Herrenwort. Eine Untersuchung über 1 Thes 4,13-18', *ST* 19 (1965), pp. 136-54.

Neugebauer, F., 'Geistsprüche und Jesuslogien. Erwägungen zu der von der form-geschichtlichen Betrachtungsweise R. Bultmanns angenommenen grundsätzlichen Möglichkeit einer Identität von prophetischen Geistsprüchen mit Logien des irdischen Jesus', *ZNW* 53 (1962), pp. 218-28.

—'Zur Auslegung von Röm 13,1-7', *KD* 8 (1962), pp. 151-72.

Neusner, J., ' "First Cleanse the Inside." The "Halakhic" Background of a Controversy Saying', *NTS* 22 (1976), pp. 486-95.

—*The Idea of Purity in Ancient Judaism* (Leiden, 1973).

—*From Politics to Piety. The Emergence of Pharisaic Judaism* (Englewood Cliffs, NJ, 1973).

—*The Rabbinic Traditions about the Pharisees Before 70* (3 vols.; Leiden , 1971).

Newton, M., *The Concept of Purity at Qumran and in the Letters of Paul* (SNTSMS; Cambridge, 1985).

Nineham, D.E., 'Eye-witness Testimony and the Gospel Tradition. I, II, III', *JTS* ns 9 (1958), pp. 13-25, 243-52; 11 (1960), pp. 253-64.

O'Brien, P.T., *Colossians, Philemon* (WBC, 44; Waco, TX, 1982).

Olford, D.L., 'Paul's Use of Cultic Language in Romans. An Exegetical Study of Major Texts in Romans Which Employ Cultic Language in a Non-literal Way' (PhD dissertation, University of Sheffield, 1985).

Orchard, J.B., 'Thessalonians and the Synoptic Gospels', *Bib* 19 (1938), pp. 19-42.

Orchard, J.B., and H. Riley, *The Order of the Synoptics. Why Three Synoptic Gospels?* (Macon, GA, 1987).

Ortkemper, F.-J., *Leben aus dem Glauben. Christliche Grundhaltungen nach Römer 12–13* (NTAbh ns; Münster, 1980).

Parunak, H.V.D., 'Transitional Techniques in the Bible', *JBL* 102 (1983), pp. 525-48.

Paschen, W., *Rein und Unrein. Untersuchung zur biblischen Wortgeschichte* (SANT; München, 1970).

Perri, C., 'Allusion Studies: An International Annotated Bibliography, 1921–77', *Style* 13 (1979), pp. 178-225.

—'On Alluding', *Poetics* 7 (1978), pp. 289-307.

Perrin, N., *The New Testament. An Introduction. Proclamation and Parenesis, Myth and History* (New York, 1974).

—*Rediscovering the Teaching of Jesus* (NTL; London, 1967).

Pesch, R., *Das Markusevangelium* (2 vols.; HTKNT; Freiburg, 1976–77).

Pfitzner, V.C., 'The School of Jesus: Jesus-Traditions in Pauline Parenesis', *LTJ* 13 (1979), pp. 22-36.

Piper, J., *'Love Your Enemies'. Jesus' Love Command in the Synoptic Gospels and in the Early Christian Paraenesis. A History of the Tradition and Interpretation of its Uses* (SNTSMS; Cambridge, 1979).

Pohle, L., *Die Christen und der Staat nach Römer 13. Eine typologische Untersuchung der neueren deutschsprächigen Schriftauslegung* (Mainz, 1984).

Polkow, D., 'Method and Criteria for Historical Jesus Research', in *Society of Biblical Literature 1987 Seminar Papers* (ed. K.H. Richards; Atlanta, 1987), pp. 336-56.

Prat, F., *The Theology of Saint Paul* (2 vols.; trans. J.L. Stoddard; 4th edn; London, 1942).

Quispel, G., 'Qumran, John and Jewish Christianity', in *John and Qumran* (ed. J.H. Charlesworth; London, 1972), pp. 136-55.

Räisänen, H., 'Jesus and the Food Laws: Reflections on Mark 7.15', *JSNT* 16 (1982), pp. 79-100.

Rawlinson, A.E.J., *St Mark* (5th edn; WC; London, 1925).

—*Paul and the Law* (WUNT; Tübingen, 1983).

—'Zur Herkunft von Markus 7,15', in *Logia. Les paroles de Jésus—The Sayings of Jesus. Mémorial Joseph Coppens* (ed. J. Delobel; BETL, 59; Leuven, 1982), pp. 477-84.

Reasoner, M., 'The Relationship of Three Old Testament Woman-at-the Well Texts to John 4:1-42' (MA thesis, Trinity Evangelical Divinity School, 1985).

Reitzenstein, R., *Hellenistic Mystery-Religions: Their Basic Ideas and Significance* (trans. J.E. Steely; PTMS; Pittsburgh, 1978).

Resch, A., *Agrapha. Aussercanonische Schriftfragmente* (Darmstadt, 1967).

—*Der Paulinismus und die Logia Jesu* (TU; Berlin, 1904).

Richardson, P., 'Gospel Traditions in the Church in Corinth (with Apologies to B.H. Streeter)', in *Tradition and Interpretation in the New Testament. Essays in Honor of E. Earle Ellis* (ed. G.F. Hawthorne and O. Betz; Grand Rapids and Tübingen, 1987), pp. 301-18.

—' "I Say, not the Lord": Personal Opinion, Apostolic Authority and the Development of Early Christian Halakah', *TynBul* 31 (1980), pp. 65-86.

—'The Thunderbolt in Q and the Wise Man in Corinth', in *From Jesus to Paul. Studies in Honour of Francis Wright Beare* (ed. P. Richardson and J.C. Hurd; Waterloo, 1984), pp. 91-111.

Richardson, P., and P. Gooch, 'Logia of Jesus in 1 Corinthians', in *The Jesus Tradition outside the Gospels* (Gospel Perspectives, 5; ed. D. Wenham; Sheffield: JSOT Press, 1984), pp. 39-62.

Richardson, P., and J.C. Hurd (eds.), *From Jesus to Paul. Studies in Honour of Francis Wright Beare* (Waterloo, 1984).

Riekkinen, V., *Römer 13. Aufzeichnung und Weiterführung der exegetischen Diskussion* (Annales academiae scientiarum fennicae dissertationes humanarum litterarum; Helsinki, 1980).

Riesenfeld, H., 'The Gospel Tradition and its Beginnings', in *The Gospel Tradition* (Oxford, 1970), pp. 1-29.

Riesner, R., *Jesus als Lehrer. Eine Untersuchung zum Ursprung der Evangelien-Überlieferung* (2nd edn; WUNT; Tübingen, 1984).

—'Jüdische Elementarbildung und Evangelienüberlieferung', in *Studies of History and Tradition in the Four Gospels* (Gospel Perspectives, 1; ed. R.T. France and D. Wenham; Sheffield: JSOT Press, 1980), pp. 209-23.

—'Der Ursprung der Jesus-Überlieferung', *TZ* 38 (1982), pp. 493-513.

Rigaux, B., *Saint Paul. Les épîtres aux Thessaloniciens* (EBib; Paris, 1956).

Robertson, A. and A. Plummer, *A Critical and Exegetical Commentary on the First Epistle to the Corinthians* (2nd edn; ICC; Edinburgh, 1929).

Robertson, A.T., *A Grammar of the Greek New Testament in the Light of Historical Research* (3rd edn; New York, 1919).

Robinson, D.W.B., ' "The Faith of Jesus Christ"—a New Testament Debate', *RTR* 29 (1970), pp. 71-81.

Robinson, J.A.T., *The Priority of John* (ed. J.F. Coakley; London, 1985).

Robinson, J.M., 'Basic Shifts in German Theology', *Int* 16 (1962), pp. 76-97.

—'Early Collections of Jesus' Sayings', in *Logia. Les paroles de Jésus—The Sayings of*

Jesus. Mémorial Joseph Coppens (ed. J. Delobel; BETL; Leuven, 1982), pp. 389-94.

—'Kerygma and History in the New Testament', in *Trajectories through Early Christianity* (ed. J. Robinson and H. Köster; Philadelphia, 1971), pp. 20-70.

—*A New Quest of the Historical Jesus* (SBT; London, 1959).

Roetzel, C.J., *The Letters of Paul, Conversations in Context* (2nd edn; Atlanta, 1982).

Roth, C. (ed.), *Encyclopedia Judaica* (16 vols.; Jerusalem, 1972).

Rudberg, G., 'Zu den Partizipien im Neuen Testament', *ConNT* (Lund, 1948), pp. 1-38.

Sanders, E.P. *Jesus and Judaism* (London, 1985).

—'Literary Dependence in Colossians?', *JBL* 85 (1966), pp. 28-45.

—*Paul and Palestinian Judaism. A Comparison of Patterns of Religion* (Philadelphia, 1977).

—*Paul, the Law, and the Jewish People* (London, 1983).

—*The Tendencies of the Synoptic Tradition* (SNTSMS; Cambridge, 1969).

Sanders, J.A., 'Dissenting Deities and Philippians 2:1-11', *JBL* 88 (1969), pp. 279-90.

Sanders, J.T., *Ethics in the New Testament. Change and Development* (London, 1975).

Sandmel, S., 'Parallelomania', *JBL* 81 (1962), pp. 1-13.

Sauer, J., 'Traditionsgeschichtliche Erwägungen zu den synoptischen und paulinischen Aussagen über Feindesliebe und Wiedervergeltungsverzicht', *ZNW* 76 (1985), pp. 1-28.

Schelkle, K.H., 'Staat und Kirche in der patristischen Auslegung von Rm 13:1-7', *ZNW* 44 (1952–53), pp. 223-36.

Schippers, R., 'The Pre-Synoptic Tradition in I Thessalonians II 13-16', *NovT* 8 (1966), pp. 223-34.

Schmithals, W., 'Paulus und der historische Jesus', *ZNW* 53 (1962), pp. 145-60.

—*Der Römerbrief als historisches Problem* (SNT; Gütersloh, 1975).

Schnackenburg, R., *The Moral Teaching of the New Testament* (trans. J. Holland-Smith and W.J. O'Hara; Guildford, 1975).

Schniewind, J., *Das Evangelium nach Matthäus* (9th edn; NTD; Göttingen, 1956).

Schoedel, W.R., *Ignatius of Antioch. A Commentary on the Letters of Ignatius of Antioch* (Hermeneia; Philadelphia, 1985).

—*The Apostolic Fathers. A New Translation and Commentary*. V. *Polycarp, Martyrdom of Polycarp, Fragments of Papias* (Camden, NJ, 1967).

Schoeps, H.-J., *Paul. The Theology of the Apostle in the Light of Jewish Religious History* (trans. H. Knight; London, 1961).

Schottroff, L., 'Non-Violence and the Love of One's Enemies', in *Essays on the Love Commandment* (trans. R.H. Fuller and I. Fuller; Philadelphia, 1978), pp. 9-39.

Schrage, W., *Die Christen und der Staat nach dem Neuen Testament* (Gütersloh, 1971).

—*Ethik des Neuen Testaments* (GNT; Göttingen, 1982).

—*Die konkreten Einzelgebote in der paulinischen Paränese. Ein Beitrag zur neutestamentlichen Ethik* (Gütersloh, 1961).

Schulz, A., *Nachfolgen und Nachahmen. Studien über das Verhältnis der neutestamentlichen Jüngerschaft zur urchristlichen Vorbildethik* (SANT; München, 1962).

Schulz, B.S., 'Die neue Frage nach dem historischen Jesus', in *Neues Testament und Geschichte. Festschrift für Oscar Cullmann* (ed. H. Baltensweiler and B. Reicke; Zürich, 1972), pp. 33-42.

Schürer, E., *The History of the Jewish People in the Age of Jesus Christ (175 B.C.—A.D. 135)* (4 vols.; rev. and ed. G. Vermes *et al.*; Edinburgh, 1973–87).

Schürmann, H., 'Die vorösterlichen Anfänge der Logientradition. Versuch eines formgeschichtlichen Zugangs zum Leben Jesu', in *Der historische Jesus und der keryg matische Christus. Beiträge zum Christusverständnis in Forschung und Verkündigung* (ed. H. Ristow and K. Matthiae; Berlin, 1962), pp. 342-70.

—*Das Lukasevangelium. Erster Teil. Kommentar zu Kap. 1, 1—9, 50* (HTKNT; Freiburg, 1969).

Schweitzer, A., *The Mysticism of Paul the Apostle* (trans. W. Montgomery; London, 1931).

—*Paul and his Interpreters* (trans. W. Montgomery; London, 1912).

Schweizer, E., *The Good News according to Mark* (trans. D.H. Madvig; London, 1971).

Scott, C.A.A., 'Jesus and Paul', in *Essays on Some Biblical Questions of the Day. By Members of the University of Cambridge* (ed. H.B. Swete; London, 1909), pp. 329-77.

Scroggs, R., *The Last Adam. A Study in Pauline Anthropology* (Oxford, 1966).

Seeburg, A., *Der Katechismus der Urchristenheit* (repr. of 1903 edn with an introduction by F. Hahn; TBü; München, 1966).

Seidensticker, P., *Lebendiges Opfer (Röm 12,1). Ein Beitrag zur Theologie des Apostels Paulus* (NTAbh 20; Münster, 1954).

Seitz, O.J.F.. 'Love Your Enemies. The Historical Setting of Matthew v.43f; Luke vi.27f', *NTS* 16 (1969–70), pp. 39-54.

Selby, D.J., *Toward the Understanding of St Paul* (Englewood Cliffs, NJ, 1962).

Selwyn, E.G., *The First Epistle of St Peter* (London, 1946).

Shepherd, M.H., Jr, 'The Epistle of James and the Gospel of Matthew', *JBL* 75 (1956), pp. 40-51.

Sibinga, J.S., 'Ignatius and Matthew', *NovT* 8 (1966), pp. 263-83.

Sidebottom, E.M., 'The So-called Divine Passive in the Gospel Tradition', *ExpTim* 87 (1975–76), pp. 200-204.

Smalley, S.S., *1, 2, 3 John* (WBC; Waco, TX, 1984).

Smith, M., 'A Comparison of Early Christian and Early Rabbinic Tradition', *JBL* 82 (1963), pp. 169-76.

—*Tannaitic Parallels to the Gospels* (JBLMS; Philadelphia, 1951).

Snyder, G.F., *The Apostolic Fathers. A New Translation and Commentary. VI. The Shepherd of Hermas* (Camden, NJ, 1968).

—'The Historical Jesus in the Letters of Ignatius of Antioch', *BR* 8 (1963), pp. 3-12.

Spicq, C., *Agapé dans le Nouveau Testament* (3 vols; EBib; Paris, 1958–59).

—'L'imitation de Jésus-Christ durant les derniers jours de l'apôtre Paul', in *Mélanges bibliques en hommage au R.P. Béda Rigaux* (ed. A. Descamps and R.P. André de Halleux; Gembloux, 1970).

Stanley, D.M., 'Pauline Allusions to the Sayings of Jesus', *CBQ* 23 (1961), pp. 26-39.

—'Significance for Paul of Jesus' Earthly History', in *Sin, Salvation and the Spirit. Commemorating the Fiftieth Year of The Liturgical Press* (ed. D. Durken; Collegeville, MN, 1979), pp. 279-88.

Stanton, G.N., 'Form Criticism Revisited', in *What About the New Testament? Essays in Honour of Christopher Evans* (ed. M. Hooker and C. Hickling; London, 1975), pp. 13-27.

—*Jesus of Nazareth in New Testament Preaching* (SNTSMS; Cambridge, 1974).

—'The Origin and Purpose of Matthew's Gospel. Matthean Scholarship from 1945 to 1980', in *ANRW* II.25.3 (Berlin, 1985), pp. 1889-1951.

—'Salvation Proclaimed. X. Matthew 11.28-30: Comfortable Words?', *ExpTim* 94 (1982–83), pp. 3-9.

Stein, R.H., 'The "Criteria" for Authenticity', in *Studies of History and Tradition in the Four Gospels* (Gospel Perspectives, 1; ed. R.T. France and D. Wenham; Sheffield: JSOT Press, 1980).

Stendahl, K., 'Hate, Non-retaliation and Love: 1QS 10.17-20 and Rom. 12.19-21', *HTR* 55 (1962), pp. 343-55.

Stock, A., 'Chiastic Awareness and Education in Antiquity', *BTB* 14 (1984), pp. 23-27.

—'Jesus, Hypocrites, and Herodians', *BTB* 16 (1986), pp. 3-7.

Strack, H.L., and P. Billerbeck, *Kommentar zum Neuen Testament aus Talmud und Midrasch* (6 vols.; München, 1922–68).

Streeter, B.H., *The Four Gospels. A Study of Origins* (London, 1936).

Strelan, J.G., 'Burden-bearing and the Law of Christ: A Re-examination of Galatians 6:2', *JBL* 94 (1975), pp. 266-76.

Strobel, A., 'Furcht, wem Furcht gebührt: zum profangriechischen Hintergrund von Rm 13,7', *ZNW* 55 (1964), pp. 58-62.

—'Zum Verständnis von Rm 13', *ZNW* 47 (1956), pp. 67-93.

Strömholm, D., 'Was the Gospel Narrative Known to the Authors of the Epistles?', *HibJ* 26 (1927), pp. 31-42.

Stuhlmacher, P., 'Existenzstellvertretung für die Vielen: Mk 10,45 (Mt 20,28)', in *Werden und Wirken des Alten Testaments. Festschrift für Claus Westermann zum 70. Geburtstag* (ed. R. Albertz *et al.*; Göttingen, 1980), pp. 412-27.

—'Jesu Auferweckung und die Gerechtigkeitsanschauung der vorpaulinischen Missionsgemeinden', in *Versöhnung, Gesetz und Gerechtigkeit. Aufsätze zur biblischen Theologie* (Göttingen, 1981), pp. 66-86.

—'Jesustradition im Römerbrief? Eine Skizze', *ThB* 14 (1983), pp. 240-50.

—'Zum Thema: Das Evangelium und die Evangelien', in *Das Evangelium und die Evangelien. Vorträge vom Tübinger Symposium 1982* (ed. P. Stuhlmacher; WUNT; Tübingen, 1983), pp. 1-26.

—'Zur paulinischen Christologie', in *Versöhnung, Gesetz und Gerechtigkeit. Aufsätze zur biblischen Theologie* (Göttingen, 1981), pp. 209-23.

Swartley, W.M., 'The *Imitatio Christi* in the Ignatian Letters', *VC* 27 (1973), pp. 81-103.

Sweet, J., 'Seed of David and Spirit of Holiness' (unpublished paper delivered to the New Testament Seminar at Cambridge University on 13 October, 1987).

Sykes, S., 'Sacrifice in the New Testament and Christian Theology', in *Sacrifice* (ed. M.F.C. Bourdillon and M. Fortes; London, 1980), pp. 61-83.

Talbert, C. H., 'The Problem of Pre-existence in Phil. 2:6-11', *JBL* 86 (1967), pp. 141-53.

—'Tradition and Redaction in Romans XII. 9-21', *NTS* 16 (1969–70), pp. 83-94.

Taylor, G., *The Witness of Hermas to the Four Gospels* (London, 1892).

Taylor, V., *The Gospel according to St Mark: The Greek Text with Introduction, Notes, and Indexes* (2nd edn; London, 1966).

—'Professor Strömholm's Riddle', *HibJ* 25 (1926–27), pp. 285-98.

Teeple, H.M., 'The Oral Tradition that Never Existed', *JBL* 89 (1970), pp. 56-68.

Theissen, G., 'The Strong and the Weak in Corinth: A Sociological Analysis of a Theological Quarrel', in *The Social Setting of Pauline Christianity. Essays on Corinth* (ed. and trans. J.H. Schütz; Philadelphia, 1982), pp. 121-43.

Tilborg, S. van, *The Jewish Leaders in Matthew* (Leiden, 1972).

Tinsley, E.J., *The Imitation of God in Christ: An Essay on the Biblical Basis of Christian Spirituality* (London, 1960).

—'Some Principles for Reconstructing a Doctrine of the Imitation of Christ', *SJT* 25 (1972), pp. 45-57.

Trevett, C., 'Approaching Matthew from the Second Century: The Under-Used Ignatian Correspondence', *JSNT* 20 (1984), pp. 59-67.

Tuckett, C.M., '1 Corinthians and Q', *JBL* 102 (1983), pp. 607-19.

—'Paul and the Synoptic Mission Discourse?', *ETL* 60 (1984), pp. 376-81.

Turner, N., *Syntax*, in *A Grammar of New Testament Greek*, III (Edinburgh, 1963).

Unnik, W.C. van, *Tarsus or Jerusalem. The City of Paul's Youth* (trans. G. Ogg; London, 1962).

Vermes, G., *Jesus the Jew. A Historian's Reading of the Gospels* (London, 1973).

—'Jewish Literature and New Testament Exegesis: Reflections on Methodology', *JJS* 33 (1982), pp. 361-76.

Vincent, J.J., 'Did Jesus Teach his Disciples to Learn by Heart?', in *Studia Evangelica*, III (ed. F.L. Cross; Berlin, 1964), pp. 105-18.

Vögtle, A., 'Röm 13,11-14 und die "Nah"-Erwartung', in *Rechtfertigung. Festschrift für E. Käsemann zum 70. Geburtstag* (ed. J. Friedrich, W. Pöhlmann, and P. Stuhlmacher; Tübingen, 1976), pp. 557-73.

Vos, L.A., *The Synoptic Traditions in the Apocalypse* (Kampen, 1965).

Walter, N., 'Paul and the Early Christian Jesus-Tradition', in *Paul and Jesus. Collected Essays* (ed. A.J.M. Wedderburn; JSNTSup, 37; Sheffield: JSOT Press, 1989), pp. 51-80.

Wanamaker, C.A., 'Philippians 2.6–11: Son of God or Adamic Christology?', *NTS* 33 (1987), pp. 179-93.

Waterman, G.H., 'The Sources of Paul's Teaching on the Second Coming in 1 and 2 Thessalonians', *JETS* 18 (1975), pp. 105-13.

Watson, F., *Paul, Judaism and the Gentiles. A Sociological Approach* (SNTSMS; Cambridge, 1986).

Webster, J.B., 'Christology, Imitability and Ethics', *SJT* 39 (1986), pp. 309-26.

—'The Imitation of Christ', *TynBul* 37 (1986), pp. 95-120.

Wedderburn, A.J.M., 'Adam in Paul's Letter to the Romans', in *Studia Biblica 1978. III. Papers on Paul and Other New Testament Authors* (ed. E.A. Livingstone; JSNTSup, 3; Sheffield: JSOT Press, 1980), pp. 413-30.

—(ed.), *Paul and Jesus. Collected Essays* (JSNTSup, 37; Sheffield: JSOT Press, 1989).

—'Paul and Jesus: Similarity and Continuity', in *Paul and Jesus. Collected Essays* (JSNTSup, 37; Sheffield: JSOT Press, 1989), pp. 117-43.

—'Paul and Jesus: The Problem of Continuity', in *Paul and Jesus. Collected Essays*. (JSNTSup, 37; Sheffield: JSOT Press, 1989), pp. 99-115.

—'Paul and the Story of Jesus', in *Paul and Jesus. Collected Essays* (JSNTSup, 37; Sheffield: JSOT Press, 1989), pp. 161-89.

—*The Reasons for Romans* (SNTW; Edinburgh, 1988).

—Review of *The Jesus Tradition outside the Gospels*, ed. D. Wenham, *JTS* ns 37 (1986), pp. 540-43.

Weder, H., *Das Kreuz Jesu bei Paulus. Ein Versuch, über den Geschichtsbezug des christlichen Glaubens nachzudenken* (FRLANT; Göttingen, 1981).

Weiss, J., *Paul and Jesus* (trans. H.J. Chaytor; London, 1909).

Welch, J.W., *Chiasmus in Antiquity. Structures, Analyses, Exegesis* (Hildesheim, 1981).

Wells, G.A., *The Jesus of the Early Christians. A Study in Christian Origins* (London, 1971).

Wenham, D., 'Being "Found" on the Last Day: New Light on 2 Peter 3.10 and 2 Corinthians 5.3', *NTS* 33 (1987), pp. 477-79.

—'2 Corinthians 1:17, 18: Echo of a Dominical Logion', *NovT* 28 (1986), pp. 271-79.

—'Paul and the Synoptic Apocalypse', in *Studies of History and Tradition in the Four Gospels* (Gospel Perspectives, 2; ed. R.T. France and D. Wenham; Sheffield: JSOT Press, 1981), pp. 345-75.

—'Paul's Use of the Jesus Tradition: Three Samples', in *The Jesus Tradition outside the Gospels* (Gospel Perspectives, 5; edited by D. Wenham; Sheffield: JSOT Press, 1984), pp. 7-37.

—*The Rediscovery of Jesus' Eschatological Discourse* (Gospel Perspectives, 4; Sheffield: JSOT Press, 1984).

Wenham, J.W., 'Did Peter Go to Rome in AD 42?', *TynBul* 23 (1972), pp. 94-102.

Westcott, B.F., *The Epistles of St John: The Greek Text with Notes and Essays* (4th edn; London, 1902).

Westerholm, S., *Jesus and Scribal Authority* (ConBNT; Lund, 1978).

Wiefel, W., 'The Jewish Community in Ancient Rome and the Origins of Roman Christianity', in *The Romans Debate* (ed. K.P. Donfried; Minneapolis, 1977), pp. 100-19.

Wilckens, U., 'Jesus' Preaching of the Kingdom of God', in *Parola e Spirito. Studi in onore di Settimo Cipriani*, I (Brescia, 1982), pp. 599-609.

—'Jesusüberlieferung und Christuskerygma—Zwei Wege urchristlicher Überlieferungsgeschichte' (ThViat 10; Berlin, 1966), pp. 310-39.

Williams, S.K., *Jesus' Death as Saving Event: The Background and Origin of a Concept* (HDR; Missoula, MT, 1975).

Wilson, S.G., 'From Jesus to Paul: The Contours and Consequences of a Debate', in *From Jesus to Paul. Studies in Honour of Francis Wright Beare* (ed. P. Richardson and J.C. Hurd; Waterloo, 1984), pp. 1-21.

Winer, G.B., *A Treatise on the Grammar of New Testament Greek* (trans. W.F. Moulton; 9th edn; Edinburgh, 1882).

Wolff, C., 'Humility and Self-Denial in Jesus' Life and Message and in the Apostolic Existence of Paul', in *Paul and Jesus. Collected Essays* (ed. A.J.M. Wedderburn; JS`NTSup, 37; Sheffield: JSOT Press, 1989), pp. 145-60.

—'True Apostolic Knowledge of Christ: Exegetical Reflections on 2 Corinthians 5.14ff.', in *Paul and Jesus. Collected Essays* (ed. A.J.M. Wedderburn; JSNTSup, 37; Sheffield: JSOT Press, 1989), pp. 81-98.

Wolff, H.W., *Jesaja 53 im Urchristentum* (3rd edn; Berlin, 1952).

Wright, N.T., ''Αρπαγμός and the Meaning of Philippians 2:5-11', *JTS* ns 37 (1986), pp. 321-52.

—' "Constraints" and the Jesus of History', *SJT* 39 (1986), pp. 189-210.

—'The Messiah and the People of God. A Study in Pauline Theology with Particular Reference to the Argument of the Epistle to the Romans' (DPhil dissertation, Oxford, 1980).

Zsifkovits, V., *Der Staatsgedanke nach Paulus in Röm 13:1-7. Mit besonderer Berücksichtigung der Umwelt und der patristischen Auslegung* (Wien, 1964).

INDEXES

INDEX OF BIBLICAL REFERENCES

OLD TESTAMENT

Genesis		*Joshua*		29.14	150
1.26-27	219	23.13	175	31.32	96
1.27	154				
2–3	83	*Judges*		*Psalms*	
3.1-7	219	2.3	175	2.11	57
		8.27	175	7.9	168
Exodus		16.30	211	14[15].3	134
15.26	128			21[22].19	49
23.4-5	100	*Ruth*		21[22].23	40, 224
34.28	121	2.16	211	33[34].15	91, 108
				39[40].7-9	40
Leviticus		*1 Samuel*		39[40].7	191
11	185, 197	16.7	188	48[49].14	175
19	181	18.21	175	49[50].20	175
19.14	175, 176,	25.31	175	50[51].6	109
	180-82			68[69]	139, 222,
19.17-18	100	*2 Samuel*			224, 225
19.18	91, 121,	23.5	211	68[69].4	224
	128, 130-			68[69].7	224
	35, 140,	*1 Kings*		68[69].8	223
	152, 170,	2.27	126	68[69].10	224
	183, 212	3.11	100	68[69].10a	223
19.34	100			68[69].10b	272
		2 Kings		68[69].21	224
Numbers		4.29	98	68[69].23	175
6.2	161	18.14	211	68[69].	
				21-28	169
Deuteronomy		*2 Chronicles*		88[89].51	224
6.5	133-35	36.22	126	105[106].	
10.4	121			36	175
10.18-19	100	*Job*		108[109]	169
14	185, 197	21.3	211	108[109].	
32.35	91, 100	22.29	216	4-5	102

108		17.13	100, 107			223
[109].28	97	20.4	95	53.11	211	
108		24.17-18	100	54.10	32	
[109].31	168	24.21	116	58.7	96	
114[116]	41	24.29	100, 107	59.17	151	
118[119].		25.21-22	91, 104			
165	175	25.21	100	*Jeremiah*		
130		29.23	216	9.23-24	45	
[131].2	216			29.7	116	
139		*Isaiah*		31.31-34	40	
[140].6	175, 181	6.9-10	192			
139[140].		8.14	174, 178,	*Ezekiel*		
19-22	169		181, 183	23.45	168	
140		8.17-18	40			
[141].6	168	11.10	234	*Daniel*		
140		21.11-12	149	11.41	175	
[141].9	175	28.16	178, 181			
146		29.13	193	*Hosea*		
[147].6	216	29.21	181	4.17	176, 181	
		45.23	164, 166	6.6	191	
Proverbs		49.6	211			
3.4	91, 118,	49.8	211	*Amos*		
	138	52.15	211	5.15	91	
3.7	91	53	211			
6.6	95	53.1	211	*Zechariah*		
6.9	95	53.4	210, 211,	13.7	49	

APOCRYPHA

Tobit		18.15	92	*Bel [Theodotion]*	
4.14-17	101			36	211
4.15	133	*Sirach*			
		6.25	211	*1 Maccabees*	
Judith		7.6	176, 181	1.47	185
5.1	181	7.34	106	1.62	185
12.2	176	9.5	175	2.55	126
		12.1-7	50, 101	5.4	175
Wisdom of Solomon		23.8	175	12.9	225
5.17-20	151	35.15 [ET			
5.18	92	32.15]	175		

NEW TESTAMENT

Matthew		5–7	51	5.9	39, 108
3.2	147	5.3	39, 56	5.10ff.	97
3.15	130	5.5	97, 154,	5.10-12	226
4.16	42		206	5.10	56, 206
4.17	147	5.7	39, 45, 89	5.11-12	97

5.11	224	7.5	93, 165	13.41-42	178
5.12	39, 95	7.6	50	13.41	176
5.13	123	7.7	39	13.57	175, 178
5.14-16	42	7.12	45, 133,	14.14	154
5.17-20	129		135	14.18	233
5.17-18	129, 137	7.21-23	166	14.30	47
5.17	129, 130,	7.21	58	15.6	137
	137, 140	7.23	58	15.7	233
5.18-19	136, 188	7.24	39	15.11	186, 188,
5.20	130, 206	8.3	188		198
5.21ff.	137	8.4	137	15.12	175, 178
5.22	39	8.17	21	15.17	186
5.29-30	179	8.20	221	15.20	186
5.29	175	9.13	49, 58,	15.24	233
5.30	175		136	15.32	154
5.34-37	38	9.36	154	16.1-4	143
5.38-48	103, 108,	10.7	147	16.3	93
	109	10.14	232	16.5-12	92
5.39-42	54, 115	10.16	33, 53, 58	16.23	178
5.39	75	10.22	95, 226	16.24-26	85
5.41	76	10.23	141	16.24	222, 226
5.43	133	10.24-25	220	16.27	89
5.44	54, 59, 72,	10.24	127	17.1-8	43
	96, 97	10.25	127	17.2	84
5.46-47	98	10.28	58	17.5	43
5.46	53, 59	10.32	58	17.27	175, 179
5.48	39, 81	10.33	226	17.24-27	112, 137
6.3	89	10.34	129	18	210
6.9-15	50	10.38	210, 226	18.3-4	177
6.10	81	10.40-41	232	18.4	107, 216,
6.12	122, 166	10.40	132, 177		29, 220
6.13	57	11.6	175, 178	18.5	177, 232
6.14	45	11.13	129	18.6	46, 47,
6.19-24	164, 166	11.19	96		175-77,
6.19-20	39	11.25-28	155		182
6.22	89	11.25-27	75	18.7	178, 180
6.24	39, 58	11.29-30	155	18.8-9	179
6.25-34	164, 166	11.29	106, 154,	18.8	175
7.1-5	171		155, 216	18.9	175
7.1-2	39	11.30	154	18.10	177
7.1	33, 45, 55,	12.7	136	18.15-20	165, 167
	163-65,	12.28	206	18.15	94
	167, 170,	12.38-42	31	18.21	94
	171, 172	12.45	44	18.23-32	127, 220
7.2	45, 56, 88,	12.50	58, 81, 94	18.23-25	123
	165	13.14-15	192	18.24	122
7.3-5	165	13.21	175	18.28	122
7.3	94, 166	13.27-28	127	18.30	122

18.32	122	24.10	175	4.12	192
18.33	156	24.13	95, 226	4.17	175
18.34	122	24.33	39	4.24	45, 88
19.6	69	24.36	148	5.34	108
19.8	137	24.43	34, 142	6.3	175, 178
19.10-12	71	24.44	141	6.6-13	16
19.19b	133	24.45-50	128	6.7-13	23
19.21	81, 137	24.38	75	6.11	232
19.29	206	24.48-50	145, 149	6.34	154
20.1-16	71	25.1-13	145	6.46	95
20.10	209	25.5-7	145	7.1-23	136, 188-
20.16	48	25.6	145, 148		90
20.26-28	95	25.14-30	88, 128	7.1-15	189
20.27	127, 200	25.15	88, 89	7.1-13	189
20.28	213, 233	25.24	206	7.2	186
20.34	154	25.26	95	7.3	188
21.5	154	25.31-46	166	7.5	186
21.21-22	39	25.35ff.	96	7.6	93
21.34-36	127	26.7	54	7.14-23	189
22.1-10	206	26.24	46, 210	7.15	71, 186-
22.3-10	128	26.31	49, 175		91, 193,
22.14	48	26.33	175		198
22.15-16	115	26.40-46	145	7.17	188
22.18	93	26.41	57, 146	7.18-19	71, 186
22.21	112, 113,	26.42	81	7.18	187
	116	26.52	112	7.19	187, 189,
22.23-33	116	26.54	210		190, 197,
22.34-46	116	26.56	210		199
22.34-40	133	26.61	192	7.23	186
22.36-39	42	27.32	145	8.2	154
22.38	136	27.34	49, 223	8.11-12	178
22.39	125	27.35	49	8.17-18	192
22.40	133, 137	27.40	192	8.34	85, 222,
23	93	27.44	221, 222		226, 227
23.3-10	92	27.46	221	8.36	58
23.3	228	27.48	49, 223	9.1	141
23.11	95	28.18-20	190	9.2	84
23.12	95, 107,			9.7	43
	216, 219	*Mark*		9.12	210
23.13	220	1.15	147	9.33-50	16
23.14	93	1.29-31	96	9.35	89
23.25-26	187, 189,	1.35	95	9.37	177, 232
	190	1.41	154	9.42	46, 175,
23.27-28	92, 189	2.15–3.6	196		176, 197
23.28	93	2.15-17	96	9.43-47	179
24	51	2.17	49, 58	9.43	32, 175
24.3	141	3.21	223	9.45	32, 175
24.9	95	3.35	58, 81, 94	9.47	32, 175

9.50	108, 178	14.37-42	145	6.41-42	165
10.9	69	14.38	57, 95,	6.42	93, 165
10.15	32		146	6.46	58
10.23-25	32	14.49	129	7.13	154
10.30	143	14.58	192	7.23	175, 178,
10.43-45	95	15.23	223		182
10.43	89	15.29	192	7.34	96
10.44	127, 213,	15.32	221, 222	7.36-50	123
	220	15.34	221	7.43	165
10.45	89, 211,	15.36	223	7.50	108
	213, 223,			8.21	58, 94
	233	*Luke*		8.48	108
11.22-23	32, 75	1.1-2	22, 66	9.5	232
11.25	45	1.52	106	9.23-24	85
12.2	127	1.78	154	9.23	222, 226
12.4	127	2.32	42	9.35	43
12.13-17	116	3.11	89	9.48	177, 232
12.13	115	4.21	129	9.58	221
12.15	93	5.32	49, 58	10.1-12	23
12.17	111-13,	6.4	200	10.3	58
	115	6.20	39, 56	10.7-8	71
12.18-27	116	6.21ff.	97	10.8	187, 232
12.25	75	6.21	106	10.9	147
12.28-34	133	6.22-23	226	10.10	232
12.28-31	42, 116	6.22	99, 224	10.11	147
12.31	26, 91,	6.25	106	10.16	132, 232
	125	6.27-38	16, 109	10.25-28	133
12.33	136	6.27-36	103, 108	10.38-42	96
12.39	95	6.27-29	103	11.2-4	50
13	144	6.27-28	54, 103	11.2	81
13.13	95, 226	6.27	72, 96, 98,	11.4	57
13.30	141		99, 108	11.20	206
13.32	141, 142,	6.28	96, 98, 99,	11.22	109
	148		102, 103	11.26	44
13.33	144	6.29-30	115	11.29-32	31
13.34	128, 145,	6.31	45	11.37-41	187
	220	6.32-35	59	11.39-41	190
13.35-36	148	6.32	53	11.39-40	189
13.35	141, 145	6.33	108	11.41	187
13.36	145	6.35	45, 97,	11.44	93
13.37	145		108	12	144
14.3	96	6.36	45, 122,	12.1	92, 93
14.21b	46		154, 155,	12.4-5	58
14.27	175		164, 166	12.8	58
14.29	175	6.37	45, 55, 56,	12.9	226
14.32-42	41		163-65,	12.33	32
14.35	95		171, 172	12.35-40	145
14.36	67, 94	6.38	45, 56, 88	12.35	145

12.37-38	148
12.37	128
12.39	34, 142
12.40	141
12.42-43	75
12.42	89
12.43-47	128
12.45	149
12.46	148
12.51	129
12.56	93, 144
12.57	165
13.15	93
13.27	58
13.35	223
14.1-24	96
14.7-10	95
14.11	95, 107, 216, 219, 220
14.12-24	206
14.13	207
14.17-23	128
14.21	207
14.27	210, 276
15	231
15.2	231, 232
16.8	148
16.10-12	58
16.13	58, 163
16.15	89
17.1	178, 182
17.2	46, 175, 176, 182
17.3-4	210
17.7-10	128
17.24	148
17.30-31	148
17.34	148
18.1	95
18.9-14	231
18.14	107, 216, 219, 220
18.30	143
18.31	210
19.10	231
19.12-27	89
19.13-27	128

19.41-44	144
20.10-11	127
20.20	93, 119
20.22	114
20.25	112, 113
20.38	163
21.8	146
21.19	95, 226
21.28	146, 147
21.31	147
21.32	146
21.34-36	159
21.34	147-49
21.36	95, 146, 147
22.22	46
22.26-27	95
22.31-32	31
22.42	81
23.2	113, 114, 119
23.36	223
23.42-43	231
24.25-27	210
24.30	53
24.35	53
24.36	108
24.39	52
24.41-43	53
24.44	129
24.46	210

John
1.4-9	42
2.17	223
4.14	42
5.23	132
6.61	175
6.61-64	178
6.63	42
6.68	42
8.7	165
8.12	42
8.26	42
8.29	222
8.34-36	128
9.5	42
10.10	42

10.28	42
11.9-10	174
12.3	54
12.27	41
12.35-36	42
12.36	148
12.46	42
12.48	132
13	127
13.3-17	220
13.10	123
13.14-15	127
13.16	127
13.20	232
13.34-35	123
13.34	42
14.9-10	42
14.26	42
15.12-13	123
15.12	42, 123
15.17	42, 123
15.23	132
15.25	223
16.1	175
16.33	109
19.17	210
19.38	223

Acts
1.1-2	63
1.6	141
1.7	144
1.14	95
1.20	223
2.10	115
2.22	63
3.5	223
3.26	233
6.1	191
6.11	191
6.13-14	191
6.14	192
7.53	126
7.58	64
8.1-3	64
8.1	68
8.32	211
9.2	132

9.3-9	66	28.2	230	3.4	109, 222
9.4	227	28.15	145	3.14	229
9.12	66	28.23	205	3.18	114
10–11	190	28.26-27	192	3.20ff.	137
10	190, 192	28.31	205	3.20-21	126
10.15	197			3.21	126
10.19-25	65	*Romans*		3.22	83
10.28	197	1	81-83	3.23	83
10.36-39	63	1.1	128, 220	3.24-25	26
11.2	67	1.2	126	3.25-26	80
11.9	197	1.3-4	26, 106	3.25	211
11.16	192	1.3	233, 234	3.26	83, 143
11.19-26	65	1.5	83	3.27-28	87
11.20	67	1.13	162	3.30	232
13.2-3	65	1.16	162, 223	3.31	105, 126,
13.46	163, 233	1.18	230		130, 196
13.47	211	1.21-22	81	4.1	68
14.22	205	1.21	81, 126,	4.13	126
15.1	67		229	4.14	220
15.5	67	1.22	88	4.23-24	139
15.7-9	190	1.23	81	4.23	105
15.19	163	1.24-32	82	4.24	26, 225
15.22-27	67	1.24	82	4.25	80, 211
15.32	67	1.25	81	5–8	78
15.40	67	1.28	81	5.1-2	204
16.1	223	1.29	126	5.1	156
16.9-10	66	1.30	82	5.2-5	95
17.31	166	1.32	81, 82,	5.3-4	227
18.9	66		126	5.5	138
18.14	209	2	130, 167	5.6-8	215
18.25-26	132	2.1	93, 125	5.6	26, 80,
19.8	205	2.1-11	172		143, 211,
19.9	132	2.1-4	173		231
19.23	132	2.4	154, 155,	5.8-9	83
20.25	205		166	5.8	26, 80,
20.35	45, 47, 63,	2.7	85, 225,		124, 231,
	192, 194		226		239
21.24	126	2.9-16	233	5.9	80
22.3	64	2.12-14	126	5.10	79, 231
22.4	132	2.13	126	5.12-19	83
22.7	227	2.17-24	88, 93,	5.12	32
23.3	163		173	5.14-19	153
23.6	64	2.17	126	5.15	26, 79
24.14	132	2.18	81, 94	5.17-18	79
24.22	132	2.21	125	5.18	204, 126
26.4-5	64	2.23	126	5.19	83, 211,
26.5	64	2.25	126		222, 238
26.14	227	2.26	126	6–8	149

6–7	128	8.26-27	94		153, 183, 236
6	79, 80, 82	8.25	225, 227	12–13.10	159
6.2-4	155	8.28	138, 157	12	79-82, 103
6.2	157	8.29	84, 154, 228, 229	12.1-2	78-86, 118, 138, 141, 151-53, 204, 222, 223
6.3-4	80, 85, 227	8.32	80, 215		
6.3	26, 80	8.34	26, 79		
6.4	79, 132	8.35	138		
6.5	85	8.36	81		
6.6	83	8.37-38	124	12.1	78-85, 155, 216, 238
6.10-11	79	8.37	109		
6.11	79	8.38	195		
6.12-13	79	8.39	124, 138	12.2	80, 81, 84, 85, 91, 111, 140, 153, 229, 238
6.12	152	9–11	78, 234		
6.13	79, 83	9.3	68		
6.14-15	126	9.4	233		
6.16-22	130	9.5	26, 68		
6.16	79, 83, 128	9.22	155, 209	12.3-8	87-89, 210, 237
6.17	25, 69, 70, 137, 160, 235, 238	9.32-33	174	12.3	82, 87-89, 94, 165, 216
		9.32	178		
		9.33	176, 181,183		
6.19	79, 82, 204	10.4-5	126	12.4-5	80, 87
		10.4	126, 130, 137	12.4	89
6.21	82			12.5	164
6.22	79	10.9-13	78	12.6-8	87, 88
7.7-11	83	10.11-21	224	12.6	90
7.12	137, 196	10.16	165, 211	12.7	89
7.22	137, 153	11.5	143	12.8	89
7.24	79	11.9-10	223	12.9-21	90-110, 119
8	159	11.9	175		
8.1-13	122	11.11	78	12.9-20	108, 114
8.2	79, 128	11.15	231	12.9-19	90
8.3-4	127	11.17-18	87	12.9-17	90
8.3	80	11.18	209	12.9-13	87, 90-96, 102, 216
8.4-5	68	11.20	87, 114, 173	12.9-10	121
8.4	82, 126			12.9	91, 94, 111, 165, 173, 203, 237, 238
8.5-10	82	11.22	154		
8.5-7	82	11.25	32, 87, 173		
8.6	79, 82, 86				
8.7	82	11.26	78		
8.8	82, 222	11.30	233	12.10-13	94
8.10	79	12–15	184, 234	12.10	87, 94, 164, 165, 203, 216, 237
8.15	67, 94	12.1–			
8.16-25	95	15.13	20, 26, 64, 76, 237		
8.17	85, 206				
8.18	143, 228	12–13	79, 138, 141, 149,	12.11	95, 220, 237
8.19-22	83				

12.12	95, 102, 226, 227, 238	13.5	119	13.14	140, 149, 152, 154, 155, 157, 158, 172, 229, 236, 238
		13.6-7	111		
		13.6	102, 114, 119		
12.13	91, 96, 102, 106	13.7	20, 33, 34, 102, 112-14, 116, 118, 119, 138, 237, 238		
12.14-21	20, 90, 103, 115, 139			14–15	87, 93
				14–15.13	161, 162
12.14-20	108			14	71, 93, 107, 121, 167, 172, 230
12.14	20, 34, 38, 74, 96-106, 109, 115, 237, 238, 240	13.8ff.	82		
		13.8-10	20, 91, 116, 121-40, 143, 152, 156, 157, 183, 237, 238	14.1ff.	137
				14.1–	
12.15-21	105-109			15.6	161, 162, 230
12.15	106				
12.16-17	87			14.1-23	87, 163
12.16	82, 87, 90, 91, 106, 164, 216, 238	13.8-9	128, 138	14.1-13	161-73
		13.8	91, 121-23, 125-27, 129, 130, 164, 208	14.1-12	172, 204, 205
				14.1-2	88, 204
12.17-21	100, 105			14.1	95, 161, 162, 209, 229-31
12.17-20	109	13.9-10	137, 212		
12.17-19	237, 238	13.9	26, 91, 118, 121, 125, 133, 135, 137, 181	14.2–	
12.17-18	111, 203			15.4	162
12.17	57, 72, 91, 107, 108, 115, 118, 138, 204			14.2-13	162
				14.2-3	161
		13.10	91, 121, 125, 127, 134, 202	14.3-4	204, 205
12.18	91, 108, 204, 237			14.3	95, 162, 163, 166, 231, 235
12.19-21	115	13.11-14	141-60		
12.19-20	104, 119	13.11-12	141, 147, 152, 237, 238	14.4	163, 166, 183, 228
12.19	91, 100, 112	13.11	127, 141, 143, 145-47, 152	14.5-6	71, 161
12.20	91, 100, 104			14.5	88, 163, 196, 204, 205
12.21	91, 108, 109, 114	13.12-14	141		
		13.12-13	149	14.6	87, 196, 228, 299
13	117, 128	13.12	143, 146-49, 151, 152, 154	14.7-9	228
13.1-7	71, 111-20			14.7-8	223
13.1-6	114			14.8-9	153
13.1-3	119	13.13	143, 145, 148, 149, 152, 154, 203, 204	14.8	152, 163
13.1	119			14.9-16	166
13.2	112, 119			14.9	166, 207, 222, 240
13.3-4	111, 114				
13.3	119			14.10-12	166
13.4	112, 119				

14.10-11	33, 164, 172		203, 204, 207, 220, 223, 235, 237	15.5	82, 87, 153, 216, 228, 229, 238
14.10	95, 163, 165, 166, 173, 177, 203, 205, 235	14.19-20	235	15.6-7	213
		14.19	108, 178, 200-204, 212, 237	15.6	228, 229
				15.7ff.	231
14.11	166	14.20-21	213	15.7-13	161, 162, 230-34, 236
14.12	164, 166	14.20	93, 161, 185, 186-		
14.13– 15.6	162		88, 193, 197-99,	15.7-9	229
14.13– 15.4	162		201, 202	15.7-8	153, 235
14.13-21	201	14.21-22	197	15.7	54, 107, 156, 162,
14.13-14	20	14.21	161, 178, 182, 201-		229, 231, 232, 238
14.13	163, 165, 166, 170, 172, 174-		203, 235	15.8-12	162, 213
	85, 197, 201-203,	14.22-23	88, 200, 204, 205	15.8-9	232
	205, 213, 235, 237,	14.22	204, 205	15.8	20, 127, 211, 230,
	238, 240	14.23	125, 204, 205, 208		232, 234, 238
14.14-21	174	15	212	15.9-13	236
14.14-15	201	15.1ff.	208	15.9-12	234
14.14	34, 93, 161, 185-	15.1-13	208-36	15.9	213, 222, 229, 234
	99, 201, 202, 213,	15.1-6	208, 214, 235, 230		
	237, 238, 240	15.1-3	122, 163, 217	15.12	234
				15.13-14	126
14.15-23	200-207	15.1	208-12, 235, 238	15.13	162
14.15-16	204, 235	15.2-3	158, 212-	15.14-15	137
14.15	124, 132,		25	15.14	70, 195
	138, 196, 197, 201,	15.2	112, 203, 212	15.15-16	162
	203, 215, 222, 229,	15.3ff.	172	15.15	160, 238
	238	15.3	17, 20, 139, 153,	15.16	79
14.16	112, 201, 203, 204,		211, 221- 24, 229,	15.18	83
	212		231, 234, 235, 238	15.19	126
14.17-18	201, 203			15.21	211
14.17	201, 203, 204, 206,	15.4	105, 139, 224, 225-	15.22-29	196
	207, 235, 237, 238		28, 238	15.30-32	196
		15.5-6	162, 228-	16.2	230
14.18	81, 201,		30	16.17	70, 178, 235, 238
				16.19	33, 83
				16.20	146
				1 Chronicles	
				1	178
				1.5	70

1.12	75	7.10-11	21, 70	10.4	124, 139
1.13	88, 215	7.10	17, 30, 69,	10.6	139
1.17–2.7	31		74, 104,	10.11	139, 225
1.17	220		190, 195,	10.13	88, 209
1.18–			198, 240	10.16	97
2.16	75	7.12	17	10.18	68, 80
1.21-22	31	7.15	198	10.24	125, 212,
1.22	178	7.19	132		217
1.23	26, 68,	7.25-28	71	10.27	187
	178, 183	7.25	17, 18, 24,	10.29	125, 167
1.26	68		74, 75,	10.30	203
1.30	151, 158		190, 240	10.31–	
2.2	17	7.36	75	11.1	212-14
2.6	81	7.38	75	10.31	213
2.7-10	155	7.39	125	10.32-33	234
2.9	138	7.40	66	10.32	203, 213
2.11-12	195	8–10	71, 161	10.33–	
2.14-15	68	8	178, 190,	11.1	132, 217
2.16	86		192	10.33	213
3.9	203	8.3	138	11	96
3.16	35	8.4-6	196	11.1	97, 213,
4.1-2	89	8.10	179		234, 235
4.2	75	8.11-13	178	11.2	96, 70
4.3-5	172	8.11	26, 80	11.18-19	63
4.3-4	167	8.13–		11.23-26	69, 76,
4.5	144, 167	9.23	213		214
4.6	125	8.13	179, 182,	11.23-25	17, 69
4.12-13	97		183	11.23	26, 69,
4.12	99	9	69, 96,		194, 196
4.16	97		198	11.24	83, 215
4.17	97, 195	9.1	64, 66,	11.31	166
4.20	205, 206		194	12.7	212
4.21	138	9.8-9	137	12.13	215, 227
5.3-4	167	9.10	105, 225	12.31	132
5.6	35	9.12	209	13	91, 156
5.7	80	9.14	21, 17, 30,	13.2	32, 75, 91,
5.12-13	167		70, 74,		195, 240
6.1	125		104, 115,	13.6	94
6.2-3	35		172, 190,	13.7	209
6.7	75		192, 198,	14.16	97
6.9-11	206		209, 213,	14.17	125
6.9-10	205, 206		232, 236,	14.20	81
6.9	35, 206		240	14.21	137
6.16	35	9.15	192, 220	14.23-24	32
6.29	35	9.19	127, 213	14.29	38
7	69, 74, 96,	9.21	131	14.34	137
	198	10–11	20	14.37	66
7.1	75, 192	10	137	15.3-7	239

15.3	26, 69, 70, 80, 211, 215
15.6	23
15.8	64, 66
15.11	67
15.20-22	153
15.24	205
15.33	35
15.36-50	47
15.45-49	83, 153
15.45	153
15.49	84, 157
15.50	205, 206
15.53	157
15.54	157
15.58	203
16.10	203
16.14	156
16.22	67, 138
16.23	195

2 Chronicles

1.3	155
1.5-6	227
1.5	226
1.6	225, 227
1.17-18	38
1.20	126
2.2-4	106
2.6-8	210
3	124
3.17-18	153
3.18	84, 154, 158
4.4	154
4.5	128, 220
4.8-11	97
4.10-11	81
4.10	85, 227
4.14	194
4.16-17	85
4.16	84, 153
5.2	157
5.3	157
5.4	157
5.9	81, 204, 222

5.10	166
5.11	114
5.14-15	80, 124, 215
5.14	68, 138, 215
5.15	80
5.16	64, 68, 76, 239
5.17	153
5.21	80, 215, 222
6.2	211
6.4	225, 227
6.6	92
6.7	92
7.1	114
7.6	106
7.9-10	228
7.15	114
8.9	17, 219, 221, 235
8.14	143
9.3	220
10.1	46, 155
10.5	83
10.6	126
10.7	75
11	183
11.1	209
11.7	216, 220
11.17	228
11.19-20	209
11.22-23	64
11.29	177, 178, 179, 182
11.31	194, 195
12.1-7	66
12.2-3	195
12.9	66
12.12	225, 227
12.15	138
13.11	216, 228
13.3	66
13.13	138, 215

Galatians

1.1	67

1.3-4	83
1.4	73, 80, 214, 215
1.9	69
1.10	67, 128, 163, 220
1.11-12	239
1.11	67
1.12	66, 67
1.13-14	64
1.15-17	64
1.16	65--67
1.17-18	65
1.18	66
1.23	67
2.2	23, 66, 67
2.4	67
2.7-9	232
2.9	68
2.11ff.	190
2.11-14	68, 189
2.12	67
2.13	93
2.16ff.	137
2.16	83
2.20	80, 81, 85, 91, 124, 214, 215
2.21	80
3.1ff.	137
3.1	17, 65, 70
3.2-3	159
3.9	97
3.10	126
3.12	126
3.13	215
3.17ff.	137
3.12	137
3.22	83
3.24	137
3.26-28	150
3.27-28	227
3.27	150-53, 157
3.28-29	150
4.4-5	73
4.4	17, 70, 234

4.6-7	206	*Ephesians*		1.10	215
4.6	67, 94	1.3	97	1.11	215
4.10	71	2.7	154	1.13	215, 218
4.19	84	2.10	202, 203	1.15	215
4.28	228	2.11	232	1.17	215
4.29	68	2.14-15	156	1.18	215
5–6	20	2.15	154	1.19	215
5	149, 159	3.16	153	1.20	215
5.3	126, 127	4.1-3	90	1.21	215
5.6	91, 132	4.2	46	1.23	215
5.10	195, 209	4.7	88	1.25	195
5.11	178	4.13-15	81, 84	1.26	215, 218
5.13-14	127, 143	4.17-24	83	1.27	214, 215
5.13	127, 131,	4.17-19	84	1.28-30	214
	138, 220	4.20-21	84	1.28	214
5.14	121, 127,	4.22-24	84, 153	1.29	215
	129-32,	4.24	153, 228	1.30	218
	135, 137,	4.25	212	2	20
	140, 152,	4.31	156	2.1-11	214-21
	212	4.32	122	2.1-5	228
5.15	127	5.2	80, 122,	2.1-4	215
5.16	132, 152		124, 132,	2.1	215, 216,
5.18	127		214		218
5.19-21	152	5.5	205, 206	2.2-4	90, 216
5.19	148	5.8	132, 148	2.2	90, 216
5.21	152, 205,	5.10	81, 222	2.3	46, 94,
	206	5.11	148		155, 216
5.22	127	5.14	145, 152	2.4	216, 217,
5.24	85	5.17	81		228
5.25	127	5.19-20	90	2.5ff.	17
5.26	209	5.22	114	2.5-13	132
6.1-5	93	5.25-27	812	2.5-11	26, 217
6.1	209	5.25	80, 124	2.5-8	17
6.2	130-32,	5.33	114	2.5	158, 216-
	140, 209,	6	147		18, 228
	210	6.5	68, 114	2.6-11	218-20
6.3	210	6.15	156	2.6-9	219
6.4-5	210	6.18	146	2.6-8	218, 221
6.4	125			2.6-7	219
6.5	209	*Philippians*		2.6	219, 221
6.6	209	1.1	128, 215,	2.7-9	106
6.7	35		220	2.7-8	235
6.10	108, 139	1.2	215	2.7	127, 211,
6.13	126	1.6	215		220
6.15	132, 153	1.8	155, 215	2.8	83, 216,
6.17	209, 210	1.9-10	94		220-22

2.9-11	221	3	20, 156		222
2.10-11	166	3.1-2	155	4.2	70, 132, 194
2.12	221, 229	3.1	156	4.3	70, 79, 81
2.13	203	3.3	155, 156	4.8	132, 232
2.17	80	3.4	151, 155-57	4.9	94, 138
2.19	195	3.5-9	156	4.12	143, 203
2.24	195	3.6	156	4.14	26
2.27-28	203	3.8	156	4.15-16	17, 21
2.29	230	3.9-10	153	4.15	121
2.30	203	3.9	153, 154	4.16	145
3.1	95	3.10	85, 153-55, 228	4.17	145
3.3	215, 218	3.11	156	5	90, 148
3.5	64	3.12-13	156	5.1-11	153
3.7-11	85	3.12	46, 154-56, 216, 226	5.1-2	70
3.8-10	67			5.1	143
3.9	83			5.2-10	145
3.10-11	152, 214, 228	3.13	122, 156	5.2	34, 70, 142, 143, 153
3.10	85, 226	3.14	156		
3.17	214	3.15	156	5.4-11	143
3.20-21	218, 219	3.16	90, 156	5.4-5	143
3.21	84, 154, 157, 219	3.20	81, 222	5.4	34, 142, 143
4.2	216, 228	3.22	68		
4.3	223	4.2	95, 146	5.5-8	145
4.5	139, 146	4.11	205, 206	5.5	143, 148
4.8	71	4.12	81, 128, 220	5.6-9	147
4.9	69, 70, 218			5.6	143, 145
4.18	80			5.7	143, 149
4.19	126	*1 Thessalonians*		5.8	143, 148, 151
		1.3	227		
Colossians		1.6	204, 227	5.9	143, 153
1.4	138	1.10	26	5.10	80, 153, 215
1.10	156	2.4	222		
1.11	225, 227	2.12	132, 152, 205, 206	5.12-22	90
1.13	205, 206			5.13	108
1.15	154	2.13	69, 132	5.15	72, 91, 107, 108, 139, 203
1.22	81	2.14-16	93		
1.24	81, 227	2.15-16	93		
1.28	81	2.15	26, 194	5.18	81
2.6	69, 228	3.1	209	5.21	38
2.7	90	3.5	209		
2.8	228	3.12	139	*2 Thessalonians*	
2.11-12	153	4-5	44, 142, 143, 158	1.4	209, 225
2.13	156	4	96	1.5	205, 206, 214
2.16ff.	137	4.1	69, 132, 194, 195,	2	142
2.16	167			2.15	70

3.5	138, 225	5.7	41	4.6	39, 106
3.6	69, 70	5.8	41	4.10	216, 219
		7.14	41	4.11-12	39, 171,
1 Timothy		8.5	228		172
1.5	92	8.8-12	40	4.12	125, 171
1.9ff.	137	10.5	40	5.2-3	39
1.15	49	10.15-19	41	5.7-8	142
1.16	154	10.25	146	5.8	146
2.6	213	10.30	91	5.9	39
4.2	93	10.33	224	5.10	39
4.3-4	195, 196	10.36	226	5.11	154, 155
4.4	197	11.5	222	5.12	38, 39, 93
4.10	224	11.26	223, 224		
6.11	226	11.33	205	*1 Peter*	
6.17	106	12.1-3	41, 226	1.4	32
		12.2	41	1.14	80
2 Timothy		12.14	108	1.15	228
1.5	92	12.24	41	1.16	40
1.12	195	12.28	205	1.22	92, 94,
2.10	209	13.1	94		123
2.11	219	13.12-13	41	1.24	40
2.12	226	13.12	41	2.1	93
2.24	128	13.13	224	2.2	81
3.11	209	13.21	222	2.6	40, 181,
3.16	225	13.22	209		182
4.1	205			2.7-8	40
4.18	205	*James*		2.8	174-76,
		1.1	128		178, 182
Titus		1.2	39	2.12	40
1.1	128	1.4	39	2.13ff.	115
1.15	197	1.5	39	2.13-25	112
2.14	213	1.6	39	2.13-17	112
3.4	154	1.9	106	2.16	128
3.5	80	1.22	39	2.17	117, 118
		1.25	74, 131	2.18	118
Philemon		2.5	39, 205	2.19-20	40
17	230, 231	2.8	39, 74,	2.19	209
			131, 171	2.20-21	226
Hebrews		2.10	125	2.21—3.1	40
1.8	205	2.11	39	2.21	215
2.10	41	2.12	131	2.22-25	211
2.12-13	40	2.13	39	2.23	97
2.12	224	2.23	39	3.8	105
2.18	41	3.1	228	3.9	40, 57, 72,
3.2-6	41	3.9-10	97		97, 107
4.15	41	3.17-18	39	3.10-12	40, 108
5.5	41	3.17	92	3.14	40
5.7-8	220, 222	4.4	39	3.16	98

3.18-22	40	*1 John*		*Revelation*	
3.20	155	1.5	41, 42	1.1	128
4.7	142, 146	1.7	132	1.3	146
4.10	89	2.5	125	1.9	225, 226
4.13	95, 142	2.6	43	2.2-3	209, 226
4.14	40, 224	2.10	175	2.14	175, 176
4.18	40	2.23	132	2.19	229
5.2-4	40	3.2-6	43	2.20	128
5.3-4	40	3.2-3	157	3.3	142
5.4	142	3.11	42, 123	3.10	226
5.5	40, 106	3.16	43, 216	7.3	128
5.6	216, 219	3.23	42, 123	11.18	128
5.8-9	31	4.7	42, 123	13.10	226
5.13	40	4.11	123	14.12	226
		4.12	123	16.15	142
2 Peter		4.21	42, 135	19.2	128
1.1	128	5.4	109	19.5	128
1.6	226			22.3	128
1.11	205	*2 John*		22.6	128
1.12	44	5–6	42	22.10	146
1.14	44	5	123		
1.16-18	43, 44				
1.17	43	*Jude*			
2.20	44	1	128		
2.21	44	14-15	43		
3.2	44				
3.10	44, 142				
3.15	154, 155				

INDEX OF ANCIENT REFERENCES

PSEUDEPIGRAPHA

Ahiqar
2.19   107

Apocalypse of Abraham
13.14   157

Apocalypse of Baruch
23.7   148
49   157
51.3   84
82.2   148
83.1   148
85.10   148

*Apocalypse
of Zephaniah*
8.3   157

1 Enoch
1.9   43

2 Enoch
44.4   101
50.3-4   101
61.2   101

Epistle of Aristeas
207   101, 133
225   101
227   101
232   101

4 Ezra
1–2   147

2.13   147
2.34-36   147
3–14   148
3.2   147
3.2b   147
4.33   141
4.44-50   147
5.50-55   148
6.7   141
6.19   147
6.25   226
8.1   48
8.3   48
8.63–9.2   141
10.19-23   148
10.48   147
14.10-13   141, 147
14.18   147
15–16   147

Joseph and Aseneth
23.9   107
28.4   107
28.14   107
29.3   107

Jubilees
36.4   101
36.9   101

4 Maccabees
2.9   101
2.14   101
7.6   185

Odes of Solomon
33.11-12   150

Psalms of Solomon
16.1   146
16.4   146
16.7   175, 179

Sibylline Oracles
3.246   128

Testament of Ashur
7.5   193

Testament of Benjamin
3.3-4   133
3.6   102
4.1-3   108
4.2-3   101
4.3   133

Testament of Dan
5.3   133, 134

Testament of Gad
4.2   133
6.1   123
6.7   101, 107

Testament of Issachar
5.2   133
7.6   101, 133

Testament of Joseph		16.2	193	*Testament of Simeon*	
17.2	123	18.14	152	4.7	123
18.2	101, 107				
		Testament of Naphtali		*Testament of Zebulun*	
Testament of Judah		8.9	133	5.3	133
14.1-8	149			6.6	133
		Testament of Reuben		7.2-4	101
Testament of Levi		6.9	133	7.2	133
3.6	81			8.3	133
14.4	193			8.5	123

QUMRAN

1QapGen		2.12	179	*1QSa*	
20.28	101	2.17	179	2.3-9	207
		2.24	216		
1QH		4.3-4	156	*4QTBenj*	
2.21	179	4.3	216		134
17.23	179	4.6-8	157		
		5.3-4	216	*4QTLevi*	
1QM		5.25	216		134
15.9	148	6.24	169		
		8.2	123	*4QTNaph*	
1QS		10.17-18	107, 168, 169		134
1.4	169				
1.9-10	148, 169	10.19-20	169	*CD*	
1.9	101	11.12	179	6.20-21	123
2.4-10	101			14.2	179

MISHNAH

m. Ab.		4.9	128	*m. Giṭ*	
1.2	124	6.1	154	5.8-9	108
1.6	169, 171				
1.12	101, 108	*m. Ber.*		*m. Pe'ah*	
2.5	169-71	4.2	180	4.19	135
2.9-10	91				
2.11	101	*m. B. Meṣ*		*m. Tem.*	
3.2	117	5.11	181	6.5	51
4.8	170				

TALMUD

b. Abod. Zar.		*b. Ber.*		28b	180
4a	117	17a	207	62a	69
6a	180, 181	23a	69		
22a	180	24a	69		

b. B. Meṣ		*b. Pes.*		40b-41a	69	
75b	181	22b	161, 181	127b	169, 171	
90a	180					
		b. Ros. Haš.		*b. Yom.*		
b. Ḥag.		16b	170	28b	128	
12b	149					
		b. Sanh.		*b. Zeb.*		
b. Mak.		55a	177, 179	102a	117	
23b-24a	134	98a	210			
		98b	210	*y. Ned.*		
b. Men.				9.41c	134	
98a	117	*b. Shab.*				
		31a	134			

OTHER RABBINIC LITERATURE

ARN		*Exod. R.*		*Pes. R.*	
2.26	134	18.12	149	14.14	193
15.1	134			*Pes. K.*	
16	101	*Gen. R.*		40b	193
		24.7	134		
Cant. Rab.				*Targ. Ps.-J. Lev.*	
2.14	53	*Mek. Vayassaʿ*		19.18	134
		1.165	128	19.34	134
Der. Er. Zut.					
3	169	*Num. R.*		*Targ. Isa.*	
		19.8	193	53	210

PHILO

Decal.		*Ebr.*		*Somn.*	
32	121		149	1.164	146
36	134			2.292	149
51	134, 138	*Migr. Abr.*			
121	134, 138	89-93	136	*Spec. Leg.*	
154	121			2.63	134
156	134	*Praem.*			
158	134	83	128	*Virt.*	
168	134			51	134
176	121	*Quaest. in Gen.*		116-18	101
		3.29	92		

JOSEPHUS

Ant.		8.58	128	*Apion*	
3.90–91	121	14.203	119	1.119	119
3.138	121			2.211-12	101

Life		*War*		3.29	53
13–14	162	2.118	111		
		2.119	124		

CHRISTIAN AUTHORS

Barnabas		*Clem. Alex. Strom.*		60.2	48
1.4	132	3.13	150	60.4	48
2.1	49			61	48
2.2	50	*1 Clement*		61.1-2	117
2.6	74	2.1	47, 48	62.2	48
4.3	48	13	56	63.2	48
4.13	49	13.1-2	56		
4.14	48, 49	13.1	45, 46, 48	*2 Clement*	
5	211			2.4	58, 59
5.1	50	13.2	45, 172	3.2	58, 59
5.5	50	13.3	48	4.2	58, 59
5.6	50	16	47, 155, 211	4.4	117
5.8	49			4.5	58, 59
5.9	49, 58	16.1-2	48	5.2	58, 59
5.12	49, 50	16.7	48	5.4	58, 59
6.6	49	16.15	47	6.1	58, 59
6.13	49	16.17	48	6.2	58
7.3	49	17.2	48	8.5	58, 59
7.5	49	18.8	48	9.6	123
7.9	49	18.17	48	9.11	58, 59
7.11	49	19.1	48	12.2	59, 150
12.10-11	49	21.8	48	13.4	59
14.4	50	22.1-8	47		
14.9	49	22.1-7	108	*Didache*	
15.1	121, 126	24.5	47	1.2	132, 135
16.9	49	30.2	48	1.3–2.1	51
17.2	49	30.3	48	1.3	59, 99
19	49	30.8	48	1.6	50
19.1	132	31.4	48	2.2	132
19.2	49	38.2	48	4.11	117
19.3	49	42.1-3	47	4.12	94
19.4	49	44.3	48	8.1-2	51
19.5	49	46.8	46-48	8.2	50, 60
19.7	117	49.1	47	8.3	50
19.11	163	49.6	232	9.2	52
21.1	49	53.2	48	9.3	52
21.3	146	55.6	48	9.4	52
21.5	50	56.1	48	9.5	50-52
		58.2	47, 48	10.2	52
Chrysostom		59.3-4	48	11.2	132
Homily	27, 224	59.3	48	11.3	51

11.4	132	5.5.2	61	6.3	54
15.3-4	51	6.1.2	61	9.2	55
15.3	51, 210	9.17.5	44	10.3	54, 225
15.4	51	9.20.1-2	61		
16	51			**Smyrn.**	
16.1	142	*Vis.*		1	54
16.5-8	51	4.1.8	61	1.1-2	54
16.5	226	4.2.6	46	1.1	53, 54, 130
				2.1	53
Epiphanius		**Ignatius**		3.2-3	54
Haereses		*Eph.*		3.2	52
30.14.5	58	6.1	117	8.1	54
		7.2	53	11.1	55
Eusebius		10.2-3	54, 155		
H.E.		10.2	54	*Trall.*	
II.23	161	12.2	55	9	54
		15.1-2	54	9.1	53, 54
Ecclesiastical History		16.1	55	12.3	55
3.36.11	52	17.1	54	13.1	55
		17.2–18.1	55	13.2	123
Gos. Eb.	58	18–21	54		
		18.2	53, 54	*Lives of Illustrious Men*	
Gos. Eg.	58, 59	19.1	53	16	52
		19.2	53		
Gos. Naz.	58	20.1	154	**Justin Martyr**	
		21.2	55	*Apol.*	
Gos. Thom.				I.15-16	51
1.47	58	*Magn.*		I.15	99
14	191	5.2	54	I.16.5	38
21	142	6.2	123	1.17	113, 115
21a	150	7.1	54	15.8	58
22	150	11.1	54	16.9	58
23	59	13.2	54	19.7	58
25	123	14	55		
37	150				
39	53	*Phld.*		*Dial.*	
55	210	3.3	54, 55	35.2	63
96	58	7.2	54	93.2	135
100	115	11.1	54		
				Mart. Pol.	
Shepherd of Hermas		*Pol.*		10.2	117
Mand.		1.2-3	54, 211		
4.1.6	61	2.1-2	53	**Origen**	
5.2.7	44	7.1	54	*De Principiis*, Preface	
12.5.4	44			8	52
		Rom.			
Sim.		4.3	54, 55		
5.4.3	61	5.1	55		

Polycarp		5.2	57	Papyri	
Phil.		6.3	57	*P. Oxy.*	
1.2	57	7.2	56	1224	99
2.2	57, 107	8.1-2	57		
2.3	45, 55,	8.2	226	*P. Ryl.*	
	172	10.1	57	76.8	167
3	135	12.3	99		

OTHER ANCIENT AUTHORS

Apuleius		Epictetus		Seneca	
Metam.		*Disc.*		*De Beneficiis*	
11.23-24	151	1.25.29	100	IV.26	100
		2.21.10	168	VII.30.2	100
Aristotle		2.21.11	168	VII.30.5	100
Decon.		3.4.8-9	100		
3	118	3.20.9	100	*De Constantia*	
		3.22.54	100	14.3	100
CH I					
27	146, 149	*Ench.*		*De Ira*	
		42	100	II.32.1-6	100
CH VII				III.5.8	100
1	146	Hippolytus			
1-2	149	*Theoph.*		*De Otio*	
		5	130	1.4	100
Demetrius				Sextus	
Eloc.		Lucian		*Sententiae*	
194	92	*Navigium*		183	172
		45	32		
Demosthenes				Tacitus	
4.47	167	Marcus Aurelius		*Annals*	
19.232	167	8.5	92	13.50	111
		Menander			
Diodorus Siculus		*Thais*		Theophrastus	
17.116.4	65		35	*Char.*	
				27.7	121
Dionysius		Plutarch			
of Halicarnassus		*Moralia*		Thucydides	
Ant. Rom.		361d, e	220	5.18	119
11.5	150	478-92	94		

INDEX OF AUTHORS

Aberbach, M. 69
Abrahams, I. 134-36, 138
Addley, W.P. 16
Aland, K. 99
Alexander, P.S. 26
Allison, D.C., Jr 16, 19, 35, 102, 107-109, 116, 121, 172, 174, 232
Althaus, P. 157
Argyle, A.W. 16, 65, 188
Aune, D.E. 24

Badenas, R. 126, 130
Balch, D.A. 75
Bammel, E. 111, 116, 200
Banks, J.S. 84
Banks, R. 129, 132, 136, 137, 188, 190
Barbour, R.S. 30
Barclay, J.M.G. 126, 127, 132
Barrett, C.K. 63, 73, 74, 80, 83, 87, 96, 97, 125, 138, 143, 157, 158, 167, 202-204, 213, 221, 225, 232-34
Barth, K. 88, 143, 217
Batey, R.A. 93
Bauckham, R.J. 19, 32, 35, 37, 43, 44, 61, 66
Bauer, W. et al. 106, 174
Baur, F.C. 17, 67
Beare, F.W. 215, 217
Beasley-Murray, G.R. 142
Ben-Porat, Z. 29
Berger, K. 122, 133-36, 193
Best, E. 21, 39, 74, 92, 96, 194, 195, 225
Betz, H.D. 17, 151, 127, 130, 131, 208, 210, 214, 221, 228, 229

Billerbeck, P. 106, 149, 154
Black, D.A. 91, 107
Black, M. 88, 113, 166, 121, 122, 187
Blackman, P. 170, 180
Blass, F. 123, 166, 221
Blomberg, C.L. 192, 197
Boring, M.E. 24
Bornkamm, G. 15, 135
Breck, J. 200
Briggs, C.A. 168
Brinsmead, B.H. 130
Brown, F. 168
Brown, J.P. 20, 121, 164, 174, 197
Brown, R.E. 41-43, 162, 197
Bruce, F.F. 16, 41, 114, 121, 125, 127, 130
Buchanan, G.W. 41, 221
Büchler, A. 170, 188
Büchsel, F. 167
Bultmann, R. 15, 17, 18, 74, 80, 98, 99, 115, 123, 129, 133, 142, 144, 147, 149, 164, 165, 176, 189, 205, 214
Burch, V. 182
Burchard, C. 122, 135
Burton, E.D. 128, 150
Butler, B.C. 50, 51

Calvert, D.G.A. 30
Calvin, J. 126
Carlston, C.E. 188, 190, 193
Carrington, P. 25, 181
Catchpole, D.R. 21
Childs, B.S. 39
Chilton, B.D. 23, 123, 210
Collange, J.-F. 215

Conzelmann, H. 15
Coombs, J.H. 28
Corriveau, R. 79, 83
Cranfield, C.E.B. 78-82, 88, 94,
    104, 106, 107, 126, 151, 152, 157,
    161, 166, 187, 191, 193, 196, 197,
    203, 204, 221, 225, 228-29, 233
Cullmann, O. 112, 195, 211

Dalman, G. 164
Daly, R.J. 80, 81
Daube, D. 90, 102, 108, 133, 136,
    189, 203
Davids, P.H. 23, 37, 39, 131, 171
Davies, W.D. 15, 16, 23, 91, 108,
    113, 121, 129-31, 136, 138, 172,
    174, 210
De Boer, W.P. 17, 208, 214
Debrunner, A. 123, 166, 221
Deidun, T.J. 185
Delling, G. 113, 121, 143
Delobel, J. 200
Denney, J. 224
Derrett, J.D.M. 119
Dibelius, M. 22, 37, 38, 65, 69, 113,
    116, 131
Dodd, C.H. 16, 25, 112, 113, 121,
    130, 135, 174, 177, 182, 194, 214,
    224
Donaldson, T.L. 30
Donfried, K.P. 58, 59, 161
Downing, F.G. 30
Draper, J. 50, 51, 66
Driver, S.R. 168
Dungan, D.L. 16, 21, 63, 72, 198
Dunn, J.D.G. 17, 20, 23, 38, 65, 66,
    79, 81, 83, 94, 96, 109, 111, 112,
    113, 189, 191, 196, 205-207, 219,
    221, 228

Ellis, E.E. 22, 30, 89, 104, 105, 234
Evans, C. 80, 81

Fannon, P. 113, 121
Farmer, W. 191
Fee, G. 97
Feine, D.P. 16, 172
Fenton, J.C. 127

Feuillet, A. 129
Fitzmyer, J.A. 99, 119, 133-35, 164,
    165, 185
Fjärstedt, B. 16, 21, 89
Fowler, H.W. 28
France, R.T. 210
Fraser, J.W. 16, 64, 68, 172, 174
Friedlander, G. 171
Friedrich, J. *et al.* 90, 111
Fuller, R.H. 134, 135
Funk, R.W. 123, 166, 221
Furnish, V.P. 15, 16, 19, 42, 79, 81,
    108, 123, 124, 127, 138, 169, 174,
    194

Gamble, H., Jr 208
Garland, D.E. 92
Georgi, D. 75
Gerhardsson, B. 23, 39, 69, 133,
    134, 136
Gewalt, D. 21
Gloer, W.H. 30, 34
Glover, R. 50, 51
Gooch, P. 21, 178
Goppelt, L. 40, 72, 80, 108, 113,
    118
Goulder, M.D. 18, 65, 66
Grant, R.M. 49, 54-56, 59
Grässer, E. 147
Grosheide, F.W. 125
Grundmann, W. 155, 216
Guelich, R.A. 98, 164-66
Guhrt, J. 177
Gundry, R.H. 21, 30-32, 36, 39, 40,
    63, 211
Gutbrod, W. 125, 137
Güttgemanns, E. 21, 22

Hagner, D.A. 45-48, 50, 59
Hahn, F. 78, 148
Hanson, A.T. 21, 91, 210, 222, 224
Harris, R. 182
Harrisville, R.A. 221
Hartin, P.J. 37
Hartman, L. 21
Harvey, A.E. 25
Hatch, W.H.P. 122, 130
Hauck, F. 161

Haufe, G. 206
Hawthorne, G.F. 24, 220
Hays, R.B. 30, 83, 210
Headlam, A.C. 113, 125, 174, 194, 228, 230, 232
Heitmüller, W. 24, 70
Hengel, M. 22, 65, 70, 75, 80, 191, 193, 194
Hill, D. 24, 165, 185
Hofius, O. 66
Holtzmann, H.J. 113
Hooker, M.D. 30, 81-83, 85, 124, 210, 218, 219
Howard, G. 83, 219, 221
Hübner, H. 127, 134, 136, 188, 193
Humbert, A. 178
Hunter, A.M. 16, 102, 107, 108, 115, 151, 172, 174, 206
Hurd, J.C. 16, 75
Hurtado, L.W. 218-21
Hyldahl, N. 82

Jackson, F.J.F. 197
Jastrow, M. 170
Jeremias, J. 22, 69, 80, 164, 185, 188, 193, 200, 210, 213
Jewett, R. 174
Johnston, G. 206, 207
Jones, H.S. 168
Jüngel, E. 21

Kallas, J. 111
Kanjuperambil, P. 102
Karris, R.J. 161, 212, 230, 234
Käsemann, E. 17, 74, 87, 96, 106, 108, 111, 113, 115, 118, 119, 121, 125, 137, 143, 157, 174, 196, 202, 217-20, 222, 223, 225, 226, 228, 230
Keegan, T.J. 16
Kelber, W.H. 75
Kennedy, H.A.A. 75
Kilpatrick, G.P. 66
Kirschner, R. 69
Kittel, G. 37, 81, 113
Klassen, W. 104
Klausner, J. 15
Kleinknecht, K.T. 211

Kloppenborg, J.S. 51, 66
Knight, G.W. 226
Knight, R. 62
Knowling, R.J. 16, 172, 174, 194, 206
Koch, D.-A. 210
Kosmala, H. 69
Köster, H. 48, 49, 51, 75
Kraft, R.A. 48
Kramer, W. 194
Kuhn, H.-W. 75
Kümmel, W.G. 113
Kuss, O. 113

Lagrange, M.-J. 81, 121, 179, 185
Lake, K. 61, 197
Lambrecht, J. 189, 191
Lane, W.L. 188, 193
Larsson, E. 17, 208, 218
Leenhardt, F.J. 78-80, 125, 157, 188, 194, 222, 231, 234
Leivestad, R. 155
Liddell, H.G. 168
Lietzmann, H. 121, 185, 221
Lightfoot, J.B. 47, 56, 128, 218
Lightfoot, R.H. 145
Lindars, B. 178, 223
Ljungman, H. 128, 129
Lohmeyer, E. 191
Longenecker, R.N. 113
Lövestam, E. 145, 146, 148, 149, 157
Luz, U. 129
Lyonnet, S. 139

MacDonald, D.R. 150
Maier, G. 39, 40
Manson, T.W. 99, 129, 144, 177
Margoliouth, G. 188
Marshall, I.H. 70, 146, 147, 218, 225
Martin, R.P. 17, 37, 215-19
Marxsen, W. 125
Mattill, A.J., Jr 192, 205
Mayor, J.B. 37
McEleney, N.J. 187, 189
Mealand, D.L. 30
Meecham, H.G. 134

Meier, J.P. 129, 162, 197
Ménard, J.E. 191
Merk, O. 156, 222
Metzger, B.M. 147, 178, 187, 208
Meyer, B.F. 129, 213, 233
Meyer, H.A.W. 158
Michaelis, W. 17, 208, 228
Michaels, J.R. 40
Michel, O. 32, 78, 96, 106, 107,
    113, 121, 125, 152, 154, 179, 185,
    210, 211, 224, 225, 228, 234
Milligan, G. 175
Minear, P.S. 38, 87, 92, 95, 145
Miner, E. 28, 29
Moe, O. 16
Moffatt, J. 40, 177, 178
Mohrlang, R. 19
Montefiore, C.G. 171, 177, 179
Montefiore, H. 139
Moo, D.J. 30
Moore, A.L. 147
Moore, G.F. 134, 136
Morrison, C.D. 112
Moule, C.F.D. 16, 65, 126, 129,
    154, 212, 218
Moule, H.C.G. 106, 222
Moulton, J.H. 37, 175, 221
Müller, K. 174, 175, 177, 182
Müller, P.-G. 62
Müller, U.B. 191
Munro, W. 16, 119
Murphy-O'Connor, J. 219
Murray, J. 114, 166, 194, 202, 203,
    233
Mussner, F. 37, 128, 209

Nababen, A.E.S. 222
Neirynck, F. 16, 20, 96, 98, 99,
    102, 113, 116-19, 133, 135, 185
Neugebauer, F. 22, 113
Neusner, J. 26, 134, 187-89
Newton, M. 185
Nineham, D.E. 23

O'Brien, P.T. 151, 154, 155
Oepke, A. 150, 151
Olford, D.L. 80, 81
O'Neill, J.C. 111, 122

Orchard, J.B. 18, 93, 142
Ortkemper, F.-J. 92, 108, 121

Pallis, A. 88
Parunak, H.V.D. 162, 201, 202
Paschen, W. 161
Perri, C. 28, 29
Perrin, N. 15, 23
Pesch, R. 22, 152, 189
Pfitzner, V.C. 16
Phillipi, F.A. 221, 228
Piper, J. 20, 79, 91, 98, 100-102,
    104, 105, 107-109, 169
Plummer, A. 213
Pohle, L. 113
Polkow, D. 30
Prat, F. 60

Quispel, G. 123

Räisänen, H. 130, 136, 185, 188,
    190-95
Rawlinson, A.E.J. 191
Reasoner, M. 30
Rehkopf, F. 123
Reitzenstein, R. 151
Rengstorf, K.H. 128
Resch, A. 19, 25, 89, 200
Richardson, P. 16, 21, 69, 75, 155,
    178
Ridderbos, H. 185
Riekkinen, V. 113
Riesenfeld, H. 23, 76
Riesner, R. 23
Rigaux, B. 226
Riley, H. 18
Robertson, A. 213
Robertson, A.T. 123, 125
Robinson, D.W.B. 83
Robinson, J.A.T. 42
Robinson, J.M. 22, 31, 75
Roetzel, C.J. 185
Rudberg, G. 90

Sanday, W. 113, 125, 174, 194,
    228, 230, 232
Sanders, E.P. 24, 25, 35, 36, 107,
    127, 135-37, 142, 147, 185, 187, 189, 232

Sanders, J.A. 217
Sanders, J.T. 106, 121
Sandmel, S. 30
Sauer, J. 20, 98, 99, 103, 104
Schelke, K.H. 117
Schippers, R. 69, 93, 217
Schlier, H. 78, 83, 87, 143, 224
Schmidt, H.W. 150, 209, 210
Schmithals, W. 15, 62, 111
Schnackenburg, R. 155
Schneider, W. 167
Schniewind, J. 129
Schoedel, W.R. 54, 56, 57
Schoeps, H.-J. 15, 151
Schottroff, L. 100, 101, 108, 115
Schrage, W. 17, 117, 121, 214, 221
Schulz, A. 208, 221, 228, 229
Schulz, B.S. 189
Schürer, E. 22, 210
Schürmann, H. 23, 98
Schweitzer, A. 18, 62, 63, 151
Schweizer, E. 135
Scott, R. 168
Scroggs, R. 83
Seeburg, A. 25
Seidensticker, P. 80, 85
Seitz, O.J.F. 99
Selby, D.J. 16
Selwyn, E.G. 25, 65, 91, 104, 142, 181
Shepherd, M.H., Jr 37
Sibinga, J.S. 53, 66
Sidebottom, E.M. 164
Siede, B. 232
Smalley, S.S. 41, 42
Smith, M. 23, 136, 187
Snyder, G.F. 54, 61
Spicq, C. 121, 138, 208
Stählin, G. 149, 175-79, 182, 215
Stanley, D.M. 16, 113, 121
Stanton, G.N. 17, 22, 66, 155, 218, 219, 221
Stauffer, E. 133
Stein, R.H. 23, 30
Stendahl, K. 104
Stock, A. 93, 200
Strack, H.L. 106, 149, 154
Streeter, B.H. 50

Strelan, J.G. 209
Strobel, A. 111, 112, 116, 117, 122
Strömholm, D. 62
Stuhlmacher, P. 20, 22, 62, 68, 69, 80, 113, 185, 213, 231
Swartley, W.M. 54
Sweet, J. 234
Sykes, S. 80, 83

Talbert, C.H. 20, 91, 219, 102
Taylor, G. 61
Taylor, V. 73, 142, 177, 189
Teeple, H.M. 23, 62
Theissen, G. 161
Tilborg, S. van 92
Tinsley, E.J. 17, 69, 208, 227
Trevett, C. 53
Tuckett, C.M. 16, 75
Turner, N. 221

Unnick, W.C. van 64
Vermes, G. 26, 73
Vincent, J.J. 23
Vögtle, A. 149
Vos, L.A. 37

Walter, N. 18, 66, 69, 206
Wanamaker, C.A. 220
Waterman, G.H. 21, 142
Watson, F. 161
Webster, J.B. 17, 208
Wedderburn, A.J.M. 16, 20, 68, 71, 73, 75, 82, 161, 191, 220
Weder, H. 73
Weiss, J. 64, 65
Welch, J.W. 200
Wells, G.A. 62
Wenham, D. 15, 16, 20, 21, 25, 34, 38, 44, 95, 98, 104, 109, 142, 147, 158, 159
Wenham, J.W. 197
Westerholm, S. 185
Wiefel, W. 161
Wilckens, U. 24, 62, 79, 87, 92, 113, 126, 148, 157, 202, 222
Williams, S.K. 80
Wilson, S.G. 15-17, 69
Winer, G.B. 223

Wolff, C. 64, 68, 69
Wolff, H.W. 210
Wright, N.T. 25, 194, 219, 220

Zeller, D. 185, 221
Zimmerli, W. 210
Zsifkovits, V. 117, 119

JOURNAL FOR THE STUDY OF THE NEW TESTAMENT

Supplement Series

10 CHRIST THE END OF THE LAW
    ROMANS 10.4 IN PAULINE PERSPECTIVE
    Robert Badenas
11 THE LETTERS TO THE SEVEN CHURCHES OF ASIA IN THEIR LOCAL
    SETTING
    Colin J. Hemer
12 PROCLAMATION FROM PROPHECY AND PATTERN
    LUCAN OLD TESTAMENT CHRISTOLOGY
    Darrell L. Bock
13 JESUS AND THE LAWS OF PURITY
    TRADITION HISTORY AND LEGAL HISTORY IN MARK 7
    Roger P. Booth
14 THE PASSION ACCORDING TO LUKE
    THE SPECIAL MATERIAL OF LUKE 22
    Marion L. Soards
15 HOSTILITY TO WEALTH IN THE SYNOPTIC GOSPELS
    T.E. Schmidt
16 MATTHEW'S COMMUNITY
    THE EVIDENCE OF HIS SPECIAL SAYINGS MATERIAL
    S.H. Brooks
17 THE PARADOX OF THE CROSS IN THE THOUGHT OF ST PAUL
    A.T. Hanson
18 HIDDEN WISDOM AND THE EASY YOKE
    WISDOM, TORAH AND DISCIPLESHIP IN MATTHEW 11.25–30
    C. Deutsch
19 JESUS AND GOD IN PAUL'S ESCHATOLOGY
    L.J. Kreitzer
20 LUKE: A NEW PARADIGM
    M.D. Goulder
21 THE DEPARTURE OF JESUS IN LUKE–ACTS
    THE ASCENSION NARRATIVES IN CONTEXT
    M.C. PARSONS
22 THE DEFEAT OF DEATH
    APOCALYPTIC ESCHATOLOGY IN 1 CORINTHIANS 15 AND ROMANS 5
    M.C. De Boer
23 PAUL THE LETTER-WRITER
    AND THE SECOND LETTER TO TIMOTHY
    M. Prior

24 APOCALYPTIC AND THE NEW TESTAMENT
   ESSAYS IN HONOR OF J. LOUIS MARTYN
   Edited by J. Marcus & M.L. Soards
25 THE UNDERSTANDING SCRIBE
   MATTHEW AND THE APOCALYPTIC IDEAL
   D.E. Orton
26 WATCHWORDS
   MARK 13 IN MARKAN ESCHATOLOGY
   T. Geddert
27 THE DISCIPLES ACCORDING TO MARK
   MARKAN REDACTION IN CURRENT DEBATE
   C.C. Black
28 THE NOBLE DEATH
   GRAECO-ROMAN MARTYROLOGY AND
   PAUL'S CONCEPT OF SALVATION
   D. Seeley
29 ABRAHAM IN GALATIANS
   EPISTOLARY AND RHETORICAL CONTEXTS
   G.W. Hansen
30 EARLY CHRISTIAN RHETORIC AND 2 THESSALONIANS
   F.W. Hughes
31 THE STRUCTURE OF MATTHEW'S GOSPEL
   A STUDY IN LITERARY DESIGN
   D.R. Bauer
32 PETER AND THE BELOVED DISCIPLE
   FIGURES FOR A COMMUNITY IN CRISIS
   K.B. Quast
33 MARK'S AUDIENCE
   THE LITERARY AND SOCIAL SETTING OF MARK 4.11–12
   M.A. Beavis
34 THE GOAL OF OUR INSTRUCTION
   THE STRUCTURE OF THEOLOGY AND ETHICS IN THE PASTORAL
   EPISTLES
   P.H. Towner
35 THE PROVERBS OF JESUS
   ISSUES OF HISTORY AND RHETORIC
   A.P. Winton
36 THE STORY OF CHRIST IN THE ETHICS OF PAUL
   AN ANALYSIS OF THE FUNCTION OF THE HYMNIC MATERIAL
   IN THE PAULINE CORPUS
   S.E. Fowl
37 PAUL AND JESUS
   COLLECTED ESSAYS
   A.J.M. Wedderburn

38 MATTHEW'S MISSIONARY DISCOURSE
    A LITERARY CRITICAL ANALYSIS
    D.J. Weaver
39 FAITH AND OBEDIENCE IN ROMANS
    A STUDY IN ROMANS 1–4
    G.N. Davies
40 IDENTIFYING PAUL'S OPPONENTS
    THE QUESTION OF METHOD IN 2 CORINTHIANS
    J.L. Sumney
41 HUMAN AGENTS OF COSMIC POWER IN HELLENISTIC
    JUDAISM AND THE SYNOPTIC TRADITION
    M.E. Mills
42 MATTHEW'S INCLUSIVE STORY
    A STUDY IN THE NARRATIVE RHETORIC OF THE FIRST GOSPEL
    D.B. Howell
43 JESUS, PAUL AND TORAH
    COLLECTED ESSAYS
    H. Räisänen
44 THE NEW COVENANT IN HEBREWS
    S. Lehne
45 THE RHETORIC OF ROMANS
    ARGUMENTATIVE CONSTRAINT AND STRATEGY AND PAUL'S
    'DIALOGUE WITH JUDAISM'
    N. Elliot
46 THE LAST SHALL BE FIRST
    THE RHETORIC OF REVERSAL IN LUKE
    J.O. York
47 JAMES AND THE 'Q' SAYINGS OF JESUS
    Patrick J. Hartin
48 TEMPLUM AMICITIAE:
    ESSAYS ON THE SECOND TEMPLE PRESENTED TO ERNST BAMMEL
    Edited by W. Horbury
49 PROLEPTIC PRIESTS
    AN INVESTIGATION OF THE PRIESTHOOD IN HEBREWS
    J.M. Scholer
50 PERSUASIVE ARTISTRY
    STUDIES IN NEW TESTAMENT RHETORIC
    IN HONOR OF GEORGE A. KENNEDY
    Edited by Duane F. Watson
51 THE AGENCY OF THE APOSTLE
    A DRAMATISTIC ANALYSIS OF PAUL'S RESPONSES TO CONFLICT IN
    2 CORINTHIANS
    Jeffrey A. Crafton

52 REFLECTIONS OF GLORY
   PAUL'S POLEMICAL USE OF THE MOSES–DOXA TRADITION IN
   2 CORINTHIANS 3.1-18
   Linda L. Belleville
53 REVELATION AND REDEMPTION AT COLOSSAE
   Thomas J. Sappington
54 THE DEVELOPMENT OF EARLY CHRISTIAN PNEUMATOLOGY
   WITH SPECIAL REFERENCE TO LUKE–ACTS
   Robert P. Menzies
55 THE PURPOSE OF ROMANS
   A COMPARATIVE LETTER INVESTIGATION
   L. Ann Jervis
56 THE SON OF THE MAN IN THE GOSPEL OF JOHN
   Delbert Burkett
57 ESCHATOLOGY AND THE COVENANT
   A COMPARISON OF 4 EZRA AND ROMANS 1-11
   Bruce W. Longenecker
58 'NONE BUT THE SINNERS'
   RELIGIOUS CATEGORIES IN THE GOSPEL OF LUKE
   David A. Neale
59 CLOTHED WITH CHRIST
   THE EXAMPLE AND TEACHING OF JESUS IN ROMANS 12.1-15.13
   Michael Thompson